The Road to Passchendaele

---✠---

THE ROAD TO PASSCHENDAELE

The Flanders Offensive of 1917
A Study in Inevitability

JOHN TERRAINE

Leo Cooper
In Association with
Secker & Warburg

First Published in Great Britain in 1977 by
LEO COOPER LTD.,
London

Re-issued in 1984 by Leo Cooper, in association with
Martin Secker & Warburg Limited,
54 Poland Street, London W1V 3DF

0 436 51732 9

Printed in Great Britain at The Pitman Press, Bath

*To all those
whose names are inscribed
on the Menin Gate at Ypres,
and to their comrades
in the cemeteries of
the Salient.*

Contents

✠

Acknowledgements

✠

The Author and Publishers are grateful to the following for permission to quote copyright material in this book; Associated Book Publishers Ltd., for extracts from *In London During the Great War* by Michael Macdonagh; William Collins & Sons Ltd., for extracts from *Hankey, Man of Secrets* by Stephen Roskill; William Kimber & Co Ltd., for extracts from *Ypres 1917* by Norman Gladden; John Murray Ltd., for extracts from *Plumer of Messines* by General Sir Charles Harrinton; Anthony Sheil Associates Ltd., for extracts from *The Fifth Army* by Sir Hubert Gough; Constable & Co Ltd., for extracts from *Home Fronts, British, French and German* by John Williams; David Higham Associates Ltd., for extracts from *The Supreme Command 1914–18* by Lord Hankey; Odhams Publishing Ltd., for extracts from *War Memoirs* by Lloyd George; Ward Lock Ltd., for extracts from *Khaki and Gown* by Field Marshal Lord Birdwood; Cassell.

Notes on Sources

✠

The published sources which I have used are readily identifiable.
Cabinet Papers are held in the Public Record Office.

The designation 'Author's Papers' requires explanation. These consist chiefly of the assembly of hitherto unpublished excerpts from Lord Haig's diary and associated papers of all descriptions which I made when researching *Douglas Haig: The Educated Soldier* (1963). Some of these have already been quoted by me in the work mentioned, or elsewhere, either in full or in part, but a great many have not; these will now see the light of day for the first time. In addition, my 'Papers' (or 'Files', or 'Collection') contain letters, diary excerpts and documents from other sources which I have gathered over a period of some thirty years.

Needless to say, everything that comes from the Haig collection (now held in the National Library of Scotland in Edinburgh) could be ascribed to the 'Haig Papers'. However, all the extracts from the same source made by Lord Blake for his *Private Papers of Douglas Haig* (1952) and by Lord Norwich (Duff Cooper) for his *Haig* (1935) should then be attributed in the same way. This struck me as unfair to two historians whose great industry has performed admirable and immensely useful spadework for all future students, as well as that procedure being somewhat unhelpful to students themselves. It therefore seemed best to indicate where, other than in the vein of original ore, each particular nugget may be found.

I must here express particular gratitude to Colonel Roderick Macleod, DSO, MC, for generous permission to draw upon his diaries and memoirs, and also on his invaluable translation of the Flanders section of the German Official Account (*Der Weltkrieg, 1914 bis 1918: Die militarischen Operationen zu lande*) and of General von Kuhl's history (*Der Weltkrieg, 1914–1918*).

Maps

———— ✠ ————

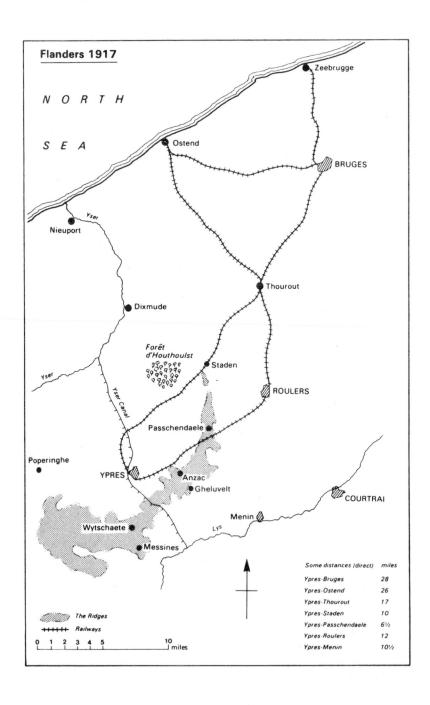

Flanders 1917

NORTH

SEA

Zeebrugge

Ostend

BRUGES

Yser

Nieuport

Thourout

Dixmude

Forêt
d'Houthoulst

Staden

Yser

ROULERS

Yser Canal

Passchendaele

Poperinghe

YPRES

Anzac

Gheluvelt

COURTRAI

Menin

Lys

Wytschaete

Messines

Some distances (direct)	miles
Ypres-Bruges	28
Ypres-Ostend	26
Ypres-Thourout	17
Ypres-Staden	10
Ypres-Passchendaele	6½
Ypres-Roulers	12
Ypres-Menin	10½

The Ridges

Railways

0 1 2 3 4 5   10 miles

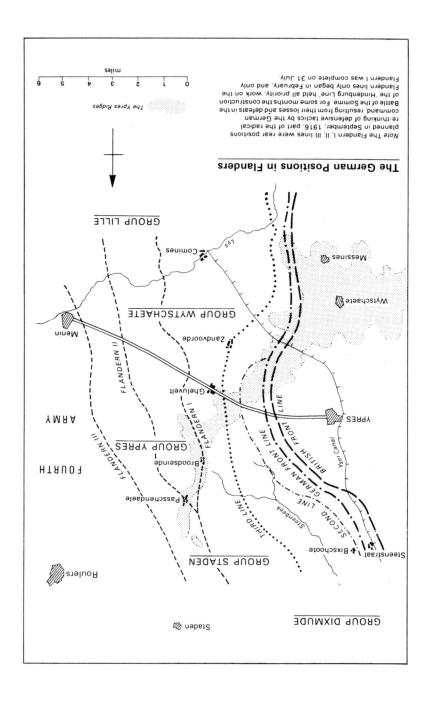

The German Positions in Flanders

Note The Flandern I, II, III lines were rear positions planned in September, 1916, part of the radical re-thinking of defensive tactics by the German command, resulting from their losses and defeats in the Battle of the Somme. For some months the construction of the Hindenburg Line, held all priority, work on the Flandern lines only began in February, and only Flandern I was complete on 31 July.

The Ypres Ridges

miles

0 1 2 3 4 5 6

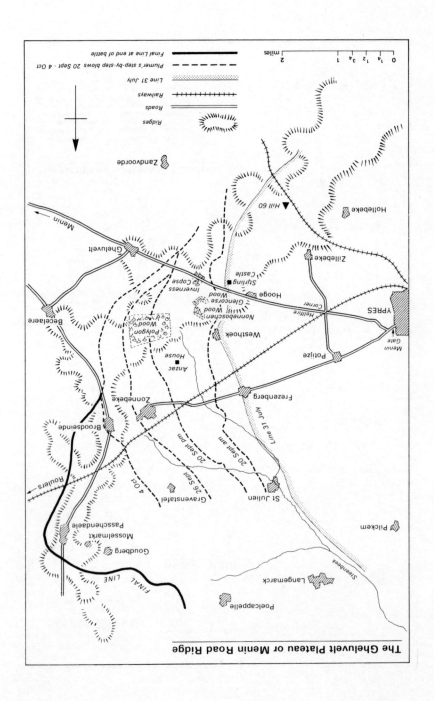

The Gheluvelt Plateau or Menin Road Ridge

Ridges
Roads
Railways
Line 31 July
Plumer's step-by-step blows 20 Sept - 4 Oct
Final Line at end of battle

miles
0 ¼ ½ ¾ 1 2

Zandvoorde
Hollebeke
Hill 60
Zillebeke
Gheluvelt
Menin
Becelaere
Inverness Copse
Stirling Castle
Hooge
Glencorse Wood
Nonnebosschen Wood
Polygon Wood
Anzac House
Westhoek
Hellfire Corner
YPRES
Menin Gate
Potijze
Frezenberg
Zonnebeke
Line 31 July
20 Sept pm
20 Sept am
Broodseinde
Roulers
Gravenstafel
26 Sept
4 Oct
St Julien
Pilckem
Mosselmarkt
Passchendaele
Goudberg
FINAL LINE
Steenbeek
Langemarck
Poelcappelle

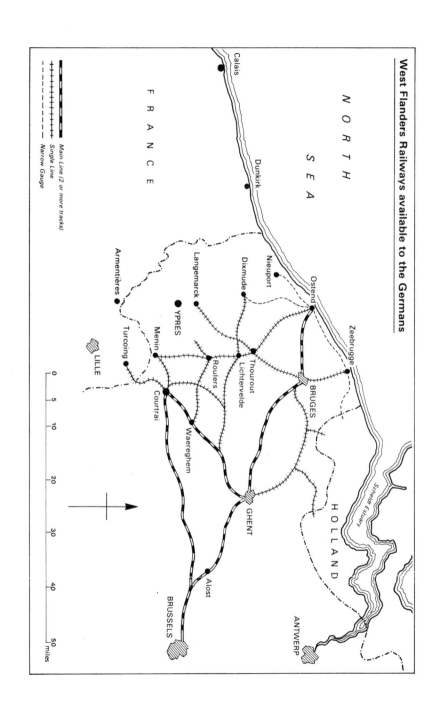

West Flanders Railways available to the Germans

Main Line (2 or more tracks)
Single Line
Narrow Gauge

NORTH SEA

FRANCE

HOLLAND

Scheldt Estuary

Calais
Dunkirk
Nieuport
Ostend
Zeebrugge
Langemarck
Dixmude
Armentières
YPRES
Menin
Turcoing
LILLE
Roulers
Lichtervelde
Thourout
BRUGES
Courtrai
Waereghem
GHENT
Alost
ANTWERP
BRUSSELS

0   5   10   20   30   40   50
miles

Introduction

✠

'All the agonies of war which I have attempted to describe were piled up in those fields of Flanders. There was nothing missing in the list of war's abominations... week after week, month after month, our masses of men, almost every division in the British Army at one time or another, struggled on through that Slough of Despond, capturing ridge after ridge, until the heights of Passchendaele were stormed and won... As a man who knows something of the value of words, and who saw many of those battle scenes in Flanders, and went out from Ypres many times during those months to the Westhoek Ridge and the Pilkem Ridge, to the Frezenburg and Inverness Copse and Glencorse Wood, and beyond to Polygon Wood and Passchendaele... I say now that nothing that has been written is more than the pale image of the abomination of those battle-fields, and that no pen or brush has yet achieved the picture of that Armageddon in which so many of our men perished.'

Sir Philip Gibbs: The Realities of War

I died in hell —
(They called it Passchendaele) . . .

Siegfried Sassoon: Memorial Tablet

No BATTLE, certainly no battle ever fought by the British Army, has attracted to itself such controversy, such odium, as 'Passchendaele', officially called 'The Third Battle of Ypres', the long-delayed British offensive in Flanders which came at last in 1917.

The critics of the Flanders offensive are numerous and powerful. Chief among them is the Prime Minister of the day, Mr (later Earl) Lloyd George. 'Passchendaele,' he wrote in his *War Memoirs,* 'was indeed one of the greatest disasters of the war . . . the battle which, with the Somme and Verdun, will always rank as the most gigantic, tenacious, grim, futile and bloody fights ever waged in the history of war.' He continues:

The tale of these battles constitutes a trilogy illustrating the unquenchable heroism that will never accept defeat and the inexhaustible vanity that will never

admit a mistake. It is the story of the million who would rather die than own themselves cowards – even to themselves – and also of the two or three individuals who
would rather the million perish than that they as leaders should own – even to
themselves – that they were blunderers. Hence the immortal renown and the
ghastly notoriety of the Verdun, Somme and Passchendaele battle-fields; the
fame won by sustained valour unrivalled in the annals of war; the notoriety
attained by a stubborn and narrow egotism, unsurpassed amongst the records of
disaster wrought by human complacency.

Lloyd George clinched this savage indictment with the verdict: 'No
soldier of any intelligence now defends this senseless campaign; certainly
not one who is not implicated by some share of responsibility for it.' Forty
years after the battle, a soldier-writer who won the Military Cross in the
First World War (but was not present at 'Third Ypres'). echoed Lloyd
George's words: 'Let those who wish try to make out a case for Munich,
but let no one seek to justify or excuse the Battle of Passchendaele.'*
    Lloyd George's supporters include Cabinet colleagues like Winston
Churchill, who was always convinced that British losses in the Third
Battle of Ypres were enormous – twice those of the Germans. Many
ex-Servicemen of all ranks from Private to Lieutenant-Colonel shared
these views; their testimonials to the 'honesty', 'candour' and 'courage' of
the ex-Premier's 'exposure of the Passchendaele horror' (as one officer
describes it) may be found in a 22-page Appendix in Lloyd George's
memoirs. In some men the anger never died; after half a century, a
correspondence, as explosive and abrasive as ever, flared up in *The Daily
Telegraph*, and in the course of it Sir Edward Beddington-Behrens
declared:

Only British valour made up for the incompetence of our cavalry generals.
Because all this happened so long ago we should not gloss over the failures of the
then existing Establishment. The useless sacrifice is remembered by all those still
living who took part in the actual fighting.†

Major-General H. Essame, himself an infantryman, wrote:

In retrospect it is amazing to me as a survivor that the infantry stuck the protracted
horror of Passchendaele as bravely as they did. Every cardinal error in their
handling was committed.‡

A Mr Alasdair MacGregor, one of the 'battalion runners' in the battle,
who 'were in a better position than anybody to know what was hap-

*Brigadier Desmond Young in *The Spectator*, 6 December, 1957
†*Daily Telegraph*, 7 July, 1967   ‡ Ibid, 10 August, 1967

pening', spoke of the 'mud-and-blood baths of Flanders', 'this murderous and mud-fast series of battles'.* Brigadier-General C. D. Baker-Carr speaks for many such men in his book *From Chauffeur to Brigadier*, where he calls 'Third Ypres' a 'bloody fiasco' which would 'ever remain an example of British stubbornness and British stupidity.'

All this verbal mud proved to be as clinging as the notorious mud of Flanders. It created an image of the battle which has been accepted and repeated by a number of historians. In the *Daily Telegraph* correspondence in 1967 Sir Basil Liddell Hart stated that 'Haig's offensive was quite unnecessary'. Major General J. F. C. Fuller, normally a most perceptive military writer, but never able to forget the miseries of being on the staff of the Tank Corps in a campaign so thoroughly unfavourable to that arm, wrote in his *Decisive Battles of the Western World*: 'To persist after the close of August in this tactically impossible battle was an inexcusable piece of pig-headedness on the part of Haig . . .' Mr A. J. P. Taylor, in his sly illustrated history of the First World War, said: 'Third Ypres was the blindest slaughter of a blind war. Haig bore the greatest responsibility. Some of the Flanders mud sticks also to Lloyd George, the man who lacked the supreme authority to forbid the battle.'

Of course, there is an opposite point of view, often expressed with equal force and much lucidity. It is not my purpose here to enter the lists; all I would wish to say at this stage is that I have found the most convincing arguments in favour of the British Flanders offensive to be the German reactions to it, summed up in General von Kuhl's memorable phrase, 'the greatest martyrdom of the war'. I have set out my own conclusions at the end of this book, and would urge that they remain there, to be considered *after* reading the book itself.

What this consists of is a documentation – evidently not comprehensive (which would require not one book, but a shelf-full) – designed to investigate whether the British offensive was, indeed, 'senseless', 'useless', 'quite unnecessary', 'blind', etc. Or was there some rhyme and reason in it after all? How *did* it come about? How was it planned? Who was really responsible for its launching? Why did it go on so long? What did it achieve? I have tried to set out here the contemporary evidence on these and other matters with as little interpolation from myself as possible, in the hope that these papers and extracts will speak for themselves, even if only to show that few occasions of such magnitude can faithfully be dismissed in one damning word or phrase. Field-Marshal Sir William

*Ibid, 14 September, 1967

Robertson, who has a knack of expressing the nub of things with deceptive simplicity, said, when it was all over: 'A correct decision was not so easy to make at the time as it appears now.' This plain truth is often forgotten, but historians ignore it at their peril.

JOHN TERRAINE
December 1976

Ramparts Cemetery, Ypres

———————————— ✠ ————————————

Headstone of 4/209A Lance-Corporal J. G. Snodgrass, New Zealand Engineers, Killed 10 December 1917.

'Sooner or later, the time will come when Private Snodgrass must advance straight to his front.' (Saying of Field-Marshal Wavell)

'Straight to his front . . .'
Half the world's diameter is far enough
To advance straight to the front –
Eh, Snodgrass?

I see they made you a lance-corporal.
Not much in that.
Of course, they paid you New Zealanders better –
But you paid best of all.

How did it happen?
What Sapper duty took you off,
Somewhere in that zone of desolation?
What maniac's gadget finished you
In the festering Salient?
Or was it a chance shell?
They dropped like ungentle rain at the Lille Gate,
Day long, night long:
No need for a 'battle' –
No need for Death to be so greedy.
Or did you scream your last conscious hours away,
Waiting for the blessed morphia
And the ultimate blackout
In a Rampart Dressing Station
Just here, beside the gate of annihilation?

What does it matter?
All these are ways in which a man
Advances straight to his front.
What does it matter –
The foreign laughter on a summer afternoon,
The children who don't know and do not care,
The strolling lovers, the old ladies
Resting their poor feet?

Was it for this
That you made that damn long journey?
I dare say not.
It doesn't matter.
'The time will come . . .'
Well, you found your time soon enough.
You did your bit.

31.V.70

I

FLANDERS

❖

FLANDERS was once one of the most important political and economic regions of Western Europe, a crossroads of trade, a strategic key. Though vassals of the French monarchy, the Counts of Flanders not infrequently followed an independent line, as their commercial and dynastic interests drew them towards France or England, the Empire or the princes of Germany. As part of the Low Countries, Flanders shared with Hainaut, Brabant, Luxemburg and the southern Netherlands the title of 'Cockpit of Europe'. France, Spain, Austria and Holland contended for its possession; English, Scots, Irish, Germans and Danes took part in their wars.

At the height of its fame, Flanders stretched from the port of Antwerp in the north, along the Scheldt estuary to Bruges (Flemish 'Brugge', connected by canal to the sea at Zeebrugge), down the coast to Ostend and Dunkirk, inland as far south as Armentières, and enclosed what became the great industrial centre of Lille, and the important towns of Tournai, Courtrai and Ghent. West Flanders, the coastal region, is a land of wide skies and flat vistas, stretching to distant horizons hidden by lines of poplar trees. It is intersected by canals, dykes and ditches, a complex system of waterways first devised by the great French engineer, Vauban, to serve the economic purposes of drainage and communication, and to make a military obstacle. This area is almost entirely at or below sea level, protected from the sea itself by sand dunes running all the way down the coast and by sluices to hold out the sea at high tide, and protected from flooding by an intricate network of drains. In 1708 Marshal Vendôme inundated the country between Bruges and Nieuport to check the advance of the Duke of Marlborough; in October, 1914, the Nieuport sluices were opened to check the German advance on the River Yser. In this level country, a spoil bank, the causeway of a road or railway, the embankment of a river or canal is a feature, any tall building a vantage point.

East and south of the old moated town of Ypres,* fortified by Vauban
as an outlying bastion of Dunkirk, the country changes. Here are found
the Flanders 'Ridges', a word which should not be allowed to over-excite
the imagination. The Staden–Passchendaele–Gheluvelt Ridge, to the
north and east of Ypres, is nowhere more than 100 feet above the plain, at
Passchendaele about 70 feet; a motorist scarcely notices that he has
crossed it, even a cyclist is only intermittently conscious of the gradient.
Yet this mild slope gives complete observation right to the ramparts of
Ypres, six miles from Passchendaele. At St Eloi the ridge bends south,
rising to 150 feet at Wytschaete, and even taking on the character of an
escarpment on the western side between there and Messines. This part of
the country is quite unlike the coastal sector; it has been likened to the
Kentish Weald – wooded, enclosed, with narrow, twisting lanes and high
hedges; it is what soldiers call 'blind country', a patchwork of small fields,
farmyards and orchards, limiting vision and promising only unpleasant
surprises. It is not unlike the Normandy 'bocage' which presented so
many difficulties to the British and Americans in 1944.

The Wytschaete–Messines Ridge drops away towards Armentières,
and the country changes again. Once more it flattens out, offering wide
horizons, but now broken by the huge slag-heaps of mining districts, like
the dark mountains of a barren planet, with pit-head machinery and tall
chimneys stabbing the skyline, and the sprawl of industrial villages across
the plain. This unprepossessing landscape continues past Béthune and La
Bassée almost as far as Arras, where it begins to fold and fall with the
chalk downs of Artois, rolling on into Picardy.

In 1914 West Flanders acquired a double fresh significance, political
and military. The Germans invaded Belgium on 4 August, and immediately began to attack the fortress area of Liége which barred their way to
France. The city itself was captured on the 7th, and the last of the forts fell
on the 17th. The next day the Belgian Army was driven from the line of
the River Gette, and began its retreat into the fortress of Antwerp. This
movement was completed on the 20th, which was also the day on which
the Germans entered Brussels. On the 21st they attacked Namur, and
two days later the garrison withdrew. This was on 23 August, the day of
the Battle of Mons and the beginning of the great retreat of the Allied left
wing. On the 24th, 25th and 26th the Belgians made a sortie from
Antwerp which was successful in drawing off some German forces from
the pursuit of the allies.

For a fortnight after this there was a respite on the Belgian front; then,

*Flemish 'Ieper'.

on 9 September, the Belgian Army made a second sortie to co-operate with the Franco-British counterattack on the Marne. The Belgian effort continued until the 13th, not achieving very much against increasing German resistance, but hastening the moment when the Germans would decide to remove this thorn from their side once and for all. The attack on Antwerp began on 4 October, and despite the support of some hastily formed Royal Marine and Naval brigades sent by Mr Winston Churchill, First Lord of the Admiralty, the city surrendered on 10 October. The Belgian field army escaped down the coast and on 14 October consolidated the line of the River Yser, which it held for the remainder of the War.

Belgium was now reduced to a slim triangle, nowhere wider than twelve miles, whose eastern face ran from Nieuport past Dixmude and Ypres to the French frontier just south of Ploegsteert. The King of the Belgians, Albert I, believed it to be politically vital to hold this remnant of his country, and Allied public opinion, enthused with stories of 'gallant little Belgium', also invested it with special importance. From a naval and military point of view it was more material that the German thrust down the Channel coast towards Calais and Boulogne had been checked, and should remain so. Thus once more the political and strategic value of West Flanders had grown out of all proportion to its size.

II

THE ORIGIN OF THE BRITISH FLANDERS OFFENSIVE OF 1917

---- ✚ ----

No part of West Flanders is tempting for military operations, despite its strategic significance. In August, 1914, however, neither its tactical drawbacks nor its strategic possibilities concerned the British Expeditionary Force. The designated rôle of the BEF was to act on the left of the French armies in their advance into Germany. It accordingly disembarked at Boulogne, Le Havre and Rouen, concentrated in the Le Cateau–Maubeuge area, and marched up to Mons in Hainaut, south-south-west of Brussels. The retreat from Mons carried it well away from Flanders, to the south-east of Paris. There, by 5 September, it found itself sandwiched between two French Armies, and in that posture took part in the Battle of the Marne.

The advance to the River Aisne was in a north-easterly direction and drew the British even further away from the sea, to a line between Soissons and Craonne. Logistically and psychologically this was a bad position for the Expeditionary Force; it was awkward of access from the British bases on the Channel coast, and it seriously compromised any degree of real independence for the British Commander-in-Chief, Field-Marshal Sir John French, whose three army corps were thus practically lost in the midst of the great French army. While the BEF was on the Aisne, its commander received a visit from Mr Winston Churchill; Sir John French wrote:

> Field-Marshal Viscount French of Ypres, *1914*;
> Constable, 1919, [henceforward 'French'], pp
> 302–5

I discussed with him fully my views as to the desirability of establishing the British Force in a theatre where they could co-operate with the Navy and link up with the troops in Belgium.* We examined the possibility of a failure to effect a decisive turning movement, and agreed in thinking that, in the last resort, we might still be able, with the flank support of the Fleet, to snatch from the enemy's possession the Belgian coastline as far, at any rate, as Zeebrugge.

When he left me on 28 September it was with a complete understanding that he would prepare the Navy to fulfil this rôle, and a few extracts from letters which I subsequently received from him will show how well he redeemed his promise.

On 26 October he writes:

. . . But, my dear friend, I do trust you will realize how damnable it will be if the enemy settles down for the winter along lines which comprise Calais, Dunkirk, or Ostend. There will be continual alarms and greatly added difficulties. We must have him off the Belgian coast even if we cannot recover Antwerp . . .'

By this time the War had taken on an entirely new aspect; the beginning of trench warfare on the Aisne had produced a stalemate; to break this, there followed the so-called 'race to the sea', an attempt by both sides to turn the western flank. As part of this operation, the BEF was transferred to Flanders in October. Antwerp fell on the 10th of that month, and the British IV Corps, which had landed at Zeebrugge and Ostend in support of the Belgians, joined Sir John French's command.

The first of the great struggles which were to make 'Flanders' such a sombre battle honour of the British Army now began: the First Battle of Ypres. Contrary to cherished British myth, this was predominantly a French battle, conducted by a French overall commander, General Ferdinand Foch. From the allied point of view, he tells us, 'it was an attempt to exploit the last vestige of our victory on the Marne.'

> *The Memoirs of Marshal Foch*, Translated by Colonel T. Bentley Mott, Heinemann, 1931, p 168.

The idea dominating our tactics was that, in view of our feeble armament, notably in artillery and machine-guns, we were powerless to break through the front of an enemy who had had time to organize the ground, construct trenches and protect them with wire entanglements. Our plan, therefore, was to forestall him, assail him while he was in full manoeuvre, assault him with troops full of dash before he could organize his defence and bring his powerful armament into play.

But attacks undertaken with this idea encountered from the very start an offensive on the part of the enemy.

---

*This is a characteristically obscure reference. At this time the only Allied troops in Belgium were the Belgians themselves. There was a British Marine brigade in French Flanders, operating between Dunkirk and Cassel under Admiralty control, in conjunction with a section of armoured cars, also manned by the Navy. The British Naval Brigades did not arrive at Antwerp until 4 October; the 7th Division (IV Corps) disembarked at Zeebrugge on 7 October, and a French Naval Brigade reached Ghent on 9 October.

The new German Chief of Staff, Lieutenant-General Erich von Fal-kenhayn (who had replaced General von Moltke on 14 September) explains the German intentions in a manner which shows that Churchill's anxieties were not ill-founded:

> General Erich von Falkenhayn, *General Head-quarters 1914–1916 and its Critical Decisions*, Hutchinson, 1919, p 29

There was no doubt about the resolute offensive intentions of the English and the French. Not only had the danger that the Germans would be finally cut off from the Belgian coast again become acute, but also the danger of an effective encirclement of the right wing. They both had to be removed unconditionally. If this, at least, was not done, then the drastic action against England and her sea traffic with submarines, aeroplanes and airships, which was being prepared as a reply to England's war of starvation, was impossible in their present stage of development.

The importance of the Belgian coast was quickly perceived by both sides, and loomed larger as the War continued. The details of the First Battle of Ypres do not concern us, but its chronology is interesting, in the light of 1917. First it should be noted that the BEF did not arrive in Flanders until October – in the case of I Corps, not until 20 October. According to the British Official History, the great encounter battle began on 19 October; it came to a major crisis on 31 October, and to its final crisis on 11 November. The weather did not play any significant part in the battle until that day, when it became 'thoroughly wintry':

> Brigadier-General J. E. Edmonds, *Military Operations, France and Belgium, 1914*, Mac-millan, 1925 [The Official History, henceforward designated *O.H.*] vol ii, p 448

Cold and rain on the 12th, 13th and 14th were followed according to the records by a little snow on the 15th; then came frost at night, hard frost on the 18th, six hours of snowstorm on the 19th and snow covering the ground on the 20th.

A German cavalry officer, Captain Rudolf Binding, billeted in the village of Passchendaele, wrote on 16 November:

> Rudolf Binding, *A Fatalist at War*, translated by Ian F. D. Morrow, Allen & Unwin, 1929, p 25

Cold storms, snowflakes that make the horses shake their heads with annoyance, warn us that we must get ready for cold weather.

To those who fought at Ypres in October and November, 1914, neither weather nor ground conditions seemed to present particular hazards. Among such people should be noted Lieutenant-General Sir Douglas Haig, commanding the British I Corps, who in the later stages of the battle was effectively the executive commander of the whole British line.

The different nationalities involved have given the First Battle of Ypres different termination dates: the French officially end it on 13 November, the British on 22 November, and the Germans on 30 November. On 27 November, unsuspectingly prophetic, Captain Binding wrote:

Ibid, p 30

A terrific struggle is going on for the crossroads at Broodseinde, south-west of Passchendaele. Generals and Colonels are flirting with the idea that to take the crossroads of Broodseinde may mean something in the history of the world.

The name of Broodseinde would be heard again.

It was on 22 November, the day on which the British battle officially ended, that Winston Churchill again wrote to Sir John French about an advance up the Belgian coast:

French, p 304

If you push your left flank along the sand-dunes of the shore to Ostend and Zeebrugge, we would give you 100 or 200 heavy guns from the sea in absolutely devastating support. For four or five miles inshore we could make you perfectly safe and superior. Here, at least, you have their flank, if you care to use it; and surely, the coast strip, held and fed well with troops, would clear the whole line out about Dixmude and bend it right back, if it did not clear it altogether.
. . . We could bring men in at Ostend or Zeebrugge to reinforce you in a hard south-eastward push. There is no limit to what could be done by the extreme left-handed push and swoop along the Dutch frontier.

Churchill was evidently unaware of the extreme exhaustion and severe numerical weakness of the BEF after the battle. His enthusiasm was infectious, and communicated itself to French when Churchill next visited him at his General Headquarters at St Omer on 7 December; French wrote:

Ibid, p 305

We discussed the situation, and were completely in agreement as to the advisability of my projected coastal advance and close co-operation with the Fleet. I told him there was fear of disagreement with the French, and that political difficulties would certainly arise. He said he did not think they were insuperable.

It appears that not everyone at GHQ shared the 'complete agreement' between French and Churchill. Major-General Sir C. E. Callwell, Director of Military Operations at the War Office, wrote:

Major-General Sir C. E. Callwell, Experiences of a Dug-out 1914–1918, Constable, 1920, p 111

The experts of St Omer did not appear to accept the scheme with absolutely whole-hearted concurrence. By some of them – it may have been a mistaken impression on my part – the visits of the First Lord of the Admiralty to their Chief hardly seemed to be welcomed with the enthusiasm that might have been expected. Whisperings from across the Channel perhaps made one more critical than one ought to have been, but, be that as it may, the project hardly struck one as an especially inviting method of using force at that particular juncture . . . The end was attractive enough, but the means appeared to be lacking.

In long-range – or, for the matter of that, short-range – bombardments of the Flanders littoral by warships I placed no trust. Mr Churchill's 'we could give you 100 or 200 guns from the sea in absolutely devastating support' of 22 November to Sir John French would not have excited me in the very least.*

However, Churchill's advocacy was powerful enough to win over his Cabinet colleagues and on 9 December the Foreign Secretary, Sir Edward Grey, sent a telegram to Sir Francis Bertie, British Ambassador with the French Government, then at Bordeaux:

French, pp 305–7

The military situation points to the advisability of shortly taking steps to prevent the Germans withdrawing their best first-line troops from the Western theatre for employment against Russia and replacing them by second-rate troops.

As some forward movement to achieve this object may be decided on, I desire to bring to the serious attention of the French Government the very strong opinion held by His Majesty's Government that British troops should be so placed in the line as to advance along the coast in immediate co-operation with our Fleet, and thus enable us, if necessary, to land further forces at any critical juncture during the operation . . .

I would point out to the French Government that the people of this country realize that the Belgian coastal positions are now held by Germany as a menace to Great Britain. They would, therefore, regard any losses entailed by an active offensive taken by our troops against these coastal positions as fully justified. British public opinion will even demand that the menace should be removed, for the forts† on the coast of Belgium are being prepared as a base of operations by

---

*As the Gallipoli campaign in 1915 revealed, Churchill never understood the unsuitability of naval guns – or rather, naval ammunition – for land warfare.

† *Sic*, but this must be a misprint for 'ports'; there were no forts on the Belgian coast.

sea and air against Great Britain especially, and this may in time hamper the safe transport of fresh troops from England to France . . .

His Majesty's Government consider it most urgent and important that this step should be taken, and you should ask the French Government to agree to it and to arrange with General Joffre for carrying it out.

The French Commander-in-Chief, General Joffre, was not to be easily moved; he considered the proposal a '*mouvement eccentrique*', and would not consent. On 1 January, 1915, however, a new factor came into calculation.

Winston S. Churchill, *The World Crisis 1911–1918*, Thornton Butterworth, 1923, Odhams Edition, 1938, vol i, p 497

The First Lord of the Admiralty to the Secretary of State for War, for transmission to the Commander-in-Chief, British Expeditionary Army.

1 January, 1915

The battleship *Formidable* was sunk this morning by a submarine in the Channel. Information from all quarters shows that the Germans are steadily developing an important submarine base at Zeebrugge. Unless an operation can be undertaken to clear the coast, and particularly to capture this place, it must be recognized that the whole transportation of troops across the Channel will be seriously and increasingly compromised.

The Admiralty are of opinion that it would be possible, under cover of warships, to land a large force at Zeebrugge in conjunction with any genuine forward movement along the seashore to Ostend. They wish these views, which they have so frequently put forward, to be placed once again before the French commanders, and hope they may receive the consideration which their urgency and importance require.

By now, however, General Joffre's strategy for 1915 had been decided: double blows in Artois and Champagne against the flanks of the great German salient in France. He wanted the British to release French troops for these attacks by taking over more line, and to participate themselves beside the French. To these wishes Sir John French felt impelled to agree, and Churchill quickly saw that this agreement spelt the end of the coastal project, though

it still held the field in British military thought up to the year 1917. At that time our resources of all kinds had greatly increased, but so also had those of the enemy.

It is appropriate that Churchill, as the prime mover, should have the last word:

Ibid, p 491

The French Government also on political grounds showed themselves strongly opposed to allowing the British armies to occupy the sea flank, or to acquire a close association with the Belgian forces. Although every point in the line where troops of different nations were in contact was a point of special weakness – a joint in the harness (*une soudure*) – the French authorities, civil and military alike, insisted on multiplying them by keeping a large French force between the British and the Belgians. These measures were not wholly inspired by the merits of the military situation.

In 1915 it was the Germans, not the British, who attacked in Flanders – the Second Battle of Ypres (22 April–25 May) – using chlorine gas clouds for the first time in the War. The British sector at Ypres was now held by the Second Army, commanded by General Sir Horace Smith-Dorrien. During the course of the battle he was removed and replaced by Lieutenant-General Sir Herbert Plumer, whose intimate acquaintance with the Flanders area now began. The British offensive fighting of the year was conducted by the First Army, under General Haig, at Neuve Chapelle, Festubert and Loos. Dissatisfaction with Sir John French's handling of the BEF had been mounting during the year, and after the last of these battles he was replaced by Haig, who became Commander-in-Chief on 19 December, 1915.

Haig took up his new appointment with two very clear ideas: first, he was conscious, to a degree unusual in the British leadership, both civil and military, of the strain that had been placed on France during the seventeen months of the War. As early as February, 1915, he was apprehensive about the weakening of the French Army. In June he received a visit from one of Joffre's staff officers, a Captain de Couvreville:

> Robert Blake, *The Private Papers of Douglas Haig 1914–1919*, Eyre & Spottiswoode, 1952 [henceforward 'Blake'], p 96; Haig's diary entry for 14 June, 1915.

One serious statement he made. This was to the effect that 'the French people are getting tired of the war'. The tremendous cost of the war, the occupation of a very wealthy part of France by the enemy and the cessation of trade and farming operations were affecting them. Everything was practically at a standstill and the whole of the manhood of the nation was concentrated on this frontier. *There was a general wish that a vigorous effort should be made to end the war by the autumn.**

*Haig's italics.

The costly failure of the French offensives of 1915 naturally increased Haig's anxieties on this score, and from now onwards the fear of French collapse was always present in his mind. At the same time he was vividly conscious of the dominating rôle of the French in the alliance on the Western Front. On 1 January, 1916, he sent for Colonel des Vallières, head of the French Liaison Mission at GHQ:

Ibid, p 122

I showed him the instructions which I had received from the S of S for War containing the orders of the Govt to me. I pointed out that I am *not under* General Joffre's orders, but that would make no difference, as my intention was to do my utmost to carry out General Joffre's wishes on strategical matters, as if they were orders.

Haig never questioned that 1916 would be the year in which his army would be required to shoulder a much larger part of the burden of war: 'There is no doubt to my mind but that the war must be won by the Forces of the British Empire.'* The new Chief of the Imperial General Staff, Lieutenant-General Sir William Robertson, was in full agreement, and worked hard to strengthen the BEF – a task made somewhat easier at first by the fact that a number of 'Kitchener Army' divisions were now reaching a state of readiness for action. So effective were Robertson's efforts to concentrate the British Empire's strength in France that nineteen divisions were added to the BEF in the first six months of the year. The question was, of course, how they should be used.

The attractions of a campaign to clear the Belgian coast, which had appealed so strongly to Churchill and French in 1914, presented themselves equally strongly to Haig a year later. It was in 1915 that Britain first experienced the potential of submarine warfare: 885,471 tons of British shipping were sunk – a small amount by comparison with the next three years, particularly 1917, but an ominous sign nevertheless. No doubt because they were so close to British shores, there was always a tendency to exaggerate the rôle of the Flanders-based U-boats. Captain Stephen Roskill has shown that in 1917 they accounted for only one third of the total sinkings, the remaining two-thirds being attributable to the flotillas at Kiel and Wilhelmshaven.† The same proportion is probably correct for 1915; but at the time the Flanders boats seemed a deadly menace. On 26 December, a week after his appointment as C-in-C, Haig wrote:

*Haig Diary, 14 January, 1916.
† See the *Royal United Service Institution Journal*, November, 1959, Captain S. W. Roskill: 'The U-boat Campaign of 1917 and Third Ypres'.

Ibid, p 120

Admiral Bacon,* commanding the Channel (with HQ at Dover), came to see me today and stayed to lunch. We discussed the co-operation of the Fleet with my Army on the Belgian Coast. He said that the front from Zeebrugge to Ostend was of vital importance to England because the Germans command the east end of the Channel from there and threaten England. We arranged to work out plans together but the time of execution must depend on General Joffre's plan for the general offensive in the Spring.

To Joffre the strategy of 1916 was already settled. On 6, 7 and 8 December there had been an inter-Allied conference at his headquarters at Chantilly, which, he wrote,

> *The Memoirs of Marshal Joffre*, translated by Colonel T. Bentley Mott, Geoffrey Bles, 1932, vol ii, p 414

. . . marks a vital date in the history of the conduct of the war. . . The outcome of these conversations was the drawing up of a document which constituted the charter of the Coalition during the winter of 1915 and the summer campaign of 1916.

It was agreed upon that a decisive result should be sought through coordinated offensives on the three fronts, Russian, Franco-British and Italian.

These offensives were to be launched simultaneously, or at least on dates sufficiently near each other to prevent the enemy from moving his reserves from one front to another.

The general action would be begun as soon as possible.

It is difficult to grasp, but essential to the understanding of all that happened in 1916 and much that happened in 1917, that this was the first *and only* time in the war that the allies formulated and tried to carry out a coordinated strategy. It was, in fact, the first effective attempt to wrest back from the Germans the strategic initiative which they had seized in the West in 1914 and on the Eastern Front in 1915. Thus what the French think of as the year of Verdun, and the British think of as the year of the Somme, and what Russians thought of as the year of General Brusilov's triumphant but costly offensive, ought really to be thought of, not in terms of these individual efforts, but as the year – the solitary year – of Coalition war. The remaining question was, where would the British effort be made? Joffre did not take long to make up his mind, though his reasoning has remained inscrutable; on the day that Haig was discussing

*Vice-Admiral R. H. S. Bacon.

the clearing of the Belgian coast with Admiral Bacon, a letter arrived
from Joffre saying:

Authors Papers:* Joffre to Haig, 25 December,
1915

. . . *l'offensive française serait grandement favorisée par une offensive simultanée
des forces britanniques entre la Somme et Arras.*

Haig was reluctant to give up the idea of making the main British effort
in Flanders. In a private memorandum entitled 'Some thoughts on the
future', he notes on 14 January, 1916:

Operations to clear the Belgian coast must be kept in view, but it is still doubtful
how best they can be fitted into the programme.

He describes the Belgian coast as 'an objective of great political and
naval as well as military importance.' With this thought in mind, on the
same day,

Blake, p 125

I asked General Plumer to consider fully the following alternatives:
(a) An attack on the Forêt d'Houthoulst with the further object of capturing the
     German railway lines about Roulers and to the North and South (Courtrai).
(b) An attack on Lille.
(c) An attack on Messines–Wytschaete ridge.
This latter would be more of a subsidiary nature and unlikely to promise any
far-reaching results.
   Sir H. Plumer said he would require three months' preparation for any one of
these attacks from the time of the final decision that such an attack was to be
carried out.

The discussion between GHQ and GQG† continued. On 26 January
Brigadier-General John Charteris, Head of Intelligence at GHQ wrote:

Brigadier-General John Charteris, *At G.H.Q.*,
Cassell, 1931 [henceforward 'Charteris'], p 132

Joffre has now written that if the big offensive does not come off until late in the
summer, he wants another, in addition to the Arras one, at the end of May. He
agrees to Flanders for our final big attack, and promises French help in it. He is
going much too far. We would be bound to have heavy casualties in the pre-

---

* See *Note on Sources*, p xi.
† *Grand-Quartier-Général*, the French General Headquarters at Chantilly.

paratory attacks, and the main attack would be weakened. But it is a great step to have got the plan for the big attack to be in Flanders. Strategically there is no doubt about that being the best place for us to attack. It strikes direct at the main railway communications of all the German armies. The Germans could not even make good their retreat. A victory, however great, on the Somme would still let them get back to the Meuse. Tactically the ground is more difficult. Most important of all is the weather. An attack in Flanders must be delivered early in the summer. June at the latest. Farther south it can be much later.

On 14 February there was another conference at Chantilly, between Joffre and his Chief of Staff, General de Castelnau, on one side, and Haig, Robertson, and Haig's Chief of Staff, Lieutenant-General Kiggell, on the other. Joffre dates the formal British agreement to make their main effort in 1916 on the Somme, attacking side by side with a French Army Group of forty divisions commanded by General Foch, from this meeting. The Flanders operation now dwindles to a mere subsidiary attack between Ypres and La Bassée, to tie down German reserves and to be launched one or two weeks before the great offensive.

All the arguments and arrangements for Allied offensives became suddenly pointless when the Germans attacked at Verdun on 21 February. Mounting casualties and heavy strain steadily eroded the capacity of the French to take the leading rôle in the Allied offensive when it came. It also became clear that the British, who had taken over the frontage of another French army to give some relief to their ally, would, despite their reinforcements, only be able to mount one major offensive – and that would be on the Somme. Flanders, however, was never quiet; the Ypres sector in 1916 was the scene of some fierce trench warfare, the Germans experimenting with new gases, and both sides busy with underground mining resulting in terrifying explosions and heavy fighting for the resulting craters.

Haig, however, never lost sight of the project of a great offensive in Flanders. In June, less than three weeks before the Battle of the Somme opened, he was again discussing with Admiral Bacon an operation against Ostend and Roulers. On 15 September tanks made their battlefield début, and three days later,

Blake, p 167

I spoke to Admiral Bacon regarding his preparations for landing on the Belgian Coast. In view of the successes obtained by the Tanks, I suggested that he should carry out experiments with special flat-bottomed boats for running ashore and landing a line of Tanks on the beach with the object of breaking through wire and capturing the enemy's defences. Such an operation would be carried out in co-operation with troops from Lombartzyde attacking eastwards. The Admiral is delighted with the idea, and is to go to the Admiralty with a view to having special boats made.

The Battle of the Somme officially ended on 18 November. Its four and a half months constituted undeniably the most destructive experience hitherto inflicted by human beings on each other. Its effect on the war was obviously profound, but susceptible to different interpretations. Among soldiers there was a certain unanimity; the new German High Command, Field-Marshal von Hindenburg (Chief of Staff) and General Erich Ludendorff (First Quartermaster-General), which had replaced Falkenhayn at the end of August, faced a sombre scene in the West:

> General Ludendorff, *My War Memories 1914–1918*, Hutchinson, 1919 [henceforward 'Ludendorff'], vol i, p 307

GHQ had to bear in mind that the enemy's great superiority in men and material would be even more painfully felt in 1917 than in 1916. They had to face the danger that 'Somme fighting' would soon break out at various points on our fronts, and that even our troops would not be able to withstand such attacks indefinitely, especially if the enemy gave us no time for rest and for the accumulation of material. Our position was uncommonly difficult, and a way out hard to find. We could not contemplate an offensive ourselves, having to keep our reserves available for defence. There was no hope of a collapse of any of the Entente Powers. If the war lasted our defeat seemed inevitable.

Another conference of Allied military representatives at Chantilly on 16 November saw the situation in much the same light; they accepted the need to renew the 'Somme fighting' which Hindenburg and Ludendorff so much feared as early as possible:

> Joffre, *Memoirs*, vol ii, p 512

They have, therefore agreed to the following:

(a) During the winter of 1916–17 the offensive operations now under way will be actively continued, as far as weather conditions on the various fronts permit.
(b) To be in a position to meet any new situation, and more especially in order to prevent the enemy from seizing the initiative of operations, the Allied Armies must be ready to undertake general offensives by the first week in February, 1917; all the resources at their disposal should be devoted to this combined action.

On 20 November the British War Committee met, and the Prime Minister, Mr Asquith, aferwards drafted a note for the CIGS. Learning that the substance of the note was to be discussed by Robertson, Haig and the First Sea Lord on 23 November, Asquith did not sign it and forward it officially, but merely laid the draft before the CIGS for information. It read as follows:

> Lloyd George, *War Memoirs*, Odhams Edition, 1938 [henceforward 'Lloyd George'], vol ii, p 1252

10 Downing Street,
21 November, 1916

After you had left the War Committee yesterday a very important discussion took place on the question of the submarine menace, and more particularly in regard to the protection of the routes through the Narrow Seas to France and Holland. The War Committee were absolutely unanimous on the very great desirability, if it is practicable, of some military action designed either to occupy Ostend and Zeebrugge, or at least to render those ports useless as bases for destroyers and submarines. There was no difference of opinion on the War Committee that the submarine constitutes by far the most dangerous menace to the Allies at the present and there appears no reason to doubt that the arrangements of the Admiralty for dealing with these craft would be immensely facilitated if the enemy could be deprived of these bases.

[A paragraph follows on the strain on the Admiralty of protecting essential sea routes.]

There is no operation of war to which the War Committee would attach greater importance than the successful occupation, or at least the deprivation to the enemy, of Ostend, and especially Zeebrugge.

I desire therefore that the General Staff and the Higher Command in France, in consultation with the Admiralty as necessary, shall give the matter their closest attention and that you will report to me personally at an early date what action you consider feasible.

Although this note never received the final authority of signature, there can be no doubt that it constitutes the true point of origin of the Flanders offensive of 1917. Ultimate responsibility is thus seen to lie where it ought to lie – with the country's political leaders. However, as we have seen, the British High Command was in full sympathy with the Government; there remained the matter of integrating British and Allied strategies. At a further meeting at Chantilly, on 29 November, this time of Army Group Commanders, including Haig, it was agreed that to begin with the British should maintain pressure on the Somme front in the direction of Bapaume. Joffre says:

Joffre, *Memoirs*, vol ii, p 515

Once the Bapaume salient was reduced, Haig's intention was to push the main body of his forces northward, so as to make an attack in Flanders and thus open the way for a disembarkation on the Belgian coast between Nieuport and Ostend.

The essential idea which governed me was that the battle of 1916 had so thoroughly disorganized the enemy's defences and the German reserves had been used up to such an extent that, if we now made a supreme effort, we could hardly fail to obtain decisive results.

Lloyd George, vol ii, pp 1250–1; Robertson to Joffre, 1 December, 1916

My Dear General,

My Government has been viewing with some anxiety the increase of German naval activity on the coast of Belgium, which clearly has for its object the interruption of communications between Great Britain and France. . . It is obvious that the maintenance of sea communication between Great Britain and France is vital to the successful conduct of the War on the Western Front, and in these circumstances my Government desire that the occupation of Ostend and Zeebrugge should form one of the objectives of the campaign next year.

The magnetism of Flanders, which had attracted the British Army since the early days of the War, was thus reinforced by powerful economic and political pressures. The strategic implications, however, now became a matter of violent dispute. If the Battle of the Somme, with all its suffering, seemed in the eyes of the military leaders of both sides to have brought the prospect of Allied victory measurably nearer, in the eyes of many politicians it had a different look. Outstanding among these was the dynamic British Secretary of State for War, Mr David Lloyd George. Sir Maurice Hankey, Secretary to the War Committee, recorded in his diary on 1 November:

Lord Hankey, *The Supreme Command 1914–1918*, Allen & Unwin, 1916 [henceforward 'Hankey'], vol ii, p 556

Lunched alone with Lloyd George . . . Lloyd George considered that the Somme offensive had been a bloody and disastrous failure; he was not willing to remain in office if it was to be repeated next year; he said Thomas,* Bissolati,* and others thought the same; they would all resign simultaneously and tell their respective

*Albert Thomas, French Minister of Munitions; Signor Bissolati, Italian Socialist leader.

fellow-countrymen that the war was being run on the wrong lines, and that they had better make peace rather than repeat the experience of 1916.

On 7 December, 1916, Mr Lloyd George became Prime Minister.

On 12 December General Joffre was appointed 'technical adviser' to the French Government. General Robert Nivelle became Commander-in-Chief of the Armies of the North and North-East.

On 26 December General Joffre resigned, and received the rank of Marshal of France.

On 27 December King George V appointed General Haig to the rank of Field-Marshal.

III

1917: THE THREADS

———————————— ✤ ————————————

INNUMERABLE and very diverse threads went to compose the pattern of 1917, the darkest year of the War. According to a man's position in the great march of events, the part of the pattern nearest him would take on this or that shade. Our purpose is to trace the thread of the British Flanders Offensive of the summer and autumn ('Flanders' for brevity) through to its end. Like all major themes this was affected by many circumstances, entangled with many other threads; it was obviously influenced by politics, by personal relations, by technological developments,* by accident, and much else. For the time being I have tried to reduce their number to five (but others will be added). They are:

> FLANDERS, often pushed into the distant background, but never entirely lost to view;
>
> SOLDIERS AND POLITICIANS, whose bad relations overhung the year like a pall of dark smoke;
>
> COMMAND CHANGES, among both soldiers and politicians, affecting every phase of the year's action, adding to its uncertainties;
>
> THE INVISIBLE ENEMY, the unseen but deadly submarine, whose performance reached a frightening peak in this year, gravely influencing decisions and deeds; and
>
> THE INVINCIBLE ENEMY, which mocked all men's efforts with frost and snow and rain; in north-western Europe a year with only a late, brief spring and no real summer at all.

---

*A striking example of this was the swaying contest between British and German aircraft designers, giving first to one side then the other the mastery of the air which was already vital and paid for at high cost by both sides in turn.

January

✠

SOLDIERS AND POLITICIANS

Colonel Repington, *The First World War 1914–1918*, Constable, 1920 [henceforward 'Repington'], vol i, p 421

Monday, 1 January

... On reading my French papers this evening I see that the Decree of 13 December, appointing Joffre *'Conseiller technique en ce qui concerne la direction de la guerre'* has been cancelled, as well as that of 2 December, 1915, which made him C in C of all the French forces. The duties hitherto performed by the French GQG are to become part of those of the General Staff of the Army at the War Ministry. Thus it seems to me that the French Cabinet intend to run the strategy of war, as L.G. obviously intends to do here. This is very serious. At the same time I get a *'projet de résolution'* from Steed,* drawn up by the French Deputy, M. Hennessy, in favour of an Allied General Staff, which seems to be part of the plan for concentrating the real direction of the war under the French. I rang up Steed tonight and found that he and I absolutely disagreed on all this affair, he holding that there was no distinction between policy and strategy (!): that Robertson and Joffre had been obstructive: that there had been a military dictatorship under the Asquith Cabinet, and so on – the usual fustian. All this because Robertson has kept strictly within his legitimate duties and has tried to keep the Cabinet from committing follies. Steed also complained – and all his ideas obviously come from Thomas and other French politicians – that Joffre and Robertson had made their plans together before the Conferences. So they did, because they would not trust them to 60 or 100 people, and they were quite right. But evidently all this is even more serious than I thought, and I am much perturbed to know what I can do or ought to do to help to save the country from the danger which has so often nearly ruined it before, namely, of having its strategy directed by a pack of ignorant politicians.

*Wickham Steed, Foreign Editor of *The Times*; Repington was Military Correspondent.

FLANDERS

O.H., 1917, vol i, Appendix 5; Robertson to
Haig, 1 January, 1917

With reference to your O.A.D. 256 of 25 December, 1916, in view of the great importance which the War Cabinet attach, as you are aware, to the capture of Ostend and Zeebrugge before next winter, I shall be glad if you will inform me whether, in your opinion, General Nivelle's plan of operations and the proposed extension of your front is likely to prevent you from undertaking the operations which you contemplate in Belgium.

COMMAND CHANGES

O.H., 1917, vol i, Appendix 2; Nivelle to Haig,
21 December, 1916

In continuation of our conversation on 20 December, I have the honour to set out below my views on the subject of our offensive of 1917 and of the modifications which I consider necessary in the original plan of these operations.

Objective. In the offensive of 1917 the Franco-British Armies must strive to destroy the main body of the enemy's Armies on the Western Front. This result can be attained only after a decisive battle, with considerable superiority of numbers, against all the available forces of the enemy.

It is therefore necessary:

– to pin down as large a proportion as possible of the hostile forces;

– to break the enemy's front in such a manner that the rupture can be immediately exploited;

– to overcome all the reserves with which our adversary can oppose us;

– to exploit with all our resources the result of this decisive battle.

Resources required. In order to carry out this programme it is essential to have the disposal of a mass of manoeuvre sufficiently strong to overcome without chance of failure all the hostile reserves available, in addition to the forces required at the beginning to pin down the enemy and break his front.

I consider that this mass should be a homogeneous force possessing full cohesion and trained for its task by the commanders who will have to make use of it . . .

Rôle of the British Armies. In sum, the rôle of the British Armies in our joint offensive should be:

1. To permit me to form without delay the mass of manoeuvre which is indispensable for the decisive battle;

2. To undertake on the front of attack which you have in mind an offensive sufficiently large and powerful to absorb a considerable proportion of the German reserves . . .

3. To participate in the general exploitation which will follow the decisive battle in another area by bringing about the disorganization of the forces in position

opposite your front and by undertaking the pursuit of the enemy within a zone on which we can decide later by common accord . . .

Finally, the plan which I have put before you does not exclude the possibility of carrying out, in case of need, the operation for the capture of Ostend and Zeebrugge, since that cannot take place until the summer.

This operation can be considered in all details in the light of the directive already adopted, and I even think that our Belgian allies ought to prepare from now onward for the rôle they will have to assume in it.

If our grand offensive succeeds, it is certain that the Belgian coast will fall into our hands as a result of the retreat of the German Armies and without direct attack.

If, on the contrary, our attacks fail, it will still be possible to carry out in fine weather* the operations projected in Flanders . . .

Accept, my dear General, the expression of my
                        most cordial sentiments,
                                          R. Nivelle

The above document embodies the 'Nivelle Plan' for 1917 which now displaced the inter-Allied agreements arrived at under Joffre's direction in November. It prescribed holding attacks to tie down German reserves by the British on the Arras-Bapaume sector, and by French forces between the Somme and the Oise, while an *attaque brusquée* on the Aisne performed the break-through which would then be decisively exploited by a mass of manoeuvre of 27 French divisions. The entire operation would be seen to be a success or failure within 24–48 hours. The significant deviation from Joffre's plan is the restoration of the main offensive rôle in 1917 to the French Armies, despite their heavy losses in preceding years.† This decision was pleasing to French *amour propre*, but not to realists in the French Army and Government; it was very acceptable, however, to Mr Lloyd George, outraged and appalled at British

---

*'à la belle saison'.

† M. Paul-Marie de la Gorce (*The French Army*, Weidenfeld & Nicolson, 1963, p 103), says:

1914	955,000 (killed, wounded and captured)
1915	1,430,000
1916	900,000
	3,285,000

The British Official History, quoting the French Official Account, gives a lower total:

to 31 December, 1915	1,961,687
1916	600,000 (approx)
	2,561,687

casualties on the Somme.* Haig's immediate comment when Nivelle explained his plan on 20 December was this:

Blake, p 188

He is confident of breaking through the enemy's Front now that the enemy's morale is weakened, but the blow must be struck by surprise and go through in 24 hours. This necessity for surprise after all is our own conclusion . . . Altogether I was pleased with my first meeting with Nivelle.

Charteris, however, recorded the meeting somewhat differently:

Charteris, p 181

20 DECEMBER.   Just back from a conference at Cassel, where D.H. saw Nivelle. Nivelle certainly sees big! The French are to do the main attack, *not* alongside of us. We are to attack to help them. This means a complete change in all our schemes. We have to take on a great deal more front-line trench, so as to set free French troops for their big effort . . . D.H. is sceptical about the French being able to deliver a decisive attack. If it fails we shall be back at the position of a year ago, with all the advantages of the Somme thrown away.

Haig evidently had understandable reservations about Nivelle's plan (as other French generals did) while being prepared to give his new colleague all benefit of the doubt. Misunderstandings, however, some serious, others less so, dogged the discussions and correspondence of the two generals about the plan. In an attempt to clear these up once and for all, Haig set down his own views of the priorities for 1917 in a letter to Nivelle on 6 January; it included this passage:

O.H., 1917, vol i, Appendix 7

It is essential that the Belgian coast shall be cleared this summer. I hope and believe that we shall be able to effect much more than that, and within limitations of time I will cooperate to the utmost of my power in the larger plans which you have proposed.

But it must distinctly be understood between us that if I am not satisfied that this larger plan, as events develop, promises the degree of success necessary to clear the Belgian coast, then I not only cannot continue the battle but I will look to you to fulfil the undertaking you have given me verbally to relieve on the defensive front the troops I require for my northern offensive.

---

*419,654. The British total to the end of 1916 was 1,120,204. According to which French total is preferred, the British loss was thus less than half or about a third of the French. It was awareness of this great discrepancy that prompted misgivings about French capacities in 1917.

In short, the first two phases of the battle cannot be of '*une durée prolongée*' as you suggest. . . If these two phases are not so successful as to justify me in entering on the third phase, then I must transfer my main forces to the north. To enable me to do this in sufficient time to carry out my plans it would be necessary that the relief of the troops on the southern part of my front should be carried out by the middle of June . . .

Thus, there is, in fact, a fourth phase of the battle to be provided for in our plans. The need to carry it out may not, and, I hope, will not, arise. But the clearance of the Belgian coast is of such importance to the British Government that it must be fully provided for before I can finally agree to your proposals.

FLANDERS

While Haig was writing this letter (which, incidentally, provided the answer to Robertson's query of 1 January) certain practical measures were already in hand.

> *O.H.*, 1917, vol ii, Appendix V; Kiggell to
> Plumer, 6 January, 1917

With reference to your G. 352 dated 12 December, 1916, giving your plan for offensive operations north of the river Lys, the Commander-in-Chief desires me to draw your attention to the following points with a view to recasting the plan.

1. The operations north of the river Lys will not take place until after the subsidiary British attacks elsewhere and main French offensive operations have been carried out. It is therefore to be anticipated that the enemy will have been severely handled and his reserves drawn away from your front before the attacks north of the Lys are launched.

Under these circumstances, it is essential that the plan should be based on rapid action and entail the breaking through of the enemy's defences on a wide front without any delay. . .

3. The object of these operations is to inflict a decisive defeat on the enemy and to free the Belgian coast.

The immediate intention is to break through the enemy defensive systems on the approximate front Hooge–Steenstraat with the object of securing the line Roulers–Thourout and, by advancing in a north-easterly direction, to threaten the coast defences in rear.

The Belgians and French will co-operate by attacking from Dixmude and Nieuport respectively.

O.H., 1917, vol ii, Appendix VI: 'Instructions for the formation of a special sub-section of the Operations Section of the General Staff', 8 January

Lieut.-Colonel C. N. McMullen.

1. You will form a special sub-section, with (Major Viscount) Gort, in the Operations (A) Section of the General Staff, with the object of working out a plan of operations to take place north of the river Lys . . .

3. You will find all the papers necessary to show the general scope of the operations. Gort will assist you in collecting these papers, which you should keep under lock and key in a separate box in my room.

Shortly, the idea is for the British to operate on the Vimy, Arras and Ancre fronts, in conjunction with attacks by the French armies. If the French are successful in driving the Germans back, we shall put all our efforts in to help them and there will be no necessity for the operations north of the river Lys taking place.

If, on the other hand, the French do not succeed in their efforts to force the Germans back and thus fail to clear the Belgian coast, the French will take over from us probably up to the Ancre river, and we shall switch as rapidly as possible to carry out our operations on a large scale north of the river Lys.

4. The object of our operations north of the river Lys is to clear the Belgian coast this summer. The War Cabinet attaches the greatest importance to the liberation of this coast . . .

6. Sir Herber Plumer made out a scheme for the northern and southern sector attacks in the shape of a steady, deliberate advance similar to the Somme battle. The Commander-in-Chief rejected this. The whole essence is to attack with rapidity and push right through quickly. It must not be forgotten that this attack will be delivered subsequent to attacks by the whole of the French armies and a portion of the British army. The Germans are likely to be disorganized and weak.

Sir Herbert Plumer is recasting the scheme, to be submitted by 31 January . . .

7. The Southern Sector attack is comparatively simple, but the Northern Sector attack requires careful thought owing to the difficulty of massing troops and guns in the Ypres Salient, also in the crossing of the canal north of the Salient . . .

8. You should get to work at once to make out the whole plan, in collaboration with the Second Army headquarters . . .

12. Consider the possibilities of surprise attack with tanks in the Northern Sector. The O.C. Tanks* is carrying out a reconnaissance of this area.

13. Remember that the Field-Marshal Commanding-in-Chief will command and control all the attacking forces – British (naval and military), Belgian and French, and conduct the operations as one whole.

*Brigadier-General H. J. Elles.

Consider the system of command. The date of attack will probably not be before 15 June.
14. When you have studied all the papers, etc., and understand the whole project thoroughly, please speak.

J. H. Davidson,*
Br.-General, General Staff

It will be seen that Haig and his staff were quite sure that in making these preparations for an offensive in Flanders, in the event of General Nivelle fulfilling less than his promise, they were carrying out the strong wishes of the British Government as expressed to the CIGS in November, 1916.† But while the above papers were being written, another inter-Allied conference was taking place in Rome.

COMMAND CHANGES

At the Rome Conference (5–7 January, 1917) the new Prime Minister, Mr Lloyd George, advanced on behalf of the British Government a strategy for the year very different from that to which his military advisers believed themselves already fully committed. In the memorandum which he circulated to the assembled delegates (and in a powerful speech) Lloyd George now advocated transferring the main Allied effort of the year to the Italian Front.

Lloyd George, vol i, pp 843–4

23.
... If (the enemy) elects to attack on this front, we propose that the Allies should concert their own plans, so that, instead of meeting the artillery armament that he calculates for, he shall find himself confronted with a vastly superior armament of Italian guns reinforced by British, and we should hope, French artillery, with their own personnel. We can put the Germans out of action just as well on the Italian as on the Western Front . . .
24. The second possible contingency is that the Allies themselves should take the offensive in this region . . . Would it not be possible to make a great and sudden stroke against the enemy by a concentration of British and French artillery‡ on the Isonzo Front, so as not only to ensure the safety of Italy against any enemy concentration, but, what is more important, to shatter the enemy's forces, to

*Brigadier-General J. H. Davidson, Head of Operations Section at GHQ.
† See p 17.
‡ The figure repeatedly mentioned was 250–300 heavy guns.

inflict a decisive defeat on him, and to press forward to Trieste and to get astride the Istrian Peninsula?

25. The strategical advantages to be gained by such action appear to be very great. It would probably be a great surprise to the enemy. The action would be fought on enemy territory. It would enable the Italians to deploy their full strength. It would compel the enemy to defend a longer line. It should, therefore, have an immediate effect in relieving the Russian, Roumanian and Balkan Fronts. It might enable the Allies to attack Pola, and probably either destroy the Austrian Fleet, or to force it to action, or drive it out to become a prey to our submarines. This in turn should hamper the enemy's submarine campaign in the Mediterranean. Moreover, it could be accomplished without any additional strain whatever upon our shipping. It would have a moral and political effect of the greatest consequence, and would be a good counter to the enemy's successes in Roumania. It would enable the Allies to take advantage of a period when the weather on the Western Front is unfavourable for the development of a great offensive.

The French and Italian delegations and their advisers did not support Lloyd George's proposals. When consulted, the Italian Commander-in-Chief, General Cadorna, conscious of the opposition of the French Government, conscious also of the strong disapproval of the British CIGS, Sir William Robertson, who was present, and aware of the very different agreement only recently signed in his name at Chantilly, made a lukewarm response to the offer. But above all it was the volte-face of the French Prime Minister, M. Aristide Briand, and M. Albert Thomas, on whose opposition to a Western offensive Lloyd George had counted, that decided the day. So firmly did they both now endorse General Nivelle's plan, and so eloquently back that general, that no senior officer from GQG was required to attend the conference. In the event:

Ibid, p 857

7. The Conference are impressed with the opportunities afforded by the Italian Front for a combined offensive by the three Western Allies. They agree that the question of assistance being given by the Western Allies to the Italian Army on the Carso should be referred to the Military Advisers of the various Governments, with a view to a decision by the three Governments concerned.

There, for a time, the matter rested. But the threads of the year were already becoming tangled, and as we shall see, the idea of a heavy blow at Austria (as he would put it, striking 'at the weakest and not at the strongest point on the enemy front') remained in Lloyd George's mind and would recur. For a while, however, he was content to let it take a secondary place, because on the way back from Rome he met Nivelle himself, and was sufficiently impressed to invite the French C-in-C to London to lay his plan before the War Cabinet in the presence of Haig. This meeting took place on 15–16 January. Aided, perhaps, by his fluent command of English, Nivelle was able to win the full support of the War Cabinet.* At the end of the proceedings, a Convention was drawn up, signed by Haig, Robertson and Nivelle; this laid down:

O.H., 1917, vol i, Appendix 8

2. The British and French Armies will take the offensive at latest on 1 April and before that date if it is possible or if the general situation requires it, in conformity with the decisions reached at the Chantilly Conference on 15 November, 1916 . . .
4. The exploitation of the successes obtained on the three fronts of attack will be carried out with the full vigour necessary to obtain a decisive result and by means of the employment, if required, of all the available reserves of the British and French Armies.
5. In case these operations do not achieve the success which is expected and which ought to be very rapidly attained, the battle will be broken off by agreement, in order to allow the British Armies to engage in other operations on a front further north, in co-operation with the Belgian Army and the French Nieuport Group.
6. These arrangements, which conform to the directives given by the French War Committee to General Nivelle, have been approved by the British War Committee, which will facilitate their execution as far as possible in respect of the means to be put at the disposal of Field-Marshal Haig . . .

This document contains the first unequivocal association of Lloyd George's Government (as opposed to his predecessor's) with the plan for a British offensive in Flanders in 1917, and its assent to that plan.

Meanwhile, however, the mood of enthusiasm produced by Nivelle's eloquence drew Lloyd George and his colleagues to the first of a number of unusual steps, described by Lord Hankey in his memoirs:

Hankey, vol ii, p 615

Immediately after the London Conference an instruction was sent to Haig emphasizing the importance which the War Cabinet attached to the utmost despatch in carrying out both the letter and the spirit of the agreement made with Nivelle. The Field-Marshal was urged to make sure that the French should not have to delay their operations owing to our preparations being incomplete.

This was the last time that a British Government would show such ardour for offensive action by the British forces on the Western Front.

*Lloyd George, Lord Milner, Lord Curzon, Mr Arthur Henderson, Mr Bonar Law.

THE INVINCIBLE ENEMY

Papers: Haig Diary

17 JANUARY.   Hard frost during night, and some snow fell.

24 JANUARY.   19° of frost registered here last night.

31 JANUARY.   Heavy snow fell during night. About 3 inches deep.

Repington, vol i, p 447

31 JANUARY.   The cold continues: the hardest winter I remember since 1880–'81.

Author's Papers: Haig Diary

26 JANUARY.   The railway situation has suddenly become worse. This morning . . . a telegram . . . was handed to me stating that from noon today only food supplies, ammunition and material for the railways could be carried – all other traffic must be stopped.

The transport crisis which now occurred was the product of several factors: the increasing strain of war needs on the Nord railway system; the blocking of the port of Boulogne for 27 days by the grounding of the steamer *Araby* on 21 December; the severity of this winter of 1916–17, when first the frost prevented all canal traffic, and then the thaw damaged the roads, compelling severe restrictions on their use. In no other year of the War did the weather play such a sinister part, as we shall observe. Meanwhile, on 29 January matters had so far deteriorated that Haig, accompanied by his Chief of Staff, General Kiggell, and Sir Eric Geddes, Director-General of Transport at GHQ, visited Nivelle at his headquarters near Beauvais. With Nivelle was M. Claveille, Minister of Communications.

Duff Cooper, *Haig*, Faber & Faber, 1935 [henceforward 'Duff Cooper'; an important source of extracts from Haig's Diary], vol ii, p 34

I walked with Claveille to the office after lunch, and made the suggestion that our technical railway men should be in touch with the French working staff. He quite agreed as to the necessity for the change.

Immediately after lunch we discussed the situation. Geddes had prepared a statement of our case as I wanted. It showed that we must have 200,000 tons carried weekly. I explained it to the conference. The discussion was most friendly, both sides being anxious to do their best.

Unfortunately, it would take more than one friendly discussion to resolve this problem, which would soon provide yet another unforeseeable entanglement of the threads of 1917. Meanwhile, through all these day-to-day preoccupations, Haig never lost sight of the more distant prospect.

FLANDERS

Author's Papers: Haig Diary

23 JANUARY.   Admiral Bacon . . . is having a special gangway made. It is some 600 yards long, and by using three of them, he calculates that an infantry division and a few guns without horses could be landed in 15 minutes.

25 JANUARY.   I discussed future plans with Kiggell, and decided:

1. General Plumer should reconnoitre the front as far as Steenstraat with a view to taking it over before the date fixed for the offensive.

2. Rawlinson* (with Uniacke as C.R.A.†) will be in command of the Army attacking north of Ypres. He should supervise preparations which will be commenced under Plumer's directions now.

3. It will require six weeks to change from the operations in the south to those in the north.

The above entries show how far ahead offensives had to be planned at this stage of the War, and how difficult it was in practice to 'switch' a major effort from one front to another – an operation always easy enough in an armchair, or in the tranquillity of subsequent memoir-writing. In the apt words of M. Briand at the time, by 1917 a large offensive had become 'nothing less than a great industrial organization'; and this it would remain as long as artillery provided the sole means of breaching the enemy's positions.

Meanwhile, one more thread was working into the pattern of the year.

THE INVISIBLE ENEMY

Lloyd George, vol i, p 709

Statistics of shipping losses, January, 1917 — 153,899 gross tons sunk.‡

Repington, vol i, p 440

24 JANUARY (*Wednesday*).   I said that any reasonable price for 500,000 to 1,000,000 rifles, which would bring into the field an equivalent number of

---

*General Sir Henry Rawlinson, commanding the Fourth Army.
† Major-General H. C. C. Uniacke, Chief of Royal Artillery, Fifth Army.
‡ British.

Russian troops, would be worth paying for. It might enable us to win the war this year, and in my view it was at present a question whether our armies could win the war before our navies lost it.

Ludendorff, vol i, pp 312–18

The Field-Marshal and myself . . . had already had under consideration, as part of our military problems, the possibility of carrying on submarine operations in the intensified form of the 'War Zone' campaign. Unrestricted submarine warfare was now the only means left to secure a victorious end to the war within a reasonable time. If submarine warfare in this form could have a decisive effect – and the Navy held that it could – then in the existing situation it was our plain military duty to the German nation to embark on it . . .

The Chief of the Naval Staff,* a friend of the Chancellor, but at the same time a warm partisan of the unrestricted submarine war, was confident that the campaign would have decisive results within six months . . .

The Chancellor's† judgment as to our military position was the same as our own. While we felt compelled resolutely to draw the inevitable and serious inference, and act on it, the Chancellor, as his nature was, remained undecided and came to such conclusions as: 'The decision to embark on the campaign depends on the effects which are to be expected from it'; and: 'If the military authorities regard it as essential, I am not in a position to withstand them'; and: 'If success beckons, we must act'.

However, with a full sense of his political responsibility, the Chancellor did advise the adoption of the campaign, as did His Majesty's other advisers. The Emperor fell in with their views and commanded that the campaign should open on 1 February.

*Admiral von Holtzendorff.
† Count von Bethmann-Hollweg.

February

✠

The Invincible Enemy

Author's Papers: Haig Diary
2 FEBRUARY.   Harder frost than ever last night.

Repington, vol i, p 452
8 FEBRUARY.   The Household Cavalry infantry battalion . . . has had heavy losses from frostbite.

Author's Papers: Haig Diary
9 FEBRUARY.   25° of frost or more in places. At Boulogne and along the coast the sands are all frozen as the tide goes back.

Flanders

On 5 February General Rawlinson reported to Haig:

Author's Papers: Haig Diary
He had seen General Plumer and fixed his HQ and those of his corps, but had not studied the problem sufficiently as yet to give any definite opinion regarding such questions as dividing the line between two armies, order of objectives etc. I told General Kiggell to arrange for photos to be taken of the woods about Hooge, Becelaere and Zandvoorde, while the snow is on the ground. These should enable us to decide on our plans for attacking this sector, possibility of using Tanks and other details.

Author's Papers: Haig Diary
10 FEBRUARY.   Some very excellent photos have been taken of the woods east of the Ypres salient as requested by me. These show a great diminution of trees since I fought there in November, 1914, and so there seems greater possibilities for the use of Tanks in that part of the ground.

After lunch I went into General Rawlinson's proposals for the operations north of Ypres. I am of opinion that it is possible to make three simultaneous attacks. The attack on right by Plumer's Army; on left by Rawlinson's Army (as proposed by Plumer) and simultaneously an attack by surprise in centre with Tanks, and without artillery preparation, to capture the high ground between Conservatory Hill and Broodseinde.

SOLDIERS AND POLITICIANS

> Michael MacDonagh,* *In London During The Great War*, Eyre & Spottiswoode, 1935 [henceforward 'MacDonagh'], pp 173–5

2 FEBRUARY (*Saturday*).   I came to Carnarvon last night for the speech which Lloyd George made this afternoon – the first to his constituents as Prime Minister . . .

The speech lasted an hour and a half. It was a masterly performance. We were made to see the big job which the Prime Minister and his Government have in hand, that of straightening out the intricate and complex War problems which confront the country – military, financial, political and economic. He impressed us with his own thoroughness. He takes the bull not only by the horns but by the tail as well. So the speech marched on to a characteristic glowing peroration. Countenance, gesture, voice – all contributed to its cumulative effect. For Lloyd George on the platform acts as well as talks. 'Time,' said he, 'is a hesitating and perplexed neutral. He has not yet decided which side he is going to swing his terrible scythe on. For the moment that scythe is striking both sides with terrible havoc. The hour will come when it will be swung finally on one side or the other. Time is the deadliest of all the neutral Powers. Let us see that we enlist him among our Allies.'

The only way to win time, he explained, was by not losing time. We must not lose time in the Cabinet nor in the Departments which carry out the decrees of the Cabinet. We must not lose time in the field or the factory or workshop. He went on: 'There are rare epochs in the history of the world when in a few raging years the character, the destiny of the whole race are determined for unknown ages.' With gleaming eyes and right hand uplifted, he solemnly added: 'This is one!' These three concluding words sent a thrill of emotion throught the crowded hall.

> Haig Diary: Blake, p 195

7 FEBRUARY.   General Maurice† . . . came to lunch . . . After lunch, I had a talk with him. From being an admirer of Mr Lloyd George, he has got to distrust him, since he has got to know him better. He says that L.G. is so sketchy, and goes into nothing thoroughly. He only presses forward the measures which he thinks will meet with popular favour. Further, M. does not think he really cares for the

*Of *The Times*.
† Major-General Frederick Maurice, Director of Military Operations at the War Office.

country or is patriotic – in fact, he does not trust him. It is, indeed, a calamity for the country to have such a man at the head of affairs in this time of great crisis. We can only try and make the best of him.

I reminded Maurice of what I told the P.M. before the Nivelle Conference in London, namely, that by employing British Divisions to extend the line to the Roye Road, we deprived the British Army of its chance of attacking in force and reaping a decisive success. We willingly play a second rôle to the French, that is, we are to make a holding attack to draw in the enemy's reserves so as to make the task of the French easier. We shall at any rate have heavy losses with the possibility of no showy successes, whereas the French are to make the decisive attack with every prospect of gaining the fruits of victory. I think it is for the general good that we play this rôle in support of the French, but let future critics realize that we have adopted it with our eyes open as to the probable consequences.

Manpower

Author's Papers: General Staff Weekly Summary for the Cabinet

8 February.   1. *Manpower*. – By far the most important feature to be noted in this week's summary is the breakdown of our own recruiting. In November last the War Office informed HM Govt that unless steps were taken *at once* to provide more men for the Army it would be impossible after April next to keep it up to strength. Such measures as have been taken have proved to be quite inadequate, and the situation foreseen by the W.O. has now arisen . . .

Repington, vol i, pp 454–8

9 February (*Friday*).   Went down . . . to No. 10 Downing Street to lunch with the Prime Minister . . .

We . . . went into the Manpower question, and I was thoroughly alarmed by the P.M.'s attitude. He seemed to me to be influenced by sentiment and prejudice, rather than by a reasoned view of the military necessities of the case, and although he had been the head and front of the demand for men under the Asquith leadership, he now seemed to me to be adopting an attitude which threatened danger for the success of our arms. He said that he was 'not prepared to accept the position of a butcher's boy driving cattle to the slaughter, and that he would not do it.' In making this sort of statement he assumes a kind of rage, looks savage, and glares at one fiercely. I suppose that his colleagues and toadies quail under this assumption of ferocity. I said that he must place himself in the position of the soldiers who had a definite military problem before them, and must know, not only how many men they could have now, but also how many during the rest of the year. All organization, strategy, and even tactics, I told him, hinged upon this decision . . .

I saw Sir W. Robertson afterwards . . . R. said that he did not intend to lose the war by giving in to the politicians, and that the Army Council had taken up a strong position on which they would stand. His view was that if it were true that we could not guarantee Haig his drafts after April – which was the present position in the event of serious fighting – then we should so inform Haig, who could then lay the matter before Nivelle, and the two would then be able to revise their plans. I strongly agreed with this line, and it may bring the War Cabinet to their senses . . .'

The Invisible Enemy

MacDonagh, pp 176–7

8 February.   The serious limitation of our food-supplies and the urgent necessity of economy in consumption were revealed by an official statement in the House of Commons today which gave members generally a shock of surprise.

The baking of brown or wholemeal bread is already compulsory, so as to make wheat go as far as possible by the use of parts of the grain which in the making of white bread are discarded. We have been advised to eat potatoes, skins and all, by a University professor, who contends that in peeling, one-fifth of the tuber as an article of food is lost. A peeress rails in the newpapers against what she calls the wasting of the food of the common people by the starching of men's collars and cuffs, rice and maize being used in the making of starch . . .

The statement was made by Captain Charles Bathurst of the Food Controller's Department. He said: 'Masters of foxhounds have decided on their own initiative to reduce substantially the number of days' hunting. They are shooting foxes and advising members of their hunts to shoot them, in order to prevent destruction of poultry and vegetables. More than that, they are prepared to slaughter a very large proportion of their hounds.'

What a recognition of the stern necessity of conserving food for human consumption! . . .

Repington, vol i, p 454

9 February (Friday).   L. G. said that the Admiralty had been awful, and the present submarine menace was the result . . . He thought that the apathy and incompetence of the naval authorities were terrible. I asked him why he did not hang somebody. He said that, at the time of the French Revolution, the heads of the incompetents would certainly have fallen. I reminded him that he and his friends had always given everything that the Navy had asked for, whereas the Army had always been starved, yet now the Army was winning the war while the Navy was losing it.

Author's Papers: Derby to Haig, 11 February

Lord Derby (Secretary of State for War) quotes to Haig Repington's 'question whether our armies could win the war before our navies lost it'*:

Rather cruel on the Navy because they are really at their wits' end as to how to deal with these submarines.

Hankey, vol ii, p 645

11 FEBRUARY (*Sunday*). Had a brainwave on the subject of anti-submarine warfare, so ran down to Walton Heath in the afternoon to formulate my ideas to Lloyd George, who was very interested. I sat up late completing a long Memo. on the subject. My Memorandum was an argument for convoys, but contained a great number of suggestions.

FLANDERS

O.H., 1917, vol ii, Appendix VII: Memorandum by Operations Section, General Staff GHQ, 14 February

Only two of the Operations Section proposals need consideration in detail here:

Rôle of the Belgians
7. The British operations should be in no way dependent on co-operation by the Belgians and need not be so. Any operation which the latter can undertake with a view to dispersal of the enemy's forces, or even subsequently to co-operate with the main attack, should be regarded as an additional asset, but no diversion should be made of British resources, which can be profitably employed either on the Ypres front or at Nieuport. . .

The Nieuport Attack and Landing
8. This operation appears to offer good prospects of success and might lead rapidly to very striking results. The paramount necessity is that it should be kept secret, especially the landing, and the method of landing now proposed renders this easy. It appears worth considering whether a report of an intended landing north of Ostend should be spread abroad prior to the Arras attack. When this is proved false subsequent rumours of operations on the coast might obtain less credence.

It is proposed that the enemy's front line system at Nieuport should be captured in the afternoon and that his second line should be attacked about 3 am on the

*See p 33.

following day. Simultaneously with the attack on the second line a landing would be effected at three points at and south-west of Middelkerke Bains by a force embarked after dark the previous evening at Dunkirk.

Zero Day for the Nieuport attack should be when the main advance has progressed so far as to afford a reasonable chance of early tactical co-operation between the two forces. This might be when our troops have reached the neighbourhood of Cortemarck or earlier if the enemy showed signs of great demoralization and disorganization.

The rôle of the landing force would be to push forward rapidly with the greatest boldness and resolution to seize certain tactical points, including those giving control of the power to inundate, and the force would be specially organized with this end in view. . .

The minimum strength of the first echelon of the landing party at each of the three points will be 5,000, and it may be possible to increase these numbers. The method of landing is from two monitors at each point by means of special pontoons under cover of a smoke screen. Tanks and other vehicles will be carried on the pontoons and the issue of troops from the pontoons will be preceded by tanks if necessary.

The initial number of divisions required for this operation is five, i.e., two to attack, two in reserve and one as the foundation of the landing force.

The latter should be a specially selected division, earmarked well in advance, and not tried too high beforehand.

It will not be necessary to take over from the French at Nieuport till the switch is decided on, but the transfer should be carried out as soon after that as troops can be made available. It will be necessary to discuss the matter with them well in advance so that plans may be prepared.

It is considered that the operations at Nieuport and the landing should be directly under GHQ.

It will be noted that the science of Combined Operations had advanced some distance since the Gallipoli landings in 1915.

COMMAND CHANGES

Haig Diary: Blake, pp 195–6

FRIDAY, 16 FEBRUARY . . . At 4.45 General Nivelle and party arrived. He was accompanied by Col. d'Alençon,* Comdt. Suzannet, and an ADC; Colonel A. seems to have great influence with Nivelle, but, unfortunately, is very anti-British in feeling.

*Sir Edward Spears, *Prelude to Victory*, Jonathan Cape, 1939, p 130 says he 'occupied the ubiquitous position, not foreseen by the French regulations, of *Chef de Cabinet*, a kind of personal assistant to the Commander-in-Chief.'

After tea, Nivelle and I had a long talk. He said he preferred to talk with me alone, rather than with Staff Officers present. Briefly, our discussion was *most* satisfactory. He was most frank. We discussed the Railway situation. I explained our difficulties; how we are only given seventy trains a day, when we require 200 to carry our minimum amount of material for the coming offensive.*

He at once sent a stiff wire to the French Government recommending that the Nord Railway Co be placed on a sound footing at once.

As regards the date of attack, he fully realized that we are dependent on the railway, but he agreed with me that *no attack should start until all our requirements had been provided*.†

From the information which he had of the Chemin de Fer du Nord, he thought that we should not be delayed more than ten days beyond the original dates agreed upon. I said that I would do my utmost to meet these views, but that my preparations depended on the amount delivered by the railways. I was much pleased with the results of our meeting as I had feared that Nivelle wished to attack in any case whether the British are ready or not. He seems now to be in complete agreement with me.

Repington, vol i, pp 465–6

TUESDAY, 20 FEBRUARY. (General Maurice) also said that Haig had been ordered to conform with Nivelle's wishes, and the latter has been anxious to attack at once before the German strategic reserve got up. Robertson had said that, as this had been done, the responsibility which formerly pertained to Haig had been assumed by those who gave him these orders, and this had made the Cabinet anxious and they were now trying to get out of it. The G.S. would now tell Haig, who was not for an early battle, that he could not count on drafts for more than two months' fighting. Haig would have to tell Nivelle, who would tell the French Government, which would wish to consult us again, and there would be another Conference, probably at Paris. M. and I are convinced that nothing will teach our politicians what war means.

SOLDIERS AND POLITICIANS

Haig Diary: Blake, p 196

THURSDAY, 22 FEBRUARY. Telegram from CIGS stating that the Prime Minister wishes to hold meeting at Calais or Boulogne next Monday regarding the railway situation here. He, Robertson, and self are to represent Gt. Britain, Briand, Lyautey‡ and Nivelle, France. I wire recommending that 'terms of reference' be drawn up for the Conference, and also suggested that Geddes attend.

*At Arras.   † Underlined by Haig.
‡ French Minister of War.

COMMAND CHANGES

Ludendorff, vol ii, pp 405–7

The general situation made it necessary for us to postpone the struggle in the West as long as possible, in order to allow the submarine campaign time to produce decisive results. Tactical reasons and a shortage of ammunition provided additional reasons for delay. At the same time it was necessary to shorten our front in order to secure a more favourable grouping of our forces and create larger reserves. . . These considerations, taken in close connection with the opening of the submarine campaign, led to the decision to straighten our front by withdrawing to the Siegfried line. . .*

Under the rubric 'Alberich' the Army Group of the Crown Prince Rupprecht† had worked out a programme for the work of clearance and demolition, which was to be spread over five weeks. If an attack on the part of the enemy made it necessary we could at any moment interrupt this programme and begin our retreat. Our first object was to avoid a battle, our second to effect the salvage of all our raw material of war and technical and other equipment that was not actually built into the position, and finally the destruction of all high roads, villages, towns and wells, so as to prevent the enemy establishing himself in force in the near future in front of our new position. Poisoning of the wells was forbidden.

The decision to retreat was not reached without a painful struggle. It implied a confession of weakness bound to raise the morale of the enemy and lower our own. But as it was necessary for military reasons, we had no choice; it had to be carried out.

Haig Diary: Blake, p 196

SUNDAY, 25 FEBRUARY.   Important developments have been taking place on the 5th Army Front. The enemy has fallen back on a front of 18,000 yds, and has abandoned the villages of Warlencourt, Pys, Irles, Miraumont and Serre. Our advanced guards met with little opposition. The question to decide is whether the enemy has begun a big movement in retreat, or whether he has merely evacuated the ground referred to above for local reasons . . .

---

*Always referred to by the British as the 'Hindenburg Line'. The Germans called the whole work the 'Siegfried Line', although one section of it (between Cambrai and St Quentin) was also called the 'Siegfried Position'. Other parts were also named from personae of the Niebelung Saga: what the British called the 'Drocourt-Quéant Switch' was the 'Wotan Position'; the section south of St Quentin and west of Laon was the 'Alberich Position'. Alberich was the malicious dwarf in the Saga, but the code-name of the withdrawal would seem to have been dictated by the name of the adjacent section of the Line, rather than by 'grim humour', as suggested by the British Official Historian (1917, vol i, p 113) and other writers. The decision to construct the Siegfried Line was taken, according to Ludendorff, 'as early as September' 1916, i.e. at the height of the Battle of the Somme.
† Field-Marshal Crown Prince Rupprecht of Bavaria.

Soldiers and Politicians

Haig Diary: Blake, p 199

Monday, 26 February.   10.45 am. I left with General Geddes for Calais. He had compiled an excellent summary of the transportation case and the questions which we wished to be settled. We talked over this in the car, and took a walk together on reaching Calais.

About 1.15 the Prime Minister (Mr Lloyd George), General Robertson and party arrived from London. M. Briand, with Generals Lyautey and Nivelle had already arrived.

Hankey, vol ii, p 615

26 February.   To Calais with Lloyd George and Robertson. Bacon took us across with quite a little fleet of destroyers to escort us, as the German destroyers had come out from Zeebrugge the night before* and were suspected of being in the Channel. Dull conference on railway matters to start with. This was followed at 5 pm by a conference that was by no means dull.

No one would dispute Lord Hankey's statement that the Calais Conference was 'by no means dull'. For present purposes I need only repeat this brief summary of what occurred, published elsewhere:†

'Lloyd George seized upon this crisis as an occasion for an inter-Allied conference, ostensibly to discuss transportation, but in reality (unknown to the British War Cabinet) to rearrange the command structure of the Western Front. In short, his object was no less than to place Haig and the British armies in France under the direct command of Nivelle. The latter and his staff were warned of this intention and drew up detailed proposals (beforehand) accordingly. They were not to know that the British Prime Minister was playing a lone hand, not only without the backing of his advisers but actually contrary to their convictions and those of his Government colleagues.

The outcome of Lloyd George's ill-considered machinations was seen at the Calais Conference on 26–7 February. It marked an important milestone in Allied war direction. Prompted by Lloyd George, Nivelle put forward proposals which would have reduced the forces of the British

---

*The Germans bombarded Margate and Broadstairs for ten minutes on 25 February.
†John Terraine: *The Great War 1914–18*, Hutchinson, 1965, pp. 284–5; a fuller account appears in Terraine, *Douglas Haig, The Educated Soldier*, Hutchinson, 1963; pp 265–76, and a comprehensive and brilliant narrative in E. L. Spears, *Prelude To Victory*, Jonathan Cape, 1939, chapters VIII and IX. The very long diary entries of both Haig and Hankey deserve close study.

Empire in France to a mere contingent in the French Army and the British Commander-in-Chief to a glorified Adjutant-General. Haig and Robertson were outraged; Lloyd George himself was somewhat taken aback. The French, when they discovered how they had been used, were much dismayed and perplexed. In the event, a compromise conclusion was reached, whereby the British Expeditionary Force retained its identity, under its own C-in-C, but Haig was subordinated to Nivelle for the duration of the offensive outlined in the great plan.'

We shall see how, stage by stage, History made a mockery of this disreputable episode. Yet nothing tangled the threads of 1917 more than this conference: it heightened the distrust between British and French Headquarters, not only for the duration of Nivelle's tenure of command, but well into 1918; and it shattered all confidence between the military and civil leaders of Britain – a grim augury for the Flanders Offensive.

Haig Diary: Blake, p 203

WEDNESDAY, 28 FEBRUARY.   It is too sad at this critical time to have to fight with one's Allies and the Home Government, in addition to the enemy in the Field.

COMMAND CHANGES

Author's Papers: Haig Diary

TUESDAY, 27 FEBRUARY.   The Fifth Army made further progress north and south of the Ancre today. Le Barque was taken last night and today Ligny was occupied, and we established ourselves in the western and northern defences of Puisieux.

Lieutenant-Colonel Spears was at this time British Liaison Officer with the Groupe d'Armées du Nord (G.A.N.) commanded by General Franchet d'Esperey. It was this Army Group that was designated to make the French subsidiary attack at the same time as the British attack at Arras (see p 24).

Sir Edward Spears, *Prelude To Victory*, Jonathan Cape, 1939 [henceforward 'Spears'], pp 204–5

On the second day of the Calais Conference, 27 February, Colonel Desticker, the Chief of Staff, had gone in to Beauvais. General Nivelle was away at the conference, but he saw General Pont, the *Major Général*,* and drew his attention to the fact that it was not only possible but likely that the Germans would extend their retreat and fall back to the Hindenburg Line on the G.A.N. front. If this

*Chief of Staff.

were so it was obvious that the plan of attack would have to be completely rehandled. The risk of bombarding empty positions and wasting an accumulated and irreplaceable supply of shells could not be run.

Everyone at the G.A.N. knew that if the enemy were allowed to withdraw to the Hindenburg Line it would be two months at least before General d'Esperey's Armies could attack him there. Colonel Desticker pointed this out to the Staff at the G.Q.G., and also drew their attention to the fact that the Hindenburg Line lay in front of the large towns of Cambrai, St Quentin and Laon, and that this would mean their probable destruction if the Line were attacked. He said that General d'Esperey was extremely anxious to be allowed to attack the enemy while they were in the act of retiring, that he believed they were about to do so, and asked that he should be given a free hand so that the opportunity, if it occurred, should not be missed.

In General Nivelle's absence no decision could be taken, but Colonel Desticker came back in a depressed mood, for he felt that General Nivelle's advisers, who showed considerable reluctance to accept the views he expressed, probably reflected the mind of their Chief. To have adopted General D'Esperey's point of view would have necessitated recasting the whole plan of operations, and this Colonel Desticker gathered was the last thing Beauvais was prepared to do. They had no alternative plan ready, nor could they have. Joffre's plan had depended upon attacking as early in the year as possible. This had been discarded in favour of a more grandiose operation. To admit that the enemy was about to retire and evacuate the salient it had been intended to pinch out, was to admit failure, that Joffre had been right and Nivelle wrong.

Author's Papers: Haig Diary

WEDNESDAY, 28 FEBRUARY.   Charteris reported that there is further evidence of the possibility of the enemy withdrawing right back to the Hindenburg line. Hutments and aerodromes have been moved back. Prisoners reported that their officers in conversation had said the Army was to move there by the end of March, and others said that they had definite orders not to do any work on their trenches or wire in the front line position . . . The advisability of launching (Nivelle's) battle at all grows daily less, and so the Calais agreement may not perhaps be of any use to him.

THE INVISIBLE ENEMY

Repington, vol i, p 467

WEDNESDAY, 21 FEBRUARY.   An experienced naval officer now at the Admiralty lunched with me to discuss submarine warfare . . . He is not at all sanguine about overcoming the menace, and thought that we should tunnel the Channel and improve our air transport service. What a prospect for the Navy! He thought that it had become a disadvantage to be an island.

Lloyd George, vol i, p 709

Statistics of shipping losses, February, 1917 — 310,868 gross tons sunk

March

---------------------------------- ✠ ----------------------------------

SOLDIERS AND POLITICIANS

The critical decisions and operations of the next few weeks were naturally all deeply affected by the Calais Conference.

Charteris, p 200

1 MARCH . . . It is all utterly wrong and unnecessary. If the French do get a great success and end the war in their next big attack, which is very unlikely, not much harm will have been done. They will claim all the credit for the whole war, as well as for this attack, but that does not matter. If the big French attack is indecisive in its result, then inevitably, as the war goes on, our army will become the biggest on the Western front (unless Lloyd George sends everybody off on side-shows), and there is bound to be interminable friction. If the French attack fails altogether, we shall have the whole weight of the German Army on the top of us, and the position will be even more difficult.

COMMAND CHANGES

As the German withdrawal continued, both the Allied Commanders-in-Chief bent their minds to interpreting its meaning, and how it might affect the plans which they had already agreed. Haig discussed the situation fully with his Chief of Staff.

Author's Papers: Haig Diary

2 MARCH. Briefly, the enemy has discovered that he is to be attacked on a front extending from Arras to near Rheims. He cannot afford to stand as he did last year on the Somme and suffer destruction. He has therefore organized the area in rear of the threatened front. To enable his troops to slip away . . . His new line called the 'Hindenburg Line' is 60 kilometres shorter than his present one, so that he will economize 12 divisions (about) once he has reached his new line. This latter is said to be immensely strong . . . His objects seem to be: To disorganize

our offensive by causing our attack to be made in the air, and so to cause us loss of time; to wear out our troops by causing us at each stage to renew our preparations for attack; to delay us (these preparations take much time to organize for each successive advance); to affect the morale of the Allies by disappointment at seeing the enemy able to escape at each successive stage, in spite of the greatest efforts made to prevent this. But the enemy means to gain victory and will spare no effort and stick at nothing. We must expect a gigantic hostile attack somewhere . . . It seems to me . . . likely that in the near future they will attack either Russia or the Ypres front . . . An attack against Ypres and the coast ports would fit in well with his submarine war; and the capture of our communications with England would mean the end of the war both for England and France! Such a blow if successful would mean decisive victory for Germany.

With such uncertainties and possibilities confronting us on the Western Front, the folly of definitely placing the British C-in-C under the orders of the French C-in-C for a specific battle (the exact nature of which cannot be foreseen) becomes more marked even than it seemed at the Calais Conference.

All these thoughts were embodied in a paper for the CIGS (O.A.D. 323) for the Cabinet's further consideration. As we shall see, the fear of a German offensive in Flanders persisted for a while; it had this foundation – a temporary concentration of some eight extra German divisions in Belgium, in case the declaration of unrestricted submarine warfare brought Holland and Denmark into the War against Germany. This was considered most unlikely, but, says Ludendorff, 'it was unwise to take any risks'.

Meanwhile General Nivelle was reaching his own conclusions about the German retreat, very different from Haig's. He accepted that the withdrawal on the front of the British Fifth Army constituted a new fact, but he emphasized that neither the front of the Arras offensive nor that of the Champagne offensive was affected:

Author's Papers: 'Directive No. 5051'; 6 March

. . . Quite the contrary, the position called 'the Hindenburg' is laid out in such a fashion that our principal attacks, in the British zone as much as in the French zone, are well aimed to outflank it and to take it in the rear.

In this respect the German withdrawal would, even if it became general, thus be to our advantage; and on this estimation I base a prime decision, which is to make no fundamental modification in the general plan of operations which has been drawn up; and in particular to adhere to the date fixed for the launching of our attacks.

Even before General Nivelle had composed this Directive there were signs that the Germans were going to withdraw on the front of the G.A.N. as well as on that of the British Fifth Army. For a week General Franchet d'Esperey urged Nivelle to allow him to attack, hoping to capture at least a portion of the German artillery before it could be removed. On 7 March he received his formal answer from Nivelle:

Spears, p 210

On the front of the G.A.N. there is no material indication which allows one to conclude that the voluntary withdrawal of the Germans will extend to this region.

There seems little likelihood that the enemy will abandon without fighting, and indeed without resisting to the utmost, one of the principal pledges he holds on our soil, that is to say the line nearest to Paris, which includes Roye, Noyon and soissons.

In any case it is impossible to base a decision on a hypothesis.

I decide therefore not to change in its general lines the plan of operations for 1917.

With only a month to go before the date came for launching his great offensive, Nivelle took comfort in the thought that if, after all, the subsidiary attack by the G.A.N. had to be called off, this would at least permit larger resources and reserves for the main attack by the G.A.R.* under General Micheler in Champagne. Everywhere there was a consciousness that the 'offensive season' was approaching.

F. S. Oliver, *The Anvil Of War*, Macmillan, 1936, [henceforward 'Oliver'], p 175

8 MARCH, 1917.   I suppose we stand on the eve of the biggest military effort in the whole range of history. Lord! what a butcher's bill there is going to be!

FLANDERS

Author's Papers: Robertson to Haig, 8 March

3. The German is out to gain time and we should make every effort to get on the move. So long as we leave him undisturbed he can do as he likes . . . We must get going in the North sooner or later and the sooner the better, if you think that that is the most likely point of attack. The enemy cannot retire there in the way he can on the Somme, while if he has any intention of attacking us there the case would be met by our attack.

Groupe d'Armées de Réserve.

Author's Papers: O.A.D. 329, GHQ to Army
Commanders, 9 March

6. The First and Third Armies will push on as rapidly as possible with the preparations for their attacks as already ordered . . .
8. The Second Army Commander will push on the offensive preparations 'n his front as already ordered. Arrangements to place extra labour at his disposal for work on roads and railways are being made.

COMMAND CHANGES

Spears, pp 212–13

Still the Belshazzars of Beauvais feasted on their dreams, while the Germans, harried by Gough* and frightened by the shadow of d'Esperey's Armies, hastened their preparations, and instead of carrying out the grand final movement on 16 March as they had intended, began quietly slipping away on the 11th in the north† and on the 13th in the south.

By the 12th there was no further need to hunt for evidence to convince the G.Q.G. The French First Army reported that on the previous day forty different villages on their front were in flames, that the Noyon water reservoir had been blown up and that there had been an explosion in Noyon Station; that the enemy had created vast inundations and many roads were already under water, and finally that nine railway bridges south of Noyon had been blown up as well as bridges elsewhere.

Of all the 'command changes' of the War, the most far-reaching took place on this day, 12 March, 1917: the overthrow of the Tsarist system, and the setting up of a Provisional Government which was in turn replaced by the Bolsheviks under Lenin. The blaze of hindsight should not blind us to the various surmises and regrets that greeted the event at the time. There is only space here for a few examples of how this further deep entanglement of the threads of 1917 then affected its observers. Admiral von Tirpitz, founder of the High Seas Fleet and Secretary of the Navy until 1916, wrote:

Churchill, *The World Crisis*, ii, p 1115

Had we been able to foresee in Germany the Russian Revolution, we should perhaps not have needed to regard the submarine campaign of 1917 as a last resource. But in January, 1917, there was no visible sign of the revolution.

*General Sir Hubert Gough, commanding the Fifth Army.
† Of the Somme.

Charteris, p 202

14 MARCH . . . The news from Russia is very bad indeed. I hope it does not mean
that they will break off the war altogether, but as you know that has been a
possibility in our mind for more than two years now. The curious thing is that most
people you meet here, and apparently most at home too, are all rather pleased
with the revolution. They say the Tsarina was a pro-Boche and had gradually got
the Tsar round to her way of thinking. Revolutions always leave a country
unstable. The Germans will certainly make capital out of this and try to get a
counter-revolution . . .

> Reginald, Viscount Esher, *Journals And Letters*,
> Nicholson & Watson, 1938 [henceforward
> 'Esher'], vol iv, p 97

PARIS, 17 MARCH . . . The Russian revolution is considered wholly good. No
revolution can be wholly good. The Tsar's abdication has been finely carried
through, and crowned by a noble and touching manifesto. But the middle-class
Girondins who have dethroned the Tsar and killed the old odious bureaucratic
system will probably themselves have their throats cut by the 'Mountain' that is
always lying in wait upon revolutions.

On 22 March Mr Bonar Law, Leader of the House of Commons, moved
the following resolution:

Lloyd George, i, p 969

That this House send to the Duma* its fraternal greetings and tenders to the
Russian people its heartiest congratulations upon the establishment among them
of free institutions in full confidence that they will lead not only to the happy and
rapid progress of the Russian nation, but to the prosecution with renewed stead-
fastness and vigour of the War against the stronghold of an autocratic militarism
which threatens the liberty of Europe.'

SOLDIERS AND POLITICIANS

At this very equivocal moment, on both sides of the Channel, in the words
of Sir Edward Spears, 'the old coat of democracy, never intended for wear
at Armageddon, was showing white at the seams'. In London, on 12–13
March, another Anglo-French conference was held, to remove some of
the misunderstandings and frictions created at Calais. How dangerous
these had become may be seen from the following:

*The Russian National Assembly.

Spears, Appendix XVIII: Telegram from Briand
to Lloyd George

7 MARCH, 1917. General Nivelle has just communicated to the French War
Committee the Memorandum of 2 March addressed by Marshal Haig to General
Robertson,* a document which calls for the following remarks by the French War
Committee . . .

Marshal Haig's repeated tendency to avoid the instructions which have been
given to him, to reopen continually the question of the offensive itself and the plan
of operations, and this at a time when these are on the point of being carried out,
would render the co-operation of the British forces illusory and would make the
exercise of a unified command impossible.

In consequence Marshal Haig should be ordered to conform, without delay, to
the decisions of the Calais Conference and to the instructions given him by
General Nivelle.

Further, it is necessary that General Nivelle should have at his disposal as soon
as possible a qualified intermediary between himself and the British Armies, in
order that he may keep himself acquainted with the possibilities of these Armies
and that he may communicate his *directives* to them. The French War Committee
insists that General Wilson, who has already fulfilled similar functions at the
beginning of the war,† be appointed to this post.

In case the War Cabinet should not see the possibility of thus remedying
without delay the grave difficulties noted above, it will not be possible for the
French Commander-in-Chief to ensure the unity of the operations on the Western
Front, and the French Government would only be able to express its great regret
at this situation.

On 9 March Haig replied to Nivelle's Directive No. 5051‡ of 6 March,
and Nivelle made certain annotations in the margin of his copy. These are
indicated by square brackets.

Spears, Appendix XIX

1. The enemy's withdrawal on the British front has undoubtedly modified very
considerably the tactical situation to be dealt with there . . . [exaggerated]
3. The proposed reinforcement of General Rawlinson§ is quite outside the original plan agreed on . . .
[The liaison to be established covers all possible plans, without its being necessary
to specify them.]

My utmost endeavours will be exerted to make the attacks I have undertaken to
launch as strong as possible, and to deliver them on the date named, subject

* O.A.D. 323; see pp 46–7.   † In 1915.   ‡ See p 47.
§ Still commanding the Fourth Army on the left of the French Third Army in the Somme
area.

always to such action by the enemy as may compel me to take special steps to ensure the safety of my Armies. From this
[Take note:- to insist on the fact that, the attack once engaged, it is necessary to make it as strong as possible, without concern for other considerations, with which it is the business of the Commander-in-Chief to deal.]
responsibility to my King and Country, and to the officers and men placed under me, I feel that nothing can release me so long as I am entrusted with the command of His Majesty's Armies in France and Flanders . . .
[That responsibility is mine, since the British Government has so decided.]

The French leaders, military and civil, were evidently unaware that in the fortnight that had elapsed since the Calais Conference, the proceedings there had found less and less favour in British eyes. At the London Conference it was clearly laid down that:

3. . . . All the British troops stationed in France remain in all circumstances under the orders of their own chiefs and of the British Commander-in-Chief.

This was the key clause of the first part of the Agreement signed on 13 March. The second (and much longer) part dealt in detail with the duties of the Head of the British Mission at GQG, the post which the French wished to be filled by Lieutenant-General Sir Henry Wilson, and which General Nivelle saw as a British Chief of Staff at GQG, i.e. another instrument of control of the British C-in-C. At the London Conference it was firmly stated:

Spears, Appendix XXI

1. As before, the object of the British Mission attached to the French Head-quarters is to maintain touch between the French and British Commanders-in-Chief.

In other words, the function of the post was liaison, nothing more. With this Nivelle had to be content, and Haig, with misgivings, signed the Agreement, first adding these two paragraphs:

I agree with the above on the understanding that, while I am fully determined to carry out the Calais Agreement in spirit and letter, the British Army and its Commander-in-Chief will be regarded by General Nivelle as allies and not as subordinates, except during the particular operations which he explained at the Calais Conference.
Further, while I also accept the agreement respecting the functions of the

British Mission at French Headquarters, It should be understood that these functions may be subject to modifications as experience shows to be necessary.

D. Haig,

Field-Marshal

Having so firmly rebuffed all the French attempts at 'taking over' the BEF, the British military leaders then considered the question whether General Wilson should be the Head of the Mission at GQG or not. As he was soon to have important threads of 1917 running through his fingers, it is worth looking at his version of this important day in detail. In the afternoon Wilson paid a visit to Robertson.

> Field-Marshal Sir Henry Wilson, *His Life And Diaries*, edited by Major-General Sir C. E. Callwell, Cassell, 1927 [henceforward 'Wilson'], vol i, p 326

13 MARCH . . . I at once made the position clear. I would *not* go unless certain conditions were fulfilled, viz: 1. Clear definition of Haig's status. 2. Clear definition of my duties. 3. A personal request on the part of Haig, Nivelle and the War Committee asking me to go. 4. My own power to resign at any moment. I added that, as he knew well, neither he nor Haig would, voluntarily, have me near them, that even when I was in Russia* evil tongues had spread reports that I had engineered all these troubles so as to get Haig or him out and to slip into their places, and that, if this was said when I was in Russia, what would *not* be said if I went to Beauvais? I said I was against taking up this appointment and would do so only if the conditions already enumerated were fulfilled. Robertson said that he would write to Haig.

At about 5 o'clock that afternoon, Wilson received a visit from Nivelle.

He enlarged upon the present futility of the connexion between him and Haig, and added that Lloyd George would like to get rid of Haig but, for the minute, the Northcliffe Press was too strong. Finally, after much talk of this description, he appealed to me 'in the name of God' to accept the post offered as I 'was the only man in England who could save a most dangerous situation'. To this I replied that I was going to see Haig at 6 o'clock, and that I had certain conditions to put forward. If these were accepted I would agree to go to Beauvais.

I then went to Haig's. Kiggell was present throughout the interview, at which I was very glad. I put the same case before him† that I had already done to Robertson, and I said that unless I could have, and retain, his complete confidence

---

*As a member of the Allied Mission, 30 January–20 February.
† Haig.

I would not accept. I told him that within a month of my going to Beauvais any number of people would tell him that I was intriguing to put him out – that in point of fact I probably could put him out if I wished – and so I advised him not to have me but to keep Clive.* Nothing that I said – and I was most open – shook him, and he agreed without hesitation to my condition that I should be allowed absolute discretion about resigning at any moment if I saw fit.

And so tonight my conditions are all fulfilled, and I really believe I could impose any others I like as regards pay, rank, staff, etc. For I am clear that they are all frightened and that they all *really* believe that I am the only man who can save the situation. The more I look at it, the less I like it, and yet I must not refuse to try. So it is settled.

No sooner were these proceedings, which had sorely tried the patience of the British soldiers concerned, concluded, than a French soldier came to grief in the whirlpool of politics. On 14 March, having been howled down in the Chamber of Deputies for suggesting that that was not the best place to air confidential information concerning Defence, General Lyautey resigned.

Haig Diary: Blake, pp 213–14

FRIDAY, 16 MARCH.   Lyautey resigned his position two days ago as Minister of War, and leaves Ministry tomorrow. It is said that Painlevé or Barthou will succeed him. Both are revolutionary Socialists. Such are the people under whom the British Army has been placed for the forthcoming offensive operations. I fancy Lyautey must have had enough of them because he read a statement in writing to the Chamber of Deputies which brought about the uproar and crisis resulting in his resignation. I am very sorry that L has gone because I found him always straightforward and an honest gentleman, which is more than I can say of most of the present politicians.

FLANDERS

Amid all these distractions, the persistent thread of British strategy was never lost to view. After Haig had made his addendum to the London Agreement on 14 March, with the approval of the War Cabinet, that body remained in session.

Ibid, p 212

I was present at its meeting and explained the general plan agreed upon by Nivelle and myself. This is to:

*Brigadier-General G. S. Clive, then and later Head of the British Mission at GQG.

1. Continue pressing enemy back with advanced guards wherever he is giving way.
2. To launch our main attacks as soon as possible.
3. But in view of the possibility of these attacks failing in the air, at once to prepare for attacks elsewhere.

As to the British Army, my plan based on the foregoing is:

1. To continue to make all preparations (as arranged) for attacks by 1st and 3rd Armies, keeping adequate reserves available either to support my 2nd Army (Ypres) or to exploit the success of our attacks near Arras. These Reserves are obtained from the 5th Army.
2. *If successful*, at Arras, exploit with all Reserves and the Cavalry.
3. *It not successful*, prepare to launch attacks near Ypres to clear the Belgian Coast. All Cavalry will be required probably if this attack is successful.

The attacks on Messines Ridge might be made in May, if desirable.

Present at the War Cabinet were:

Lloyd George, Milner, Curzon, Henderson, Balfour, Derby, Gen. Robertson and Colonel Hankey (the Secretary).

This was the second occasion on which Lloyd George's Government was fully associated with the plan to clear the Belgian coast in the summer of 1917.*

Author's Papers: O.A.D. 337, GHQ to Army Commanders, 16 March

7. Second Army will study and report what action is possible in the direction of Langemarck with the troops available and in co-operation with the Belgian Army in the event of the enemy being defeated elsewhere and thus being compelled to weaken himself on the Belgian and Second Army fronts.

The preparations for the Messines-Wytschaete attack will be continued . . .

It is a further indication of the inexorable quality of a major offensive at this stage of the War that the first studies and preparations for an attack on the Messines Ridge, at the southern flank of the Ypres Salient, had begun in February, 1916, and the first of the great mines which were the feature of the initial attack was completed in April, 1916, fourteen months before the attack was actually launched.

Author's Papers: Haig Diary

17 MARCH.   I told Army commanders that in my opinion enemy might either:
1. Counter-attack from the Hindenburg line if our advance was conducted carelessly; or

*See p 30.

2. Make a sudden mass attack in Flanders, using the recent divisions sent there from Germany, and the additional 15 or 20 divisions which his withdrawal from to the Hindenburg line will set free.

We must be prepared for either or both of these operations.

COMMAND CHANGES

In the East and in the West, change was in the air. On 15 March the Tsar Nicholas II abdicated and three hundred years of Romanov rule in Russia came to an end. Two days later M. Aristide Briand, whose Government was already shaken by the departure of Lyautey, in turn resigned.

Haig Diary: Blake, p 214

SUNDAY, 18 MARCH . . . M. Ribot is carrying on as 'President du Conseil' under M. Poincaré's supreme direction. M. Barthou is said to be trying to form a Government with Painlevé as Minister of War. But what a crowd of fickle changeable people are the French Deputies. Gen. Lyautey must have had a most difficult position in a Government of political jugglers with a Chamber of semi-lunatics!

Wilson, i, p 330

18 MARCH . . . Briand resigned the night before last, and no one yet appointed. So Russia is in revolution and has no Tsar, and France has no Government. Nivelle and his staff absolutely indifferent, even amused, at the fall of Lyautey and Briand.

The French ministerial crisis was not resolved until 20 March, when M. Alexandre Ribot became Prime Minister and M. Paul Painlevé Minister of War.

FLANDERS

Author's Papers: Haig Diary

20 MARCH.   I discussed situation with Kiggell. If enemy is retiring to Douai – Marquion – Hindenburg Line, and hold it in force, some time will be required for our preparations for attack. By the time these are completed, he will retire again! I am therefore in favour of at once going on with our preparations for attacking near Ypres. This may not suit the French!

Author's Papers: Wilson to Haig

20 MARCH.

2. If enemy goes on retiring (Nivelle) wants you to tell him what you think it all means, and what you think we ought to do in the future . . .

4. N. wants to know about your Messines scheme so as to see whether he can fit in operations of his own if the retirement of the Boches knocks out the original scheme of great offensive.

Author's Papers: Haig to Nivelle

21 MARCH.

My dear General,

        . . . If the enemy continues to hold the line Lille–Douai–St Quentin–Laon, I presume your G.A.R. will attack that line, in flank and rear, from the south and it will still be my task to break through it towards Cambrai.

If, however, the enemy continues his retirement beyond that line, I propose to develop as quickly as possible a strong offensive on the front of my Second Army. The full front of attack there would extend from Messines to Steenstraat. For this from 35 to 40 divisions in all would be required and some two months would be necessary to complete preparations. The attack could, however, be divided into two phases, taking the portion south of the Ypres–Comines railway first and the portion to the north of that later.

For the first phase (south of the Ypres–Comines railway) 16 divisions and 5 or 6 weeks' preparation should suffice.

The objective of the attack would be to reach the general line Courtrai–Roulers–Thourout as quickly as possible, opening the Dixmude defile to the Belgians, and forcing the enemy to evacuate Belgium.

A simultaneous attack along the coast from Nieuport would of course be highly advisable in combination with the operation described. Our Navy would also assist in any way possible, and I am sure that, under the assumed conditions, I should have all the help and cooperation that your Armies could give.

In ordinary weather the ground would be quite fit for operations by the time my preparations could be complete, and indeed in fine weather it would be quite passable before that – probably by the end of this month.

It is still quite possible that the enemy may anticipate any attack on my Second Army front by taking the offensive in that area himself . . .

Yours very truly,

D. Haig

Field-Marshal

The Invincible Enemy

Spears, p 263

The weather continued to be abominable. There never had been such a spring. Snow day after day.

Author's Papers: Haig Diary

22 MARCH . . . The ground (at Ypres) is very wet for the most part and the digging of starting trenches at this season of the year is out of the question.

Oliver, p 178

22 MARCH . . . One most unfortunate thing is the weather. In this respect Providence has been fighting against the Entente ever since last September.

Spears, p 276

It was heart-breaking, this unbelievable weather. It seemed as if the gods of the north had collected all the hail, rain, snow and mists from East Prussia and Pomerania to hurl at us in their endeavour to help the field-grey hordes.

Command Changes

Wilson, i, p 332

23 MARCH.   Nivelle came to see Haig at 8.30 am, and had 1¾ hours interview with him, I being present. All went most amicably. We discussed the situation, and we all agreed that appearances now pointed to the Boches standing on the Hindenburg Line, and therefore that Micheler's attack from about Soissons–Rheims, and Haig's attack Arras–Vimy will hold good. The difficulties of roads, rails, river crossings, etc, etc, all well discussed. Then Haig explained his alternative of attack Messines–Ypres, which will take two months to prepare. Then we discussed the Belgians. Then the Italian situation, where Cadorna seems to have given up his promised offensive on the Carso because of his fear of a Boche attack from the Trentino. A nuisance. The whole tone of Haig and Nivelle was a good as it could be.

Charteris, p 204

25 MARCH . . . We are near the end of the German retreat. They are right back to their entrenched lines in most places. The next great change is to be the big attack next month.

Soldiers and Politicians

Haig Diary: Blake, pp 214–15

24 MARCH.   M. Painlevé, the new French Minister of War, arrived at 7.30 pm and stayed the night . . .

After dinner, I had a long talk with P. He is a pleasant bright little man. Said to be a great mathematician and an extreme Socialist. He is most anxious, he says, to keep on the most friendly terms with the British. Hence his visit to me the day after he took over his office. I thought it was nice of him coming to see me so soon, and I was most friendly. I gather that General Pétain is a favourite of his. He questioned me closely about Nivelle. I was careful to say that he struck me as a capable General, and that I was, of course, ready to co-operate with whoever was chosen by the French Government to be their C in C. I said my relations with Nivelle are and have always been excellent.

The Calais Conference was a mistake, but it was not Nivelle's fault.*

We talked on pleasantly till a very late hour. A bad evening for a late talk, as the clocks were advanced an hour at 11 pm for Summertime, and so I was done out of an hour's sleep.

Charteris, p 203

25 MARCH.   Things have straightened themselves up a little better than they were immediately after the Calais mess-up, chiefly I think, owing to the fact that Nivelle's own position is very insecure. He is not having an easy time with his politicians. He deserves it in a way. He appealed to Caesar and Caesar now seems inclined to cuff him. Our own particular Caesar at No. 10 is for the moment not so unfriendly.

Command Changes

Ibid, pp 204–5

26 MARCH.   There are strong rumours of riots in Germany. If they are even half-true the end may be near. The first signs of the real defeat of Germany will be the fall of morale of her people, and then the commencement of revolution. But the news from Russia shows a much worse state there than even these rumours,

---

*Haig continued to believe in Nivelle's complete innocence, despite mounting evidence to the contrary. No doubt he was much influenced by Lord Esher, who had conducted enquiries into the background of the Calais Conference in Paris, and who had told Haig on 10 March (after a conversation with Lyautey): 'Lloyd George took the sole initiative.'

which are, of course, exaggerated, show of Germany. I saw the Russian Attaché at Paris last week. Usually an optimist, he is now very depressed. The Grand Duke Nicholas,* he said, though straightforward and resolute, is ignorant and unintelligent. The Provisional Government cannot, he thinks, last. Now that the 'dignity' that has always hedged the Tsar has been defiled, he does not think the troops will fight or the nation wish to go on.

SOLDIERS AND POLITICIANS

Repington, i, 499

WEDNESDAY, 28 MARCH.   I said that when the secret history of these times came to be written, people would be surprised to learn that far more time and energy were expended by British and French soldiers in fighting their own politicians than in fighting the enemy. If the politicians would only go on leave and allow the soldiers to carry on, victory was assured, but that I thought that the politicians were doing their best to lose the war.

THE INVISIBLE ENEMY

Oliver, p 178

22 MARCH.
3. *Submarines and Food*. The submarine campaign is going on gaily. It is serious and likely to become more so, but there is not yet any appearance of it being fatal . . .

Hankey, ii, p 648

30 MARCH.   Personally I am much worried about the shipping outlook owing to submarines and the inability of the Admiralty to deal with it, and their general ineptitude as indicated by their stickiness towards any new proposal. I have many ideas on the matter, but cannot get at Lloyd George in regard to it as he is so full of politics. I am oppressed by the fear I have always had that, while moderately successful on land, we may yet be beaten at sea. Something like a million tons of the world's shipping have been lost in the last two months – and that takes a lot of replacement.

Lloyd George i, p 709

Statistics of shipping losses, March, 1917 — 352,344 gross tons sunk

*Uncle of the Tsar, and Commander-in-Chief of the Russian armies until 1916.

April

— ✠ —

April, 1917, was a month of many decisions.

The Invincible Enemy

> Repington, i, p 505

Sunday, 1 April.   Heavy fall of snow this morning. This winter seems endless.

> Author's Papers: Haig Diary

Monday, 2 April.   Cold wind. Very wintry looking.

> Charteris, p 207

3 April.   Another day of disheartening weather, the country is under a blanket of snow, the heaviest we have had this year. It is as bad for the Germans as for us, but if it continues it will make our advance much more slow and will very seriously interfere with the French.

> Spears, p 327

Mud, the implacable enemy of the soldier, was rising up in a sea about him.

Now a new thread entered the pattern of 1917, a thread which was to have incalculable significance in the history of the world.

America

> President Woodrow Wilson, speech to Congress,
> 2 April, 1917

The world must be made safe for democracy. Its peace must be planted upon the tested foundations of political liberty.

> MacDonagh, p 188

3 April, 1917.   Tremendous news today! Wilson, President of the United States, asked Congress yesterday to declare war against Germany!

Charteris, p 207

3 APRIL . . . So America has come in! That is the best world news we have yet had
in the whole war. If there was ever any doubt about the ultimate issue, it must be
ended now even for the most pessimistic. The war may be over before America
can bring her armies over here; but if it goes on beyond this year, we shall have an
almost inexhaustible reserve of manpower to draw on.

Ludendorff, ii, p 415

It was not a matter of surprise to me that the United States joined the ranks of our
enemies. I had reckoned upon her doing so, provided the balance of war continued in our favour, even if the unrestricted submarine campaign had never been
opened . . . America was led by economic interests ever more and more to the
side of the Entente, for England had surrendered to her the position she had
hitherto enjoyed as the first capitalist power in the world. The Entente was deeply
in America's debt, and their defeat would have involved her in heavy loss.

COMMAND CHANGES

On 4 April Lieut-General Sir Henry Wilson met for the first time the new
French Minister of War, M. Painlevé.

Wilson, i, p 335

I was not much struck with his appearance, but he seemed sensible. What I did not
like was the attitude towards Nivelle. Not that he said anything against him, but he
insisted on the right to discuss matters with Nivelle's subordinates, and named
Pétain, Micheler and Franchet. If he discusses Nivelle, or Nivelle's plans, with
these men it will certainly end in trouble. He is supposed to be an admirer of
Pétain's and an enemy of Nivelle's. I asked him if he was going to make Pétain his
Chief of Staff, and he said that that had been his intention but that his colleagues
had put him off, saying, in effect, that Pétain would run him instead of his running
Pétain.

   On 4 April General Nivelle issued a characteristically bombastic Directive to his armies, prescribing deep exploitations as though the Germans
were as good as beaten. Yet on that very day they gave strong indications
of the contrary, making a brilliantly successful attack of their own at
Sapigneul* which penetrated to the French second position, and winning
ground which it took over a week to regain. But that was not the worst of
it.

*On the front of the French Fifth Army, about 5 miles east of Berry au Bac.

Spears, pp 331–2

The day after the main French attack had been launched, I learned that during the Sapigneul fighting the Germans had captured an order which gave away a great deal of the French plan. It seems incredible that a document covering so wide a field should have found its way into the front line, but the determination to exalt morale was the cause of this folly. So as to inflame the imagination of the men, it had been decided that they should be informed, towards the end of March, of the grandiose operations in which they were about to take part.

The order in question not only gave the detailed objectives of the regiment to which it was addressed . . . Worse still, the composition of the VII Corps and everything concerning its attack on Brimont, together with the plans and man-oeuvres of three other corps and of the Russian Brigade, were all given in this fatal document.

Haig Diary: Duff Cooper, ii, p 83

THURSDAY, 5 APRIL . . . Nivelle said that he is very pleased with the way in which the situation is developing, and is full of confidence.

Nevertheless, it was on this day that Nivelle told Haig that Micheler had asked for a 48-hour delay in the attack, because of the weather, and Haig himself was glad to make a 24-hour delay in his own attack at Arras for the same reason. Meanwhile, Nivelle's troubles did not abate. On the same day Colonel Messimy, French Minister of War in 1914, and now commanding the infantry component in a division of the Tenth Army, addressed a formidable document to M. Ribot, the Prime Minister:

Spears, pp 356–8

The GQG, faced with an entirely new situation, has only made the minimum alterations in its plan . . . As always, and this has been proved in the past, the GQG is showing complete optimism and colossal powers of self-deception. It is now about to commit a grave error which may have irreparable consequences for France . . . As a Deputy, as a former Minister for War, and as a leader responsible for the lives of 10,000 men I demand that the Government, before the operations begin, should consult with and hear the opinions of the Group Commanders, either separately or together, beginning with the one who will lead the French Armies to the attack, General Micheler.

Charteris, p 208

6 APRIL . . . Esher tells me that Nivelle's position is even more precarious than we had realized. A strong section of the Government wanted to forbid the French offensive altogether. Several of Nivelle's own generals are against it. Nivelle had great difficulty in holding his own. What a commentary on the Calais Conference!

Unless Nivelle has a big success he will certainly fall. Some of our gunners who have been to the French front are very doubtful about the French chances. I hope and pray they are wrong. Failure now would throw everything back for many months, probably a year.

Messimy's demand that the Government should consult Nivelle's Army Group Commanders, irregular though it was, could not be ignored in view of his stature and authority. The meeting took place on 6 April* in the Presidential train at a siding in the station of Compiègne, where GQG had transferred itself three days earlier. President Poincaré himself presided; he was accompanied by the Prime Minister, Ribot, the Minister for War, Painlevé, the Minister of Marine, Admiral Lacaze and the Minister of Munitions, Thomas. They met Nivelle with Generals Micheler (GAR), Franchet d'Esperey (GAN), Pétain (*Groupe d'Armées du Centre*, GAC) and de Castelnau, just returned from Russia to command the *Groupe D'Armées de L'Est* (GAE). General Micheler was understood to be the strongest critic of the Nivelle Plan, but in the presence of his Chief he entirely failed to make a case. General D'Esperey sounded a note of caution about the likely results of the offensive, but did not advise calling it off, reminding his hearers that the British were already committed.† General de Castelnau, coming fresh to the scene without intimate knowledge, could only support his C-in-C. It was left to General Pétain to state categorically that there would not be a break-through. General Nivelle offered to resign, but was dissuaded by the united politicians. In an atmosphere of almost complete misunderstanding the offensive was not cancelled, and the meeting broke up. General Spears, who was at Compiègne and spoke to some of those who had been present at the conference that afternoon, writes:

Spears, pp 376–7

The celebrated Conference of Compiègne was over, its only obvious result a lessening of the authority of the Commander-in-Chief.

It is difficult at first sight to see why a meeting purely negative in its results should have obtained such notoriety. The fact that it brought to a head bitter dissensions and exposed without remedying them deep divergences of opinion, is but a poor claim to a special niche in the fane of history; nor is it for these reasons

*This should have been an auspicious day, the day of the formal American declaration of war.
† The British preliminary battle bombardment at Arras had begun at 6.30 am on 4 April and had already used a vast number of shells. It is some indication of the magnitude of these battles that the artillery 'softening-up' programme at Arras (25 March–8 April) used 2,687,653 shells, and the remainder of the battle from 9 April used a further 4,261,500.

that the proceedings have attracted so much attention. It is because the Conference of Compiègne stands as a monument to the inefficiency of democracy at war, to the helplessness of Ministers facing technicians, and their total inability to decide between different professional opinions . . .

6 April epitomizes the terrible disability from which democracies, even when fighting for their existence, are unable to free themselves. What this weakness in the supreme direction of the war cost the Allies in lives and money can never be computed.

Spears, p 437

The Compiègne Conference was the inevitable result of the earlier one held at Calais. The seed planted at Calais bore fruit at Compiègne. The British forces were under the orders of the French Commander-in-Chief, but the French Commander-in-Chief was under the control of the French Cabinet, who in an emergency such as had occurred, did not hesitate to use their powers without reference to the British Government. It was now quite evident that our Cabinet had abdicated its powers in favour not of a French general but of the French Government.

Wilson, i, p 336

6 APRIL . . . I hear that the Government, aided by Pétain, wanted to force Nivelle to abandon his great offensive, and have a small one instead. Nivelle stood firm and won. What time of day for such a proposal, and Haig not consulted.

If events in France were shrouded in doubt and uncertainty, with prospects of fresh Command Changes, the great change in Russia continued to baffle all observers.

Repington, i, p 509

FRIDAY, 6 APRIL.   Played Bridge with Countess Torby, and she drove me back to Hampstead. She was perfectly furious about the Revolution, and declared that all the Russian officers who came over here assured her that there would be a counter-revolution very soon, and that the Revolution would be put down.

THE INVINCIBLE ENEMY

Author's Papers: Haig Diary

SATURDAY, 7 APRIL . . . Ground in bad state, but day was fine with drying wind.

Spears, pp 393–4

8 APRIL.   The morning of Easter Sunday was lovely. Not a cloud in the sky. A

sharp frost had solidified the mud of the previous evening . . . Night fell, and it became very much colder . . . The weather was obviously breaking . . . There were some icy rain-squalls.

Spears, p 394

9 APRIL.   Towards morning snow interspersed with sleet began to fall. It was very cold.

COMMAND CHANGES

Blake, pp 215–16, Haig to Robertson, 8 April

Very many thanks for your kind thought in writing to wish me 'Good Luck' on the eve of battle. I appreciate this very much.

Yesterday I was all round the Corps in 1st and 3rd Armies who are attacking – I have never before seen Commanders so confident, or so satisfied with the preparations and wire cutting. Today is lovely weather – so I hope things will turn out all right.

I hear Nivelle has had trouble.

Charteris, p 210

8 APRIL.   We are again on the eve of battle; although it is only to help the French it is a big thing. Three corps, each with four divisions, are making the main attack, and the Canadians are attacking on their left. The big French attack is being held back on account of the weather, but will not make very much difference to us, so far as the immediate fighting is concerned, always provided that the French Government does not at the last moment succeed in overruling Nivelle, and stop the attack altogether; if they do that we shall have the whole German Army on our heads here in a month.

Ludendorff, ii, p 421

On the 9th, after a short but extraordinarily intense artillery preparation, our army encountered a powerful attack, led by tanks, on both sides of the Scarpe. Some of our advanced divisions gave way. The neighbouring divisions which stood firm suffered heavy losses. The enemy succeeded before noon in reaching our battery positions and seizing heights which dominated the country far to the east . . .

. . . The battle of Arras on 9 April was a bad beginning for the decisive struggle of this year.

10 April and the following days were critical. The consequences of a break-through of 12 to 15 Kilometres wide and 6 or more kilometres deep are not easy

to meet. In view of the heavy losses in men, guns and ammunition resulting from such a breakthrough, colossal efforts are needed to make good the damage . . . A day like 9 April threw all calculations to the winds.

Wilson, i, p 337

9 APRIL.   The news tonight of our attack is that we have got to our objectives and have taken 10,000 prisoners and 50 guns. Vimy Ridge is at last in our hands. This is a good beginning towards the 300,000 prisoners that I want this summer.

Haig Diary, Blake, p 216

MONDAY, 9 APRIL . . . Our casualties are estimated at 16,000. This is small considering the three successive strong positions, each one deeply wired, which have been taken.

THE INVISIBLE ENEMY

While the Army was scoring its great triumph at Vimy on 9 April, Rear-Admiral William S. Sims of the US Navy, who had just arrived in England, was talking to the First Sea Lord, Admiral Sir John Jellicoe.

Rear-Admiral W. S. Sims, The Victory At Sea,
Murray, 1927

After the usual greetings, Admiral Jellicoe took a paper out of his drawer and handed it to me. It was a record of tonnage losses for the last few months. This showed that the total sinkings, British and neutral, had reached 536,000 tons in February and 630,000 tons in March; it further disclosed that sinkings were taking place in April which indicated the destruction of nearly 900,000 tons. These figures indicated that the losses were three and four times as large as those which were then being published in the Press. It is expressing it mildly to say that I was surprised by this disclosure. I was fairly astounded; for I had never imagined anything so terrible. I expressed my consternation to Admiral Jellicoe.

'Yes,' he said, as quietly as though he were discussing the weather and not the future of the British Empire, 'it is impossible for us to go on with the war if losses like this continue.' . . .

'It looks as though the Germans were winning the war,' I remarked.

'They will win unless we can stop these losses – and stop them soon,' the Admiral replied.

'Is there no solution for the problem?' I asked.

'Absolutely none that we can see now,' Jellicoe announced.

THE INVINCIBLE ENEMY

Charteris, p 212

10 APRIL . . . The one unfortunate thing is the accursed weather. It has broken again, and we are having snow and rain. Just now it is practically a blizzard.

Spears, p 426

The heaviest snowfalls of the whole winter occurred on the 10th, 11th, and 12th. Indeed the weather remained very bad until the 20th.

SOLDIERS AND POLITICIANS

Author's Papers: Robertson to Haig, 6 April

Glad to say that the troubles here regarding you a few weeks ago are quite past, and all is now very well so far as you are concerned . . .

[Reference here to criticisms of Generals Sir Archibald Murray, Egypt and Palestine front, and Sir George Milne, Salonika.]

The P.M. is the arch-conspirator. *No* General is good enough for him. He is always producing some story he hears from people who can talk and who are back from the various theatres. However, all is now well all round once more.

Charteris, p 213

11 APRIL . . . I have never seen D.H. so stirred by success before, and he has been most kind and complimentary about our little part in the show. It means a great deal to him personally, though I do not think that weighs much with him. After all this trouble at Calais, however, there is no doubt in any of our minds that the Prime Minister would have got rid of him out of hand unless this show had been a success. It is a success, indeed it is more than a success, it is a victory.

Haig Diary, Duff Cooper, ii, p 86–7

15 APRIL . . . Will history ever forgive the members of the War Cabinet for declining in January, 1917, to have any confidence in the power of the British Army to play its part with credit on the Western Front? Almost every week gives us fresh indications of the decisive effect of the Somme Battle on the German Army and the German plans.

COMMAND CHANGES

Repington, i, pp 514–15

FRIDAY, 13 APRIL . . . (Robertson) is very uneasy about French politics, and declares that when Nivelle fights he will fight with a halter round his neck, as Pétain disapproves of the offensive, and he and Painlevé, with others, are said to be distrustful of Nivelle. R. likes Nivelle, and thinks him straight and frank,* but does not know whether he has the qualities for his present position. If Painlevé succeeds Ribot, Pétain may get the Command-in-Chief, but R. says that it is absurd to change the Commander with every change of Government.

Author's Papers: Robertson to Haig, 14 April

Poor Nivelle is going into action with a rope round his neck . . . No more foolish or cruel thing can be done than to crab a man's plans once they have been decided upon and approved. In fact no plan should ever be crabbed. It should either be accepted or rejected, and if accepted criticism should be practically silent.

FLANDERS

It would not be surprising, in this month of crowded action, if the Flanders project had been entirely lost to sight. But such was not the case.

Blake, p 216, Haig to Robertson, 8 April†

The grave question I have to decide within the next few weeks is whether the present operations are likely to result in freeing the Belgian ports by the late summer. If, say, by the end of May, we are still before the line Lille–Valenciennes–Hirson–the Meuse, then preparations should be begun for the switch elsewhere.

On 6 April General Smuts, then a member of the Imperial War Cabinet, visited GHQ on behalf of that body. According to Lloyd George,

Lloyd George, i, p 909

Sir Douglas Haig seems to have taken advantage of the visit to impress upon General Smuts the importance of an offensive to clear the Flanders coast. He came back full of the idea.

*See p 59 f.n.
†See p 66.

On his return to London, General Smuts made a full report to General Robertson.

Repington, i, pp 515–16

FRIDAY, 13 APRIL . . . R. passed on to me some interesting advices from an important person. The latter does not think that we are taking the position due to us from our financial, naval, and military pre-eminence in the war, and complains that French policy is untrustworthy, and their plans always changing. He is disposed to think that after the present, or rather coming, French offensive ends, we should make the French take over more of our line and mass a force in the North to sweep up the coast and march towards Holland. He also says that France has drained us of all our troops, and that we have no great strategic reserve left such as the Germans now possess, and that, therefore, we cannot easily repair a mistake or strike a new blow.* Much of which is very true, but I think a great attack in the North poor strategy . . . because the Low Country positions amongst the rivers and canals, and with rain and mud, would be difficult and costly to force.

THE INVINCIBLE ENEMY

Spears, p 458

14 APRIL. The weather, always the abominable weather, was the fiendish, relentless ally of the Germans.

Ibid, p 485

During the whole night of the 15th–16th it poured with rain. Water deepened the puddles at the bottom of the trenches, ran in streams down the roads, and churned up the soil in the fields where troops and guns were standing, until these were gluey, sticky, reeking, stinking quagmires, lit by the sudden vivid flares of bursting shells and heaving like boiling porridge under the shock of explosions.

Water dripped off the steel helmets of hundreds of thousands of men cowering in the trenches or marching down the muddy roads, and soaked into their blue cloaks until they were heavy and stiff.

The rain beat down on hutments and hospitals. It drove into the faces of the artillery observers, blinding them as they peered into the night. Its icy contact numbed thousands of Senegalese almost to lifelessness.

COMMAND CHANGES

Spears, p 482

15 APRIL. Before starting off again into the freezing night, listening to the rain

---

*On 29 March, according to Repington, the number of troops (other than those in hospital) in the U.K. was 1,384,000. The number of officers and men in France on 1 April (other than coloured labour) was 1,822,274.

beating down, I made some notes in my diary: they are before me now. They began 'The offensive cannot succeed.'

Haig Diary, Blake, pp 217–18

MONDAY, 16 APRIL.   The French launched their long-delayed attack this morning on a front of 25 miles on the River Aisne . . . Reports were at first very favourable. Later it was said, 'Enemy counter-attacked very strongly and ground gained was lost.' French claim 10,000 prisoners, but the attitude of French officers attached to my Staff makes me think that they are not quite satisfied and that the much talked of victory has not been gained by the French up to date. It is a pity that Nivelle was so very optimistic as regards breaking the enemy's line.

Ludendorff, ii, pp 424–6

16 APRIL.   (The French) broke through at various points on the Chemin des Dames and forced us to withdraw with heavy losses from the Vailly salient to the heights of the Chemin des Dames . . . Meanwhile offensives in Champagne had also been opened, directed against the heights of Moronvilliers. One division gave way, and we lost the heights which formed a key position. When the French attempted to descend the northern slope they were exposed to our artillery fire, which mowed them down and brought them to a standstill . . . The crisis of the April battle had been survived. In these battles the French infantry had attacked in close formation, and its losses had been appalling. Both on the Aisne and in Champagne General Nivelle again attempted to score a victory. By this time our line was once more re-established and consolidated, so that on both fields of this great double battle the new offensive came to grief with heavy loss.

Haig Diary, Blake, p 218

TUESDAY, 17 APRIL.   I could get no details from the French Mission as to results of today's fighting. This is always a bad sign, and I fear that things are going badly with their offensive

Wilson, i, p 338

17 APRIL . . . So far, the great attack has been a failure. Of course, all this will greatly shake confidence in Nivelle, and my opinion is that unless the Fourth and Fifth armies pull off a real success Nivelle will fall and that we shall have Pétain here. Painlevé will certainly aim towards that.

The Invisible Enemy

MacDonagh, pp 188–9

15 April . . . The following official announcement is made:

'We are authorized to state that, realizing the urgent need for economy in food, and particularly in breadstuffs, their Majesties the King and Queen, together with the Household and servants, have adopted the scale of National Rations since early in February.'

The Times publishes this as an introduction to a new and more restrictive Public Meals Order, issued by the Food Controller, which comes into operation today. It applies to hotels, restaurants, boarding-houses and clubs. A meatless day is to be observed weekly. No meat, poultry or game is to be served on Tuesdays in London, and on Wednesdays in the country. On five days of the week potatoes are prohibited. Bread at any meal is restricted to two ounces . . . It is suspected by the public generally that the scarcity is due, at least in part, to the withholding of potato stocks from the market by home growers and dealers in foreign imports in the hope of prices rising still higher. My own view is that it is to be attributed more to the activity of enemy submarines. The shortage of bread is also due to the sinking of cargo-ships carrying wheat.

Charteris, pp 215–16

17 April . . . Repington has been here . . . He was very alarmed about the submarine menace, and gave it as not only his own opinion, but that of people who ought to know more about it than he does, and whom he had met, that there would be a serious shortage of food in England if the war went on through this autumn. He is very sarcastic about the Navy, and not at all hopeful about what the attitude of the people would be if they are faced with real personal hardship. He thinks that a lack of bacon would depress Great Britain even more than the biggest casualty list.

Author's Papers, Derby to Haig, 18 April

The state of affairs now existing is really very bad indeed, and we have lost command of the sea.

Command Changes

Author's Papers: Haig Diary

Thursday, 19 April . . . The great error was that N. and his staff gave out that they were going to advance a long way very quickly. Hence there is a feeling of disappointment everywhere in France at the results of Nivelle's operations.

Author's Papers: Robertson to Haig

20 APRIL.

My dear Haig,

... Nivelle's prophecy of doing the trick in 24 to 48 hours and then pushing up a lot of other divisions was always to my mind most ridiculous and I could never understand why he should have made such a statement. It is coming home to roost now and will be his undoing if he is not careful. It was a very silly theory for him to have advanced and he seems to have entirely wasted the lessons of the last two years and a half. You know, I imagine better than most people, that every war has its own peculiarities, and in certain important respects is totally different from its predecessors. To my mind no war has ever differed so much from previous wars as does the present one, and it is futile, to put it mildly, hanging on to old theories when facts show them to be wrong. At one time audacity and determination to push on regardless of loss were the predominating factors, but that was before the days of machine guns and other modern armament . . . I cannot help thinking that Nivelle has attached too much importance to what is called 'breaking the enemy's front'. The best plan seems to me to go back to one of the old principles, that of defeating the enemy's army . . . and that means inflicting heavier losses upon him than one suffers oneself. If this old principle is kept in view and the object of breaking the enemy's army is achieved the front will look after itself, and the casualty bill will be less. I apologize for breaking out in this manner into a sort of Staff College lecture . . .

Yours very truly,

W. Robertson

Haig and Robertson were correct; the mischief lay in Nivelle's rash promises rather than in actual failure on the battlefield. In the words of the British Official History:

O.H., 1917, i, p 498

The French had sought a breakthrough, and they had completely failed to achieve it. From other points of view they had gained considerable advantages. By 20 April they had in their hands over 20,000 prisoners and 147 guns; the railway from Soissons to Reims was freed; the enemy had been driven out of the Aisne valley west of the Oise–Aisne Canal; the German second position had been captured south of Juvincourt; and in Champagne some of the most important of the 'monts' had been taken. The German counter-attacks, successful at the beginning, were becoming less and less so as time went on.

By 25 April French casualties had reached over 96,000. This was not an unusual number for a large offensive,* but it was not what public

*In March–April, 1918, in 40 days of offensive against the British, the Germans had over 348,000 casualties.

opinion was expecting, and the sense of shock and resentment was intensified by the evident lack of medical preparation, resulting in great hardship for the wounded.

Spears, p 507

16 APRIL.   These were not the men the nurses expected, were used to; mangled, but gallant and very courteous. These men were broken in spirit as well as in body; not a laugh among them, not a smile of greeting. They were discouraged as French wounded had never been discouraged before.
'It's all up,' they said, 'we can't do it, we shall never do it'. '*C'est impossible*', and the words whispered from ashen lips swept over the rows of stretchers like a cold gust rustling dead leaves and dead hopes in a cemetery.

And so another new thread of dire significance entered the patttern of the year.

FRENCH MORALE

Esher, iv, pp 103–4: Esher to Derby, 17 April

There are certain things that you and the Prime Minister should know and digest: . . .
4. The discouragement and fatigue, physical and moral, of the French women, especially of the peasant and working class.
5. The growing reluctance of the French soldier to go over the parapet.

The deductions, I want you to understand, the most candid and thoughtful Frenchmen draw from these undeniable facts are that we have arrived at a psychological moment when discouragement may lead to any sort of acquiescence in any sort of peace rather than continue the war . . .

Russia has collapsed as a state organism; Italy is torn by conflicting sympathies and hopes and fears; France is very, very tired.

SOLDIERS AND POLITICIANS

Wilson, i, p 339

19 APRIL . . . I told (Haig) that my feeling was that Lloyd George and Painlevé were determined to take a more active command of the major operations of the war, and that Painlevé was determined to get rid of Nivelle, and to replace him by Pétain, whose mental attitude was to sit and do nothing and wait for the Americans. I praised Nivelle, and said it would be a dangerous thing if the French Army were to think that Lloyd George had joined with French politicians to *dégommé*

Nivelle. He showed me a short note that he had written to Lloyd George on the necessity of going on with the present attacks. The note was good; but I could have made a much stronger and more convincing case about the danger of Italy and Russia running out, and the danger of prolonging the war and thus giving the Boche submarines more chance.

Author's Papers: Robertson to Haig, 20 April

The French Ministers are worse than ours in the way they are prone to jump about from one plan to another. Poor Nivelle has not had a proper chance, going into battle with the knowledge that his plan was thought to be not a good one.

Wilson, i, p 340

20 APRIL . . . a meeting today in Paris, and discussion with Painlevé and Nivelle as to whether the present offensive should be stopped. However, Haig's letter, and Robertson's help, and Nivelle's determination have prevented this disastrous state of things from happening. But the Frock Coats are to have another meeting in ten days, when, I fear, unless we get a theatrical success, the matter will be much more acute. I had a long talk with Nivelle before dinner. He was depressed . . . I told him that he and Haig must meet next week and put up a joint paper against the Frocks when next they meet.

Duff Cooper, ii, p 105: Esher to Haig, 21 April

Yesterday I spent some hours with Lloyd George, and we lunched on the balcony of the Crillon in the sunshine. He has entirely changed his point of view as to the respective merits of the chiefs of the Allied Army, their staffs, and powers of offence. It is almost comic to see how the balance has turned. For the moment I do not think *you* could do wrong. This instability of vision (if you can use such a phrase) is L.G.'s great weakness. With his tremendous vitality and indestructible spirit it is a source of danger. But luckily he never displays infirmity of purpose. He suffers from over-elasticity of mind which is a rare enough fault on the borderline between vice and virtue.

THE INVINCIBLE ENEMY

MacDonagh, p 189

FRIDAY 20 APRIL.   It is a day of pearly Spring.

Charteris, p 218

21 APRIL . . . Today for the first time it is real spring weather, a very pleasant change. The trees are bursting into bud and the sun has brought out the birds. War seems very futile.

Soldiers and Politicians

Wilson, i, p 340

23 April . . . (Nivelle) told me that all sorts of Cabinet Ministers, Members of the Chamber and others were getting passes for the Front and going down there and seeing Pétain, etc, then going back with fantastic tales. All this is undermining discipline and playing the mischief, and is also making Nivelle's position very difficult.

Wilson, i, p 341

24 April . . . I told (Haig) that I thought the *civiles* were determined to get the upper hand, and then to go in for the Pétain school of squatting and doing nothing, so as to avoid loss.

Flanders

Haig Diary: Blake, p 219

Tuesday, 24 April. I left Bavincourt* at 1.30 by motor for Amiens where I met General Nivelle at 3 pm . . . We at once went to a small room upstairs by ourselves, and I put my view of the situation to him. Briefly, my points were as follows:

1. The French Government had told the British Prime Minister that if a distinct success were not obtained in the first few days of attack on the Aisne, they intended to stop offensive.
2. In view of submarine campaign, it was most necessary to clear the Belgian Ports soon, at any rate before Autumn.
3. This could be done either directly by operating from Ypres, or indirectly, by operating towards Charleroi–Liège.
4. We are at present carrying out the latter plan,† and I am prepared to use every effort to break the Hindenburg Line and take Cambrai; but for this to be successful, the continued action of the French Army is essential.
5. I requested him to assure me that the French Armies would continue to operate energetically, because what I feared was that, after the British Army had exhausted itself in trying to make Nivelle's plan a success, the French Govt might stop the operations. I would then not be able to give effect to the other plan, viz, that of directly capturing the Northern Ports.

Nivelle assured me that neither he nor his Government had any intention of stopping the offensive.

*Haig's Advanced Headquarters during the Battle of Arras.
† At Arras; the Second Battle of the Scarpe was fought on 23–4 April, 2,500 prisoners being taken at a cost to the British of nearly 10,000 casualties.

Command Changes

On 25 April M. Painlevé dined with Sir Henry Wilson and Lord Esher, Lord Duncannon, Wilson's ADC, also being present.

Wilson, i, p 342

25 April . . . We four talked till 11.30. The upshot of the whole thing is that I believe Nivelle is done.

Esher, iv, p 109

Paris, 25 April . . . Painlevé told us that he had made up his mind to supersede Nivelle.

Haig Diary, Duff Cooper, ii, pp 94–5

Thursday, 26 April.   . . . I left at 9 am by motor for Paris . . . M. Painlevé was delighted to see me, but he appeared quite excited, and from his conversation I gathered that he had persuaded himself that the French had been beaten on the Aisne. He assured me that whatever happened the French Government would loyally discharge their duties towards the British Army, that there would be no change of plan, and that the offensive would be maintained. I gathered, however, that he wished to replace Nivelle by Pétain. I told him of the plan agreed upon between Nivelle and myself regarding clearing the Belgian coast before winter. He stated definitely that there would be no delay in carrying it out . . .

At 3 pm I saw M. Ribot at the Quai d'Orsay. He is a tall old man of eighty years of age. A dear old thing, but I should think too old to deal with these tricky French politicians . . . He stated that in his opinion this was no time for making a change in the command. He asked my opinion. I said any change in command during a battle was to be deprecated, that I had no knowledge of what Nivelle was supposed to have failed in, but that I was delighted to work with any General whom the French Government appointed as their Commander-in-Chief. He asked me about Pétain's merits, but I of course could not discuss this. I said I knew him very slightly and had not had any opportunity of judging his military qualities.

Wilson, i, p 343

26 April.   Haig arrived at 2.15. He went off to see Painlevé, then Ribot, and I saw him again at 4.30 . . . Haig had gone to Ribot and had told him that all was going well, and Ribot agreed that nothing should be changed, and that this was not a good moment to change the C in C. So Haig is delighted with himself. My own opinion is that Painlevé, who was not present at the Ribot interview, spoke the Cabinet mind much more truly than Ribot, and that the Cabinet do not keep Ribot informed of the state of affairs. We shall see.

Repington, i, p 541

THURSDAY, 26 APRIL . . . Painlevé is having a hard time to induce his Cabinet to accept Pétain, and is furious because Sir H. Wilson came to see him uninvited, supporting Nivelle and criticizing Pétain severely. Ribot is pro-Nivelle, and Briand angry at Nivelle being upset; but Nivelle has failed, and the Government have to meet the Chambers on 22 May.

Wilson, i, p 343

27 APRIL . . . Esher telephoned about 11.30, to say that Haig had had another interview with Painlevé, who had confirmed Ribot by saying that there was no intention of changing the present plan. Nothing was said about Nivelle . . . But I remain always of the same opinion that Painlevé will *dégommé* Nivelle and put in Pétain, and that operations will at once be changed. Neither Ribot nor Painlevé understand what they are doing, and both are out to save their skins.

Repington, i, pp 541–2

FRIDAY, 27 APRIL . . . Reached Pétain's HQ, where several officers were assembled. I was shown into the garden, where Pétain and another general were walking about. Pétain greeted me kindly and then introduced his comrade as General Nivelle. I was at a loss to know whether Pétain or Nivelle knew of Pétain's new appointment, but, in fact, as it turned out afterwards, Pétain and I knew, but Nivelle did not. There was, therefore, a certain comedy about the deference which Pétain and I showed to the supposed but already fallen Commander-in-Chief . . . Nivelle was very pleasant and agreeable, but he lacks Pétain's character, and was plainly under the latter's influence. It was like pupil and master, and there was no doubt which was the dominant spirit.

Charteris, p 219

28 APRIL . . . Apparently Nivelle is to go, although D.H. urged that he should be retained, on the grounds that any change now will only mean further dislocation. It is very generous of D.H., considering all that has happened in the past, to try to save Nivelle. D.H.'s view is that Nivelle, now that he has learned that things do not always happen as one would like them to happen, will be a much easier man to deal with than before, and that the devil you know is better in any event than the devil you do not know.

Author's Papers: Haig Diary

SUNDAY, 29 APRIL . . . Message from Paris stated that Pétain had been offered and accepted Chief Command of French Armies of North and North-East.* He described his tactics as 'aggressive/defensive' – the basis is to avoid losses and wait American reinforcements.

*Actually Pétain was appointed Chief of the General Staff, with extended powers, on 29 April, only becoming C-in-C on 15 May.

Haig Diary: Blake, p 222

29 APRIL.   (GHQ), Haig to Sir William Robertson:
Pétain calls it the 'Aggressive/Defensive', and doubtless in his mind he figures the
British Army doing the aggressive work, while the French Army squats on the
defensive!

Repington, i, pp 550–1

SUNDAY, 29 APRIL . . . Went to see Painlevé in the evening, and heard that Pétain
had today been definitely appointed CGS of the Army and would come to Paris.
He had been offered this or CGS to Nivelle, and had naturally chosen the first,
and I feel sure that it will be with such extended powers that he will have full
control.

FLANDERS

Author's Papers: Haig Diary

29 APRIL . . . I told (Kiggell) that in view of the French Govt having decided to
remove Nivelle, we must expect that the action of the French Armies will be
limited to minor offensives, in which no large losses are likely. There was thus no
object in our pushing on to Cambrai. Such a position will cause a salient in our
line, and will only be reached after considerable losses. It will not lead to decisive
results . . .
  We ought to aim
1. At reaching a good defensive line . . .
2. At preparing several attacks to go in by surprise so as to hold the enemy and
   wear him out.
3. At launching Ypres attack, for which troops should be economized.

Blake, p 222: Haig to Robertson, 29 April

I shall send you a paper tomorrow night giving my views on the situation.
Meantime, I think the time has now come for me taking up our 'alternative plan'
in earnest, and to this end we should ask the French to relieve some of our
Divisions on our right, while we relieve their Divisions on the Belgian coast. But
pressure on the German Army must not be relaxed in the meantime. This seems
to me of first importance for the success of *our* plan.

On 29 April General Smuts, his visit to the Western Front completed,
drew up a paper for the attention of his War Cabinet colleagues, entitled
*The General and Military Situation and Particularly that on The Western
Front*. Having dealt with the general situation and with the Salonika,
Mesopotamia and Palestine fronts in more detail, General Smuts then

turned to the Western Front, and in the course of a lengthy analysis wrote:

Lloyd George, i, p 915

I feel the danger of a purely defensive policy so gravely that I would make the following suggestions in case the French carry out such a policy. In that case we should make them take back a substantial part of their line now occupied by us. As they would require no great reserve for offensive purposes, they would be in a position to do so. Our forces should then be concentrated towards the north, and part should go to the rear as a strategic reserve, while the rest should endeavour to recover the northern coast of Belgium and drive the enemy from Zeebrugge and Ostend. This task will be most formidable, especially if both the Russian and French lines remain passive, and every pressure should be exerted to induce them to be as aggressive as possible, even if they cannot actually assume the offensive. But, however difficult the task, something will have to be done to continue our offensive, and I see more advantages in an offensive intended to recover the Belgian coast and deprive the enemy of two advanced submarine bases, than in the present offensive, which in proportion as it succeeds in driving the enemy out of France will make the French less eager to continue the struggle beyond that goal.

This was the third time that the project of a British offensive in Flanders in the summer of 1917 was formally drawn to the attention of the War Cabinet, this time by one of its own members (see pages 30 and 54–5).

AMERICA

Blake, p 222: Haig to Robertson, 29 April

Whoever the nominal or actual C in C may be, we will be confronted with one and the same policy, namely, that of the French Government. Their policy, I feel pretty certain, is to be based on avoiding losses while waiting for American reinforcements.

COMMAND CHANGES

Repington, i, p 550

SATURDAY, 28 APRIL ... All that I saw of (Pétain) confirmed me in my belief that he is the best leader in France, and combines the qualities of science, judgment and character to a higher degree than any of the other generals whom I have met. I admire Painlevé – this deputy of the extreme Left – for his courage in selecting him.

THE INVINCIBLE ENEMY

Repington, i, p 550

SUNDAY, 29 APRIL . . . A glorious spring day, the first after many months of the worst winter that I remember.

FLANDERS

Haig Diary: Blake, p 222

MONDAY, 30 APRIL . . . I rode back to Bavincourt with General Gough, who stayed to lunch. It was nice riding across the fields, soil nice and dry. The season is so late that buds are only just beginning to show. Yet the day was hot!

After lunch I explained to Gough that I am preparing for the Ypres operations, and that he would command the northern half of those operations, including the landing force.* He must keep this absolutely secret, but is to study the scheme which Colonel McMullen† (his former Staff Officer) would explain to him. Admiral Bacon is attending a trial of 'Tanks' today, so I sent Gough off at once to Eris (Tank HQ) to see the Admiral and McMullen.

THE INVISIBLE ENEMY

Duff Cooper, ii, p 101: Robertson to Haig, 26 April

The situation at sea is very serious indeed. It has never been so bad as at present, and Jellicoe almost daily announces it to be hopeless. There may soon be a serious shortage of food in this country, and this has to be taken into consideration in regard to all theatres of war.

Wilson, i, p 344

29 APRIL . . . Hankey gave me dreadful figures of damage done by submarines.

Hankey, ii, pp 649–50

29 APRIL . . . In one way this has been one of the most dreadful weeks of the war, owing to appalling mercantile losses from submarines. These have depressed me

---

*Probably because General Rawlinson's Fourth Army was still engaged beside the French Third Army against the Hindenburg Line.
† See p 27.

very much, but at last, when it is almost too late, the Government are taking action. I spent the whole morning dictating a long Memo. to help Lloyd George, who has undertaken to investigate the whole question at the Admiralty on Monday. I also had a long talk on the telephone with Stamfordham* about the Press attacks on the Admiralty, though in my opinion these attacks are largely justified. For example, a few weeks ago they scouted the idea of convoy. Now they are undertaking it on their own initiative, but apparently want weeks to organize it, though this at any rate might have been done earlier. They don't look ahead. As Fisher has recently written to me, the problem is 'Can the Army win the war before the Navy loses it?'†

Hankey, ii, p 650

30 APRIL . . . At last Lloyd George has set himself to tackle the submarine question seriously . . . This morning Lloyd George and I went to the Admiralty and spent the whole day there very pleasantly, lunching with Jellicoe and his wife and four little girls – Lloyd George having a great flirtation with a little girl of three. I spent the whole evening up to 8.30 pm dictating a long report, embodying a large reconstruction of the Admiralty and more especially of the Admiralty War Staff.

Lloyd George, i, p 709

Statistics of shipping losses, April, 1917 — 526,447 gross tons sunk

*Lord Stamfordham, the King's Private Secretary.
† Actually, this was Repington's mordant question, now obviously doing the rounds; see p 32.

May

—————————————————— ✦ ——————————————————

It is important to remember that although the high drama of the British offensive at Arras and General Nivelle's ill-fated enterprises on the Aisne and in Champagne was over, fighting continued at a sharp and costly intensity almost until the end of May on the British front, and well into July on the French. The British Third and First Armies fought the Third Battle of the Scarpe on 3/4 May; between 3 and 17 May the Fifth Army fought a Second Battle of Bullecourt (a name of evil memory); minor operations on the Third and First Army fronts continued until 24 May. The French won a considerable success along the Chemin des Dames Ridge on 5 May, provoking no less than seventy German counter-attacks during the next eighty days (according to a report by the Director of Military intelligence to the War Cabinet on 25 July).

All this activity shows how difficult it was to break off major battles at will; yet the real preoccupations of British GHQ were now elsewhere.

FLANDERS

Author's Papers: Haig to War Cabinet, O.A.D. 428: 'The Present Situation and Future Plans', 1 May

We must maintain the offensive* for at least 2 or 3 weeks more, but limiting our efforts to what we may hope to accomplish with comparatively little loss. The French must be prevailed on, for similar reasons, to do at least as much, acting on the same principles.

After Italy and Russia have come in† the French and ourselves must still maintain sufficient activity – but no more – to keep the enemy in expectation of serious attack, and thus hold him to this front, so that he may be unable to reinforce his other frontiers, where his forces at present are not too great for Italy and Russia to cope with successfully.

*At Arras.
† In accordance with the agreement of the Allied Military representatives at Chantilly, 16 November, 1916; see p 13.

Preliminary measures to enable me to undertake operations to clear the Belgian coast have been in hand for some time and are fairly well advanced; as soon as Russia and Italy have come in my main efforts must be concentrated on completing these measures so that the operations may be commenced at as early a date as possible.

To give these operations a reasonable chance of success, however, it is necessary firstly that the French should take over at least as much of my front as·I took over from them since General Nivelle assumed command, and as much more as possible.

[References follow to the Nieuport sector, where the amphibious operation was intended, though this was not mentioned because of the need for secrecy; to the need for a French subsidiary offensive 'simultaneously with my proposed attack in Belgium'; the need for reinforcements of men and heavy guns; the need for an agreement with the Belgians.]

To summarize the foregoing:

The guiding principles on which my general scheme of action is based are those which have proved successful in war from time immemorial, viz, that the first step must always be to wear down the enemy's power of resistance until he is so weakened that he will be unable to withstand a decisive blow; then to deliver the decisive blow; and, finally, to reap the fruits of victory.

The enemy has already been weakened appreciably; but a long time is required to wear down such great numbers of troops composed of fine fighting material, and he is still fighting with such energy and determination that the situation is not yet ripe for the decisive blow. Our action must therefore continue for the present to be of a wearing-down character until his power of resistance has been further reduced . . .

Under the conditions I have stated success in this attempt is now, in my opinion, reasonably possible and would have valuable results on land and sea; while even if a full measure of success is not gained we shall be attacking the enemy on a front where he cannot refuse to fight, and where, therefore, our purpose of wearing him down can be given effect to – while even a partial success will considerably improve our defensive positions in the YPRES salient and thus reduce the heavy wastage which must otherwise be expected to occur there next winter as in the past.

This most important paper, formally addressed to the War Cabinet three months before the main offensive began, constitutes the fourth involvement of that body in the Flanders project (see pages 30, 54, 79), yet there is no record of it ever being discussed.*

*It must be said at once that this was not due to indolence. The War Cabinet met twenty-five times in May, some meetings dealing with as many as 17, 18, 19 or 20 agenda items, one

On 2 May Colonel Repington was talking to General Foch, at that time without active employment.

Repington, i, p 556

We discussed operations in the West and elsewhere . . . I found that Foch had ideas about the low country near the coast, and I advised him to keep away from them. He got out the maps and we had a discussion on the subject.

COMMAND CHANGES

Charteris, p 220

1 MAY.   D.H. is back from Paris. It seems more than doubtful whether the French will open another attack or continue with the present one. Exactly what we feared has happened. The French now want us to take up the whole burden of active operation on this front. Nivelle will go . . . Poor Nivelle! One cannot help being very sorry for him. With all his faults, he did take a big view of things, and he certainly did not seek to spare his own army. He staked everything on this one battle and has lost.

Esher, iv, p 113: Esher to Derby

2 MAY.   It is thought that Painlevé and Pétain in the same building is a juxtaposition that will not last long.

Haig Diary: Blake, pp 226–7

3 MAY.   At 10 am I called on General Pétain at his Office in the Invalides. The same room as that in which I was received by General Joffre in June, 1914, before the war. Pétain took over the duties of a new appointment yesterday, viz, Chief of the General Staff. Nivelle is practically ousted . . .

I had a long talk with Pétain. He was Professor of Infantry Tactics at the French Staff College, and is a very capable soldier according to all accounts . . .

[A lengthy discussion of future plans followed; Haig asked Pétain to relieve six British divisions, and make holding attacks to tie down German reserves.]

(No. 150, 30 May) with no less than 24. The subjects discussed ranged from the condition of Russia or Ireland to Liquor Restriction or a proposed increase in the Dog Tax. Some members of the Cabinet became extremely exhausted, Lord Curzon in particular (always a hard driver of himself) being described as 'on the verge of a nervous breakdown'. The truth is that the War Cabinet system, though far better than anything previously known, was not yet sufficiently streamlined for war direction, so that when the question of the main British effort of the year arose with urgency, a new committee had to be set up to examine it.

Pétain replied that he entirely agreed with my view and plans. The one difficulty was the question of effectives. But he would consider the question and let me have his reply in writing. He was anxious to do his utmost to help me in every possible way.

I found him most clear-headed and easy to discuss things with. There is always the difficulty, however (which one has always had in agreements with the French), to know to what extent we can depend on the French to carry out their attacks.

In this case, if the French do not act vigorously, the enemy will be free to transfer his reserves to oppose our attacks in the north . . .

At 9.30 pm I saw the Prime Minister with General Robertson. The former is afraid that the French Government is not going to act offensively. He is here, he says to press whatever plan Robertson and I decide on. Rather a changed attitude for him to adopt since the Calais Conference!

                                        Repington, i, p 557

THURSDAY, 3 MAY . . . Went to see Haig at 3 pm. He was immensely pleased with his first talk alone with Pétain today, and this gave me great satisfaction. They had got on very well, and had been entirely agreed, as I expected.

SOLDIERS AND POLITICIANS

A year of amazing conferences – Rome, Calais, London, Compiègne – now produced yet one more, in keeping with the rest, in Paris, now at last basking in the full warmth of Spring.

                                        Esher, iv, p 113: Esher to Robertson, 2 May

It is hard to say whether your views and Pétain's will be found in harmony; and still more whether his somewhat imperious character will not clash with yours. We shall see.

There is also some doubt whether, when once established here in Paris, this General will submit to the daily interference of the Ministers, and the 'heckling' of the members of the Army Commission, whom he has treated contemptuously before now and whom he openly reviles.

That he possesses a vigorous personality is beyond question . . . If what many say of him is true, Painlevé may yet rue the day when he pressed for his appointment.

                                        Repington, i, p 556

WEDNESDAY, 2 MAY . . . Foch thought that France was headless politically, and urged me to tell L.G. to take the lead and adopt a strong line after consulting Haig and Robertson.

On 4 May the broad agreement arrived at between Haig and Pétain the previous day was formally ratified, with a further proviso (promoted, no doubt, by the swarming indiscretions which had surrounded the Nivelle Plan):

Haig Diary: Blake, pp 227–8

4 MAY ... Plan to be kept a perfect secret. Governments not to be told any details concerning the place or date of any attack, only the principles.

At 12.30 we were entertained to lunch by M. Ribot (*Président du Conseil*) at the Quai d'Orsay ... In spite of food restrictions we were given a real democratic feast.

After lunch I walked with L.G. across the Seine to the trees of the Champs Elysées, expecting Robertson to join us under the shade for the day was very hot. Wully,* however, found the combination of new breeches, riding boots, a big lunch and the hot sun too much for him to face a walk! So he got into a car after walking a few yards and went direct to the hotel ...

At 3 pm the Conference met at the Quai d'Orsay. Gt Britain was represented by Mr Lloyd George, Lord Robert Cecil† with General Robertson, Admiral Jellicoe and myself, while for France were M. Ribot, M. Painlevé (Minister of War), Bourgeois,‡ Admiral Lacaze, with Generals Pétain and Nivelle. The two Generals agreed to and accepted a document drawn up by Robertson giving the results of this morning's meeting to which all the Generals gave their assent previously.

Mr Lloyd George made two excellent speeches in which he stated that he had no pretensions to be a strategist, that he left that to his military advisers, that I, as C in C of the British Forces in France, had full power to attack where and when I thought best. He (Mr L.G.) did not wish to know the plan, or where or when any attack would take place. Briefly, he wished the French Government to treat their Commanders on the same lines. His speeches were quite excellent.

M. Ribot replied and quite agreed, but mentioned the great losses of the French Army since the war began. M. Painlevé also spoke and said that his views had been misinterpreted. He was all in favour of an offensive, but only differed from those who planned the last attacks in the question of methods of execution. He concurred in the necessity for putting in large attacks but on wide fronts with limited objectives.

The Conference passed off in the most friendly spirit and all stated that they were united in the determination to attack vigorously, and carry on the war '*jusqu'au bout*'.

Repington, i, p 560

SATURDAY, 5 MAY ... Robertson said that he was better pleased with the Conference than with any other that had preceded it. We had taken the lead, and

---

*Robertson's nickname.   † Minister of Blockade.
‡ M. Léon Bourgeois, French politician.

laid down the terms, and all the soldiers were in agreement . . . All are very
pleased with Pétain.

Esher, iv, p 114: Esher to Haig, 6 May

(Lloyd George) has shelled off his Gallic proclivities in a remarkable degree. He
has got to distinguish matter from form, and his notions of French superiority in
everything are obliterated. He sees, with his serene Celtic forgetfulness, the
British Commander-in-Chief and the British soldier through a more gracious
stratum of air.

On Sunday, 6 May Lloyd George, Lord Robert Cecil and Hankey
dined with Haig at the latter's headquarters.

Charteris, p. 223

7 MAY . . . At present (Lloyd George's) line is outspoken praise of everything in
the British Army in France, and especially of D.H. He compares us now with the
French, very much to the disadvantage of the latter, and says he trembles to think
what would have happened if we had been held up with them. I longed to point out
that if the Calais Conference agreement in its first form had held, we probably
should have been held up just the same, but refrained, as I am not supposed to
know anyting about that most disreputable of all intrigues . . .

FLANDERS

Blake, pp 228–9: Haig to Nivelle, 5 May

I feel sure you realize the great importance to all the Allies of making a great
effort to clear the Belgian coast this summer. The enemy's submarine operations
have become such a serious menace to the sea communications, on which all the
Allies are so dependent for many of their requirements, that the need to deprive
the enemy of the use of the Belgian ports is of the highest importance and
demands a concentration of effort. The forces at my disposal are insufficient to
enable me to undertake the operations necessary for the purpose in view. I
therefore hope that you may be able to relieve the troops on a portion of my front.
To enable you to do this with a minimum of inconvenience, however, and to avoid
delay, I propose to divide my operations into two phases as explained below . . .

(a) Continuing to engage and wear out the enemy on my present battle-front
    (ARRAS–VIMY) by attacking definite local objectives from time to time with
    such forces as I can make available for this purpose.

(b) Concentrating a force of sixteen divisions and an adequate amount of artillery
    with a view to the delivery of an attack on the MESSINES–WYTSCHAETE RIDGE
    during the first days of June. This attack will have as its object the capture of

the high ground and observation, thus securing the right flank and preparing the way for the undertaking of larger operations at a subsequent date directed towards the clearance of the Belgian coast . . .

Charteris, p 223

6 May . . . We go back to our original plan (northern offensive), but after a loss of two months of most valuable time.

On 7 May Haig communicated the satisfactory results of the Paris Conference to his Army Commanders, and indicated what the future rôles of their Armies would be. Meanwhile less agreeable influences were at work.

FRENCH MORALE

Sir Edward Spears, *Two Men Who Saved France*, Eyre & Spottiswoode, 1966, p 87. In this was published for the first time a paper written by General Pétain in 1926, entitled *A Crisis Of Morale In The French Nation At War*, 16 April–23 October, 1917, from which this and other extracts are taken; henceforward 'Pétain', with page references to Spears):

On 4 May a number of sudden desertions occurred among members of an infantry regiment* in action in the Chemin-des-Dames area. In the quarters of a colonial regiment† due to take part in an attack in the same sector *the men noisily refused to fight*, an action clearly provoked by the circulation of leaflets on which were blazoned such inflammatory slogans as 'Down with the War!', 'Death to the Warmongers!', etc.

THE INVISIBLE ENEMY

MacDonagh, pp 191–2

3 May. A Proclamation by the King, exhorting His subjects to food economy was read from the steps of the Royal Exchange at noon today by the Common Crier of the City . . . This shows that the gravest danger of the food situation is the scarcity of bread arising from the sinking of wheat-ships. The activity of enemy submarines has been intensified. As the Germans originated piracy of the air, they

* 321st Infantry Regiment, 133rd Infantry Division.
† 43rd Colonial Infantry Regiment, 2nd Colonial Infantry Division.

have now restored piracy of the sea – sinking without warning . . . The Germans are said to be bent on starving us out before the United States can effectively come to our aid. I know that in Government circles deep anxiety prevails. Famine is feared. The stocks of wheat are down to nine weeks' supply.

Lord Beaverbrook, *Men And Power*, Hutchinson, 1956, p 158: US Ambassador Walter Page to President Wilson, 4 May

At the present rate of destruction more than four million tons will be sunk before the summer is gone. Such is the dire submarine danger. The English thought that they controlled the sea; the Germans, that they were invincible on land. Each side is losing where it thought itself strongest.

Repington, i, p 560

SATURDAY, 5 MAY . . . Admiral Jellicoe, who sat next to me, told me that the Huns were turning out 3 submarines a week and that we were catching 3 or 4 a month, and, on the whole, had destroyed 2 submarines a month since the war began. We build 6 to 7 destroyers a month, and lose 2 a month from accidents mainly. He wants 500 to cope with the submarines.

Repington, i, pp 561–2

SUNDAY, 6 MAY . . . I had a talk with the American Admiral, Sims, whom I thought a good and modern flag officer and sure to do well. He told me that he had been shown a chart giving the places where submarines had been seen and had sunk ships. The mass were in S. Irish waters, and off the Scillies, and a few near Brest. He is to work this area, and expects to drive the submarines 100 to 200 miles out to sea, as they are not dependent on local bases. He will soon have fifty destroyers . . . We caught two submarines last week, of which one was recharging on the surface by night. This makes a noise which can be heard five miles away, and one of our submarines heard it, stole up under water, and sank the Hun, a few men only escaping.

Esher, iv, p 115: Esher to Haig, 6 May

It is time that something was done at the Admiralty. There has been no critical or creative movement within its antique walls since the war began. That celebrated phrase of Mahan's about Nelson's ghostly, storm-tossed fleet has been the Navy's undoing.*

*Admiral A. T. Mahan (U.S.N.): 'Those far distant, storm-beaten ships, upon which the Grand Army never looked, stood between it and the dominion of the world.' *The Influence of Sea Power On The French Revolution And Empire*, 1892.

FLANDERS

Author's Papers: Haig Diary

10 MAY . . . General Plumer came to lunch today. Afterwards he explained his plan of attack and received my approval. I called his attention to the new German system of defence. The enemy now fight not in, but for his first position. He uses considerable forces for counter-attacks. Our guns should therefore be registered beforehand to deal with these latter. Our objective is now to capture and consolidate up to the range of our guns, and at once to push on advanced guards to profit by the enemy's demoralization after the bombardment. No delay should take place in doing this.

O.H., 1917, ii, pp 416-17: Second Army Operation Order No. 1, 10 May

1. Under instructions from the Commander-in-Chief and with a view to enforcing the enemy to withdraw reserves from the main battle front (Vimy–Arras),* the Second Army will capture the Messines–Wytschaete Ridge on a date (Zero) which will be fixed later . . .
4. . . . It is imperative, in order to effect surprise and to capture enemy guns, that the attack should be pushed through without delay in one day.
5. The attack will be made at dawn (the exact hour will be notified later).
6. The initial advance will be assisted by the explosion of mines on each corps front. The mines will be fired at zero hour.
7. Two battalions of the Heavy Branch Machine Gun Corps (Tanks) will assist the operations.
8. The preliminary bombardment will be 5 days . . .
11. Acknowledge.

C. H. Harington,
M.G.G.S. Second Army

Wilson, i, p 349

11 MAY . . . I went to see Pétain. He was quite civil, but not expansive. He said that changes in the High Command were going to take place tomorrow, and that from tomorrow he (Pétain) was the man responsible for plans, and that he would send Haig an answer to his letter of the 5th on Monday next. Pétain is against relief of our divisions by French divisions even up to the Omignon River. This, I pointed out, was only a matter of one division and had already been settled for Monday next, to which, after argument, he reluctantly agreed. He is opposed to Haig's plans of attack. He is opposed to our taking over from the XXXVIth Corps

---

*This, of course, is quite untrue; the Battles of Arras would be over before the Messines attack was launched. The statement must therefore be read as a reflection of the British Army's preoccupation with secrecy, after what it considered the unforgivable talkativeness of the French earlier in the year.

at Nieuport. He is opposed to big attacks, and favours small fronts and great depths, and some successes which, he says, the Army and France require. He is very pessimistic about his effectives of 6, 7, or 8,000 to the divisions, and says that if he can't get men from America or Poland he must reduce the number of his divisions. He is going to consider whether we should not take over line from the French, instead of the French from us, as he thinks that we do not hold nearly enough front. He told me that the Belgians would not allow us to go to Nieuport, and that Poincaré had thrown up his arms in dismay at the proposal, and that Poincaré and the King of the Belgians were agreed on this point.

I summed up by telling Pétain some home truths. I said that the two Prime Ministers, the two C in Cs, Robertson and he, had come to certain clear decisions *en principe* on 3 and 4 May, and that the two C in Cs were to work out the details without further interference. Now, on the 11th, he admitted that there was absolutely no one in France who could answer Haig's letter of the 5th.* But he told me that tomorrow (12th) he would have the power; and at the same moment he told me that he disagreed to every single thing agreed to on the 3rd and 4th, and did not propose to carry these decisions out. I pointed out that we could not carry on like this, nor could we beat the Boches by such procedure, and therefore it was essential that Haig and he should meet as soon as possible.

This remarkable entry marks the beginning of one of the most fatal misunderstandings of a year not lacking in such things. I have attempted some analysis of its complicated causes in my book *Douglas Haig: The Educated Soldier*, pp 296–304.

COMMAND CHANGES

Wilson i, p 350

11 MAY . . . After seeing Esher, I motored down here to Compiègne and telephoned the substance of all this (the above) to Kiggell, and wired it to Robertson. Then, at 10.30, I got a telephone from Esher to say that Nivelle was to remain C in C. At 10.35 Weygand† telephoned to say that, at a meeting in the morning, it was practically decided that Pétain should come down here and that Foch should succeed him in Paris. Lastly, at 10.45, Nivelle rang me up from his house asking me to come and see him; he told me that he was going to remain C in C, and he laughed like a boy when I told him that Pétain had said he was taking supreme command tomorrow. Of course, all this is most unsatisfactory and can't last.

*See p 58.
† General Foch's Staff Officer.

Wilson, i, p 350

12 MAY . . . As I said in my letter,* it all comes to this. Haig sends proposals to Nivelle. On this, Nivelle puts up his complementary proposals, which he submits for approval to Pétain and Painlevé. In effect, therefore, Haig submits his proposals for approval to Pétain. This is exactly the situation which I foresaw when I went to London, and against which I warned both Lloyd George and Robertson time after time; it is a state of affairs which I would not tolerate for a moment. I said in my letter to Robertson that I hoped to see daylight in a few days. Till then we must go carefully, as Nivelle may assert himself, or go away, or anything may happen.

Haig Diary: Blake, p 230

14 MAY . . . I had arranged by Nivelle's request to meet him in Amiens tomorrow morning, but at dinner-time I received a telephone message from him requesting me to cancel the engagement because the whole position of affairs seemed so obscure. In fact, I gather that he is unable to answer my letter, and cannot really say what the French Army will and can do!

In reply to my message to CIGS I received the following: 'Prime Minister desires me to remind you of War Cabinet's intentions to support your policy as was in fact done by him at the recent Paris Conference, but on express condition that the French also play their full part as agreed upon at our Conference with Nivelle and Pétain. He is anxious that you should clearly realize this in your discussion with Nivelle, because Cabinet could never agree to our incurring heavy losses with comparatively small gains, which would obviously be the result unless French co-operate whole-heartedly, Chief of Imperial Staff.'

This telegram is evidently meant to strengthen my hand at my conference with Nivelle which was fixed for tomorrow but is now postponed.

Robertson's telegram constitutes the fifth association (albeit conditional) of the War Cabinet with the Flanders Offensive.

Repington, i, p 567

WEDNESDAY, 16 MAY.   This morning came the news that Pétain is to succeed Nivelle, and that Foch is to be CGS at Paris in Pétain's place.

FRENCH MORALE

Charteris, p 224

15 MAY.   I was in Paris yesterday and dined with Esher, who gives most alarming acounts of the situation there. He says the morale of the whole nation is badly affected by the failure of their attack. The Military Attaché† confirmed this.

*To Robertson.   † Colonel Leroy-Lewis.

Pétain, p 87

On 16 and 17 May serious trouble . . . broke out in a battalion of Chasseurs,* and in an infantry regiment† in a reserve position on the Aisne. These unhappy incidents multiplied to a point where *the safety and cohesion of the whole army were in jeopardy*.‡

FLANDERS

Blake, pp 231–2: O.A.D. 449, Haig to Robertson, 16 May

In reply to your (telegram) of 12 May, my views on the present situation, as affecting the operations of the Armies under my command, are as follows:

The opinions expressed in my No. O.A.D. 428 of 1 May,§ still hold good, viz, that action of a wearing-down character must be continued; that pressure on the present offensive front must be gradually relaxed; and that my efforts must be concentrated on completing preparations for clearing the coast this summer.

My action since 1 May has been, and continues to be, guided by the above stated views . . .

The Italians are already committed to an offensive¶ although I am not yet aware what results may be expected from it.

The only question I have to consider now, therefore, is how far, if at all, the situation in Russia . . . may necessitate any alteration or modification in my plans for the immediate future.

In view of this and other uncertainties in the existing situation, I had already decided to divide my operations for the clearance of the Belgian coast into two phases, the first of which will aim only at capturing certain dominating positions in my immediate front, possession of which will be of considerable value subsequently, whether for offensive or defensive purposes.

Preparations for the execution of this first phase are well advanced and the action intended is of a definite and limited nature, in which a decision will be obtained a few days after the commencement of the attack.

It is very unlikely that the Russian situation will develop with sufficient rapidity to enable the enemy to mass forces large enough to render it useless to enter on the execution of this first phase, but if he should succeed in doing so, it will be within my power up to the last moment to abandon the intended attack.

The second phase is intended to take place several weeks later, and will not be

*25th Battalion of Chasseurs-à-pied, 127th Infantry Division.
†32nd Infantry Regiment, 18th Infantry Division.
‡Pétain's italics.
§See pp 83–4.
¶The Tenth Battle of Isonzo, in which Italian casualties, according to Cyril Falls, were 157,000, Austrian 75,000.

carried out unless the situation is sufficiently favourable when the time for it comes.

It will be seen, therefore, that my arrangements commit me to no undue risks, and can be modified to meet any developments in the situation. Meanwhile they enable me to maintain an offensive proportionate to the forces at my disposal, which, in my opinion, is necessary in order to prevent the initiative passing to the enemy.

COMMAND CHANGES

Author's Papers: Telegram, Robertson to Haig, 16 May

Your O.A.D. 447 of yesterday. War Cabinet ask me to impress upon you the necessity of seeing the General who is really responsible for deciding on combined operations with you. Previously you had proposed to see NIVELLES [sic] and now that PÉTAIN has replaced him Cabinet do not quite understand why you propose seeing FOCH. Will you please say if you have reason to believe FOCH is the supreme military authority in the matter. Cabinet think PÉTAIN is more likely to be this authority as he is nominee of present government. Whoever you may see Cabinet ask me to emphasize the necessity of insisting upon full co-operation on the part of French armies and I think if you remain very firm you will ensure it while on the other hand any sign of intention on your part to embark on costly operations whether the French really do so or not may result in our fighting practically alone. To this or to a plan which contains the danger of it the Cabinet could not agree. Your difficulty is fully appreciated but Cabinet wish to make their view clear and also to afford you support in insisting upon the French fighting.

Ibid: Robertson to Haig, 17 May

The Cabinet are quite consistent in the desire to support our views as to the necessity for continuing real offensive action, but at the same time they are equally desirous of the French doing their share, because if they do not it is quite clear that you will have all the German divisions which can be scraped together on the top of you, and we shall find ourselves at the end of the year with depleted divisions and the French will not. This will not be good from many points of view.

It is a very difficult matter for you to deal with, because of course you cannot guarantee that the French will do what they promise, but you can form a pretty good idea; and at any rate you should make your doubts known to the Cabinet if you have any.

The upshot of all this was yet another conference, no less fateful than those that had gone before. This time the venue was Amiens.

Author's Papers

Record of Conference held at AMIENS at 3 pm on Friday, 18 May, 1917

Present:

British —   The Field-Marshal Commanding in Chief
                   Lt-General Sir H. H. Wilson, KCB, DSO (Chief of the British
                   Mission at French Headquarters)
                   Brig-General J. H. Davidson, CB, DSO (Operations, GHQ)

French —   General Pétain, Commander-in-Chief of the French Armies of
                   the North and North-East
                   General Debeney, Chief of Staff
                   General des Vallières, Chief of the French Mission at British
                   Headquarters
                   Lt-Colonel Serigny, French HQ Staff

(Haig asked for and received Pétain's credentials.)

F-M Sir Douglas . . . read a telegram, No. 34467, from the CIGS, dated the 14th
       Haig   instant* . . . and stated that he wished to have an assurance
                  from the French that their co-operation on the other fronts
                  would be whole-hearted.
General Pétain   stated that the French would co-operate whole-heartedly with
                  the British in accordance with the assurances given at the PARIS
                  conference.
                  On being questioned as to the form which this co-operation
                  would take, he stated that he had four main operations in
                  course of preparation:
                  1. An operation to secure the crest of the CHEMIN DES DAMES to
                     be undertaken by the VIth Army. This will involve an attack
                     of 6 divisions on a front of 7 or 8 kilometres and would be
                     followed by an attack made by the Xth French Army a few
                     days later on a front of 4 kilometres.
                     The above operation will take place on or about 10 June and
                     will be preceded by small preliminary attacks to gain the
                     necessary positions of departure for the assaulting troops.
                  2. An operation on a large scale with the object of disengaging
                     RHEIMS. This operation would involve attacks by two armies
                     from SAPIGNEUL to MORONVILLIERS. The total front of attack
                     is approximately 25 km. The date of this attack would be
                     made to coincide approximately with that of the main Brit-

*See p 93.

ish offensive from the YPRES salient, viz., about the end of July.

3. An operation north of VERDUN to secure certain positions of importance on a front of 10 km. No date could be given regarding this attack as the question of the movement of heavy artillery from other fronts was involved.

4. An operation was being prepared in ALSACE, but no details were given of this, nor were any dates mentioned.

He stated that the French would not undertake any attack to capture ST QUENTIN, as he considered that such an operation was too difficult.*

F-M Sir D. Haig then read a paper in French aloud describing the British plan of operations north of the River LYS after the capture of the MESSINES–WYTSCHAETE Ridge. He subsequently handed the paper . . . to General Pétain, together with two maps illustrating the operations. He emphasized the importance of the French undertaking active operations about 1 July, pointing out that from that date onwards the British activity on the ARRAS battle front would subside.

General Pétain stated that he would study the British plan and would send his remarks on it to Field-Marshal Sir Douglas Haig as early as possible. He again stated that he would do all he could to co-operate with the British operation in the North and that he regarded it as the main operation; and he added that he would do his utmost to attract as many hostile divisions as possible. He proposed to visit the Field-Marshal in about a fortnight's time.

(Signed as correct by Haig on 19 May)

Haig Diary: Blake, p. 232

18 MAY . . . I asked (Pétain) straight, 'Did the French intend to play their full part as promised at the Paris Conference? Could I rely on his whole-hearted co-operation?' He was most outspoken and gave me full assurance that the French Army would fight and would support the British in every possible way.

I then went into my plans and gave him a copy of them with two maps.

He replied to the questions given in my letter of 5 May as follows: 'That I could take over the Coast Sector whenever I liked, and dispose the two French Divisions thus relieved as I judged best.'

He could not agree to relieve my troops S. of Havrincourt as I had asked. Instead he would place a Corps of four Divisions to operate with the Belgians. These, along with the two Divisions from the Coast Sector, make at total of six

*The French were unwilling to cause the complete destruction of St Quentin, already badly damaged in the course of General Humbert's unsuccessful attacks in April.

French Divisions to work with six Belgian Divisions, i.e., twelve Divisions. These would be under the King of the Belgians who would be given a French Chief of Staff and a French Commander of Artillery.

Pétain suggested either General Anthoine or General Hély d'Oissel for the post of C. of S. I could choose whichever I preferred. I left the selection to him (Pétain). The C. of S. will be ordered to carry out my instructions . . .

As regards Pétain personally, I found him businesslike, knowledgable, and brief of speech. The latter is, I find, a rare quality in Frenchmen!

On the whole, I considered the meeting much more satisfactory than I had reason to anticipate.

It is difficult to exaggerate the importance of this conference. It will be appreciated that its instigation by the War Cabinet sets the seal on the involvement of that body in the British Flanders offensive. And the difference between General Pétain's detailed plans for French participation and his remarks to Wilson on 11 May (pp 91–2) will also be noted. Pétain did frankly admit at Amiens that he did not believe in far-distant objectives, but was quite clear that the British Army must attack. (see *O.H.*, 1917 ii, p 27)

It is now clear that, under the guise of candour and accord, Pétain was being very far from frank with his British colleague. He was making promises which he must already have known that it would be exceedingly difficult to fulfil. His motives, it must at once be said, were those of a patriotic Frenchman, unwilling to reveal, even to an ally, the frailty of his countrymen, and unwilling to risk, even with a brother soldier, a potentially disastrous security leak (what a change from the days of Nivelle!). And Pétain was not the only one to practise such a deception; nor was Haig the only one to be misled. Lord Derby was visiting France at this very time.

Cabinet Papers, CAB 23/2: War Cabinet No. 144, 23 May

French Military Policy

The Chief of the Imperial General Staff stated that he had received information from the Field-Marshal Commanding-in-Chief to the effect that he had had a very satisfactory meeting with General Pétain, and he was of opinion that the French fully intended to act up to their part in the offensive and give wholehearted co-operation.

The Secretary of State for War then proceeded to report to the War Cabinet the result of his visit to France. He stated he had seen Sir Douglas Haig, who had assured him that his meeting on the previous day with General Pétain had been most satisfactory, and that the latter had given him an assurance that the French would continue to make real attacks on a fairly wide front with limited objectives.

Sir Douglas Haig also stated that he was expecting to receive from General Pétain full particulars in writing as to the forces to be employed, &c.

Lord Derby then informed the War Cabinet that he afterwards proceeded to Paris, where he had seen M. Painlevé, who had given him similar assurances to those given by General Pétain to Sir Douglas Haig. Lord Derby was perfectly satisfied that there was every intention on the part of the French Government to give full effect to these promises, although M. Painlevé had stated that the Government were somewhat disturbed at the low state of their reserve of men.

Lord Derby had also seen General Pétain, who confirmed the assurances given by him to Sir Douglas Haig.

Counting on the firm promises of his ally, believing that he now had the cordial support of his Government, and confident of the abilities of his army, Haig pressed forward the preparations for the Flanders offensive. A factor, however, of which there had already been ominous warnings, now began to make itself increasingly felt.

MANPOWER

Oliver, p 187

17 MAY, 1917

We are terribly short of men; that is the mischief . . .

We keep a huge army in England to repel an invasion which can't possibly be on a large scale. That seems to me a sad waste . . .

Repington, i, pp 568–9

SATURDAY, 19 MAY.   Went to see General Geddes* in the afternoon to talk recruiting. From 1 January to 18 May they have collected 295,407 general service men and 172,343 others, a total of 467,750, which is not bad in itself, but between 4 April – when Robertson asked for 500,000 men before the end of July – and 18 May, they have only got in 93,000 men for general service, and this is less than 60,000 a month, at which rate R. will only have half his requirements at the end of July. Geddes seems to count on 100,000 more, however, from the new law for re-examination of the rejected, and on more men again by combing general service men from Home Defence, and from the rear in France, while he has designs on the boys of $18\frac{1}{2}$, saying that the German boys of $17\frac{1}{2}$ will be fighting this summer. By these shifts Geddes hopes to go a long way to get the men needed, but

*Brigadier-General Sir Auckland Geddes, Director of Recruiting at the War Office, later Director-General of National Service.

not all R. asked for and by the date specified, and this is only to keep up strengths, and allows nothing for new divisions which Geddes and I concur in thinking necessary.

We then went into the question where the men of military age, 18 to 41, now are in civil life. There are 3½ millions of them. There are 728,705 temporarily exempted, including 226,705 in certified occupations, 196,000 for domestic reasons, and 126,000 appeals outstanding. There are 628,000 under the Ministry of Munitions; 527,000 exempted by the Colliery Courts; 236,000 on the railways, including 50,000 under 25; 115,000 of low medical categories, C3 etc; 211,000 unexpired notices, etc; 85,000 men badged by the Admiralty, and 37,000 by the War Office; 61,000 men holding trade cards, 88,000 men of the transport trades, 47,000 of the public utility services, and 40,000 absolute rejections. There are many other headings. Geddes thinks he ought to get 300,000 out of the M. of M., 100,000 from the railways, 200,000 from the mines, and so on. He reckons the class of the year to be 364,000, but only counts on 240,000 to serve, as some 60,000 will not pass fit, he thinks, and 60,000 will be in exempted occupations. Geddes still wants the men of 41 to 50.

Esher, iv p 116

Bavincourt,
19 May

Derby arrived late last night. He is excited and pessimistic over affairs in England. The food supplies, manpower and strikes worry him. The spectre of revolution stands behind his chair.

FRENCH MORALE

Charteris, p 225

19 MAY.   The news today is not good. The French are having very serious trouble in their own army.

Pétain, p 88

19 MAY.   In a Chasseur battalion* south of the Aisne three armed companies staged *noisy demonstrations* in cantonments.
20 MAY   Two complete infantry regiments† in the Chemin-des-Dames sector refused to obey orders. Individual *acts of insubordination* were reported in an infantry regiment‡ in the same area.

---

*26th Battalion of Chasseurs-à-pied, 166th Infantry Division.
†128th Infantry Regiment, 3rd Infantry Division; 66th Infantry Regiment, 18th Infantry Division.
‡90th Infantry Regiment, 17th Infantry Division.

21 and 22 May: In an infantry regiment* resting in the Tardenois district an attempt was made by agitators to stir up trouble among the men. *Delegates were elected to present at headquarters a protest against a continuation of the offensives*; a group of trouble-makers marched to the divisional depot and created a disturbance. Nearby, in another infantry regiment† in the same division, *groups of soldiers turned on their officers, sang the Internationale and threw* stones at them.‡

FLANDERS

Author's Papers: Haig Diary

19 MAY . . . I told (Gough) to move his Hqrs to Loewe Château (north of Poperinghe) on 31 May. The date on which he is to take over his command will be on some date after the Messines attack is launched and must depend on the development of that attack.

Repington, i, p 571

MONDAY, 21 MAY . . . I gave (Robertson) a warning to keep out of Low Country fighting, and said that I had warned Foch when he disclosed ideas to me in this sense. I said that you can fight in mountains and deserts, but no one can fight in mud and when the water is let out against you, and, at the best, you are restricted to the narrow fronts on the higher ground, which are very unfavourable with modern weapons. I reminded him of our past failures in the low-lying lands, and urged him to keep away from them. He listened so attentively that I think some operation in this sense may be in the wind.

Author's Papers: Haig Diary

22 MAY. I saw Sir Herbert Plumer, commanding Second Army at 9.45 am for a few minutes. He is in very good spirits now that his Second Army occupies the first place in our thoughts! I find him a most pleasant fellow to work with and Harrington (sic) (head of the G.S.) and all his Staff work very kindly with GHQ. All are most ready to take advice . . .

During the day Haig visited two Corps Headquarters in Second Army, II Corps (Lieut-General Sir Claud Jacob) and X Corps (Lieut-General Sir Thomas Morland) and four divisions.

On the whole, there is a fine spirit in the Corps I saw today, but I felt that the leaders had been on the defensive about Ypres so long that the *real offensive spirit* has to be developed. I went into each Brigadier's plan today as well as those of the GOC's Divisions. I also saw Trenchard§ re the Flying Corps and Artillery.

*267th Infantry Regiment, 69th Infantry Division.
† 162nd Infantry Regiment, 69th Infantry Division.   ‡ Pétain's italics.
§ Major-General H. M. Trenchard, commanding the Royal Flying Corps; later Lord Trenchard, founder of the Royal Air Force.

COMMAND CHANGES

Charteris, p 225

19 MAY.   Foch . . . has amazed us all by suggesting as one of his first expressions of opinion in his new office that Henry Wilson is now not fulfilling any useful purpose at French GQG and should go. I could have understood it if he had followed that up by asking for him at Paris. Not a bit of it! He wants him anywhere except near himself!! These were D.H.'s and W.R.'s feelings when they took over their respective charges, and so H.W. goes home. But he will bob up again, for 'Satan finds mischief still for idle hands to do'.*

Author's Papers: Wilson to Haig

20 MAY
My General,
    I had a long talk with Pétain this afternoon and as I raised some important points I want to give you my general impressions:
    In order to impress on him the necessity for replying with great care and in great detail to the plan of operations and the maps which you gave him on the 18th at Amiens, I put the following case to him:
    I said that the arrangements for the Messines affair and his simultaneous action have already been settled, but must be recorded in writing; but as regards your larger operation the French proposals for simultaneous action were much too vague and must be worked out in detail – length of fronts, objectives, number of divisions, *and* period, or length of time, over which fighting would be continued; for unless you were fully satisfied with the volume and duration of the French attacks we might, conceivably, find ourselves . . . in a very uncomfortable and to me rather dangerous situation due to: the nerves of both countries a little bit on edge owing to, (a) Russia's inability to help, (b) no real solution to the submarine having been found, (c) the near approach of another winter, (d) failure of the whole Salonika conception, (e) heavy losses due to continuous fighting, (f) coal famine in Paris, (g) other similar reasons . . .
    I said that in our efforts to disengage Ostend and Zeebrugge if England got it into her head that the French had failed to help us at the critical moment of the campaign it was easy to see that a really bad feeling might be started which would be disastrous to the War.
    I painted the picture as vividly as my French would permit, so as to make Pétain put his *real* cards on the table. He listened very attentively and then asked me for my solution.
    I replied that in my opinion he must do one of two things:

*Wilson 'bobbed up' first as British Military Representative at the Supreme War Council (November) and then as CIGS (February, 1918).

(a) Attack, perhaps with a less number of divisions but still, attack practically all the time we were engaged

or

(b) Explain *now* that for certain reasons, which he must specify, he would confine himself to much smaller operations divided into much shorter periods of fighting.

He replied somewhat as follows:

1. Owing to his holding much too long a line, and our holding much too short a one, he could not attack with anything approaching the number of divisions you had at your disposal. (Here is the reason of his wish to revise the points of junction!)

2. He was opposed to any operations with such distant objectives as those which the Admiralty and our Cabinet were asking you to carry out – but he added that this was no business of his.

3. He would try and employ up to twenty-five divisions in operations during the summer.

4. He was going to substitute the Verdun offensive instead of the Rheims–Moronvilliers offensive which he had originally intended to synchronize with your big offensive. He hoped to employ 18 divisions.

5. His attacks at Craonne, at Verdun, at Moronvilliers, or elsewhere would be for strictly *limited* objectives, and when objectives were gained the whole movement would automatically cease.

6. He did not believe in another Somme.

In short that my proposal at (a) was impossible whilst that at (b) was the course which he proposed to adopt, making each operation as big as he could but ceasing the fighting when the objective was gained.

I told him that this being the case it was quite possible that the ill-feeling, which I feared, might really come into existence unless he stated his whole case and made clear beyond all possibility of doubt *exactly* what he was prepared to do and that he neither could nor would do anything more.

He agreed and said he would submit those paragraphs to me before he signed the letter in order to see if I thought them sufficiently clear.

I liked Pétain today; he was clear and decided and when he saw what I was at he thanked me – I had spoken very openly – and told me he had not thought of that aspect but he now saw the necessity for a clear and unequivocal statement. He reminded me that you had asked him to express an opinion on your projects, but this he would never do, but he said to me that, with the amount of assistance he could give, our Cabinet was setting you an impossible task.

Oh dear, what a long letter and I am afraid rather confused but I have just tried to jot down, in sequence, the result of my conversation. I don't like to have it typed. I am so sorry for you!

Henry

Wilson, i, pp 354–5

20 MAY . . . I had a very interesting interview with Pétain. I wanted to impress upon him the danger of allowing Haig to carry out his big offensive towards Ostend, an operation which will cost him very heavy losses over many months' fighting, if the French are not going to do likewise . . . He told me that, in his opinion, Haig's attack towards Ostend was certain to fail, and that his effort to disengage Ostend and Zeebrugge was a hopeless one. So I replied that this made it all the more imperative for him to make his position and his plans absolutely clear. He entirely agreed, and said that he would not sign the letter he was writing to Haig until he had shown it to me, and I had approved.

Author's Papers: Pétain to Haig, 23 May

M. le Maréchal,

With reference to our interview of 18 May, I have the honour to inform you that I am in agreement with you as regards the execution of the plan of operations set out in the scheme which you handed to me at Amiens, only excepting the following points:

1. [A point of detail concerning the Franco-Belgian command.]
2. [A reference to an alternative attack on the Hindenburg Line.]
3. It remains understood that the French armies will carry out, in order to assist the British attacks, two successive offensives, one about 10 June, on the front of the VIth Army, corresponding to the British attack on Wytschaete-Messines, the other on the front of the Xth Army, in the middle of July, during the operations north of Ypres.

    In addition, the present activity on the Chemin-des-Dames and on the plateau of Moronvilliers has the effect of tying down important enemy forces, both artillery and infantry, on our front.
4. [A reference to the question of reliefs.]

Wilson, i, pp 355–6

23 MAY . . . I read this morning Pétain's answer to Haig's paper given to Pétain on the 18th at Amiens. This answer apparently went to Haig yesterday by De Vallières (sic), although Pétain had promised to show it to me before he sent it. I object strongly to this answer, both to its tone and to its substance. In tone it smacks a little of a superior writing to an inferior, and in substance it absolutely ignores Haig's suggestions as to dates for French offensives, and he only has two attacks (Craonne and Verdun) instead of the three (Craonne, Rheims and Verdun) which he promised at the Amiens Conference. Finally, he fixes the last (Verdun) attack for July 15th, without consulting Haig who had asked for 1 August. Then he comes to a dead stop, never mentioning any further operations during the autumn, nor even that he cannot carry any out.

Of course, this is quite hopeless. There is no sign of combined operations at all. No mention of the Boches being able to bring over divisions from Russia, no subordination of the French plan to ours, nothing but Haig's plan and Pétain's plan, which happen to come off in the same year.

Haig Diary: Blake, p 233

26 MAY . . . Sir H. Wilson from Compiègne and stayed the night. He struck me as not quite friendly with Pétain. Wilson finds fault with P.'s letter to me. He would like to see Pétain acknowledge more fully that his position is subordinate to mine. I think it would be a serious mistake for me in any way to indicate to the French C in C that he is 'playing second fiddle'. As a matter of fact, he knows it and has promised to support me in every possible way. Besides it was Nivelle's adoption of such an attitude towards me which caused so much friction between our respective Staffs.

   I told Wilson that the important thing for him is to find out how the orders given by Pétain to his Army Group Commanders are being interpreted – what attacks are being prepared? What do the troops intend to do? Are the attacks to be serious ones on a considerable scale and to last a long time or not?

The apparent complete failure of real communication between Haig and Pétain and the senior Liaison Officer between them persisted. It can only be accounted for by the personal factor: the firm belief of many senior British officers, Haig and Robertson among them, that Wilson was an intriguer and fundamentally unreliable. Pétain was certainly equivocating; on the day after Wilson's visit, 27 May, Haig received another letter from the French Commander-in-Chief. It was mainly concerned with the Belgian rôle; their King had decided that they should not take part in the offensive until it had made sufficient progress, of which he was to be sole judge. Pétain pointed out that this implied certain modifications of the Amiens agreement; he defined the separate British, French and Belgian zones of attack; he placed a purely French army of six divisions directly under Haig's command; he suggested a new written agreement, to which the Belgians should be a party. Nowhere did he cast doubt on the offensive as such. Haig commented that this letter seemed 'most satisfactory and indicates a desire to work wholeheartedly with me'.

FRENCH MORALE

Esher, iv, pp 117–18: Esher to Robertson, 24 May

There is very little doubt that the French people are showing signs of wear and tear. To ignore this is wilfully to close one's eyes to the facts. In every quarter, in town and country, you find symptoms of fatigue, of war-weariness, of discontent.

The bright animation with which the people looked forward to the 'great offensive' of 1917 has died out of their faces, and those who have large knowledge and insight into the secret heart of France tell you that the unconscious purpose of the nation is moving away from absolute to qualified victory. It is just as well to envisage the truth, if truth it be.

Charteris, p 225

25 MAY . . . The news from Russia is a little better this morning, but one can no longer hope for anything really good from there. Things are better in the French army but at a heavy price. They are giving every man ten days' leave every four months; that means something like a quarter of a million permanently away from the front line. Our own total on leave is not a quarter of that. It means definitely that we cannot expect any great help from the French this year.

Pétain, p 88

25 MAY.   In the Vosges, up to that time completely untroubled by the outbreaks, one section of an infantry regiment* refused to embus for the front. They were incited to this act of defiance by their own sergeant.
26 MAY.   Three infantry regiments† of a division recalled to the front after a rest period in the Aisne sent representatives to join *in discussions at which plans for an attempted general mutiny were being hatched.*‡

MANPOWER

Author's Papers: Robertson to Haig, 26 May

It is necessary that you and I should have a talk over your proposed plans in order that there may be no misunderstanding as to what they involve. I say this from the point of view of manpower, regarding which the outlook is not good by any means. Lord Derby and I had a long talk with the Prime Minister last night on the subject and as an indication what the position is I may say that the Prime Minister told us that he was afraid *the time had now arrived when we must face the fact that we could not expect to get any large number of men in the future but only scraps.*§ He said this was because of the large demands for ship-building, food production, and *labour unrest*,§ and I am afraid that there is no getting away from the fact that there is great unrest in this country now as a result partly of the Russian revolution. There have been some bad strikes recently¶ and there is still much dis-

*54th Infantry Regiment, 12th Infantry Division.
† 224th, 228th, 329th Infantry Regiments, 158th Infantry Division.
‡ Pétain's italics.   § Haig's italics.
¶ According to Lloyd George, during 1917, 'there were 688 disputes, affecting 860,727 work-people, and causing the loss of 5,966,000 working days.' (*Memoirs*, ii p 1148) The most serious strike was that of engineers engaged on munition work at Barrow in March–April, which was only settled by invoking the Defence of the Realm Act. It was this strike which caused Lord Derby to tell Haig on 27 May: 'The Government is really scared . . .' (Author's Papers)

content. An announcement even appeared in some of the newspapers yesterday with regard to the calling together of a committee of workmen and soldier delegates to consider the political situation. This shows the way the wind is apt to blow.

Blake, pp 233–4: Haig to Robertson, 28 May

Your letter of 26 May in which you tell me that the Prime Minister stated that we could not expect to get any large number of men in the future but only 'Scraps' is very serious reading.

I presume the General Staff will point out clearly to the Government what the effect of such a decision is likely to be. It would be well also to indicate what the results of our present operations might reasonably have been had our Divisions here been maintained at full strength. Briefly, the offensive in the Arras front could have been maintained at full pressure, at the same time as the attack in the north. And, in my opinion, the enemy would undoubtedly have been forced to withdraw to the line of the Meuse.

As to what the effect of the curtailment of Drafts in the future may be (as foreshadowed in your letter), it is difficult to estimate until we know what is meant by 'only scraps'. There seems little doubt, however, that victory on the Western Front means victory everywhere and a lasting peace. And I have further no doubt that the British Army in France is capable of doing it, given adequate *drafts and guns.**

Another conclusion seems also clear to me, and that is that the Germans can no longer attack England by means of a landing on her coasts. Consequently the time has now arrived for sending every available trained man to reinforce the Divisions now in France.

For the last two years most of us soldiers have realized that Great Britain must take the necessary steps to win the war by herself, because our French Allies had already shown that they lacked both the moral qualities and the means for gaining the victory. It is thus sad to see the British Government failing at the XIIth hour.†

AMERICA

Author's Papers: Derby to Haig, 27 May

(Lloyd George) further added that we must limit our attacks and wait till the Americans came – In other words we are to do exactly what he urged me to tell the French they were *not* to do. We may get some sort of modification of this but I am not sanguine.

Wilson, i, p. 357

27 MAY . . . Winston in great form, and evidently in high favour with Lloyd George . . . his great plan for the moment is to delay any attempt at a decision on

---

*Haig's italics.   † See *Douglas Haig: The Educated Soldier*, p 322

this front till the Americans come over – say 12 to 18 months. He developed this at length, using both good and silly arguments, all mixed up.

Esher, iv, pp 120–1: Esher to Haig, 30 May

A true appreciation of Winston Churchill – of his potential uses – is a difficult matter. The degree in which his clever brain will in future fulfil its responsibilities is very speculative. He handles great subjects in rhythmical language, and becomes quickly enslaved by his own phrases. He deceives himself into the belief that he takes broad views, when his mind is fixed upon one comparatively small aspect of the question.

At this moment he is captured by the picture of what 1918 may bring forth in the shape of accumulated reserves of men and material, poured out from England in one great final effort, while at the same time a million Americans sweep over Holland on to the German flank. He fails to grasp the meaning to England, to France, to Europe, of a postponement of effort through the long summer that was crammed full of anticipated expectations, and a still longer winter . . .

The power of Winston for good or evil is, I should say, very considerable. His temperament is of wax and quicksilver.*

THE INVINCIBLE ENEMY

Repington, i, p 567

WEDNESDAY, 16 MAY . . . Spent the rest of the day in the country, which was looking very bonny. The show of blossom on all the fruit trees is unimaginably fine in all the orchards.

Ibid, i, p 574

WHITSUNTIDE. (26–9 MAY) . . . Wonderful weather. The country looks splendid. I never saw such a show of buttercups. The gardens looking beautiful. Is there a war?

FRENCH MORALE

Pétain, pp 88–9

27 MAY.   Demonstrations and disturbances occurred in an infantry regiment† out of the line in Lorraine. In the Tardenois district the men of an infantry regiment‡ *shouted seditious slogans, sang the Internationale, and insulted and molested their officers while the regiment was embussing.*

*Churchill became Minister of Munitions on 16 July.
† 298th Infantry Regiment, 63rd Infantry Division.
‡ 18th Infantry Regiment, 36th Infantry Division.

28 MAY. *A serious extension of indiscipline and mutiny* was reported from six infantry regiments, a battalion of Chasseurs, and a regiment of dragoons stationed on the Aisne and farther south.*
29, 30 AND 31 MAY.   The situation deteriorated and indiscipline spread to the majority of the regiments of eight divisions† and to a colonial artillery regiment,‡ all of which had been in action in the Chemin-des-Dames sector or were about to be sent back there.

COMMAND CHANGES

Wilson, i, pp 358–9

31 MAY . . . Then Foch began to talk about myself. He said that Pétain was opposed to my remaining at GQG as he looked on me as a Nivellite, though in truth, as Foch said, all that had happened was that I had accurately diagnosed Pétain's mind and character. Foch rather astonished me by telling me that he had spoken of this to Robertson, who had said that no doubt Haig would fit me out with a Corps; to which Foch had replied, 'Is that your idea of making use of Wilson?'

THE INVISIBLE ENEMY

Ludendorff, ii, p 427

The submarine campaign again achieved good results in April and May and relieved our Western Front.

Lloyd George, i, p 709

Statistics of shipping losses, May, 1917 — 345,293 gross tons sunk

*4th, 82nd, 313th Infantry Regiments, 9th Infantry Division; 224th, 228th Infantry Regiments, 158th Infantry Division; 129th Infantry Regiment, 5th Infantry Division; 66th Battalion of *Chasseurs-à-pied*, 9th Infantry Division; 25th Dragoons, 1st Cavalry Division.
† Units of the 5th, 6th, 13th, 35th, 43rd, 62nd, 77th and 170th Infantry Divisions. It will be seen that by now twenty infantry and one cavalry division had been affected at different times during May.
‡ 3rd Regiment of Artillery, 1st Colonial Corps.
  All italics are Pétain's.

June

———————————— ✠ ————————————

For the Flanders offensive of 1917, June was the month of decision; the battle of words (which has continued ever since) now rose to its first crescendo. Lloyd George tells us:

It had been stipulated by the War Committee in 1916 that the military experts should report to them after they had concluded their examination of the idea of an operation to clear the Flemish coast.* Such 'instructions' as were given by the Asquith Government were orders to report. The fact that such a report was never submitted before June, 1917, may be due to the final plans not having been settled before that date.

It is necessary to interrupt the flow of Lloyd George's exposition at this point to remark that plans were scarcely likely to have been settled, since Allied policy had been entirely reversed at the turn of the year with the full approval of himself and M. Briand; since British strategy had, at his own insistence, been fully subordinated to that of General Nivelle; and since the chief British effort so far had, as a consequence, been in support of Nivelle's disastrous offensive (the Battle of Arras which had only just ended, at a cost of 158,660 British casualties).

Lloyd George continues:

That, however, did not prevent preparations on the most tremendous scale being made from December onwards. They were revised and re-revised. Not one of the various plans or proposals was brought to the notice of the War Committee until June, 1917.†

This statement, as we have clearly seen by now, was entirely untrue; but what is true is that it was only now, in June, that the War Cabinet at last bent their minds to the most serious business of the year. The sense of being 'taken by surprise' by it was undoubtedly strong within them, and was never entirely eradicated, as Lloyd George's Memoirs show; the

———————————————————————————

*See p 17.   † Lloyd George, ii, p 1255.

fault, however, lay only with themselves, and the unnecessary drudgery with which they filled their days. We shall shortly have first-hand corroboration of this.

FLANDERS

Wilson, i, p 359; 2 June

(Foch) wanted to know who it was who wanted Haig to go on 'a duck's march through the inundations to Ostend and Zeebrugge'. He thinks the whole thing futile, fantastic and dangerous, and I confess I agree, and always have. Haig always seems to think that when he has got to Roulers and Thorout he has solved the question. So Foch is entirely opposed to this enterprise, Jellicoe notwithstanding.

On the previous day General Gough had established his Fifth Army headquarters in the Château of La Louvie, a couple of miles north of Poperinghe. He and his staff were now concerned with the preparation of the northern sector of the offensive in all its intimate detail.

General Sir Hubert Gough, *The Fifth Army*, Hodder & Stoughton, 1931 [henceforward 'Gough'], pp 196–7

The plans for the Battle of Passchendaele (as it was sometimes called) were most thoroughly studied. A memorandum drawn up by Major-General J. H. Davidson at GHQ dealt with our operations and was submitted to me. It recognized the fact that a properly-organized attack on such a front as we could operate on could penetrate an enemy's position to the depth of a mile or so, but that after that the attack would be completely held up. Further advance could only be gained by a second deliberate and organized attack, to be followed by others of the same nature. I agreed in the main with these conclusions, and we all realized that, given such a front as that on which we were attacking, a deep penetration of the enemy's position could only be achieved by a succession of organized attacks, and that we must recognize that several days must elapse between each of these.

Sir William Robertson visited me about this time and I told him that I did not look for a 'break-through' nor for rapid and spectacular success, but I envisaged a series of carefully organized and prepared attacks, only gaining ground step by step, and that it would be a month (given fine weather) or perhaps two, before we were masters of the Passchendaele–Staden Ridge. At the time he saw the soundness of this forecast.

On 6 and 7 June Gough held conferences with his new Corps Commanders, Lieut-General Sir Claud Jacob (II Corps), Lieut-General Sir

Herbert Watts (XIX Corps), Lieut-General Sir Ivor Maxse (XVIII Corps), and Lieut-General the Earl of Cavan (XIV Corps).

Gough, pp 193–5

The details of the operations which lay before us were considered, and a slight change in the plan was made; it was proposed to pivot on the left flank with the French, while the right flank advanced along the Passchendaele Ridge. This would eventually bring our general direction northwards to clear the Houthoulst Forest, and Roulers would thus cease to be an objective of the Fifth Army.

On 16 June the Commander-in-Chief held a conference at Lillers. At this our Intelligence Department* announced that the Germans had 157 divisions on the Western Front, and that 105 of these had been employed and severely handled in the period since 1 April, covering the French attack under General Nivelle, the Arras battle, and the Battle of Messines. Sir Douglas again impressed on the Second Army that all its resources would be required to protect the right of the Fifth Army.

The original plan had been for me to capture the high ground on my right, as a separate preliminary operation. At this conference, however, I told the Commander-in-Chief that I would prefer to make this attack part and parcel of the major operations, as a partial attack, even if successful, would only throw the troops employed into a very pronounced salient, and expose them to the concentrated fury of all the German artillery, and to this change the Commander-in-Chief agreed.

The significance of these two conferences will emerge later. In *Douglas Haig: The Educated Soldier* I wrote:

'It is extremely difficult to understand why Haig did agree to this change in the plan. It was anything but 'slight' – it was fundamental; moreover, it ran counter to all Haig's own ideas; he realized this, when it was too late. We can only conclude that this was another example, and this time a disastrous one, of his principle of allowing the utmost freedom of action to the man actually entrusted with operations.' (p 338)

FRENCH MORALE

Pétain, pp 94–5

Example of a violent outbreak in a regiment of the line† : *1–3 June*
    Another type of *outbreak was violent in character and the spirit animating it was revolutionary.*‡

----

*ie. GHQ Intelligence, headed by Charteris.
† 23rd Infantry Regiment, 41st Infantry Division.   ‡ Pétain's italics.

Here again our example is an infantry regiment, with a first-class record and reputation and forming part of a crack division. After much hard fighting during the battle of the Somme, it was not sent back to rest as it had been led to hope that it would be. Instead, it was moved to the Argonne sector, where it suffered heavy casualties during the winter of 1916–17. It took part in the April offensive, achieving an appreciable but exceedingly costly success. It was then kept for five weeks in the line, although nearly all the neighbouring units were sent back to be reconstituted. Finally, it was sent to rest in the Tardenois area and was looking forward to catching up on its arrears of leave, when, after only a few days, on the afternoon of 1 June, the order came to return to the trenches.

At 1 pm on that day, angry protest broke out in the camp. The Colonel and the other officers rushed to the scene, but their attempts to control the disorder had little or no result. At 5 pm a procession was formed and moved off to the strains of the Internationale. *The Brigade Commander, who acted with energy, was given a violently hostile reception and greeted with cries of 'Kill him!' Insults were hurled at him. He was pushed and jostled. The stars on his cuffs and his epaulettes were ripped off, as was the flag on his car.* * The Divisional Commander succeeded with difficulty in forcing his way to the town hall, in front of which the mutineers were assembled. He was unable to make himself heard above the shouts and was forced by threats to postpone the regiment's departure for the front. Meanwhile, *some of the mutineers had armed themselves with wire cutters and cut the barbed wire round the punishment centre.* * The prisoners were released and one of them, a lawyer, and editor of a trench newspaper, became the guiding spirit of the revolt. 'Friends,' he told his rescuers, 'I am delighted that our movement has met with such success. We shall not be alone. I have channels of information which enable me to tell you as a fact that this evening twelve divisions have taken the same action as ourselves. Cars from Paris have set out for every sector with the mission of bringing this good news to all our comrades.' The mutineers, still shouting murderous threats against their Brigadier, broke the windows and doors of the town hall with paving stones, overturned the lorries in the streets, broke the windows of houses and forced the occupants to join them.

The morning of 2 June began rather more calmly, though crowds of drunken soldiers were still milling about in disorderly mobs, singing the Internationale and sporting red flowers in their jackets. *The organizers of the outbreak had had numerous posters stuck up on the walls bearing the words: 'Vive la Paix au nom de toute l'Armée!' ('Long live Peace, in the name of the whole Army!')** with the result that, that evening, a new mob of demonstrators, about 2,000 strong, were repeating the exploits of the evening before, *with red flags flying** and shouts of 'Long live the Revolution! Down with the war! Long live Peace! Down with tyrants!'

On 3 June and during the next few days the regiment was moved in lorries to another camp, and the trouble subsided – far more quickly than could have been hoped – as the principal trouble-makers lost their hold over the men. Very soon

*Pétain's italics.

the agitation had died down altogether and the men had returned, without exception, to the path of duty.

Haig Diary: Blake, pp 234–5

SATURDAY, 2 JUNE. The 'Major-General'* of the French Army arrived about 6.30 pm and stayed to dinner. His name is General Debeney. He brought a letter from General Pétain saying that he had commissioned him to put the whole situation of the French Army before me and conceal nothing. The French Army is in a bad state of discipline.

Debeney then stated that the French soldiers were dissatisfied because leave had been so long suspended. Leave must consequently be opened at once. This would prevent Pétain carrying out his promise to attack on 10 June! The attack would take place four weeks later. Then I discovered by questions that the attack promised already for the middle of July was the one which would be launched.

So really that attack of 10 June will not be made by Infantry – only by Artillery! However, the Germans are now counter-attacking the French with considerable vigour in Champagne† so I hope no reserves will be able to come to Flanders to oppose my attacks.

This profoundly important entry reveals another grave misunderstanding. I have elsewhere‡ described the passage 'put the whole situation . . . before me and conceal nothing' as 'a misleading phrase in a misleading speech'. A careful reading of what follows, in the light of what we have seen of Pétain's own account of the development of the mutinies, shows clearly that a great deal was being concealed from Haig. Pétain admitted as much to him when they met at Chantilly after the war on 3 April, 1919: 'The state of the French Army was much worse than he had dared to tell me at the time' (Blake, p 360). It is a matter of speculation how Haig would have acted, had he known the full truth (as he supposed he did); what cannot be doubted is that the concealment of it was a serious matter.

Wilson, i, p 359

4 JUNE. I saw this morning the notes made at the conference the day before yesterday, when Debeney went up to see Haig. They are disquieting. The French attack for 10 June is cancelled, because the morale of the French troops is such that it cannot be carried out. Debeney said that the fighting at Moronvilliers and the Chemin des Dames had used up a very large number of divisions, that in consequence of this all leave had had to be stopped, and that the men wanted leave and must have it. He hoped that the attack for July (Verdun) would still be

---

*Pétain's Chief of Staff. † See p 83.
‡ *Douglas Haig: The Educated Soldier*, p 305.

carried out, but said that the Marshal must understand that no infantry attack would take place anywhere for at least a month. Gun and aeroplane attacks, yes; but infantry attacks, no. This endorses and underlines all that I have been saying for the last month or more, and I think, and hope, that it will finally dispose of Haig's idea of taking Ostend and Zeebrugge. For if the French continue to feel the strain like this, we must expect them to ask us to take over some more line.

Author's Papers: Haig to Pétain

6 JUNE
My dear General,

With reference to your letter No. 21444, of 23 May, I understand from the information given me by General Debeney, on the 2nd instant, that the operation intended by you to take place about 10 June cannot be carried out, but that the operation proposed for the middle or end of July still holds good, the date depending, of course, on the situation in Flanders.

While appreciating the reasons which have necessitated a modification of your plans as previously agreed on, I rely confidently on everything in your power being done to retain the enemy's units now in your front and to wear them out.

As regards the possibility of future operations to free the mines at LENS, I fully appreciate the importance of this and am giving it full consideration.

As I informed General Debeney, it appears to me important that the necessary preparatory work in the STEENSTRAATE sector should be taken in hand as soon as possible, but this can, no doubt, be done behind a screen of Belgian troops as you propose, in order to deceive the enemy.

The date you propose (10–20 June) for the relief of your troops in the NIEUPORT sector seems likely to suit me well, but I will communicate with you as regards the exact date after the MESSINES attack has taken place.

Yours very truly,

D. Haig
Field-Marshal

Cabinet Papers, CAB 23/3: War Cabinet No,
156, 6 June
Members of War Cabinet present: Mr Lloyd
George, Lord Curzon, Lord Milner, Mr George
Barnes.

Trouble in French Army
5. The Director of Military Operations* reported that there was serious trouble, practically amounting to mutiny, in a number of French regiments, partly as the result of Socialistic propaganda, partly on the ground that native troops had been

*Major-General F. Maurice.

allowed to fire on strikers in the neighbourhood of Paris.* It was hoped that this disaffection would be set right in five or six days.

A thread of fresh confusion now enters the pattern of 1917, a subject of vital importance, but susceptible of drastically conflicting interpretations.

CONDITIONS IN GERMANY

Author's Papers: Haig Diary

SATURDAY, 2 JUNE.   Extracts from German correspondence which we have recently captured are the most encouraging I have yet read: hunger, want, sickness, riots, all spreading in the most terrible manner throughout the Fatherland.†

The date of this entry will be noted: the very day that Debeney informed Haig of the French Army mutinies.

Charteris, p 226

3 JUNE.   The pleasure we have been taking in revolutionary tendencies in Germany, and in captured documents that enlarge on those tendencies, have (sic) had a rude shock. Our own country seems to be tainted with the same disease. I have just had sent to me a circular letter which Ramsay MacDonald and his crew of peace-at-any-price maniacs has issued to all Trade Unions, calling them to a conference 'to do for this country what the Russian Revolution has accomplished in Russia' . . ‡ Of course, this particular effort of our defeatists cannot be taken seriously. The chief thing they want is probably the 2s 6d from 'each delegate' attending the conference: but it helps one to put a juster value on some similar captured German documents. We have probably been giving them too much importance.

Author's Papers: Haig to Army Commanders, 5 June

O.A. 799

For issue down to Corps Commanders only, and by name, and *not to be communicated to the Press.*

---

*One of the contributory factors to the mutinies in May was a rumour that Annamite troops from Indo-China (Vietnam) stationed in Paris had opened fire on French civilians. As luck would have it, there was, indeed, a disturbance on 4 June, when Annamites were involved in a fracas with some women in a café on the Boulevard Bessières, and one woman was killed.
† See Appendix I.
‡ This was the famous (or notorious) Leeds Convention of June, 1917, attended by some 1,150 delegates, who considered it 'to be the British equivalent of the Soviet, the Council of Workers' and Soldiers' Deputies, at Petrograd'. Apart from a telegram to the Petrograd Soviet, pledging itself 'to work through its newly constituted workers' and soldiers' councils for a democratic peace', the Convention achieved nothing. It has been called 'one of the great pseudo-events of British left-wing history' (Colin Cross, *Philip Snowden*, Barrie & Rockliff, 1966, pp 157–8).

After careful consideration of all available information I feel justified in stating that the power of endurance of the German people is being strained to such a degree as to make it possible that the breaking point may be reached this year.

The chief mainstay of the German people at present is the hope of starving England by the submarine campaign. With far less self-denial at home than the Germans have been enduring for some time this hope is doomed to disappointment. Suspicion that this is so is spreading in Germany and as this suspicion gradually turns to certainty the feeling of hopelessness which is already evident in Germany will tend to grow beyond control.

If, during the next few weeks, failure to stop the steady, determined, never-wearying advance of our Armies is added to a realization of the failure of the submarine campaign the possibility of the collapse of Germany before next winter will become appreciably greater.

In short, while it cannot be regarded as a certainty that final victory will be reached this year, the great efforts already made have undoubtedly brought it so near that it may be attained; and even one great and striking success, combined with general activity and steady progress on the whole front and a secure hold of all that has already been won, will have far-reaching results.

Despite the distress in Germany and the short rations in the German Army we must still reckon on desperate efforts being made by the enemy to hold on in the hope of outlasting the determination of the Allies. But we have already overcome similar efforts on the SOMME, on the ANCRE, and at ARRAS. We are able to do so again. Every fresh success brings us nearer to the end of the long and desperate struggle; and we are now justified in believing that one more great victory, equal to those already gained, may turn the scale finally, and, at the least, will have even a greater effect than previous victories in Germany and on the World's opinion generally.

This success will be gained, as it has been gained in the past, by the steady and unquenchable determination of all, co-operating with skill, to beat down all opposition to our advance, and to hold firmly what is won.

I request that all ranks may be informed by their officers how far on the road to victory the splendid efforts already made have brought us and how a careful and unbiased examination of the evidence shows the present situation to be.

Ludendorff, ii, p 446

I deeply regretted the events which took place in Germany in the spring and summer of 1917, as I did all other manifestations of weakness. They were bound to react unfavourably on our conduct of the war, and therefore on the subsequent peace. Looking back I can see that our decline obviously began with the outbreak of the Revolution in Russia. The Government was oppressed on the one hand by the fear that it might spread to Germany and on the other by the knowledge of their inability to revive the resolution and warlike ardour of the people, waning as they were through the combination of innumerable circumstances. No doubt our precarious military position and, later, the want of success achieved in the submarine war, of which some people had unfortunately been too confident, made it more difficult to rouse our energy. It was obvious that it suffered from these causes.

But after all, owing to the collapse of Russia, our position in the summer of 1917 was better than that of the Entente. We were justified in being hopeful. But there were other reasons for our spiritual decline. The Government lacked the resolution to deal energetically with abuses. And behind it there was the Reichstag, with no united will, in part sincerely anxious about our future, in part merely striving for power from selfish reasons.

FLANDERS

> Author's Papers: Captured Corps Order of German 'Wytschaete Group', received by Haig on 1 June

2(a) The unconditional retention of the independent strong points, Wytschaete and Messines, is of increased importance for the domination of the whole Wytschaete salient. These strong points must therefore not fall *even temporarily* into the enemy's hands.

> Haig Diary: Duff Cooper, ii, pp 115–16

WEDNESDAY, 6 JUNE . . . I visited hqrs Second Army at Cassel and saw General Plumer. I went round the offices with him and shook hands with the principal staff officers, and wished them luck in tomorrow's attack.

All seemed very pleased and confident. I thanked Plumer for the thorough methodical manner in which he had made his preparations for the attack, and I wished him success.

At Bailleul I saw General Godley,* commanding II Australian Corps, and his staff. All were full of confidence.

It was now past 1 o'clock, so we halted for lunch on the top of Mont Rouge, where a hut with a telescope had been arranged for me to use on the days of battle.

About 2.30 I called at hqrs IX Corps and saw General Hamilton Gordon.* He and his staff seemed in excellent form. Thence I went to Abeele and saw General Morland,* commanding X Corps. The same feeling prevailed here.

Subsequently I visited hqrs VIII Corps (Hunter-Weston*). I saw Brig-General Ward, the CRA, who has done excellent work in pushing his guns forward. Before Ward arrived, 3 weeks ago, the attitude of this corps was too defensive, and the guns were too far back.

*Lieutenant-General Sir Alexander Godley (his command was actually II Anzac Corps); Lieutenant-General Sir Alexander Hamilton Gordon; Lieutenant-General Sir Thomas Morland; Lieutenant-General Sir Aylmer Hunter-Weston.

At Château Lovie I saw General H. Gough. The headquarters of Fifth Army is now here. He is delighted with his palatial residence after nearly a year in a smelly farm at Toutencourt. He says all the corps commanders are anxious to get to work at once in preparing for the attack. I told him it was necessary to wait for the results of General Plumer's operations against Messines. It was possible that we might be able to exploit our success quickly, and reach a position which would materially help his (Gough's) operations.

Lastly I saw General Jacob (commanding II Corps) at Steenvoorde. He gave a good report of the 30th Division under Major-General W. de L. Williams, and said he was ready to exploit the success of the Wytschaete operations on the first opportunity.

The preliminary bombardment for the Battle of Messines had begun as far back as 21 May, and the intensive stage had begun on 31 May.* With the infantry assault, delivered on 7 June, the Flanders Offensive of 1917 opened. The feature of this day's attack was the explosion of nineteen great mines under the Messines-Wytschaete Ridge at zero hour, 3.10 am.

O.H., 1917, ii, p 54 f.n.

To a German observer the spectacle appeared as 'nineteen gigantic roses with carmine petals, or as enormous mushrooms, which rose up slowly and majestically out of the ground and then split into pieces with a mighty roar, sending up multi-coloured columns of flame mixed with a mass of earth and splinters high into the sky.' German Official Account xii, p. 453.

Norman Gladden, *Ypres 1917*, William Kimber,
1967, p 61

With a sharp report a rocket began to mount into the daylit sky. A voice behind me cried 'Now'. It was the hour, and that enemy light never burst upon the day. The ground began to rock. My body was carried up and down as though by the waves of the sea. In front the earth opened and a large black mass mounted on pillars of fire to the sky, where it seemed to remain suspended for some seconds while the awful red glow lit up the surrounding desolation. No sound came. My nerves had been keyed to sustain a noise from the mine so tremendous as to be unbearable. For a brief spell all was silent, as though we were so close that the sound itself had leapt over us like some immense wave. Almost simultaneously a line of men rose from the ground a short distance in front and advanced away towards the upheaval, their helmets silhouetted and bayonets glinting in the unearthly redness . . . There was a tremendous roar and a tearing across the skies as the barrage commenced with unerring accuracy.

*Between 26 May and 6 June the artillery preparation for the Battle of Messines expended 3,561,530 rounds.

General Sir Charles Harington, *Plumer Of Messines*, John Murray, 1935, pp 90–2; in 1917 Major-General C. H. Harington was Chief of Staff of the Second Army

The attack was delivered at 3.10 am on 7 June.

The nineteen mines on the front of attack, containing 957,000 lbs of explosive, were fired at zero, blowing up large portions of the enemy's front line and support trenches, and causing great demoralization and loss of the garrisons of the trenches.

The artillery barrage opened simultaneously, and the infantry advanced to the assault after the debris and shock of the mines had subsided.

Previous to the day of attack, six Brigades, R.F.A., five 6-in howitzer batteries and a 60-pdr battery had been placed in action as far forward as possible without being actually in view. These batteries did not open fire till zero hour.

Owing to the previous effective wire cutting and trench bombardment, the infantry were able to carry the whole of the enemy's front-line system within a few minutes. Following closely the artillery barrage, our troops pressed on up the western slopes of the ridge with scarcely a pause, and within three hours of the commencement of the attack had stormed the crest of the ridge along the whole front of the attack . . .

About 2.30 pm the enemy attempted to launch a local counter-attack just north and south of Messines, but was driven back by our artillery, rifle and Lewis-gun fire.

At 3.10 pm a further advance was made against the Oosttaverne Line* by fresh troops supported by tanks, which had been brought forward after the line east of Messines and Wytschaete had been captured. These troops advanced through the original assaulting columns and pushed down the eastern slopes of the ridge. Within an hour the Oosttaverne Line had been captured with the exception of a small portion east of Messines, which fell into our hands on the following morning.

Haig Diary: Blake, p 236

THURSDAY, 7 JUNE.   Battle of Messines.

Soon after 4 pm I visited General Plumer at his HQ at Cassel, and congratulated him on his success. The old man† deserves the highest praise for he has patiently defended the Ypres Salient for two and a half years, and he well knows that pressure has been brought to bear on me in order to remove him from the Command of Second Army.

*The final objective of the Second Army.
†In 1917 Plumer was 60 years old; Haig was 56.

I left him about 5 pm. Before I came away he had received news of the capture of the Oosttaverne Line.

The operations today are probably the most successful I have yet undertaken.

Charteris, pp 226–7

8 JUNE.   We attacked again yesterday, and again had a very great success . . . The whole attack went like clockwork. Everything exactly as it was intended and exactly at the time intended; a very great feather in the caps of Plumer and Harington. They are a wonderful combination, much the most popular, as a team, of any of the Army Commanders. They are the most even-tempered pair of warriors in the whole war or any other war. The troops love them. When a division is rattled for any reason, either because of very heavy casualties or because it thinks it has had unfair treatment, it is sent to the Second Army, and at once becomes as happy as sandboys . . . D. H. referred to Plumer last night as 'his most reliable Army Commander'. High praise for both of them, for nobody knows where Plumer ends and Harington begins.

This is the first big attack they have brought off and it could not have been better. We have taken 7,000 prisoners and over 50 guns, and our casualties are less than 10,000; altogether a remarkable day . . .

The one depressing thing is that all this should have been done at the beginning of the fighting this year, and not now when half the year is gone. We are two months later than we should have been.

Field-Marshal von Hindenburg, *Out of My Life*, Cassell, 1920, p 267

Violent attempts on our part to restore the situation by counter-attacks failed under the murderous, hostile artillery fire which from all sides converted the back-area of the lost position into a veritable inferno. Nevertheless, we again succeeded in bringing the enemy to a halt before he had effected a complete breach in our lines. Our losses in men and war material were heavy. It would have been better to have evacuated the ground voluntarily.

Ludendorff, ii, p 429

The 7th of June cost us dear, and owing to the success of the enemy the drain on our reserves was very heavy. Here too, it was many days before the front was again secure. The British Army did not press its advantage; apparently it only intended to improve its position for the launching of the great Flanders offensive.

Lloyd George, ii, p 1248

The capture of the Messines Ridge, a perfect attack in its way, was just a useful little preliminary to the real campaign, an *apéritif* provided by General Plumer to stimulate the public appetite for the great carousal of victory which was being provided for us by GHQ.

AMERICA

Esher iv, pp 122–3; Esher to Lloyd George, 5 June

You cannot reconcile waiting for American armies with the anxiety of the masses to get a decision speedily. Every attempt to explain the situation here that I have seen is confused and uncritical. None penetrate below the surface of Paris gossip to the secret longing of the masses to have done with war.

The supreme risk of allowing the people, and the armies that are so subtly interwoven in sentiment with the people, to think that they must 'wait for America', is that the soldiers will insist upon returning to their homes – like their 'brothers in Russia'.

Haig's Diary: Blake p 237

SUNDAY 10 JUNE . . . General Robertson (CIGS) left after having a talk with me and Kiggell after Church. A night's reflection and Duncan's* words of thanksgiving for our recent victory seemed to have had a good effect on him. He was less pessimistic and seemed to realize that the German Army is in reduced circumstances. I again urged the need for increased activity by the Allies *all round*.† There must be no thought of staying our hand until America puts an Army in the field next year. We must press the enemy now, as vigorously as possible by every means at our disposal on the Western Front.

Cabinet Papers, CAB 23/3: War Cabinet No. 160, 11 June

Probable Arrival of American Forces
14. The Secretary of State for War informed the War Cabinet that General Pershing‡ stated that the Americans would have from 175,000 to 200,000 men in the field by November.

*The Rev G. S. Duncan of the Church of Scotland, Haig's chaplain.
† The 10th Battle of the Isonzo ended on 8 June (see p 94 f.n.); the last Russian offensive of the War was to begin on 1 July.
‡ General John Joseph Pershing, commander of the American Expeditionary Force, arrived in London on 8 June.

Blake, pp 237–8: Haig to Lord Derby, 12 June

I am so glad to hear that you think well of the American General, but I do beg of you to do your utmost to prevent our Government delaying to take action until the American Army is in the field. We heard in 1916 the same argument used regarding the advantages of waiting till Russia should be ready this year! There is no time like the present. Do your utmost to turn the present very favourable military situation in France to account.

Soldiers and Politicians

Cabinet Papers, CAB 23/16: Note by Lord Milner to War Cabinet, 7 June

It seems to me that there is urgent need of a fresh stock-taking of the whole war situation. War Policy is after all the chief business of the War Cabinet. Many and very difficult domestic questions, all no doubt arising out of the war, have latterly taken much of our time and threaten still further to absorb it.* Ireland, the Labour Unrest, Food, Liquor, the increasing difficulty of distributing our diminishing stock of Manpower – all of them complicated and aggravated by an uncertain Parliamentary situation – make increasing demands upon us. And yet, greater and more urgent than any of them or all of them, put together, is the necessity of reviewing our war policy as a whole, and making new plans to meet a wholly new situation.

Three or four months ago we had a War Policy. As a result of the Conferences at Chantilly, Rome, Petrograd, a fairly definite and quite hopeful plan of coop- eration between the Allies had been evolved. It held out good prospects of success in a subsidiary but still important theatre, i.e. the trilateral attack upon Turkey in Armenia, Mesopotamia and Palestine. The defection of Russia has completely destroyed these prospects. On the other hand, the entrance of America into the war has introduced a new factor, of great ultimate promise but small immediate value. What are we going to do to fill up the time before the weight of America can be thrown into the scale? How do we hope to get the greatest benefit from her assistance in the long run?

Lord Milner questioned whether 'another million or two' on the Western Front would be America's best contribution to the War, suggesting as an alternative 'an overwhelming effort in the air'.

It may be said that the whole position is so full of uncertainties that no plan is possible. I admit that any plan we may make today is liable to be completely upset

*See p 84 f.n.

by developments at present incalculable. Nevertheless it cannot be right to go on without any plan at all. How do we now stand about Palestine, about the Balkan campaign, about the continuance of the offensive on the Western Front?* I don't know that we have made up our minds about any of them. I feel as if we were just drifting, and as if there was some danger that, in view of the preoccupation of a number of grave but nevertheless minor domestic questions, we might continue to drift.

The remainder of Lord Milner's Note is concerned with politics and strategy in the Balkans.

Cabinet Papers, CAB 23/16: War Cabinet No. 159a, 8 June

It was pointed out by the Prime Minister that up to the present time the Government had been guided in their war policy entirely by the views of their naval and military experts. He himself had always felt some misgivings about this course owing to the fact that in a large number of instances all through the war the advice of the experts had proved to be wrong. Recent events had confirmed the view that, like everyone else, they were not infallible.

Cabinet Papers, CAB 23/3: War Cabinet No. 159, 8 June

Cabinet Committee on War Policy
13. In view of the recent important changes in the international situation, the War Cabinet considered that the time had come for reviewing our policy as a whole and forming fresh plans. They decided that
             A small Committee, composed as follows:

> The Prime Minister,
> Lord Curzon,
> Lord Milner,
> General Smuts,
> Sir Maurice Hankey (Secretary),
> should investigate the facts of the Naval, Military, and Political situations, and present a full report to the War Cabinet.

Blake, p 239: Sir William Robertson to Haig, 13 June

There is trouble in the land just now. The War Cabinet, under the influence of L.G., have started, quite amongst themselves plus Smuts, to review the whole

---

*What had become of Haig's Memorandum to the War Cabinet of 1 May (pp 83–4)?

policy of the war, and to 'get at facts'. They are interviewing different people singly, and sending out to Departments various specific questions to be answered. All this instead of first settling on the policy and then telling me and Jellicoe to carry it out, if we can. However, they will have to fetch up at us sooner or later, and then the trouble will begin. But to forewarn you of what is in the air so that you may be ready for them next week, the L.G. idea is to settle the war from Italy, and today the railway people have been asked for figures regarding the rapid transfer of 12 Divisions and 300 heavy guns to Italy! They will never go while I am CIGS, but all that will come later . . .

P.S. We have got to remember, as we do, that the Government carry the chief responsibility, and that in a war of this kind many things besides the actual Army must be considered. Having remembered this, however, we are entitled to see that unsound plans are not adopted – or all other plans may come to nought.

FRENCH MORALE

Lloyd George, ii, p 1294

It must be remembered that we were not placed in full possession of facts which would have justified our taking a stronger line. In the course of the discussions that took place between the War Policy Committee of the Cabinet and the Commander-in-Chief and the Chief of the Imperial Staff and the conversations before and after the formal meetings, Ministers were misled on several critical points.

First of all we were misled as to the French attitude towards the offensive.* This was vital, for without their active and whole-hearted co-operation the attack could not hope to succeed . . .

The salient facts as to the condition of the French Army and the extent of the demoralization in its ranks were also withheld or minimized.

Haig Diary: Blake, p 236

THURSDAY, 7 JUNE . . . At 5 pm I met General Pétain in his train at Cassel Station. He had seen the King of the Belgians this morning and was on his way back to Compiègne. Our interview was most satisfactory. General Rucquoy was also present as representing the King of the Belgians. Pétain brought a document embodying the points already agreed upon between us by correspondence regarding the forthcoming operations in Flanders. This document, or 'protocol', was read aloud by me and was finally signed by the three of us. It placed the French six Divisions entirely under my orders, appointed General Anthoine† to command

*See p 98.
† General Anthoine's force was to be known as the French First Army.

them, and left all points remaining in doubt to be decided by me. Altogether I found Pétain most anxious to help in every way, and thoroughly businesslike.

Pétain and I then had a private talk. He told me that two French Divisions* had refused to go and relieve two Divisions in the front line because the men had not had leave. Some were tried and were shot. The French Government supported Pétain. They also refused to allow the leading French Socialists to go to Stockholm for a Conference with German Socialists.† The situation in the French Army was serious at one moment but is now more satisfactory. But the bad state of discipline causes Pétain grave concern.

Cabinet Papers, CAB 23/16: War Cabinet No. 159a, 8 June

The War Cabinet received a verbal report from General Sir Henry Wilson, the head of the British Mission at French General Headquarters on the subject of the general feeling in the French army and nation in regard to the war. General Wilson expressed grave doubts as to whether we could count on the continued resistance of the French army and nation until such time as effective military assistance could be received from the United States of America, a period he put at 12 to 18 months. In support of this view he mentioned the fact that the French Commander-in-Chief had been compelled to relinquish the big French attack timed to take place on 10 June in concert with the British attack on the Messines ridge. From General Wilson's information and from information from other sources the War Cabinet gathered that this decision was partly due to the reason that General Pétain could not absolutely rely on his men. General Wilson did not confirm the rumours which had reached the War Cabinet that an incident had occurred in the French army amounting almost to a mutiny, but he said there was a good deal of unrest which resulted in large numbers of applications for leave of absence. He suggested that leaders of the type of Marshal Joffre or General Nivelle might have risked the attack on 10 June, but General Pétain had nothing of the gambler's instinct and would not take a gambler's chance. General Wilson expressed the belief founded on his knowledge of the French character and temperament that General Pétain could not hold the French army together through another winter without some real success, whether military or diplomatic. Pressed by the War Cabinet as to his personal views on the prospect of a considerable military victory he admitted that he could see no reasonable prospect of this in Mesopotamia, or Egypt, or on the Western front, with the possible exception of Flanders, where he understood that Field-Marshal Sir Douglas Haig was hopeful. In Flanders, however, the prospects of a big success would be considerably reduced if the French could not develop an attack on a large scale in concert with the British offensive. Commenting on a statement that was made to the effect that General Pétain was alleged to believe in the possibility of an allied

*Actually 54 divisions were affected, according to Pétain.
† An international Socialist conference, organized by a Dutch-Scandinavian committee.

success in the Balkans, General Wilson pointed out that General Pétain had no responsibility for or special knowledge of that theatre of operations. He further expressed the view that before long the British Government would be approached by the French Government with a request to take over a further section of the line on the Western Front. A case based on a comparison of the numbers of bayonets would be made out, which it would be very difficult to resist.*

Hankey, ii, p 671

8 JUNE.   The new feature in the situation today is that Henry Wilson came to the War Cabinet this morning to warn us that the French would not stick it much longer, and Pétain had to fail in his promise to carry out an offensive on the 10th in support of Haig's attack on the Messines Ridge. This report is confirmed more or less by Esher, and has made us all very anxious.

Esher, iv, pp 124–5; Esher to Lord Derby, 8 June

The stormy light from Petrograd has illuminated some dark corners of French mentality, both military and civil. The army is in a state far from satisfactory. The men are discontented, captious and beginning to long for peace.

The incisive reality of the whole situation is that D.H.'s dogged pertinacity may enable us to bring Germany to her knees, in the sense that after hard hammering they may agree to reasonable terms of peace.

Pétain, p 97

The mutinies took many forms . . . and reached their peak on 2 June, when seventeen outbreaks were reported. The situation remained serious up to 10 June, with an average of seven incidents a day. During the rest of the month the daily average was one. In July the total fell to seven incidents altogether, in August to four, and in September to one.

COMMAND CHANGES

Haig Diary: Blake, p 234

FRIDAY, 1 JUNE.   H. Wilson writes from Compiègne that 'he is beginning to feel that he is not doing much good there'. I also hear privately from London, that

---

*According to a report submitted by the CIGS to the War Policy Committee in response to questions put to him on 12 June (W.P. 4) the comparative figures were:

British: 62 Infantry divisions + 5 cavalry divisions, with a combatant strength of 1,127,300 (ration strength: 1,658,000) held 85 miles;

French: 109 infantry divisions + 17 brigades (= 8½ divisions) + 7 cavalry divisions, combatant strength 1,310,000 (ration strength: 2,170,000) held 335 miles.

Painlevé has again stated to Derby and also to the Prime Minister that H.W. is not welcome to them! H.W. is classed as 'a Nivellite' and so doubtless the atmosphere is not very congenial to him now that Nivelle is in disgrace.

Wilson, i, p 359; 2 June

Then I discussed my own position here, and Foch was quite clear that I ought to go and ask for a command. He said that Pétain did not particularly want me, and that with Nivelle's departure all had changed. It is abundantly clear that I cannot stop here. But when I told Foch that Haig wanted me to go to Paris, I found that he was against that also.

So he does not want me – and he really is my friend.

Haig Diary: Blake, p 235

TUESDAY, 5 JUNE.   Sir H. Wilson arrived from Compiègne and stayed the night. By his request General Foch (his old friend) found out whether Painlevé and Pétain wanted him (Wilson) to give up his appointment as head of the British Mission. Foch's reply was that he 'would do better service by going'! I told Wilson to go to London to see Lord Milner. In the meantime it was possible that a new French Minister of War might be appointed in Paris vice Painlevé.

Haig Diary: Blake, p 237

MONDAY, 11 JUNE.   Sir H. Wilson arrived about 10 pm from England. He considers it best to resign his appointment as Head of the British Mission at GQG because the French Minister of War does not get on with him. I concur in his decision.

Wilson's appointment at GQG terminated on 26 June.

FLANDERS

Haig Diary: Blake, p 236

SATURDAY, 9 JUNE.   I had a long talk with Robertson. He wished me to realize the difficult situation in which the country would be if I carried out large and costly attacks without full co-operation by the French. When Autumn came round, Britain would then be without an Army! On the other hand it is possible that Austria would make peace, if harassed enough. Would it not be a good plan, therefore, to support Italy with guns? I did not agree. Altogether I thought Robertson's views unsound. I told him that I thought the German was now nearly at his last resources, and that there was only *one sound* plan to follow, viz, *without delay* to

1. Send to France every possible man.
2.   ,,   ,,   ,,   ,,   ,,   aeroplane.
3.   ,,   ,,   ,,   ,,   ,,   gun.

The first meeting of the War Policy Committee of the Cabinet, set up on 8 June (see p 123) took place on 11 June. According to Lord Hankey,* 'the Committee managed to hold sixteen meetings between 8 June and 20 June (actually 20 July) when the results of the inquiry were laid before a full meeting of the War Cabinet, and the final conclusions were reached'. The Report itself (in CAB 27/6) is, curiously enough, dated 10 August. At the first meeting the full Committee of four members was present (with Hankey as Secretary) and those also attending were Sir William Robertson and Lieutenant-Colonel E. L. Spiers (as Sir Edward Spears then spelt his name). Spears, who is described in Hankey's Notes as 'Liaison Officer with General Foch', but calls himself 'head of the newly created British Military Mission to the French Government', opened the proceedings with a lengthy report on the state of the French Army and nation (see pp 140–2).

Sir William Robertson then described the recent interchange of views he had had with General Foch, who . . . had said that the French Army was at present not out for any big offensive, and that it would be folly to attempt it, but they were both agreed that the Allied armies could not sit still and do nothing. In the case of the British Army this was especially important, because at present the prevailing opinion in the British Expeditionary Force was that they could beat the Germans by themselves. Hence, we must maintain an offensive spirit, and such operations as that against the Messines Ridge were very suitable for this purpose. Although General Foch held the view that great attacks against a distant objective were not at present practicable, the French were quite prepared for less ambitious offensive operations. He and General Foch had both felt that they must keep hard at it, more particularly because Germany was in great difficulties . . .

Sir William Robertson said he had also seen Sir Douglas Haig, who was very satisfied with the progress he had made. He was coming over in a few days, and no doubt the War Cabinet or the Committee would like to see him. His future plans were being based on the general lines approved by the War Cabinet. Sir William Robertson stated, however, that, in his opinion, it would be desirable to modify Sir Douglas Haig's orders to a certain extent, owing to the changed situation, unless, after hearing what the Admiralty have to say, the War Cabinet prefer to

The Supreme Command 1914–1918, ii, p 673

maintain their former instructions. The instructions to which he referred were the following, communicated by the Secretary to the War Committee on 26 November:

> 'There is no operation of war to which the War Committee would attach greater importance than the successful occupation, or at least the deprivation to the enemy of *** and especially ****.'*

(The names of the places are well known to the Committee.)

A lengthy discussion on prospects in Italy then took place, followed by a brief reference to America, in the course of which Robertson 'doubted if we could count on more than a dozen divisions next year'.

The Prime Minister said that the Committee must think out the whole position. Whatever we did must be thorough, and we must have no fiddling. The Committee would have to hear the Admiralty and go exhaustively into the shipping situation, as well as the Salonica and Palestine situations, the overland route to the Balkans, and they should not dismiss from view the possibility of some bargain with the Italians. In his view the great defect of the War had been that we have always hit the enemy at his strongest instead of his weakest side. If we had concentrated against Austria earlier in the War we might have knocked her out and isolated Germany. In his opinion, our strategy must be considered again without any preconceived ideas. This was the only chance of rescuing ourselves from a tight place. The news from Russia was very discouraging and Colonel Spiers, an officer of great knowledge of the French, actually talked of a Revolution in France. On the other hand, he could see no serious indication of cracking in Germany. The Germans were stronger on the Western Front than ever in men, and guns, and leadership. Nothing but bold determined action could save the cause of the Allies. We had a very difficult and long voyage in front of us.

>   Cabinet Papers, CAB 27/6: Second Meeting of
>   the Cabinet Committee on War Policy, 12 June

Proceedings opened with a discussion of the desirability of greater mobility of resources on the Western and Italian fronts; 'a permanent Board of Allied Strategy' was suggested.

The War Policy Committee then discussed on a map the chances of the British operations being attended with success, and it was decided that they should take an early opportunity to see Field-Marshal Sir Douglas Haig and hear his views on the subject. It was pointed out, however, that Sir Douglas Haig was by nature an

*See p 17.

optimist. In order to judge his psychology you had only to study the history of recent campaigns. He had been equally optimistic before Neuve Chapelle, Festubert, Loos, and the Somme. What the War Policy Committee wished to avoid was a series of costly operations as the result of which we would have no more to show than after the Somme last year. While the Italian operation made an appeal to some Members of the Committee, it was felt that very likely it might only lead to the same sort of results as had been achieved on the Somme, and that the question required very careful investigation.

After a short discussion of the questions to be put to various experts, the First Sea Lord, Admiral Jellicoe, and the CIGS came in.

Admiral Jellicoe laid great stress on the importance of rendering submarine bases untenable. The question was discussed at some length. It was generally agreed that as a policy of perfection the most hopeful plan would be to clear the enemy out from land bases, but it was pointed out that if this was to involve a loss of hundreds of thousands of men, perhaps without achieving the object, it would not be worth while attempting. The question was discussed as to how far, particularly during the summer months, the bases on the Belgian coast could be rendered untenable by attack from the sea. The First Sea Lord, while admitting that the recent bombardments of Ostend and Zeebrugge had been extraordinarily successful, pointed out that it had been necessary to wait nearly six months before the exact circumstances favouring an attack of this kind in regard to tide, wind, meteorological conditions, &c, could be realized, and that even during the summer months it was impossible to count on repeating the operation very frequently.

The Prime Minister read a letter which was received during the meeting from Admiral of the Fleet Lord Fisher, reminding him of Lord Fisher's advocacy of a coast operation in January, 1915, and urging that it should be taken up.

The Committee ended by discussing a report on Italian artillery and the prospects of capturing Trieste.

Author's Papers; Haig to Robertson, 12 June

O.A.D. 478   Present Situation and Future Plans

My action since 1 May has been in accordance with the views and intentions expressed in my Nos. O.A.D. 428, of that date,* and O.A.D. 449, of 16 May†

A modified pressure has been maintained, with good results, on the ARRAS and VIMY fronts and arrangements to continue this for the present have been made.

The first phase of the operations for the clearance of the Belgian coast (capture of the MESSINES – WYTSCHAETE Ridge) has been carried out with complete success,

*See pp 83–4.   † See pp 94–5.

and is of considerable importance in facilitating preparation for a further advance and in improving our defensive position round Ypres.

Arrangements have been made to take over from the French, at an early date, the sector now held by them on the Belgian coast.

French troops have already taken over my southern front as far north as the OMIGNON River; and by agreement with General Pétain, instead of relieving my troops between the OMIGNON River and HAVRINCOURT as proposed by me, French troops will take over a portion of the front now held by the Belgians on my immediate left and will co-operate in my Northern operations.

General Pétain is also arranging for offensive operations on other portions of his front, on a sufficient scale to prevent withdrawal of German forces to oppose my advance; and, well prepared and supported by artillery, the operations intended by him should prove effective in wearing down the enemy opposed to him.

It will be seen, therefore, that, with one exception, the conditions specified by me in my memorandum of 1 May (No. O.A.D. 428, paragraph commencing at the foot of page 3) have been, or are being, fulfilled.

The one exception I allude to is the completion of my divisions to establishment and the provision of guns required to complete my armies to the scale agreed upon.

With the drafts and guns already promised, however, I consider, on present indications, that it will be possible to carry through at least a portion of the operations intended, and my plans and preparations are being made to advance by stages so arranged that, while each stage will give a definite and useful result, it will be possible for me to discontinue the advance if and when it appears that the means at my disposal are insufficient to justify a further effort.

Success in the first stage alone will improve our positions round YPRES so greatly that the saving in normal casualties during the winter will probably far more than counter-balance the casualties to be expected in capturing the objectives aimed at. Moreover, from the experience of previous attacks made by us this year, the German casualties in defence are likely to exceed ours in attack, while the moral gain from another defeat of the Germans will count for much, and at the present stage of the war may open up far-reaching possibilities.

I am accordingly pushing on my preparations for the Northern operations, but these cannot be complete for some time* and the scope of my plans can and will be adjusted as may be necessary to future developments in the situation.

I take this opportunity to submit for the consideration of the War Cabinet the following remarks on the general situation and the deductions I draw as to the conduct of the campaign in France.

According to reports, the endurance of the German nation is being tested so severely that discontent there has already assumed formidable proportions. The German Government, helped by the long disciplinary training of the people, is

*GHQ contemplated the next stage of the offensive taking place 'about the end of July'.

still able to control this discontent; but every fresh defeat of the German armies, combined with a growing realization of the failure of the submarine campaign, increases the difficulty of doing so, and further defeats in the field may have unexpectedly great results, which may come with unexpected suddenness.

The German army, too, shows unmistakable signs of deterioration in many ways and the cumulative effect of further defeats may at any time yield greater results in the field than we can absolutely rely on gaining.

I attach notes on these points, as an Appendix to this paper.

From a careful study of the conditions, I feel justified in stating that continued pressure with as little delay as possible certainly promises at least very valuable results; whereas relaxation of pressure now would strengthen belief that the allies are becoming totally exhausted, and that Germany can outlast them. Waning hope in Germany would be revived, and time would be gained to replenish food, ammunition, and other requirements. In fact many of the advantages already gained by us would be lost, and this would certainly be realized by, and would h? e a depressing effect on, our armies in the field who have made such great efforts to gain them.

The depressing effect in France would be especially great and especially dangerous. At the present crisis of the war French hope must have something to feed on. The hope of American assistance is not sufficient for the purpose. It is still too far distant and the French at the moment are living a good deal on the hope of further British successes. They can and will assist in these by keeping the enemy on their front fully employed, wearing him down, and preventing him from withdrawing divisions to oppose to us. But they feel unable at present to do more than this, and it is useless to expect it of them – although any considerable British successes, and signs of a breakdown in the German power of resistance, would probably have an electrifying effect.

That the British armies in France are capable of gaining considerable further successes this year I am confident, as are all ranks under my command; it is only the extent of the success possible that is in doubt, and that depends mainly on three factors, viz:

Firstly, on whether the War Cabinet decides to concentrate our resources on the effort.

Secondly, on the degree of help given by Russia.

Thirdly, on the extent to which the German resolution and power of endurance stand the great strain they are undergoing.

The first of these factors lies within the power of the War Cabinet. The second to some extent, and the third to a very great extent, depend on their decision.

It is my considered opinion, based not on mere optimism but on a thorough study of the situation,* guided by experience which I may claim to be con-

---

*On information supplied by Charteris. In *Douglas Haig: The Educated Soldier* (p 311) I wrote: 'All through the year there was a discrepancy, sometimes very substantial, between what Charteris thought privately, and what he proffered to Haig as a basis for the latter's

siderable, that if our resources are concentrated in France to the fullest possible extent the British armies are capable and can be relied on to effect great results this summer – results which will make final victory more assured and which may even bring it within reach this year.

On the other hand I am equally convinced that to fail in concentrating our resources in the Western theatre, or to divert them from it, would be most dangerous. It might lead to the collapse of France. It would certainly encourage Germany. It would discourage our own officers and men very considerably. The desired military results, possible in France, are not possible elsewhere.

I am aware that my motives in stating this may be misunderstood, but I trust that in the interests of the Empire, at what is undoubtedly a critical period in the war, whatever value the War Cabinet may attach to my opinion may not be discounted by any doubt of such a kind. I have reason to believe that the Commanders-in-Chief of British Forces in other theatres of war are entirely in agreement with the view that the Western Front always has been and will remain the decisive one.

The correct strategy, to pursue, in accordance with the teaching of every great exponent of the art of war, is clear under such conditions.

In my opinion the only serious doubt as to possibilities in France lies in the action to be expected of Russia, but even that doubt is an argument in favour of doing our utmost in France with as little delay as possible.

Russia is still holding large German forces and every week gained makes it more impossible for the enemy to transfer divisions to the West in time, if we act promptly.

There is still room for hope of increased Russian assistance, and successes in the West will surely increase the prospects of it.

A passive attitude in the West, or mere minor successes, would not encourage the Russians; and delay under such conditions may make matters worse in Russia instead of better.

In conclusion, I desire to make it clear that, whatever force may be placed at my disposal, my undertakings will be limited to what it is reasonably possible to succeed in.

Given sufficient force, provided no great transfer of German troops is made, in time, from East to West, it is probable that the Belgian coast could be cleared this summer, and the defeats on the German troops entailed in doing so might quite possibly lead to their collapse.

Without sufficient force I shall not attempt to clear the coast and my efforts will be restricted to gaining such victories as are within reach, thereby improving my positions for the winter and opening up possibilities for further operations here-after if and when the necessary means are provided.

plans.' I added that the correct assessment of the extent to which the Central Powers were weakening in mid-1917 'involved subtleties which Charteris did not possess' – and unfortunately the brilliant Brigadier-General G. M. W. Macdonogh, Director of Military Intelligence at the War Office, was ill at this juncture.

A definition of the term 'sufficient force' must depend on developments in the general situation; but provided that does not grow less satisfactory than at present I estimate that even the full programme may not prove beyond reach with the number of divisions now at my disposal, if brought up to and maintained at establishment of men and guns. An increase in the forces available would, of course, give still greater prospects of complete success.

Appendix to O.A.D. 478:

SUMMARY:

1. The course of events in Russia has not, so far, justified Germany in moving any considerable number of troops from the Eastern to the Western theatre.
2. Even if events in Russia should take a marked turn for the worse, it is unlikely that Germany could move more than 20 divisions, at an average rate of 2 divisions per week, from the Eastern to the Western Front.
3. Of the divisions at present on the Western Front not more than 35 remain fresh for offensive operations. 105 divisions have been worn out by the battle and have probably lost an average of not less than 40% of their infantry.
4. Germany is within 4 to 6 months of a date at which she will be unable to maintain the strength of her units in the field.
5. The pressure of economic conditions on the nation at large is increasing and has definitely extended to the ranks of the Army.
6. There is a marked and unmistakable fall in the morale of the German troops.

From all these definite facts, it is a fair indication that, given a continuance of circumstances as they stand at the present and given a continuation of the effort of the Allies, then Germany may well be forced to conclude peace on our terms before the end of the year.

This remarkable document embodies the core of Haig's thinking about the Flanders offensive. His motive has been described as 'a strange belief that he could defeat the German army single-handed in Flanders'.* From this and foregoing documents it is clear that there was no question of 'single-handed'; wisely or unwisely, Haig expected help from the French; he hoped for help from the Russians; the Italians had already made one effort, and would soon make another. It is, however, also clear that Haig was convinced of the possibility of beating Germany in 1917, and of the vital need to do so. His statement, as may be supposed, produced prompt reactions in London.

*B. H. Liddell Hart, *History Of The First World War*, Cassell, 1970, p 426

Author's Papers: Telegram, Robertson to Haig,
13 June

I cannot possibly agree with some of the statements in the appendix. For example,
extent of depletion of enemy reserves and deduction given in final paragraph. I
hope, therefore, you will agree appendix not being circulated to War Cabinet . . .
It would be very regrettable at this juncture if different estimates of enemy
resources were presented to War Cabinet as it would tend to destroy value of your
sound appreciation.

Blake, p 239: Robertson to Haig, 13 June

What I do wish to impress on you is this:– Don't argue that you can finish the war
this year, or that the German is already beaten. Argue that your plan is the best
plan – as it is – that no other would be *safe* let alone decisive, and then leave them
to reject your advice and mine. They dare not do that. Further, on this occasion
they will be up against the French.

Conditions in Germany

Ludendorff, ii, pp 448–9

In utter disregard of the destructive intentions of the enemy, the idea of peace by
reconciliation made ever greater progress among the German people. It was
swallowed most eagerly by those who feared the effects of victory on their
political aspirations. During May and June a number of delegates, with facilities
from the Government, undertook journeys to Stockholm,* Austria–Hungary and
Switzerland. We walked into the traps of the Entente. I was against these journeys
and so was the Commander-in-Chief in the Marches.† The Emperor decided in
favour of them, and the deputies of the General Staff in Berlin had to prepare the
passports. Count Czernin‡ also sent the Socialist leaders of Austria–Hungary to
Stockholm.

From there, supported by the Russian Revolution, the labouring classes of the
hostile states were to be called upon to proclaim and carry out the 'Reconciliation
of Mankind'. These endeavours revealed woeful ignorance of human nature, and
certainly took no account of the spirit of the enemy nations, nor of our own; they
did, however, in some cases pursue decidedly revolutionary objects. No impression was produced on the enemy, but with us and in Austria the fighting spirit was
weakened more and more. Confidence in our own strength was lost.

*See p 126 f.n.
†Prince Leopold of Bavaria, commanding the Eastern Front.
‡Austrian Foreign Minister.

F<small>LANDERS</small>

Haig Diary: Duff Cooper, ii, pp 120–1; Army
Commanders' Conference, 14 June

I stated that there was no departure from the plans I had outlined at the conference of 7 May, viz. the British and French will wear down and exhaust the enemy by attacking (by surprise as far as possible) at points where an attack is not expected. Finally, the British will strike the main blow, probably in the north.

Underlying the general intention of wearing out the enemy is the strategical idea of securing the Belgian coast and connecting our front with the Dutch frontier.

The nature and size of the several steps which we take towards that objective must depend on our *effectives* and the replacement of *guns*.

Roughly these steps are:

(a) Capture the bridgehead formed by the Passchendaele–Staden–Clercken ridge.

(b) Push on towards Roulers–Thourout, so as to take the German coast defences in the rear.

(c) Land by surprise on the Ostend front in conjunction with an attack from Nieuport.

If our effectives or guns are inadequate, and progress is delayed, it may be necessary to call a halt after (a) is gained.

Meantime, it is desirable to mislead the enemy as to our next point of attack. With this end in view, the Second Army will operate towards Comines and clear the triangle between the Comines canal and the river Lys so as to give the impression of the intention to turn Lille on the north, while our First Army operates against Lens with a view to turning Lille on the south. Secrecy is most important, but it is difficult to conceal preparations on so large a scale. The best plan seems to be to prepare simultaneously several points for attack: thus the situation becomes similar to the case of the pea under one of three thimbles.

Author's Papers: Haig Diary

F<small>RIDAY</small>, 15 J<small>UNE</small> . . . CGS (with Davidson) brought me proposals regarding the divisions to be used in the northern operations. With a few exceptions, all had been heavily engaged in the Arras battle. I ordered the list to be revised . . . It is most important to employ all divisions equally and fairly, all round.

Author's Papers; Haig to Robertson, 17 June

O.A.D. 502

To assist the War Cabinet in considering the various possible courses of action open this summer, I submit, in continuation of my O.A.D. No. 478, of the 12th instant, the following, fuller, statement of my views as to the strategical advantages which would be gained by successful operations to secure the Belgian coast.

Even a partial success in the operations for which I am preparing will give very useful results, apart from the effect on the German army and nation of another defeat.

A very limited advance will enable our guns to make OSTEND useless to the German navy, and will, at the same time, render DUNKIRK – one of our most important ports – immune from long-range hostile gunfire.

The enemy's communications with the coast are not numerous, and run through such a narrow space between our lines and the Dutch frontier that an advance sufficient to bring the ROULERS–THOUROUT railway within effective range of our guns would restrict his railway communications with the coast to those passing through GHENT and BRUGES.

A short further advance, bringing us within effective heavy-gun range of BRUGES, would most probably induce the evacuation of ZEEBRUGGE and the whole coastline.

The consequences of extending our front to the Dutch frontier would be so considerable that they might prove decisive. Following on the successes we have already gained such a failure to stop our advance would leave little room for German hope of successfully opposing our further advance, even if temporary exhaustion imposed a halt on us for a time.

Realizing this, the enemy would find himself faced by a most serious situation. His main lines of retreat run through bottlenecks north and south of the ARDENNES, and any reasonable possibility of our being able to continue the advance on GHENT and BRUSSELS would probably suffice to determine the enemy to undertake a retreat, if not to accept our terms at once, in view of the dangers and difficulties of retreat under such conditions.

In addition, as neutrals would recognize the imminence of a German collapse, it is conceivable that the attitude of Holland towards us might be such as to add seriously to the German anxieties.

At present it is not in our power to give Holland any direct help if Germany committed a breach of neutrality against her. With the Germans driven from the Belgian coast, and our flank resting on the Dutch frontier, however, the situation would be very different; and if Holland then decided to join the allies a way would be opened to turn ANTWERP and the German lines through Belgium completely, and to sever the German Lines of Communication through LIEGE.

Germany would then have to choose between accepting terms, or undertaking a retreat likely to prove disastrous, or attempting to forestall the danger by violating Dutch territory. If she had failed to stop our advance, it is reasonable to assume that she would not have sufficient forces left at her disposal to justify the last mentioned course.

In short, it is clear that very great possibilities will be opened up by the operations now in preparation. These operations have long been recognized as offering the possibilities stated whenever we had sufficient strength to carry them out. If it be questioned whether that time has yet come my considered opinion, as stated in my paper of the 12th instant, is that by concentration of our resources now the operation has sufficient prospects of success this year not only to justify our undertaking it, but – in view of the general situation – to make it most advisable to do so. Even if the full measure of success is not gained I see no reason to doubt that the results attained will at least be sufficient to have a great effect on Germany and her allies, who will realize that, although a respite has been gained, it is likely to be a short one.

Comparing this operation with anything that we might do in other theatres its advantages are overwhelming.

It directly and seriously threatens our main enemy, on whom the whole Coalition against us depends.

It is within the easiest possible reach of our base by sea and rail and can be developed infinitely more rapidly, and maintained infinitely more easily, than any other operation open to us.

It admits of the closest possible combination of our naval and military strength.

It covers all the points which we dare not uncover, and therefore admits of the utmost concentration of force; whereas, for the same reason, any force employed in any other theatre of war can never be more than a detachment, with all the disadvantages of detachments.

Even a short advance along the Belgian coast, in addition to considerable moral results, would assist our navy appreciably in securing our lines of communication; while the value of that coast to the enemy as a base for air raids against England would be reduced in proportion to the extent of our advance.

In no part of any theatre of war would so limited an advance promise such far-reaching results on Germany, and through Germany, on her allies and on neutrals.

In short, after the fullest consideration, it is my earnest conviction that the arguments in favour of the course I propose in comparison with the possibilities open in any other theatre of war are incontrovertible. In other theatres we can only employ detachments, seeking to attain results by indirect methods, and under most difficult conditions of maintenance. Time and space considerations would be so unfavourable to us that if any indirect threat appeared dangerous to Germany it would be well within her power to take timely steps to counteract it either by direct attack on us at a more vital point or by moving troops to meet our indirect threat.

Lastly, while an increase in our forces in the Western theatre would have an encouraging effect on France, where encouragement is of very high importance now, any reduction of our forces here at this juncture might have most serious consequences.

I cannot urge too strongly the importance of a whole-hearted concentration of our forces for the purpose in view.

Amid the uncertainties of war one thing is certain, viz, that it is only by whole-hearted concentration at the right time and place that victory ever has been or ever will be won.

In my opinion the time and place to choose are now beyond dispute. We have gone a long way already towards success. Victory may be nearer than is generally realized if we act correctly now. But we may fall seriously short of it if at this juncture we fail to follow correct principles

This was the final document in the 'small mountain of paper'* on which Haig rested his case for pursuing the Flanders offensive, before thrashing out the whole matter face to face with the War Cabinet in London two days later.

Haig Diary: Blake, p 239

Sunday, 17 June. I left at 12 noon and reached Calais by motor at 1 o'clock. After lunching there, I left by destroyer at 2 o'clock for Dover. Admiral Bacon came to Calais to meet me and returned with me to Dover. He is whole-heartedly with us, and has urged in writing to the Admiralty the absolute necessity for clearing the Belgian Coast before winter. We left Dover by special train at 3.30 pm and reached Charing Cross at 5.20 pm.

French Morale

Cabinet Papers, CAB 27/6: First Meeting of the Cabinet Committee on War Policy, 11 June

Colonel Spiers gave the Committee a description of the present position in the French Army. He said that a short time ago two whole regiments, that is to say, six battalions in all, had mutinied. There had also been some trouble in other regiments.

Spears's French informant had obviously been to some trouble in planting this 'information', because he then related the incident – probably fictitious – in great detail to the Cabinet Committee.

The regiments concerned had not taken part in the recent offensive, and had been quartered in the region of Épernay, which was apparently a centre of sedition. In fact, it was believed that the whole movement was organized by civilian influences in the interior of France. Then there had been rumours that Colonial troops were

*Douglas Haig: The Educated Soldier, p 332

to be used against the strikers, and Colonel Spiers had been informed that if this occurred the French troops said that they would move against the Colonial troops. There had also been the Annamite troubles in Paris. At Lyons also there had been a curious incident, as rumours had got about that British troops resting there were to be used against strikers. Colonel Spiers then recapitulated the measures taken to suppress the mutiny.

This passage also suffers from the limited nature of Spears's information; it concludes with an attack on the French Government's feebleness by 'High Military Officers to whom Colonel Spiers had spoken', which was no doubt true.

Colonel Spiers said that the reasons for the trouble in the French Army were as follows:

1. Disappointment at the Aisne offensive, which was very general because so much had been promised, and the French had really believed that they were going to drive the Germans out of France:
2. The bad news from Russia. France had been very much in love with Russia, and when the men in the trenches read the continual bad news in their newspapers it depressed them and made them want to follow the example of the Russian Revolutionists:
3. The French Army was very tired; there was a general lassitude:
4. There were too many old men in the trenches. These were tired and made no secret of the fact:
5. There had been too many changes in the Higher Command, not only in the Chief Command, but among the Armies. General Nivelle had put in his men and now General Pétain had replaced them by his own men. During the recent disturbances no General Officer or Staff Officer had been able to appear among the disaffected troops.

The remedies which had been taken by the French Government, Colonel Spiers said, were as follows:

1. More troops were to be taken out of the line to rest:
2. There was to be more leave:
3. The classes of very old men were to be dismissed:

The effect of all this would inevitably be a demand for France to hold a shorter front.

Colonel Spiers added that the situation had, for the moment, been extraordinarily improved by the British success at the Messines Ridge, which had greatly cheered up not only the French Army but the whole country. There was no doubt now that we were the mainstay of the French nation. He apprehended serious results in the event of a German offensive against the

French. He did not suppose that the effect of our success would be of very long duration, but the arrival of American troops might be expected to stimulate the French. Colonel Spiers urged that the French situation would have to be very carefully watched, since a comparatively small incident might lead to very serious trouble and possibly even to a Revolution which, if it occurred, would take the form of anarchy, since there was no commanding individual to control the situation.

In reply to questions put to him by the War Policy Committee, Colonel Spiers stated that the intended offensive on 10 June had been postponed by General Pétain with very great distress. The reason given for the postponement was that the Germans were attacking so hard on the front where it was to have taken place that sufficient German troops were already diverted there from opposing the British. The real reason, however, was that the recent disturbances had broken out in a division in that very area. If the British response to the abandonment of serious efforts by the French was to go into winter quarters, so to speak, the effect on French opinion would be very bad, particularly if the Germans should then attack. Colonel Spiers felt sure, however, that before very long the French would themselves recover sufficiently to undertake considerable attacks. If the Russian offensive was a complete failure, the effect on the French Army would also be very depressing, but Colonel Spiers suggested that possibly results might be represented as better than they really were. Colonel Spiers, when pressed by the Prime Minister, was not willing to risk his reputation that the French would put up a really big fight which would compel the Germans to turn and face them and so ease the situation in front of the British Army. He considered, however, that they would be able to keep up a considerable effort. Moreover, by means of long rests, leave, etc, he thought the French should be able to keep their Army together and to maintain it through the winter. M. Painlevé, whom Colonel Spiers had seen, had not thought much of the recent trouble in the Army.

It is clear that the whole French War Ministry, political and military leaders alike, was engaged in a large act of dissimulation. Spears continued with a brief report on French internal politics, concluding:

The attention of the Committee was drawn to the danger of upsetting the present French Government as there was no good alternative Government from our point of view. The French President had lost influence; M Briand was, to some extent, discredited, and M. Clemenceau was too old. The only alternative to the present Government was M. Caillaux, and his advent to power would mean peace.*

*A somewhat highly coloured, and in certain respects inaccurate (eg. the date) account of this episode may be found in *Two Men Who Saved France*, pp 43–7. The passage of almost fifty years, and perhaps a somewhat illegible pocket diary will suffice to account for the discrepancies.

Across the Channel, Sir Henry Wilson spent the next ten days saying goodbyes to friends along the French front. On 16 June he was at General de Castelnau's headquarters.

Wilson, i, pp 362–3

He is anxious about the future. He says that there is no doubt that the morale of the men is not good, that the two Russian brigades, who will now neither fight nor work, are doing great harm, that Painlevé is useless and dangerous and chiefly to blame for the present state of affairs . . .

He said that the constant changes in command were playing havoc, and he absolutely agreed with me that victories, military or diplomatic, must be obtained. He did not believe in anything better than Messines–Wytschaete being possible on this front, and that was not enough.

Wilson and his ADC, Lord Duncannon, continued their journey through the Vosges to the Swiss Frontier, forming a very clear picture of the French mood as they went along:

All day, the Lord and I talked with no end of people of all sorts of rank, and always the same story. The fighting army (i.e. the younger men) are tired and depressed; the women are ditto; be careful.

Just the same story. Be careful, don't ask too much, and gain some successes. Always the same story.

I talked with Laguiche and his staff, with Boisveedy's staff, with infantry officers, with civilians – always the same story. Also Duncannon, talking to everyone, finds the same thing.

Back to Wesserling to lunch with General Boyer. I had a long talk with him again, and with his Chief of Staff, and again I got exactly the same impression. Some successes must be obtained to keep the French in.

In London, outside a restricted Government circle, even normally well-informed people had no inkling of the true state of affairs.

Repington, i, pp 584–5

TUESDAY, 19 JUNE. . . Met Philip Sassoon* yesterday, who told me of troubles in the French Army bordering on mutiny, from sheer war-weariness I suspect . . .

Met Lieut Pernot at my club afterwards. He brought a charming message for me from General Foch . . . I said that I saw in the German Press that Pétain was busy at Verdun, and Pernot did not deny it. There has been serious trouble in two French regiments, and the mutiny had been firmly repressed. Things were all right

*Sir Philip Sassoon, Haig's private secretary.

now. It was the Press making out that the French had been so badly beaten that
caused the trouble.

Author's Papers, Esher to Robertson, 20 June

Causes having different values have lowered the morale of the French Army. The
withholding of leave from officers and men, a deficiency in the supply of red wine,
an exaggerated pessimism as to the results of the Champagne offensive so tact-
lessly fostered throughout the Army for political purposes, the contagion of the
Russian revolutionary propaganda, and war weariness caused by the prospect of
waiting until the American Army materializes, have produced grave mutinous
outbreaks that have given occasion for considerable anxiety.

The attitude of the Army, and the physical condition of the civil population,
have led to the narrowing of the War aims of France to the restitution by Germany
of Alsace and Lorraine. Nothing else greatly matters to the people of France, and
it is difficult to imagine, should the offer of these provinces be made by Germany,
that the French Army or the French nation would carry on the War for objects
that would appear to them subsidiary or alien.

FLANDERS

In his *War Memoirs*, Lloyd George is at great pains to preserve the
myth of the War Cabinet being kept in ignorance of the plans for the
Flanders Offensive. Referring to the setting up of the War Policy Committee on 8 June, he says:

Up to that date the Flanders project had never been submitted to the examination
of the Government by the Chief of the Imperial General Staff or the
Commander-in-Chief. It was understood that GHQ had such a project in con-
templation, but, to use the Commander-in-Chief's words, it would not be undertaken 'unless the situation was sufficiently favourable for it when the time came.'

On 19 June, a meeting of the Committee was held to discuss the matter.*

We have already sufficiently noted how wide of the mark (and of the
truth) is this suggestion that 19 June marks the first real involvement of
the War Cabinet in the Flanders campaign. It is entirely in keeping with
Lloyd George's method of exposition that, instead of quoting the copious
material submitted by Haig to the Government before that date, he uses,
to present Haig's argument, a document which did not come into exis-

*Lloyd George, ii, p 1272

tence until 5 July, and was then addressed, not to the Government, but to the Army Commanders.

Fortunately, however, Hankey's notes of the proceedings are now available for inspection, and supply some valuable correctives to Lloyd George's version. All the members of the War Policy Committee were present, joined by the Conservative leader and Leader of the House of Commons, Mr Andrew Bonar Law. Robertson and Haig also attended throughout.

> Cabinet Papers, CAB 27/6; 7th Meeting of the Cabinet Committee on War Policy, 19 June, 11 am

The Prime Minister said that Sir Douglas Haig's Memorandum of 17 June* together with his previous Memorandum of 12 June† provided a very powerful statement in favour of the plans he wished to carry out.

Sir Douglas Haig stated that he was making his preparations on the lines indicated in the Memoranda to give effect to the instructions of the War Cabinet. (The Committee then adjourned to a raised map which Sir Douglas Haig had brought with him, and the Field-Marshal explained his plans in full detail.)

In a further bracket the security-conscious Hankey adds that he did not consider it advisable to reproduce the detailed plans in his secretarial Notes. Lloyd George, in his memoirs, provides a tableau at this juncture:

> When Sir Douglas Haig explained his projects to the civilians, he spread on a table or desk a large map and made a dramatic use of both his hands to demonstrate how he proposed to sweep up the enemy – first the right hand brushing along the surface irresistibly, and then came the left, his outer finger ultimately touching the German frontier with the nail across.‡

In Douglas Haig: The Educated Soldier I wrote: 'Lloyd George never forgave that finger-nail.' Now, however, with the Notes of the meeting before me, what strikes me is that at the time neither Lloyd George himself, nor any of his colleagues, appears to have noticed the wandering finger, or questioned its meaning (or lack of meaning) in any way. Was all this only another play of Lloyd George's lively imagination?

At any rate, Haig concluded his exposition with another plea that his army should be kept up to strength in men and guns, and with the firm statement that:

*O.A.D. 502, pp 137–40
†O.A.D. 478, pp 131–35
‡Lloyd George, ii, p 1277

Both the French and the Belgians were in agreement on the plan and were ready to co-operate.

The Committee then discussed the relative numbers of the various combatants on the Western Front.

A short discussion on manpower and gun-power followed, with Haig producing evidence of a certain deterioration in the German artillery, and both he and Robertson also referring to evidence that the Germans were having difficulty in maintaining their supply of ammunition.

The Prime Minister remarked that this was a very satisfactory piece of information. He pointed out that the Allies' superiority in men was only 15 per cent and without the Belgians and Portuguese it was only 10 per cent. In heavy guns we had no superiority at all. He then asked Sir Douglas Haig for an estimate of the losses he anticipated in the offensive as planned, and he reminded him that on the Somme our losses had amounted to an average of 100,000 a month.

Sir Douglas Haig said that his original estimate had been for a loss at the rate of 100,000 men a month. He was encouraged, however, to hope for less losses, owing to the small rate of loss of some of the divisions engaged at the Battle of Messines. In one corps the three divisions had reported respectively only 40, 50 and 90 dead.

The Prime Minister reminded the Committee that the total British losses since 7 April were not much less than 200,000, which was not very far short of 100,000 a month.

A brief discussion of the Battle of Arras then took place, with Haig pointing out that heavy casualties had been incurred through the British having to go on attacking in order to support Nivelle in accordance with the Calais agreement.

Lord Curzon asked if Sir Douglas Haig had enough men apart from guns to carry the operation through?

Sir Douglas Haig said he was prepared to start with the men now at his disposal, but he wished to occupy a certain position ('Clercken Ridge' later pencilled in the margin) before he proceeded with the operation. He said that the plan promised success, although, of course, no soldier could say that any operation of war was a certainty. He pointed out that it was only the beginning of a very great strategical operation.

Lord Milner agreed in the importance of the operation, but said his only doubt was whether we could carry the entire operation through.

The Prime Minister said that the Committee were all agreed that it was a splendid conception and they would like to undertake it. Their only doubt was whether it was practicable at the present time.

General Smuts pointed out that the answer was supplied by the last paragraph of W.P. 3* as follows:

'A definition of the term "sufficient force" must depend on developments in the general situation; but provided that does not grow less satisfactory than at present I estimate that even the full programme may not prove beyond reach with the number of divisions at my disposal, if brought up to and maintained at establishment in men and guns. An increase in the forces available would, of course, give still greater prospects of complete success.'

A short and somewhat desultory discussion then ensued on the subjects of, first, a disappointing short-fall in British gun-production, and secondly, French and German manpower reserves.

Thereafter, however, the proceedings became much more business-like, sticking to the main point, and I propose to give them at length, precisely as reported by Hankey.

Lord Curzon asked that the following questions might be answered:

1. What are the forces at Sir Douglas Haig's disposal for his proposed operations?
2. Could Sir William Robertson guarantee to maintain that force with men and guns?
3. Was there any prospect of obtaining the additional forces which Sir Douglas Haig said were required to give still greater prospects of complete success?

Sir Douglas Haig said that he was concentrating 42 divisions in the North. A large proportion of these had not been engaged this year in offensive operations on our front. He was also encouraged by the relatively easy success at the Messines Ridge which, instead of weakening the divisions engaged had gone far to strengthen their morale. He stated that the French had placed 6 divisions and the guns and aeroplanes of an Army under his command for this operation. The Belgians would also co-operate, but would not be called on to advance until a comparatively late stage of the first phase of the operation. Including the French and Belgians the total force available for the operation would be 54 divisions.

Lord Curzon pressed that an answer might be given to his second question.

Sir William Robertson stated that he anticipated no difficulty in the supply of ammunition, and that we might hope to keep the present number of guns of the more important natures up to strength, provided none were sent elsewhere. As regards men, the Army in France is now 20,000 to 30,000 men below establishment. Between now and the middle of August the War Office hoped to be able to send 150,000 men. He considered the position to be sufficiently favourable to justify undertaking the operations in the manner proposed by the Field-Marshal

*O.A.D. 478 was indexed as War Policy Document No. 3.

Commanding-in-Chief, that is to say, to proceed methodically and consider the situation before making each fresh bound. As to additions, he proposed to send the 67th Division from home, as the Canadians were not inclined to send their 5th Division.

Sir Douglas Haig pointed out that if the War Cabinet ordered a defensive attitude to be adopted until next spring the first phase of the proposed operation was necessary in order to protect Dunkirk, which is now an important base, against long range bombardment.

Mr Bonar Law asked whether, supposing the Germans concentrated the bulk of their forces in front of us the French would be able to spare any troops or to make a big effort to support us.

Sir Douglas Haig referred the answer to this question to the Prime Minister.

The Prime Minister said that according to his information they could not be counted on to make any very great effort.

Sir Douglas Haig said that General Pétain had given him an undertaking that he would attack simultaneously on a front of 25 kilos. The bombardment, in the event of such an attack, would last for a week or two. The result of all experience in recent offensives has been to show that it was useless to allow the infantry to advance until artillery superiority had been gained. The necessities for a successful infantry attack were supremacy (a) in the air and (b) in the preliminary artillery battle. As regards the deficiency of the French in infantry it must be borne in mind that a long preliminary bombardment mystified the enemy so that he never knew what was coming or when an infantry attack would develop, and was obliged to maintain reserves to meet it.

The Prime Minister asked Sir Douglas Haig how many divisions he proposed to employ simultaneously for the capture of his first objective.

Sir Douglas Haig said he would require about 12 divisions, including two French divisions on the (North) left flank, and British divisions in the protection of the right flank. It would be impossible to employ the whole of his 42 divisions simultaneously at the outset of this attack. He contemplated employing at most 12 divisions at the outset, and then another 12 to relieve them.

Lord Milner asked whether he might not have to use the whole of his 42 divisions in order to reach his first objective?

The Prime Minister remarked that this would imply a failure of the attack.

Sir Douglas Haig reminded the Committee that on the Vimy Ridge one division had advanced six miles and captured three fortified villages without a check, and without of course being relieved.

The Prime Minister asked whether this was not due to the fact that the Arras attack was a surprise?

Sir Douglas Haig said that that might be the case but one received very conflicting reports from the enemy. He had it in writing that the enemy's failure at Arras was attributed to his delay in starting counter-battery work.

Mr Bonar Law asked whether the German divisions, which Sir Douglas Haig showed on a map to be very thick in the region of Arras, could not be brought up against his new front very rapidly.

Sir Douglas Haig pointed out that the relief of a division in the front line takes time and also that the enemy's railway communications were not very numerous between the particular front selected and the proposed point of our own attack.* At present the enemy only had 13 'fresh' and 35 'used' divisions in Reserve. (He then gave the Committee a full explanation on a map of the position of the German divisions and reserves.)

The Prime Minister said that he was sure the Germans would fight desperately for the defence of the position Sir Douglas Haig proposed to attack, and he suggested that the British army would really be engaged against the main strength of Germany.

Sir Douglas Haig pointed out that the question had also to be considered of how many divisions the Germans could employ on the ground. As far as Ostend our communications were superior to those of the enemy. Another consideration was the morale of the troops.† That of the Germans in front of us was poor. At Messines the Germans had known we were about to attack and had made every preparation to resist us and had determined to hold the position, but, nevertheless, had been completely defeated.

Lord Curzon asked whether Sir Douglas Haig could rely on General Pétain to act with sufficient vigour to hold the Germans in front of him?

Sir Douglas Haig said that General Pétain declared that he could operate in such a way as to do more than hold them.

The Prime Minister questioned the value of the French attack. He said the Germans would probably believe that General Pétain did not intend to press it and would arrange their forces accordingly. General Pétain's operations might be of some value, but not equal to a really decisive attack to meet which the enemy would have to mass great reserves.

Sir Douglas Haig said that General Pétain's operations were very different from those designed by General Nivelle, in which he had never had much confidence.

Lord Curzon pointed out that if Sir Douglas Haig's plan were adopted, it would be the great and decisive move of this year. At the end of it we should be practically exhausted for the year, and in making our decision we must remember that it would be the supreme military effort for 1917. He understood Sir Douglas Haig's case to be that there was no other theatre where such good results could be achieved, that the conditions were favourable, and that we should, therefore, act here and now.

*This is one of many passages corrected by Haig, usually in the interests of clarity. In this case, however, the meaning remains obscure.
† A summary of impressions by a member of the American Relief Committee in Belgium is appended, with the conclusion: 'The morale of the German troops is bad; they realize they are beaten, but live in the hopes that something will turn up to save them from disaster.' The report cites deterioration of uniforms and reduced rations.

Sir Douglas accepted this summary of his case, except that in his view the Army would be by no means exhausted by the operation. If we did not attack this year the enemy would; we should then probably lose the same number of men and guns without any advantage.

The Prime Minister disputed this and quoted the statement in regard to ammunition as an answer to Sir Douglas Haig. He felt no doubt that we could hold the enemy even if he did attack.

Sir Douglas Haig said the plan he had explained to the Committee was the best he knew of. It was necessary for us to go on engaging the enemy. He was quite confident he could reach the first objective he had mentioned, although nothing was certain in war, and he could give no absolute guarantee. He believed his troops were also confident. In regard to the distance to be crossed in order to reach his objective he again reminded the Committee of the incident of Vimy Ridge, where one division had advanced six miles without stopping.

The Prime Minister reminded Sir Douglas Haig that at that time the Germans were awaiting a tremendous attack by General Nivelle, and had concentrated very large forces to meet it. On this occasion, however, they would anticipate our attack and concentrate their forces in front of us, because they would not believe that General Pétain meant business. He pointed out that by the time the first objective had been reached even if this took no more than a month, which was a sanguine estimate judging by previous experience, there would not be very much more time for further fighting before the weather rendered it impossible. It was clear that we must make all our efforts in this offensive or else attack elsewhere.

Sir William Robertson agreed that we must make our full effort if we undertook the operation at all.

Sir Douglas Haig also agreed. He said that this was the decisive point, and that everything must be concentrated here. He then referred to two alternative minor attacks which he had prepared as part of the general policy of wearing out the enemy.

Mr Bonar Law said that the problem for the Committee to decide was whether we should get enough out of this attack to justify it.

Lord Milner said that to get the enemy away from the Belgian coast was worth half a million men.

Lord Curzon then referred to two memoranda that had been circulated by the First Sea Lord, putting certain naval considerations which, in his view, had weight.

The Prime Minister said the question really was whether we should do this operation this year or postpone it to another year. He asked whether, supposing the Government decided that they could not find the means of carrying out the whole operation, Sir Douglas Haig could only carry out the first part of the operation.

Sir Douglas Haig replied in the affirmative. All he had told his Army Commanders was that our objective was the Ridge which he had indicated on the raised map, but that further developments would depend upon the general situation.

General Smuts said that as he understood Sir Douglas Haig's proposal it was first to aim at the first objective he had named, which, having regard to the morale of our troops and the morale of the enemy he considered he ought to be able to get. When he had captured that position he would be in a good position for considering further operations.

Sir Douglas Haig concurred in this statement.

General Smuts then inquired as to the possibility of using our aerial superiority to bomb the enemy's communications.

Sir Douglas Haig replied that the communications were very favourable for bombing. Moreover, owing to the flatness of the country our aerial supremacy could be very effectively utilized for artillery observation.

General Smuts then summed up the advantages of the proposed expedition (sic) as follows:

1. We should be working towards a very valuable ultimate objective:
2. We should protect Dunkirk:
3. We should be operating in a region where the enemy's communications were not very good.:
4. Our aerial superiority could be used very effectively.

Sir Douglas Haig concurred. He pointed out, however, that it was always necessary to wear down the enemy before we could hope to exploit any success.

General Smuts agreed in this, but said that if you could have a strategical objective at the same time it was an obvious advantage.

Lord Milner pointed out that while we were wearing the enemy down he was also wearing us down.

General Smuts then raised the question as to whether the German losses are heavier than ours and asked what evidence there was of this?

Sir Douglas Haig said they had the evidence of the captured company rolls, which all pointed in one direction.

General Smuts pointed out that the latest estimate of our losses since 7 April was 182,000; the French were somewhat greater. So that the Allied total was about 400,000. The Germans had lost about 70,000 prisoners to us; supposing their losses to have been on the same scale as those of the Allies they must have lost half a million men.

Sir Douglas Haig said that he understood that the Chief of the Imperial General Staff had received an estimate from a neutral country somewhat similar to this. (There was then some discussion on the subject of the German casualty lists and the question of their correctness or otherwise.)

The Prime Minister asked General Robertson and Sir Douglas Haig to realize our own difficulties in regard to manpower. We were now reduced to the point where we had to scrape up men where we could. Every time we scraped any in there was trouble in the House of Commons or a strike. The last strike, which had been due to calling up men from munition works, had lasted three weeks and had seriously put back the output of Sir Douglas Haig's guns. Then we had ordered a medical re-examination of rejected men. The result of this was that on Thursday in the House of Commons there would be the severest attack on the War Office that had yet been delivered. If we dip in one place for recruits they said: No, these are agricultural men; and so it was everywhere. All the newspapers without regard to party joined in the agitation. There was no place from which we could take men in large quantities without facing a serious trouble. He could assure Sir Douglas Haig that the Committee were most anxious to support him. They recognized that his brilliant successes had given him a right to demand their support. The Russian Revolution, however, had had a very unsettling effect in all countries, and there was a good deal of talk of revolution everywhere. He was rather afraid of being drawn into a military enterprise before we were ready for it. He did not want to fail, and did not want to go in for it unless he was sure that it could be carried through. The alternative was to face a tremendous row in the country in regard to men. The real question was whether we should undertake the operation this year or next year.* In this connection he asked Sir William Robertson and Sir Douglas Haig to bear in mind that on the Allied side we were sustaining the whole burden of the War. The United States of America had not yet developed their resources, and by the end of the year would not have more than 150,000 or 160,000 men in France. The burden on us, therefore, was very great, and it was very important not to break the country. Yesterday the Committee had been considering the shipping situation, and there again the demand for men was more insistent every day. He wanted the country to be able to last. He did not want to have to face a Peace Conference some day with our country weakened while America was still overwhelmingly strong, and Russia had perhaps revived her strength. He wanted to reserve our strength till next year. He quite understood Sir Douglas Haig's point of view, but the Committee had to consider whether it would not be better to hold our hand until the French Army had been resuscitated by the intervention of America.

Haig Diary: Blake pp 239–40

TUESDAY, 19 JUNE . . . I saw the CIGS at 10.45 am and then walked to Lord Curzon's Office (Privy Council) for a meeting of the War Cabinet at 11 am. We discussed the military situation till 1 o'clock when the Prime Minister left to marry his daughter. The members of the War Cabinet asked me numerous questions, all tending to show that each of them was more pessimistic than the other. The Prime Minister seemed to believe the decisive moment of the war would be 1918. Until then we ought to husband our forces and do little or nothing, except support Italy

*Lloyd George probably hoped that if the Flanders offensive were deferred his own plan for a knock-out blow at Austria would be carried out, and the Central Powers would then collapse. He must later have deeply wished that this sentence could be struck out of the record.

with guns and gunners (300 batteries was the figure indicated). I strongly asserted that Germany was nearer her end than they seemed to think, that *now* was the favourable moment for pressing her and that everything possible should be done to take advantage of it by concentrating on the Western Front *all* available resources. I stated that Germany was within six months of the total exhaustion of her available manpower, *if the fighting continues at its present intensity*. To do this more men and guns are necessary.

Doris and I lunched with Philip* at his house in Park Lane. At 2.30 pm I had a talk with Sir William Robertson at the War Office and at 3 pm called on General Smuts by appointment at 2 Whitehall Gardens. I was with him till 4 pm. He does not know a great deal about strategy but is anxious to support Robertson and myself. The Prime Minister, he said, was afraid that my plan would exhaust the British Army by the winter, and without gaining victory.

Two meetings of the War Policy Committee took place on 20 June. The first was concerned with German air activity; a raid on London by Gotha bombers on 13 June had caused 162 deaths and injuries to a further 432 people. Public opinion and the Government were deeply disturbed, and at this meeting the Committee interrogated Major-General Trenchard closely on possible countermeasures. Trenchard spoke to a carefully prepared brief, only two paragraphs of which need now concern us.

Andrew Boyle, Trenchard, Collins, 1962, pp 221–2

The capture by us of the Belgian coast would be the most effective step of all, as, in addition to increasing the distance to be traversed, it would force the German machines either to cross territory occupied by us, when going and returning (a considerable advantage to us), or to cross neutral territory, where our Secret Service could doubtless establish means of giving us warning quickly.

The next most effective step is to inflict the utmost damage on the enemy's sheds and machines behind the Western Front. The amount which can be done is limited by the number and capacity of machines and pilots available in France. Increased activity on the Western Front serves the double purpose of assisting the armies in overcoming the enemy and at the same time reducing his power to send expeditions to England.

The Government nevertheless preferred to conciliate public opinion by withdrawing two fighter squadrons from the Royal Flying Corps in France, with the immediate effect of increased German air activity against the rear areas of the BEF.

*Sir Philip Sassoon.

The second War Policy Committee meeting (No. 9) began at noon, and continued the Flanders debate, the same people being present as on the previous day. Proceedings opened with a short discussion of German strengths before and after the Battle of the Somme, based on information supplied by Robertson. He then read a formal statement of his considered opinion of the relative merits of an attack on Austria and an offensive in Flanders. The full text of this statement is printed in the Appendices to Chapter LXIII of Lloyd George's *War Memoirs* (Odhams Edition, vol ii, pp 1461–3); here I propose only to summarize the now familiar arguments and quote the conclusion.

CAB 27/6

20 JUNE, 1917
2. Personally, I have been sceptical of Austria making a separate peace, as her whole future depends upon her relations with Germany to whose wheels she is tied in a variety of ways, economic, industrial, political, etc . . .
4. It would, of course, be a great advantage if we could completely dispose of Austria, but Germany knows this as well as we do and she may be depended upon to try and support Austria, if and when she is in danger.

Robertson then discusses the proposal to send 75 batteries of heavy artillery from the British front in France to Italy. The move would take not less than six weeks, and could not be concealed; furthermore,

We have but two railways into Italy, one of which – the Mont Cenis – is not very good, whereas the enemy has five . . . The enemy can therefore always hope to beat us, if he wishes to, in concentrating superior forces on the Italian front.

He develops the argument of Germany's advantage in possessing the interior lines, the hazards of being forced to assume the defensive in the West, and the need to encourage Russia, herself about to attempt a new offensive. He concludes:

9. The conclusion I have arrived at, taking the broadest possible view of the general situation, is that our chances of obtaining good results are certainly no greater in Italy than they are in the North, while the risks involved are much greater in the former place than in the latter. I deprecate as strongly as anyone our incurring heavy casualties without a corresponding return, but the plan as outlined by the Field-Marshal should secure us against this mistake. I have shown, and I understand the War Cabinet agree, that we must continue to be aggressive somewhere on our front, and we ought of course to do this in the most promising

direction. The plan provides for this and will enable us to derive a real advantage till the enemy shows signs of weakening, while at the same time it permits of our easing off if the situation so demands. No doubt the enemy will fight as hard as he possibly can, and he will use as many troops and guns as he possibly can, but he will also do these things on the Italian Front rather than see Austria decisively defeated. I do not for one moment think that Germany is as yet near the end of her resources in men or material. I think she may yet take a great deal of beating, and that it is necessary France should be aggressive as well as ourselves. On the other hand, Germany may be much nearer exhaustion, both on the fronts and at home, than we imagine, and there are many indications of this. Doubtful situations such as the present one have always arisen in war, and great mistakes have been made by endeavouring to find a fresh way round as soon as the strain begins to be felt.* We should be on our guard against this mistake.

10. I am therefore in favour of continuing our present plan on the chance of getting a success in the north, not only because of the military situation but also because of the necessity of trying to improve the air and sea situation, and I am consequently averse from diverting any of our resources to Italy. We should, however, do all we can to provide Italy with means for increasing her ammunition supply, as she already has far more guns than she can keep employed, and in this connection I would remind the War Cabinet that there is no reason why Italy should remain inactive throughout the winter, as operations can continue on the Isonzo up to the end of January.

Lord Curzon asked whether, by the last paragraph, Sir William Robertson meant that we could, if we wished, help the Italians at some later date?

Sir William Robertson replied that we could consider it.

Sir Douglas Haig said that his views had been asked as to the expediency of delaying our main attack as planned by him until 1918 in order that the British army might still be strong in that year. He himself knew the situation at the present moment, but could not forecast the future. He considered the present moment favourable. He was fully in agreement with the Committee that we ought not to push in attacks that had not a reasonable chance of success, and that we ought to proceed step by step. He himself had no intention of entering into a tremendous offensive involving heavy losses. His plan was aggressive without committing us too far.

(Sir Douglas Haig then read the following paper . . .)

Like Robertson's, Haig's memorandum is printed in Lloyd George's memoirs in full (pp 1464–6); like Robertson's, it covers much familiar ground, so I propose to treat it in the same fashion.

Haig begins with a fairly detailed examination of German strengths and

*Lloyd George here notes: 'Where? Scipio – Sherman – Wellington.' It is a pity he offers no explanation of this note.

dispositions on the Western Front, railway capacities, etc, drawing him to the conclusion that

The Allies will have a considerable superiority in infantry on the front of attack – probably not less than two to one . . .

In guns and ammunition, judging by experience and information from captured orders, etc, our superiority will be even greater; while in the air we may regard our superiority as still more assured. The last mentioned factor is of immense importance from the points of view of artillery efficiency, information, damage behind the enemy's lines, and general morale.*

Turning to the proposed attack on Austria, he says this:

It has always been accepted as the most effective form of war to attack and destroy the enemy's strongest forces as soon as possible if there is a reasonable prospect of success. If there is not a reasonable prospect of success the next best course is to weaken the enemy by holding his main forces and attacking his weaker ones, if that be possible. The possibility depends, however, firstly on being able to hold his main forces, and secondly, on being able to defeat his weaker ones.

If we were to detach largely to Italy it is probable that we could still hold the Germans on the Western Front, but it is not certain and it would depend much on the French.

It is at best very uncertain that we could defeat Austria.

Haig then repeats Robertson's argument of the advantage of the interior lines, adding a fresh thought with the hint that, against Germans at any rate, the Italians might prove not to be entirely trustworthy. He concludes:

A decision to transfer troops to Italy would mean abandonment of our offensive in Belgium; a consequent gain of time to Germany; very dangerous disappointment in France and to some extent in Russia; small prospects of success against Austria supported in all probability by German troops; a possibility of reverses on the Western Front; and a possibility of still more serious reverses on the Italian Front.

Against all this we have a reasonable chance of success in Belgium which may have greater results than even a bigger success against Austria, and which at least may be expected to open the way for greater results subsequently.

It is not impossible that Germany aims at inducing us to detach from the Western Front – that is a very usual form of war, often employed with telling

*This proved to be all-too-sadly true, as we shall see.

effect. But whether she is deliberately trying so to induce us or not, there seems no doubt that our wisest and soundest course is to continue to wear down the German forces on the Western Front, as we are undoubtedly able to do.

Lord Curzon asked whether, when Sir Douglas spoke of having a reasonable chance of success, he merely meant that he expected to capture his first objective?

Sir Douglas Haig replied that he referred to the complete operation which he had explained to the Committee on the previous day.

Lord Curzon then pressed that the First Sea Lord should be called in to explain his case.

The Prime Minister and Lord Milner both said that they were quite satisfied with the case as made out by the First Sea Lord in the papers he had circulated to them.

The Prime Minister said he had no doubt whatsoever about the desirability of carrying out Sir Douglas Haig's plans if it [sic] was reasonably likely to succeed and was practicable.

General Smuts said that he had had a long talk with the First Sea Lord in order to ascertain what importance he attached to the proposed operations. Admiral Jellicoe had replied that, in his paper, he had, if anything, understated the case. He himself had not up till then been aware of the extent to which the Germans could use the bases on the Belgian coast.

(The First Sea Lord entered at this point).

Admiral Jellicoe, in reply to Lord Curzon, who asked him to develop the case he had made in the two papers circulated to the Committee, said that two points were in his mind, the first was that immense difficulties would be caused to the Navy if by the winter the Germans were not excluded from the Belgian coast. He could not develop the reasons for this better than he had already done in the papers circulated.* The position would become almost impossible if the Germans realized the use they could make of these ports. The enemy already had 3 squadrons of destroyers based on Zeebrugge and might increase them to six. If he came out in a concentrated force he could wipe the ships on patrol out of existence. The largest force which he had hitherto sent out at a time was one flotilla, and that was divided. If he came out concentrated he could sweep up the naval forces on patrol, which never exceeded a strength of 7 destroyers and 2 flotilla leaders. He could also attack the French craft, monitors, and the cross-channel coastal traffic.

In reply to Mr Bonar Law, the First Sea Lord said that about one dozen small German submarines were based on the Belgian coast. They were situated so close to our East Coast war channel that they could operate there every night, and we had information to show that their minelaying submarines carried out a regular routine. These mines were a constant danger to our patrols, and only last week we had lost a destroyer from this cause. The second point he felt was that if we did not clear the Germans out of Zeebrugge before this winter we should have great

*Listed as W.P. 10 and W.P. 11.

difficulty in ever getting them out of it. The reason he gave for this was that he felt it to be improbable that we could go on with the war next year for lack of shipping.

The First Sea Lord also pointed out that the German position on the Belgian coast was very bad from the point of view of our air position. For the moment we had lost the command of the air over the sea as the Germans had a better seaplane than we had. Only yesterday two of our seaplanes had been destroyed by the enemy and the Rear-Admiral Commanding at Dover said he could not maintain an aerial seaplane patrol without better machines.

The Prime Minister said that the most serious point in Admiral Jellicoe's remarks was the statement that we could not continue the war next year for lack of shipping.* This statement made in such a quarter must be tested. If it was accurate then we should have far more important decisions to consider than our plans of operations for this year, namely, the best method of making tracks for peace.

Admiral Jellicoe adhered to his statement and quoted in support of it a paper by the Shipping Controller. He also asserted that he had made a similar statement before the War Cabinet earlier in the year.

The Secretary then produced War Cabinet 85, Minute 8, which was the statement referred to by the First Sea Lord, but the Prime Minister pointed out that it was a much less formidable statement than that which Admiral Jellicoe had just made.†

Haig Diary: Blake, pp 240–1

A most serious and startling situation was disclosed today. At today's Conference, Admiral Jellicoe, as First Sea Lord, stated that owing to the great shortage of shipping due to German submarines, it would be impossible for Great Britain to continue the war in 1918. This was a bombshell for the Cabinet and all present. A full enquiry is to be made as to the real facts on which this opinion of the Naval Authorities is based. No one present shared Jellicoe's view, and all seemed satisfied that the food reserves in Great Britain are adequate. Jellicoe's words were, 'There is no good discussing plans for next Spring – We cannot go on.'

Lloyd George, ii, pp 1298–1304
CAB 27/6: Tenth Meeting of the Cabinet Committee on War Policy, 21 June

It was at the tenth meeting of the War Policy Committee, on 21 June, that Lloyd George put forward his case against the Flanders offensive and

---

*In his *War Memoirs* Lloyd George says: 'This startling and reckless declaration I challenged indignantly, but the First Sea Lord adhered to it.'
† In War Cabinet 85, Minute 8 (2 March, 1917; CAB 23/2) we find:
'The possibility of continuing to the end of 1917 and during 1918 would depend mainly on the extent to which we could guarantee the food supply of the United Kingdom by setting aside a definite reserve of ships for this purpose, and on the possibility of reducing the obligations of the Navy and of our shipping on the various overseas campaigns, as advocated in the First Sea Lord's Memorandum of 21 February.'

in favour of the attack on Austria with the greatest effect. In his memoirs he quotes the speech he delivered that day at great length, using the secretary's notes transposed back into the first person singular. It will be seen that it falls into two distinct parts: the argument *against* Flanders is very powerful indeed, and hindsight, of course, lends it even greater weight; the argument for attacking Austria, however, tends somewhat to weaken the force of the previous section, giving it an air of special pleading, and hindsight here turns against Lloyd George. Despite its great length, because of its importance I have thought it best to reproduce it *in extenso*, putting the sections from CAB 27/6 in square brackets. Lloyd George said:

I had devoted many hours of anxious consideration to the plans put forward by Field-Marshal Sir Douglas Haig, and supported by the Chief of the Imperial General Staff, and on the previous evening I had discussed the question very fully with my colleagues. I felt that at this stage it would be desirable to make Sir Douglas Haig and Sir William Robertson acquainted with the conclusions which I had reached, and I expressed the hope that they would give careful thought and full weight to the considerations which I was going to place before them. My view was that the responsibility for advising in regard to military operations must remain with the military advisers. Speaking for myself, and I had little doubt that my colleagues agreed with me in this, I considered it would be too great a responsibility for the War Policy Committee to take the strategy of the War out of the hands of the military. This made it more important that the military advisers of the Government should carefully weigh my misgivings as the head of the Government in regard to the advice they had tendered. If, after hearing my views, and after taking time to consider them, they still adhered to their previous opinion, then, subject to the condition they had themselves suggested as to breaking off the attack if it did not work out in accordance with expectation, we would not interfere and prevent the attempt.

I entreated Sir Douglas Haig and Sir William Robertson to remember that a most momentous decision had now to be taken and that a wrong step might bring disaster to the cause of the Allies.

The first point which I raised was that I felt somewhat disturbed at the recent change of attitude on the part of the Chief of the Imperial General Staff. I reminded the Committee that at the Paris Conference of 4 and 5 May, I had discussed the question with Sir William Robertson and the latter had himself felt some misgivings in regard to aggressive operations unless the French were able to co-operate with a strong offensive. My own doubts at that time had been due to the collapse in Russia and the consequent ineffectiveness of the Russian Army and the opposition of Generals Alexeieff* and Pétain. General Robertson, how-

*Russian Chief of General Staff.

ever, had expressed the view that if the French would undertake really serious offensive operations, by which he meant some such operations as our own, calculated to hold a fair proportion of the German reserves on the French Front, then he was prepared to agree to an offensive.

[Although the Prime Minister's own misgivings had not been entirely removed, he had, nevertheless, subordinated his views to those of the military advisers, and he felt sure that General Robertson and Field-Marshal Sir Douglas Haig would both recognize that he had fought their policy right through at the Paris Conference.* When he had arrived at Paris, General Pétain had made promises almost identical with those which he now made, namely, to make considerable attacks on fairly wide fronts, but he had been unwilling to attempt anything on a large scale. General Robertson had advised that this was not sufficient, and that it would be folly to undertake a big attack unless the French really meant business. The Prime Minister had based his attitude at the Conference on this advice, and had insisted on a written undertaking by the French Government to continue the offensive on the Western Front in accordance with the principles agreed to by Generals Pétain, Nivelle, Robertson and Field-Marshal Haig.]

Now General Pétain had found himself obliged, for reasons which were really beyond his control, and for which he could not be blamed, to go back on his undertaking. In consequence, there had been no big French offensive operation in concert with the attack on the Messines Ridge. Hence, it appeared to me that Sir William Robertson had made a very serious change in his advice in agreeing to Sir Douglas Haig's plan, which involved the commitment of 42 divisions in an attempt to fight right through to a depth of 20 miles, while the French contented themselves with relatively minor operations further to the south.

I then turned to an examination of the prospects of success. I pointed out that failure would be a very serious business. All the world would recognize, if Sir Douglas Haig only succeeded in reaching his first objective, that our operations had failed to realize their full scope. I felt that we were not in a position to play with the disintegrating forces that were operating in all belligerent countries on both sides, but more especially on the side of the Allies, owing to the hopeless position of Russia. Every one would know that we were aiming at a much greater prize than Sir Douglas Haig's first objective and that the real object of our operations was to clear the Belgian coast. Only that morning I had noticed an extract from the *Frankfürter Zeitung*, which showed that our intentions were already realized in Germany. [If we only succeeded in advancing 7, 8, or 10 miles, and we sustained heavy casualties while the enemy remained unbroken in front of us, the effect would be very bad throughout the world.]

In reckoning up our chances of success I pointed out that we must advance 15 miles before we could really begin the first operation for freeing the Belgian coast. What reason, I asked, was there to believe that we could first drive the enemy

*See pp 86–8.

back 15 miles and then capture a place ten miles away? For a success on this scale one of the following conditions was essential:
1. An overwhelming force of men and guns.
2. That the enemy should be attacked so strongly elsewhere that his reserves would be drawn off;
3. That the enemy's morale should be so broken that he could no longer put up a fight.

None of the above conditions obtained at that time.

The numerical superiority of the Allies on the Western Front, including 25,200 Portuguese, 18,000 Russians, who were forming Committees and talking revolution, and 131,000 Belgians [who were not first class troops], did not exceed 15 per cent. More than this, however, the French did not in their present temper count as available for any offensive enterprise on a great scale. They were a little out of hand and wanted rest, so that the French Government had been obliged to grant them extended leave. In comparing the value of the French and German soldier, it had to be remembered that the French soldiers represented one out of six of the population,* whereas the Germans only included one out of eleven, which must make a difference in quality. The French Army included all kinds of material in the line that were on the ration strength but did not constitute soldiers.

[Lord Curzon suggested that Colonel Spiers had not painted quite so dismal a picture as the Prime Minister in regard to the morale of the French Army.

The Prime Minister said that he himself had certainly drawn the conclusion from the evidence of General Wilson and Colonel Spiers that the French Army would not be ready for some time to put really heavy pressure on the enemy. It had to be borne in mind that they had really never had a victory.†]

I myself did not pose as an expert in strategy but, nevertheless, I understood that an overwhelming superiority in men and material was agreed by all strategists as essential to success in an offensive, particularly under modern conditions. I agreed that we might very likely make a success of a first attack, but assaults on the German lines were like hitting india-rubber.

I reminded the Committee that during nearly three years of war I had never known an offensive to be undertaken without sure predictions of success. Similar reasons to those given now had always been adduced as to why we should do better than last time, and I had always been told that by applying the lessons of the past we should succeed. This experience had not unnaturally made me feel sceptical. On this occasion I was more especially sceptical, owing to the lack of numerical superiority, to which I had already alluded. I pointed out that in heavy guns we were barely equal to the enemy. It was true that we were told we had a good deal more ammunition than the Germans, but I asked whether the Germans

*De la Gorce (*The French Army*, p 103) says that 7,800,000 Frenchmen were called up, 'or about one-fifth of the total population', but this includes men mobilized for agriculture and munition factories. By comparison, the total enlistments of the British Empire were 9,496,170, of which the United Kingdom accounted for 6,211,427.
† Apparently it occurred to no one to change this extraordinary statement.

had not ample supplies of ammunition for the defensive. According to my experience, in the present war, something like a superiority of five shells to one was required for the offensive as compared with the defensive. To try and break the enemy's army with no material superiority in men or guns, with no adequate support from the French, with Russia broken, with the Germans able to exchange fresh divisions brought from the Eastern Front for the divisions already shattered on the Western Front – (a point which appeared to me to have been lost sight of in those calculations) – why should we succeed? I asked why we should anticipate a greater measure of success on this occasion than in the Battle of the Somme, where we had only succeeded in making a dent of five or six miles? Yet our military advisers were just as sanguine then as they were now.

I said I was told that the experience of Arras and Messines rendered success more likely. I agreed that these operations had both been very brilliant. In both, however, there had been an element of surprise. I reminded the Committee, however, that in the case of the Battle of Arras, the main attack was to have been delivered by the French further to the south, and consequently the bulk of the German reserves had been accumulated in front of General Nivelle's main attack. [Moreover, after the first victory at Arras our troops had made no serious advance.

Sir Douglas Haig interpolated that the moment he realized that the French attack had failed he desisted from following up his success.

The Prime Minister said that in that case he would withdraw this point. Nevertheless] in my view all that the Battle of Arras demonstrated was that with surprise you could obtain an advance of five or six miles. It provided, however, no illustration or proof of what you could do when the Germans were concentrating their main reserves behind their lines, as they would to meet the attack now contemplated. In regard to the Battle of the Messines Ridge, I pointed out that the mines had provided an element of surprise.

A brief and unilluminating discussion then followed between Lloyd George and Haig about the extent to which the mines had taken the Germans by surprise at Messines. The Prime Minister remained unshaken in the belief that neither Messines nor Arras offered

[ground on which to base a confident anticipation of success in the proposed operations. It was true that you might conceivably obtain a success, namely, the clearance of the Belgian coast.

The chances, however, were against such a success.] The cost in human life would be very heavy, and failure would react widely at home and abroad, while the Army would be seriously weakened. [He was afraid that the effect might be similar to that produced by the German attack on Verdun. There the enemy had had an overwhelming superiority in artillery, but the French, by constantly changing their men, had succeeded in frustrating the attack. The Germans had made a steady advance, but had failed to reach their objective.* The effect had been absolutely disastrous in Germany; it had had a very bad effect on the morale of the German people, which had sunk to its lowest ebb; there had been universal discouragement and confidence in their military advisers had been lost. The success had been merely one of capturing posts, but there had been an entire failure to capture the real objective. This was precisely what he feared in connection with the coming attack, namely, that it would lower the morale of the people, weaken the Army, and, above all, undermine confidence in the military advisers on which the Government acted. [sic] For these reasons I urged the Chief of the Imperial General Staff and the Field-Marshal to pay me the compliment of considering the above case and of giving me an answer, not that day, but after they had taken a few days to think it over.

Concluding this part of my statement, I said that none of my colleagues, whether they were in favour of or opposed to the adoption of Sir Douglas Haig's plan, were sanguine of success.

I then said: The question will be asked: Does this rejection of Sir Douglas Haig's plan mean that we are to do no more fighting on the Western Front? The answer was in the negative. It was not the Committee's business to suggest alternatives, but that of the military advisers. Nevertheless, I would like to ask our military advisers to consider two alternatives.

The first of these was to adopt what might be called the Pétain tactics, namely a punch here and there and a process of wearing down the enemy by that means. We had plenty of ammunition and could punish the enemy heavily. Having in view the privations of the Germans, the prospect of a big reinforcement from America and a regeneration of the Russian Army, the enemy, feeling that time was against him, might be considerably damaged and discouraged by such a course.

The second alternative was to undertake an operation which was, in the first place military, and, in the second place, diplomatic, with the object of detaching Austria from Germany, namely an attack on the Austrian Front.

I felt that the fatal error which had been committed in the present war had been continually to attack where the enemy was strongest. Surely it was a mistake to deliberately aim our spear against the thickest part of the enemy's armour. If we had made efforts earlier in the War to knock out Austria we should be in a far

---

*Lloyd George was constitutionally incapable, then or at any other time, of grasping the reasoning behind Falkenhayn's offensive at Verdun: 'Within our reach behind the French sector of the Western Front there are objectives for the retention of which the French General Staff would be compelled to throw in every man they have. If they do so the forces of France will bleed to death – as there can be no question of a voluntary withdrawal – *whether we reach our goal or not.*' (My italics.) The German objective at Verdun in 1916 was thus neither the city nor the forts; it was the French Army itself – just as Grant had made the Army of Northern Virginia the objective of the Army of the Potomac in 1864–5, as Hiag and Joffre considered the German Army to be their objective in the 'wearing-out fight' on the Somme, and as the Germans should have clung to the Red Army as their objective in 1942, instead of pursuing the illusion of geographical gains. The difficulty, of course, with this attrition strategy is to make it seem real to public opinion and civilian government, both of which prefer simpler and more comprehensible targets on which to fasten attention.

better position now. I felt, however, that we had another chance of effecting this. There was not the smallest doubt that Austria was anxious to be out of the War. This was not a matter of conjecture, but of absolute knowledge. Austria, however, was not willing now to pay the price demanded by the Allies, although if another heavy blow were struck against her she might be brought to accept our terms. I pointed out the difficult internal situation of Austria, with about half her population disaffected. I compared it with the position that this country would occupy if Wales, Scotland, and either the South or the East of England had a hostile population, whilst only a patriotic and bellicose core remained in the centre. The account that had reached us of the sessions of the Austrian Chamber showed that the nation was sulky. This appeared to offer a special opportunity for a military and diplomatic success. The prize was far the biggest in sight. If Austria could be forced out of the War, Bulgaria and Turkey would automatically have to go out. [The umbilical cord of the Central Alliance would be cut and] no more ammunition would reach Bulgaria and Turkey and both would have to make terms. Next year the whole of the forces now locked up in Salonika, Mesopotamia and Egypt would be set free for operations on the Western Front. Moreover, Italy would then be bound to support us, for I did not contemplate co-operation with Italy without a bargain that, if Austria was reduced to terms, Italy should support us in our attacks against Germany. How then was this result to be accomplished?

[It was his belief that Trieste was the only thing which stood between Italy and a separate peace with Austria. He had reason to believe that Austria would be willing to cede the Trentino now, but not Trieste. If Trieste were captured Austria would have to appeal to a population that was half Slav to recapture it. They would refuse to do it. The Magyars also did not care about Trieste. Neither the Hungarian nor the Slav would sacrifice themselves to recover it.* The question arose as to whether success in this attack was feasible. Comparing it with Sir Douglas Haig's plan he pointed out that in order to achieve success in the latter our army must advance, first 15 miles, and then 10 miles. On the Italian Front, however, an advance of 7 miles or a little more would place Trieste at the mercy of the Allies. In their last attack the Italians had got to the foot of Mount Hermada. A successful attack on the Hermada front would place Trieste at their mercy.] I then pointed out that the Italians had enormous resources of men, but an insuf-

---

*This was another of Lloyd George's blind spots. A modern historian, Norman Stone (*The Eastern Front 1914–1917*, Hodder & Stoughton, 1975) writes: 'Italy was the major enemy as far as almost all the peoples of the Habsburg Empire was concerned. Czechs, Germans, Slovenes, Croats were alike enthusiastic to fight Italian pretensions . . . The heroic defence of the frontier against Italy had given the peoples of the Monarchy a cause that united them as no other did . . .' Closer to the time (*Out of my Life*, Cassell, 1920) Field-Marshal von Hindenburg put it even more succinctly: 'In Galicia . . . Austria-Hungary was fighting only with her head, whereas against Italy she was fighting with her whole soul.' Lloyd George himself, by the time he came to write his memoirs, no doubt with unpleasant memories of disputations at the Paris Peace Conference, preferred to leave out this predilection for taking Trieste. As late as 1945–6, its possession by Italy proved to be a serious bone of European contention.

ficiency of guns. The Austrians were unaccustomed to any bombardment on the scale experienced on the Western Front and probably the first time they were exposed to it they would succumb. Taking into consideration the great Italian preponderance of men, the addition of heavy guns that they lacked should give them a chance of success.

If success was achieved on the Italian Front, I believed that victory in the War was assured. A separate peace with Austria would then be practicable, and having eliminated Austria from the War, Germany would be at our mercy.

[He asked the Committee particularly to consider the effect of the Austrian operation on Russia. If Russia went out of the War while Austria still remained in we could not win. If the Eastern Armies of Germany were released we should have no chance of eventual victory. The United States of America might in time place half a million men in the field, but if Russia had gone out of the War, Germany could bring $1\frac{1}{2}$ million men to the Western Front.* The Allies could not bring so large a force from anywhere. We should then have an inferiority both in men and guns in the West and this meant defeat. Hence the vital necessity of the hour was to get Austria out of the War in order to give Sir Douglas Haig a chance of victory next year.]†

(Sir Douglas Haig, being asked by me at this stage whether he had any hope of victory this year, at once replied that in his view he would have a very good chance of victory this year. Only today he had received information that the German companies were from 50 to 70 strong as compared with an original establishment of 250, that a regiment (German 163rd) refused to attack on 18 June, that a proportion of men of the 1919 class were already in the companies at the front, etc.)

I welcomed Sir Douglas Haig's sanguine views, but did not personally attach great importance to this sort of information.

Continuing the main thread of my argument, I stated that I was very seriously alarmed about the Russian situation. [All our information showed that the position there was thoroughly bad. Only that morning he had read the statement of a Russian doctor who wished to enlist in the British Army, and who frankly stated that Russia was by now to all intents and purposes out of the War. This report was confirmed by all the information that reached us. If Russia made a separate peace, he would be almost inclined to agree with the First Sea Lord that the War could not be continued next year. At any rate, you could not in those conditions achieve complete victory.]

Our aim therefore should be to get Austria out. General Delmé-Radcliffe‡ had

*In fact matters worked out almost exactly opposite to this prognostication. Thanks to Ludendorff's Eastern ambitions, Germany was only able to bring some 500,000 men from East to West after the Peace of Brest-Litovsk, while American ration strength in France rose to 1,876,000 at the Armistice.
† This interesting paragraph is summarized in the *War Memoirs* as follows: 'I then called attention to the peril we should be in if Russia went out of the War leaving Austria still fighting. It might even endanger the prospect of ultimate victory.'
‡ British Liaison Officer with Italian GHQ.

expressed the view that, if we sent men and guns to the aid of the Italians, we could secure secrecy as to their movements, and had suggested various expedients for doing so. If the Germans came to the assistance of the Austrians, then you would be fighting them and wearing them out. [But this would be taking place at the expense of the Italians and not of our men.] Up to now, our losses, and those of the French, had been very heavy, but this was not the case with the Italians. It would be the first time that the Italian resources of manpower had been properly utilized to pull their weight in the War. The French and ourselves had no substantial numerical superiority over the Germans, and it would be very advisable for the Allies at last to make use of the great Italian superiority in men.

Lord Curzon remarked that the Italians themselves had entirely failed to make proper use of their great numerical superiority over the Austrians. I pointed out that this was due to the fact that the Italians never had any superiority in gun-fire until their last attack, and on that occasion they had been short of ammunition, and had been compelled to break off their attack for this reason. We, however, had the ammunition as well as the guns. I asked the Chief of the Imperial General Staff to take a day or two to think these matters over, and begged him carefully to weigh the points which I had put. Personally, I said, even if my colleagues agreed, I would not be willing to impose my strategical views on my military advisers, but I had felt that I would not be doing my duty if I concealed my great misgivings about the advice they had given. If, after full reflection, they advised against the suggestions I had propounded I would, nevertheless, support them. I felt, however, that we were at the parting of the ways. I believed that one course would lead to victory and the other course to a hopeless and costly struggle bringing us no nearer victory.

Sir W. Robertson said that the first note he had made had been to ask to have time to prepare his reply. He and Field-Marshal Sir Douglas Haig both fully appreciated the great responsibility which lay on me. He agreed that this might be the greatest decision in the War, and he wished to say that neither he nor Sir Douglas Haig resented any of my criticisms or suggestions. He would do his best to answer the questions, but he pointed out to the Committee that an officer of 41 years' soldiering is bound to base his views partly on military experience and instinct and knowledge of the service, and similar considerations which it was difficult to formulate briefly in writing.

[One point to which he wished to refer today was that of economy of our resources. The War Office had been hammering away at this subject for a long time, and only three months ago they had sent a letter to all Generals impressing on them the importance of this. They fully realized that we could not win and might lose unless we made the best use of everything, not only of men but supplies, material, horses, petrol, &c. This War was not being fought only by armies, and all waste and superfluities must be cut down to the utmost.

In order to make quite sure as to what the Prime Minister referred in his allegation of a change of advice, he restated the Prime Minister's proposition in a form agreed to by the Prime Minister.*

Lord Curzon asked that the following three minor points might be considered by General Robertson and Sir Douglas Haig:

1. If they adhere to the advice they have already given will they consider the possibilities of more active co-operation by the French, either tactically on the spot or elsewhere, and more particularly whether such co-operation could not be given after Sir Douglas Haig has succeeded in reaching his first objective?

2. The possibility that the Prime Minister's plan for an attack on the Italian Front, if not adopted at once, could be carried into execution a little later on?

3. The possibility and desirability of asking the French to send guns to Italy as well as ourselves?

General Smuts pointed out in regard to the second question that if it was suggested to the Italians that we might co-operate later they would do nothing. They ought, however, to attack the Hermada in concert with our attack in the North. They had the necessary superiority and ought to be able to capture it.]

The Committee then briefly discussed Long Distance Bombing Operations and favoured the proposal to bomb Mannheim.†

So ended a momentous meeting, at which Lloyd George had demonstrated his full strength as an advocate (Haig described it as 'a regular lawyer's effort to make black appear white'‡) and his weakness as a director of military policy (by comparison, for example, with his considerable skill as a director of domestic policy, soon to be tested to its limits). The debate, however, was by no means ended. What must strike the modern student with sadness is the extent to which a group of men, all of them responsible, patriotic and diversely talented, had fallen into opposite camps, barely capable of communicating with each other. Responsibility for this can only lie with the Prime Minister, and the deep mistrust which he had engendered at the Calais Conference and subsequently during his honeymoon with General Nivelle. This now meant that although the War Policy Committee would have to digest many more words, no departure was made on either side from positions already firmly adopted. One extremely serious aspect of this was that the evidently very different views of the condition of Germany held by Haig (based on Charteris) and Robertson (based on Macdonogh) were never properly discussed and resolved, because of their fear that any apparent

---

*The opacity of these two paragraphs suggests that Hankey was finding the strain of minuting both the Committee and the War Cabinet distinctly heavy.

†A reprisal for the raid on London as a sop to public opinion, against the advice of Trenchard.

‡Duff Cooper, ii, p 125

crack in their united front would be exploited by Lloyd George for his own purposes.

Haig was the first to draw up a reply to Lloyd George; he kept it relatively brief.

Author's Papers: W.P. 18, Haig to Robertson, 22 June

As desired by the Prime Minister I have given very careful thought to the views which he expressed yesterday at the meeting of the War Cabinet, when I had the honour of being present.

I am fully alive to the momentous effect which the decision now about to be taken by the Prime Minister and his colleagues must have on the future course of the war, and so on our Country.

I also thoroughly realize the grave responsibility which rests on me in tendering advice and formulating plans for operations on the Western front.

Consequently, in view of the deliberate opinion expressed by the Prime Minister that he has 'grave misgivings of the advice' which he had received from his Military Advisers, I have again most carefully reviewed the opinions which I have expressed in the various documents submitted to me since the 1st May last for the information of the War Cabinet.

This further investigation of the problem has confirmed me as strongly as ever in those opinions.

Once again Haig rests his case on his view of the state of the German Army, on his evidence of its numerical weakness, shortage of matériel and even food, due to the serious economic condition of Germany, and its declining morale, concluding:

In fact, the optimistic views I hold and the advice which I have given are justified by the present condition of our opponent's troops.

I therefore must confidently adhere to the advice which I have given to the War Cabinet, and which I summarized in my note of 12th inst. as follows: 'If our resources are concentrated in France to the fullest possible extent, the British Armies are capable, and can be relied on, to effect great results this summer – results which will make final victory more assured and which may even bring it within reach this year.'

On the other hand I am equally convinced that to fail in concentrating our resources on the Western theatre, or to divert them from it, would be most dangerous. It might lead to the collapse of France. It would certainly encourage Germany. And it would discourage our own Officers and men very considerably.

Robertson, whose post kept him in closer daily contact with Lloyd

George, felt that the latter's great oration had been, to a large extent, directed personally against himself. He wrote later:

> Field-Marshal Sir William Robertson, *Soldiers and Statesmen 1914–1918*, Cassell, 1926, p 242, f.n.

The procedure followed by this Committee was, I think, unique in the annals of military history, and it reminded one more of the Law Courts than a Council Chamber. Instead of being received as a military chief, the accuracy of whose views, so far as they were military, were not in dispute, I was made to feel like a witness for the defence under cross-examination, the Prime Minister appearing in the dual capacity of counsel for the prosecution and judge.

Robertson accordingly framed his reply to Lloyd George at much greater length and considerably more combatively than Haig. Once again, it covers much familiar ground, which I shall summarize. He deals first with Lloyd George's accusation that he had changed his attitude towards the Flanders offensive since the Paris Conference in May:

> W.P. 19, 23.VI.17; CAB 27/7

In the first place I submit that Sir D. Haig's plan does not involve 'the commitment of 42 divisions in an attempt to fight right through to a depth of 20 miles, while the French content themselves with relatively minor operations further to the South.'

I do not now, and I did not at Paris, advise aiming at distant objectives, *coûte que coûte*, but at wearing the enemy down 'and if and when this is achieved to exploit it to the fullest extent possible'. On the 20th instant I repeated that 'it is necessary the French should be aggressive as well as ourselves'. It is admitted by the War Cabinet that we must continue to be active somewhere on the Western Front, and I consider now, as I did at Paris, that Sir Douglas Haig's plan does this in a direction which, if the enemy weakens, can be exploited to very great advantage, while at the same time it permits of our modifying our operations if the situation demands. The ultimate objective is undoubtedly the Northern Coast, but I certainly do not advocate spending our last man and last round of ammunition in an attempt to reach that coast if the opposition which we encounter shows that the attempt will entail disproportionate loss.

Robertson next dealt with the question of French participation, noting that 'our latest information is that General Pétain is satisfied that he has the disaffection trouble in hand', that the French were, in any case, making a contribution to the offensive itself, and concluding:

It seems to me that we must give the French the opportunity to fight.* If they do not fight we must act accordingly, and the plan will permit of this. In any case, French defection is not a good reason for sending British troops to another theatre, for Germany may counter us by heavily attacking the French, and under the assumption that they will not fight this attack might be disastrous to the Entente.

A lengthy passage then re-iterates Jellicoe's insistence on 'the absolute necessity of turning the Germans out of Northern Belgium at the earliest possible moment. It must be done during the present Summer.'

The next point is Lloyd George's scepticism about predictions of success by the military advisers.

I, myself, do not remember making any sure predictions of success, if by that is meant the defeat of the German Army or even the breaking through of the enemy's line and reaching points many miles beyond. I certainly did not as regards the Somme, nor as regards our April operations. On the contrary I always told the War Cabinet that Nivelle's predictions were absurd. Further, our operations in April were not primarily intended to do more than to create an opportunity for the French to deliver the crushing blow. But both the Somme and the April operations were successful in wearing down the enemy, and this has always been a necessary preliminary to decisive defeat. The Messines operations were completely successful. As regards the future, I make no sure prediction of reaching the Belgian Coast. I suggest that our plan should be to press on in that direction, and think that the chances of our securing good results are certainly no greater in Italy than they are in the north, while the risks involved are much greater in the former case than in the latter. Our chances of complete success in the north depend largely upon what the French and Russians do, and upon German morale. I admit that the Germans still have plenty of fight in them but not as much as they had, whereas our own troops have more. Also, the Germans have been told in their Press that Messines is the last battle of which we are capable, and if we have another Messines, followed we may hope by still another, the effect will not tend to hearten either the German troops or the German people.

Robertson then applied himself to Lloyd George's dictum, that the 'fatal error' of the war 'had been continually to attack where the enemy is strongest'.

This statement compels me to say, with full respect and without any attempt at recrimination, that the greatest of all errors was that of not providing before the

*See Appendix II.

war an Army adequate to enforce the policy adopted. To our absurdly weak
pre-war Army can be attributed practically all the difficulties which now face us.
Until this year we have not had the means to attack with the hope of getting a
decision, and therefore we have had no choice in the point of attack.

Putting this governing factor aside, my reply to the statement is that the best
military course is to defeat the strongest enemy since this brings with it the defeat
of the weaker, but I agree that if there is no reasonable prospect of success against
the strongest enemy the next best course is to defeat the weaker, if that is possible.
To do this, however, it is necessary to hold the front against the strong enemy so as
to prevent him sending troops to reinforce the weak one, otherwise the attempt to
fight the latter merely leads to fighting the former in another place, and that after
all the dislocation involved by a change of plan . . . To keep the Germans on the
Western front we must fight and fight hard. We could not fight hard enough if we
sent a large force to Italy.

The next questions arising were Lloyd George's idea of adopting
'Pétain tactics', and of driving Austria out of the war by capturing Trieste.

As regards the 'Pétain tactics' I do not understand that General Pétain claims
any greater peculiarity for them than that they are not the Nivelle tactics, which
we have always thought to be absurd. Pétain's tactics are to attack on a wide front
with limited objectives, and so to wear down the enemy. This is what we are
aiming at.

Concerning the Trieste operation, Robertson once more reminded the
Committee that 'Germany is no doubt just as anxious to keep Austria in
the war as we are to get her out'; that possession of the interior lines
would enable the Central Powers, if necessary, to concentrate 90 divisions in the Italian theatre; and added that the physical difficulties of the
Isonzo front were much greater than in Flanders. He continued:

I know really very little of Cadorna's qualifications. He has not shown any
marked ability in the war as yet, and for the British Government to entrust the fate
of the war to him seems a very serious step. It is agreed that the War Cabinet is
now about to take, perhaps, the greatest decision of the war, and I feel it my duty
to quote what I said to them when the British Armies were placed under the
command of General Nivelle: 'It causes me very grave anxiety as to our final
success in the war. The next battle may well govern the final issue, and we have
placed our troops under a Commander, a foreign officer, who has yet to prove his
fitness for so great a command.' I feel this anxiety even more at the present stage
than in February last.

In my opinion there is no chance whatever of gaining a great success on the

Isonzo unless we send a considerable number of divisions as well as a large amount of artillery. It is notorious that the Italians are miserably afraid of the Germans. They themselves have confessed as much.

Robertson added that any large reinforcement of the Italian theatre would take months; that the configuration of that theatre, with its two fronts on the Isonzo and in the Trentino, made it peculiarly difficult to obtain a decision there; that he doubted whether even the capture of Trieste would cause Austria's collapse; and if it did, whether Italy really would help the Allies against Germany.

She is too afraid of German troops, and her relations with France we know are not good. Once she gets Trieste is she not likely to make peace herself? She came into the war to fight Austria, not Germany, and for a long time was not even theoretically at war with her.

Summing up, Robertson said that he saw no other alternative than those proposed, i.e. an attack on Austria, or the Flanders offensive, and of these he believed the latter to be the right selection.

It is a source of deep regret to me that I cannot advise the adoption of the policy so greatly desired by the Prime Minister, for I fully recognize the responsibility which he has to carry. My own responsibility, I may add, is not small in urging the continuance of a plan regarding which he has 'grave misgivings', but I can do no other than say that to abandon it and to attempt to seek a decision in Italy seems to me to be unsound.

The remainder of Robertson's paper dealt with the three minor points raised by Lord Curzon on 21 June.

These, then, were the dialectical battle lines: the Prime Minister's position, backed by Bonar Law and to a lesser extent Lord Milner, and the military advisers' position, backed by Smuts and to a lesser extent Lord Curzon, both now fixed in a rigidity as immovable as the Western Front itself. The final exchanges, showing tempers somewhat strained on both sides, took place on 25 June.

CAB 26/6; Eleventh Meeting of the Cabinet Committee on War Policy

Proceedings opened with a report by Lloyd George on his meeting with M. Albert Thomas, who had just returned from Russia, and described the situation there as 'fairly encouraging'. The Committee then turned to the Western Front.

The Prime Minister said that Sir Douglas Haig's Memorandum (W.P. 18) expressing his views, as requested by the Cabinet Committee on War Policy at the last meeting after considering the remarks of the Prime Minister, was a very encouraging document . . . The paper by the Chief of the Imperial General Staff (W.P. 19), however, inspired less confidence. Sir William Robertson's comment on the Prime Minister's suggestion that the fatal error that had been committed in the present war had been continually to attack where the enemy was strongest, namely, that the greatest of all errors was that of not providing before the War an army adequate to enforce the policy adopted, did not appeal to the Prime Minister personally. He himself had proposed Conscription in 1911 in writing. The proposal had not met with much military support,* and had eventually been dropped. This argument, therefore, made no appeal to him.

What the Prime Minister wished to know was whether the responsible military advisers of the Government considered that the chances were in favour of success attending Sir Douglas Haig's operations. He realized that no one could be sure, but before making this all-important decision the War Cabinet would require an assurance that there was a reasonable prospect of success. Field-Marshal Sir Douglas Haig's Memorandum was quite clear on this point. He wished to know whether Sir William Robertson shared this feeling. The Chief of the Imperial General Staff was the constitutional military adviser of the Government, and it was important that the Government should be clear as to what his view was.

Lloyd George read out passages from the papers submitted by Robertson and Haig which, he felt, indicated some discord between them.

The Field-Marshal was confident of success. He wished to know whether Sir William Robertson felt an equal confidence and shared Sir Douglas Haig's views of success.

Sir William Robertson pointed out that the result depends, to a certain extent, on circumstances which he cannot control, for example, the co-operation of France and Russia. He admitted that he had deliberately used somewhat guarded language in order not to encourage excessive hopes, and because the Prime Minister had stated on the 21st instant that during the years of the war many offensives had been preceded by sure predictions of success on the part of the soldiers. He himself, as CIGS, had made none, and to meet the allegation had

*The General Staff examined the question of compulsory service in 1910, and concluded that in the unsettled state of European affairs it was impracticable, and likely to increase the danger to the State. See Lord Haldane's autobiography, Hodder & Stoughton, 1929, p 196.

perhaps watered down his confidence a little too far.* He and Sir Douglas Haig had written their Memoranda entirely independently, but afterwards they had compared notes, and the Field-Marshal had expressed general agreement in his views.

Sir Douglas Haig confirmed this, and stated that, taking the paper as a whole, he agreed with it.

Sir William Robertson then pointed out that Sir Douglas Haig's view was somewhat different from his. He was in a much better position to judge the local situation, as he knew the morale of his own troops and that of the enemy. He himself, however, was bound to take a wider outlook and to give weight to many factors outside the purely local situation.

Lord Curzon pointed out that both Sir William Robertson and Sir Douglas Haig advised the same strategical plans. They had written independently and naturally their temperamental difference must affect their manner of stating their opinions. Although Sir Douglas Haig, with his personal experience of the morale of his own troops and those of the enemy was rather more sanguine, and Sir William Robertson was rather more cautious, the important thing to remember was that the policy they advised was identical.

Mr Bonar Law said that the point on which he understood the Prime Minister to require Sir William Robertson's opinion was as to whether we could take Ostend.

Sir William Robertson replied that his opinion was that Sir Douglas Haig's plan was the best course to adopt, and that he would not advise its adoption if he did not think it had a reasonable chance of success, but of course he could not guarantee success.

Mr Bonar Law pressed for a more direct answer to his question.

Sir William Robertson then said all the answer he could give was that he adhered to the following statement in Sir Douglas Haig's Memorandum:

'If our resources are concentrated in France to the fullest possible extent, the British armies are capable, and can be relied on to effect great results this summer, results which will make final victory more assured, and may even bring it within reach this year.'

He considered there was quite a good chance of success if France and Russia would pull their weight. If we were to stop taking the offensive altogether, Russia would probably go out. Hence, this was the right direction in which to move.

The Prime Minister, at this point, called attention to the fact that General Foch considered it desirable to send guns to Italy.

Sir William Robertson said he hoped that General Foch would do so.

Lloyd George once more raised the question whether Robertson was now going back on the advice he had tendered for the Paris Conference in

---

*Here, and later in the discussion, we see another evil result of the mistrust and consequent lack of frankness engendered by Lloyd George's methods of dealing with his military advisers.

May. Would the French really support the British offensive with their whole strength? He drew attention to an official proposal to withdraw men from the French Army to remedy a deficiency of 400,000 in agriculture.

M. Thomas had taken the same view as himself, that the French don't intend to fight, and was going back to France with the intention of doing his best to make them fight. M. Thomas was in complete agreement with Sir Douglas Haig's ideas, but considered that his plan would have no chance of success unless the French would fight. M. Thomas, however, required a fortnight in which to feel his way . . .

Sir William Robertson pointed out that the object of the Prime Minister's visit to Paris at the beginning of May had been to make the French fight. With this object in view he had perhaps exaggerated a little the necessity of a great French effort.*

The Prime Minister then asked what would be Sir William Robertson's view if the French refused to fight; had he changed his mind, was there any half-way house between a complete offensive and a defensive?

Sir William Robertson said he had not altered his view from that given at the Paris Conference as quoted above, but the Paris statement must of course be read as a whole.

The Prime Minister said he was convinced the French would let us down unless M. Thomas was able to convince them to the contrary, and he thought it very desirable to allow him the time he required to prepare the ground. In the meanwhile, Sir Douglas Haig could continue his preparations. At the end of a fortnight, the moment would be favourable for a fresh meeting with the French in order to put further pressure on them, and M. Thomas had agreed with this view.

Sir William Robertson pointed out that, in the meanwhile, the decision of the Paris Conference of 4 and 5 May, to continue the offensive on the Western Front in accordance with the principles agreed to by the Generals, and to devote the whole of the forces of the two Governments to the purpose, held the field.

The discussion then briefly descended into minutiae and became somewhat desultory.

Sir William Robertson pointed out that the French could not be expected to undertake an attack against a distant objective. We ought to be satisfied if they would use all their available forces as General Pétain had undertaken to do.

The Prime Minister agreed that he would be satisfied if they would do this. What we ought to do was to put to the French the alternative that if they would not use all their available forces and fight their hardest, we would not fight either.

*See p 174 f.n.

Mr Bonar Law pointed out that it was not unnatural if the French, who had sustained such tremendous losses, took the line that it was our turn to do the fighting.

Sir William Robertson pointed out that without fighting we could never win the War.

Mr Bonar Law said that he had heard rumours that the French Government might be out of office in a fortnight . . .

(After some further discussion on the details of Sir Douglas Haig's plan, and a reference to the raised map, the Committee reached the following decision):

1. Field-Marshal Sir Douglas Haig should continue his preparations for the present:
2. In the meantime M. Thomas should be left free to use his influence and prepare the ground with the French Government, and at the expiration of about a fortnight a fresh Conference should be held at which the French Government should be pressed to use all their available forces in co-operation with Sir Douglas Haig.

(The Committee then discussed the policy with regard to the bombing of distant towns.)

So ended, on a highly equivocal note, one of the most significant strategic debates of the war.

Charteris, p 231

21 JUNE.   The longest day of the year, and we have not yet even begun the really big effort. Six months ago I thought that by this time we should have been near peace. Now it looks as if nothing can prevent another full year of war . . . We fight alone here, the only army active. We shall do well, of that there is no reasonable doubt. Have we time to accomplish?

AMERICA

Appendix to War Cabinet 164, 15 June; CAB 23/3; Forecast of the Arrival of American Land Forces in France

4. *Time*. The first division – 20–25,000 men – should be in France by end July (America says end June). The second by end of August, and after this a division per month may be calculated upon, making six divisions, or 120–150,000 men, by the end of 1917.

During next year favourable circumstances may allow of further speeding up, but it is safer to calculate on the same rate of progress, and to count on twelve divisions coming over in 1918 . . .

12. *Conclusions*. To sum up, leaving all matters of sea-transport out of the question, it seems probable that America can have an army of 120,000–150,000 men in France by 1 January 1918, and 500,000 men by the end of 1918. That these figures for 1918 may, under favourable circumstances, be improved upon.

That the question of the supply of guns requires particular attention, a sound decision and a thorough development of production.

(Signed) Tom Bridges,
Major-General.

Repington, i, pp 581–2

SUNDAY, 17 JUNE. General Tom Bridges, our military representative, recently with Balfour's Mission to America, leaves for France today, and I went to see him in the morning at 27 Chesham Street. He had given his views to the War Cabinet, and Curzon had described it as the most depressing statement that the Cabinet had received for a long time . . . The Cabinet were expecting a million, and were proportionately depressed. I said that this report would incline the Cabinet to peace, but Tom said that this could not be helped as he had to report what he believed to be the truth.

The first American troops to arrive in France landed at Brest on 25 June; the following day an anonymous correspondent of *L'Illustration* watched another contingent come ashore at Saint-Nazaire.

Richard Thoumin, *The First World War*, Secker & Warburg, 1960, pp 357–8

From the quay, I watched the scene as the Star Spangled Banner was hoisted while the band played the national anthem and the soldiers stood at attention on every deck of the ship, thus marking their arrival on French soil by a traditional patriotic gesture.

With their olive-green uniform, their broad-rimmed felt hats, their pocketed belts and their appearance reminding one of the cowboys of the American West, they brought a new and picturesque note into our war atmosphere . . .

One of these soldiers, still excited from the day's events and somewhat exhilarated by our French wines, which were new to him, met one of my friends on his way to camp and quite seriously told him: 'I have come to fight all the kings!' (*In vino veritas*) . . .

To 'fight all the kings' is what the Americans would call 'a big contract'. We won't ask that much from the man. Let him take care of the King of Prussia, and he'll have done his job.

FRENCH MORALE

Repington, i, p 590

MONDAY, 25 JUNE . . .   In the late afternoon called on Sir W. Robertson at the War Office . . . He saw nothing for it but to go on hitting the enemy with all the men and guns that could be had. I agreed. He thought that Pétain would soon help, and he was fighting hard now,* though at the Boche instance. He thought that Pétain must be much exercised about the mutiny. He agreed that only two regiments were concerned badly, but some others had engaged in conversations.† All his news from Russia was bad, and he said that Foch had the same news from his man.

Esher, iv, pp 126–7; Esher to Derby, 26 June

All along the French lines the troops are tired and discontented. There are unpleasant signs of disintegration, and the patriotic officers fear decomposition of the armies as the result of German propaganda, war-weariness, inaction and weak administration.

You remember a caricature in the early days of the war that had a great vogue, called '*Pourvu que les civils tiennent*'. Curiously enough the reverse is the case just now. It is a case of '*Pourvu que les poilus tiennent.*'

After all the sacrifices made and the glory achieved it would be a sad ending if the Russian example was followed in France. That the danger is real you may infer from the stoppage of all 'leave' to Paris for soldiers and officers under field-rank, and from the timid attitude of the Government towards the mutinous troops.

The French *permissionaires* have two stock phrases: 'If the English want to win the war, let them win it themselves.' 'If the politicians and civilians want Alsace and Lorraine, let them go and take them.'

Unless the war ends before the winter the maintenance of order in Paris and consequently throughout France will depend upon a good supply of coal. Deprived of fuel, the French people will put an end to the war and accept a *paix blanche*.

We shall be lucky if it is no worse. Revolution is never very deep under the surface in France. The crust is very thin just now.

Haig Diary, Blake, p 242

THURSDAY, 28 JUNE.   I had a long talk with Sir Henry Wilson. He thinks that by the British continuing the offensive is the only way to save France. The French Army is in a state of indiscipline not due to losses but to disappointment.

---

* See Appendix II, pp 349–50, but why did Robertson not think it worth while saying this to the War Policy Committee?
† Here again one sees how tight-lipped the usually talkative French could be when it suited them. It is perfectly clear that *no* British officer had any idea of the full extent of the collapse of French morale.

Wilson, ii, pp 1–2

28 June. I had a long talk with Haig this morning. He told me that the War Committee had only given him authority to go on making his arrangements for an offensive, that Albert Thomas (just back from Russia) was going to report on the state of France in a fortnight, and that the War Committee would then decide whether to let Haig attack or not. The Committee were going to send for me, and very much, if not everything, would depend on what I said, and he wanted to know.

I told him the same as I told Kigg last night, viz: that I did not think the French would be able to make another serious attack this year under Pétain's leadership, but that they would fight all right defensively, and would help all they could by simulating attacks, and that, as one of our main objects now was to keep the French in the field, I was absolutely convinced that we should attack all we could, right up to the time of the mud, and should then be prepared to take over.*

I told Haig that if he was successful in his attacks, and he later on got the chance of disengaging Ostend and Zeebrugge, or of disengaging Lille, he was not to hesitate for a moment, but should disengage Lille. Haig told me that in his opinion, if he disengaged Ostend and Zeebrugge, he would form such a salient there that the Boches could not remain in front of the French. However, he was satisfied with what I was going to say to the War Cabinet.

He was most nice to me, begged me to do something with my 'great brains', and said that there was always a bed and a welcome at his headquarters for me.

Lloyd George, in his memoirs (pp 1265–70) confuses Wilson's first report on the French Army to the War Cabinet on 8 June (which had, in fact supplied him with ammunition to oppose Haig's plan during the great debate of 19–25 June) and a second similar report to the War Policy Committee on 3 July in order to build up his case that the Government's military advisers were deliberately suppressing information about the French in order to win approval for the Flanders offensive.

The fog of doubt and deception surrounding French affairs remained very dense indeed.

Author's Papers: Esher to Haig, 30 June

The French troubles in the Army are quieting down. Pétain seems to have been firm and sensible.

Pétain, p 103

Altogether, between May and October, 412 men were condemned to death by the Courts Martial, 203 of whom were sentenced in June, 386 for offences against

*Wilson presumably means 'take over more line' – a matter on which, he knew, the French were very insistent.

military law or for acts of rebellion and twenty-six for common law offences. In consequence of the large number of free pardons and communted sentences, *only seven men were, in fact, executed immediately, by order of the Commander-in-Chief, and only forty-eight after the Head of State had confirmed the sentence.**

The stern penalties imposed on the self-confessed leaders of the mutiny, on trouble-makers and those convicted of serious acts of violence, had a deterrent effect which was all the more striking in that they followed so swiftly on the heels of the crimes themselves. They were also enough, though comparatively few in number, to put a stop to the dangerous activities of the agents of revolutionary propaganda.

MANPOWER

Author's Papers: Haig Diary, 28 June

We are now 99,000 infantry short of establishment.

FLANDERS

Ibid

General Gough came to see me . . . We discussed his proposed plans. I urged the importance of the right flank. It is in my opinion vitally important to occupy and hold the ridge west of Gheluvelt in order to cover our right flank, and then push along it to Broodseinde. The main battle will be fought on or for this ridge† so we must make our plans accordingly. The main difficulty seems to be at the beginning of the attack in advancing from a comparatively small salient to the attack of a wider area.

I impressed on Gough the vital importance of the ridge in question, and that the advance north should be limited until our right flank has really been secured on this ridge.

Ibid, 29 June

Haig visits Fifth Army Corps commanders, beginning on the right with II Corps (Jacob):

*Pétain's italics; he adds in a footnote: 'Of these fifty-five executions, only thirty were concerned with the re-establishment of morale.'
† This proved only too sadly true; for the divergences between GHQ and Fifth Army see *Douglas Haig: The Educated Soldier*, pp 338–340.

I emphasized the importance of securing the Gheluvelt ridge to cover the right flank . . . (Jacob) is confident of success . . .
(Watts, XIX Corps) quite confident of reaching his objectives . . .
(Cavan, XIV Corps) Everything is all right and the troops are in grand spirits.

Ibid, 30 June

Robertson had been visiting the French leaders; he reported to Haig that Foch 'adheres to the Paris Conference, that is to use all available forces in co-operation with us.' He recorded disappointment with Pétain:

I could not quite make out what his line was . . . he talked like a man without a jot of confidence as to the future.

Oliver, p 197, 28 June

We are at present in one of these periods when we are holding our breath and waiting for great events. I expect before this letter reaches you we shall have dealt some big blow somewhere. From the newspaper reports about the cannonading north of Ypres I should imagine that it is going to be in that quarter. It is as anxious a time as has ever been during the war. The splendid thing, however, is that the British army in France is imbued with a spirit of absolute confidence in being able to smash the Hun.

General der Infanterie Hermann von Kuhl,* *Der Weltkrieg, 1914–1918*, Berlin: Weller; trans. Col R. Macleod [Author's Papers]

One asks oneself the question whether that which, to our loss, we had neglected to do at WYTSCHAETE could now, having been taught by experience, be carried out in Flanders? Would it be possible in this coming battle to avoid the first blow by a planned withdrawal to a rearward position? The examination of this question in the conference which took place at the end of June led to the conclusion that a withdrawal in Flanders, having regard to the peculiar local conditions, would not be advantageous . . .

From this it is clear that principles of war cannot fit every situation and can never be hard and fast rules. What might, without doubt, have been possible at

*Chief of Staff to Crown Prince Rupprecht of Bavaria, commanding the Northern Group of Armies: Fourth (von Armin) in Flanders, Sixth (von Falkenhausen) in Artois, Second (von der Marwitz) in Picardy.

WYTSCHAETE, was not right at Ypres . . . In Flanders a halt had to be called against further withdrawals so that the U-boat bases could be protected.

THE INVISIBLE ENEMY

Lloyd George, i, p 709

Statistics of Shipping Losses, June, 1917 — 398,773 gross tons sunk.

July

─────────────────────── ✠ ───────────────────────

Flanders

Haig Diary: Blake, p 242

1 July. Colonel de Bellaigue* reported on his visit to Compiègne. General Pétain told Robertson that he is in full agreement with me regarding my proposed operations in France and Belgium; also that the French Army will attack, and support me 'to the fullest extent possible' during my operations.

Author's Papers: Haig Diary, 1 July

General Neil Malcolm (Gough's BGGS) came to lunch. If General Anthoine cannot be ready on the date fixed, Gough wishes to wait, rather than modify our plans. As the French delay is due to want of railways, I told Kiggell to arrange to give them more help. But I am averse to postponing, so I told Malcolm to make out a plan for holding back the left of the Fifth Army, while the right takes the Gheluvelt ridge.

Haig Diary: Blake, pp 242–3

2 July. I discussed with General Anthoine the date on which he would be ready. He seemed anxious about the state of morale of his gunners, because many of his heavy guns had come straight from the battle on the Aisne, and they must be sent on leave and given 'repos'. This being so, I arranged to send a brigade of infantry to make the emplacements for the French guns; and also some 'labour battalions' to move the ammunition from the broad to the narrow gauge railways. 'Even with this help it is possible that he may not be ready', he said. I assured him that I would never ask him and his troops to attack until they all felt that they were ready and able to take the position in their front.

───────────────

*Successor to General Des Vallières as Head of the French Mission at GHQ.

CAB 27/6; Thirteenth Meeting of the Cabinet
Committee on War Policy, 3 July

Robertson reported on his recent visit to the French military leaders. He said that Cadorna had asked Foch for a large number of British and French guns with ample ammunition for the 1918 campaign.

He had also discussed the question of the Western Front with General Foch, and his interview on this subject had been satisfactory. General Foch was all for making the French do their utmost, and had shown himself a strong supporter of the policy agreed to at the Paris Conference of 4 and 5 May.

Sir William Robertson had then proceeded to General Pétain's Headquarters. When he arrived General Pétain was away, but he saw his Staff, whose attitude was entirely satisfactory from our point of view. The French divisions and guns which had been promised to cooperate with our Army had already gone North, and 18 to 20 divisions were being concentrated for the main French attack.

Subsequently, General Robertson had seen General Pétain, but had been somewhat disappointed with his attitude. He found it difficult to induce him to talk much of the forthcoming operations. His conversation was mainly of diplomacy and the desirability of getting Turkey and Bulgaria out of the War.

FRENCH MORALE

Ibid

Sir William Robertson, in the course of his visit, had formed the impression that the French were very much dejected. One of the main causes of their depression appeared to be the devastation of their country.

Robertson described some of the damage he had seen.

Also there was great dissatisfaction everywhere with the French Government and their recent removal of many of the French Generals and Staff Officers which had had a very disquieting effect on the Army. General Pétain had urged the great importance of a success. When Sir William Robertson reminded him of our success at Messines and of the encouraging effect that the arrival of the first contingent of Americans ought to produce, General Pétain had said that the effect of this would not last long. General Pétain had said that there was no leader in the country. Sir William Robertson urged that the War Cabinet should do all they can to sustain and encourage the French, and that no time should be lost in doing this.

The Prime Minister said that Sir William Robertson's information fully confirmed Colonel Spiers's letter which had been circulated to the War Cabinet. The effect on his own mind was that he ought to make another visit to Paris.

Conclusion.   It was decided that M. Mantoux* should be sent to Paris to see M. Thomas and ascertain whether the moment was favourable for a visit by Mr Lloyd George.

FLANDERS

Author's Papers: O.A.D. 538, Haig to Army Commanders, 5 July

1. The general situation at present is favourable to the attainment of considerable results in the offensive operations we are about to undertake.

Russia has resumed active operations, apparently with excellent results and on a considerable scale.† The effect on the Russian people of the successes gained is reported to be such as may lead to the development and maintenance of still greater efforts.

Before the Russian attack the endurance of the Central Powers and their allies was based on three main facts: hope that Russia would make peace, or at least remain inactive; confidence in the power of the German armies to hold their 'impregnable' positions; and belief in England being starved into submission by the submarine campaign before the armies of the United States could take the field in strength.

We know that German faith in the submarine campaign must soon be abandoned entirely. Confidence in the invincibility of the German armies has already been so severely shaken that it cannot survive many fresh defeats. And hope of Russian inaction has now been dispelled.

Coming at a moment when the heavy attacks the enemy has been making on the French front have failed to achieve success,‡ and when he is looking with grave anxiety to a resumption of the British offensive and to the possibility of renewed attacks by our French and Italian allies, this sudden resumption of a dangerous offensive on the Eastern front is a very heavy blow to him.

We were justified in hoping for success with the possibility of great results from our next offensive before we had this convincing evidence of Russia's intention and ability to fulfil her whole duty to her allies. We are still more justified in this

---

*M. (later Prof) Paul Mantoux, official interpreter, who was to be chief interpreter at the Paris Peace Conference in 1919.
† The last Russian offensive, organized by the Minister of War, Alexander Kerensky, opened on 1 July with delusive success. By 13 July the Russians claimed over 37,000 prisoners, but when the Germans counter-attacked a few days later, the Russians soon collapsed in rout. However, fighting did continue both on the Galicia front and in Bukovina (beside the Rumanians) through July and into August.
‡ See Appendix II.

hope now, and our plans must be laid to exploit to the full the possibilities of the situation.

With this object the following instructions are issued in confirmation and amplification of those already given to Army Commanders:–

2. The Fifth Army, assisted on its right by the Second Army and co-operating on its left with the French and Belgians, is first to secure the PASSCHENDAELE – STADEN Ridge.

To drive the enemy off that Ridge from STIRLING CASTLE in the south to DIXMUDE in the north is likely to entail very hard fighting lasting perhaps for weeks; but as a result of this we may hope that our subsequent progress will be more rapid.

3. Subject to modifications necessitated by developments in the situation, the next effort of the Fifth Army, with the French and Belgians – after gaining the Ridge mentioned above – will be directed north-eastwards to gain the line (approximately) THOUROUT–COUCKELAERE.

4. Simultaneously with this advance to the THOUROUT–COUCKELAERE line the Fourth Army, acting in combination with naval forces, will attack the enemy about NIEUPORT and on the coast to the east of there.

5. The Fourth Army and the forces attacking the line THOUROUT–COUCKELAERE will afterwards operate to join hands on the general line THOUROUT –OSTEND and to push on towards BRUGES.

6. Operations eastward, and towards LICHTERVELDE, from the PASS-CHENDAELE–STADEN Ridge will be required to cover the right flank of the advance on THOUROUT; and possession of the high ground between THOUROUT and ROULERS will be of importance subsequently to cover the flank of the advance on BRUGES.

7. In the operations subsequent to the capture of the PASSCHENDAELE – STADEN Ridge opportunities for the employment of Cavalry in masses are likely to offer.

8. The Second Army will cover and co-operate with the right flank of the Fifth Army as already ordered and will be prepared to take over gradually the defence of the main Ridge from the Fifth Army, possibily as far as PASSCHENDAELE or even to a further point.

The Commander of the Second Army will also be prepared with plans to develop an advance towards the line WARNETON–MENIN, or to push forward on the right of the Fifth Army to the line COURTRAI–ROULERS (throwing out a flank guard along the line of the LYS), if circumstances should render such movements desirable as the situation develops.

9. As far as can be foreseen at present the main operations after the capture of the STIRLING CASTLE–PASSCHENDAELE–DIXMUDE Ridge will be those directed towards OSTEND and BRUGES.

In those circumstances our resources, to the utmost possible limit, will be concentrated on those operations; and, provided the degree of success gained is sufficient to justify it, we must be prepared to reduce the garrison of the remainder of our line to mere outposts with a few centrally placed reserves.

The Commanders of the Armies south of the River LYS will accordingly be prepared with plans to release as large forces as possible to ensure the success of the main operations. Those plans should be so designed as to admit of a gradual withdrawal of forces to the north as the situation develops.

Meanwhile as much activity as possible will continue to be displayed along our defensive front, in order to wear down and deceive the enemy, thus preventing any transfer of his forces from that front.

10. The above outline of possibilities is issued to enable Army Commanders to foresee and prepare for what may be required of them. The progress of events may demand modifications or alterations of plan from time to time and – especially in view of the comparatively short period of fine weather which we can count on – our progress before winter sets in may fall short of what would otherwise have been within our power this year.

The general situation is such, however, that the degree of success gained and the results of it may exceed general expectations, and we must be prepared for the possibility of great developments and ready to take full advantage of them.

11. The extent of the success gained will depend much on concentration and continuity of effort at the right time and place, and the necessary concentration must be attained by a bold reduction of force at other points, and by ensuring that to the utmost possible every fit man takes his place in the ranks. Army Commanders will satisfy themselves that, during the coming offensive, no man fit to be in the ranks is employed elsewhere without most urgent and necessary reason.

12. The drafts available to replace casualties are limited in number and in the great struggle before us it is essential that, without in the least degree relaxing the strength and continuity of our efforts, we shall conserve the energy of our officers and men so that we may outstay the enemy. For this the utmost use must be made of all means of offence and defence at our disposal. All ground gained must be held, by rifle and bayonet alone if no assistance is obtainable from other arms. In the attack, more especially in the earlier attacks, each step must be thoroughly prepared and organized. Every advance must be carried out steadily – but none the less vigorously – with thorough combination and mutual support between the troops employed. The tendency of isolated bodies of troops to dash forward beyond the reach of support must be held in check. This tendency, springing from the finest motives, is of the greatest value if controlled and used for adequate objects, whereas if uncontrolled and misapplied it leads to the loss of many of the most gallant officers and men without the gain of compensating advantages.

Conducting our operations on these principles, as has been done with such success on so many previous occasions during the past twelve months, we may look forward with confidence to still greater successes in the near future.

Haig has frequently been accused of over-optimism. This document, in its broad scope, and despite the many qualifications contained in it, is probably the most wildly optimistic to which he ever put his signature. This we may attribute to Pétain's repeated reassurances of French help and the deceptive initial success of the Russians. Whether Haig would have written in the same terms a fortnight later, we cannot tell; it is possible that he might have done, because by then he would know that the Germans, in order to counter-attack the Russians, had withdrawn 4 divisions from the Western Front – 'the last troops in this war to be sent from west to east over Groener's well-organized railways'.*

Despite its overall optimism, however, the final paragraph of Haig's paper shows that he did have doubts about the execution of the plan. Gough's latest biographer tells us that a considerable difference of opinion had developed between Fifth Army HQ, planning for deep advances, and Operations Section, GHQ, advising more deliberate and less ambitious attacks.† The irony is that the method outlined here by Haig is practically identical with that later employed by Plumer.

Repington, i, pp 605–6

THURSDAY, 5 JULY ... Saw Sir W. Robertson afterwards about the Mesopotamia Report and the Indian Army system ... We had a little talk on other matters. Some French divisions are in the north to help Gough. I said that I did not think that the choice of Gough for this particular operation was good, much though I admired his gifts. R. was inclined to agree, and wished that Plumer, who knew every stone in the north, had been placed in charge.

Author's Papers: Haig Diary

5 JULY. Charteris reported this morning that the enemy is apparently in ignorance of our preparations north of Ypres, and has not yet moved any extra troops to meet us there.

O.H., vol ii, p 141

The opening offensive of the Flanders campaign was more clearly heralded than any other British or French offensive during the War. In one respect the obviousness of the intention was an advantage; for it caused German O.H.L. to hurry every available man and gun to Flanders instead of taking advantage of the failure of the Nivelle offensive to crush the French army by a counter-stroke.

The Official Historian is, of course, incorrect about O.H.L.; as we have seen, 4 July was the day of the big German effort along the Chemin des Dames.

*Cyril Falls: *The First World War*, Longmans, 1960, p 266. General Groener was Chief of the Field Railways.
†Anthony Farrar-Hockley, *Goughie*, Hart-Davis, MacGibbon, 1975, pp 216–18

Soldiers and Politicians

> CAB 27/6; Fifteenth Meeting of the Cabinet
> Committee on War Policy, 6 July

Forthcoming Allied Conferences
The Prime Minister said he had heard from M. Thomas in the sense that he was
not quite ready for a conference . . .

The Western Front
General Smuts pointed out that the Committee on War Policy had reached a
hypothetical agreement that if the French would attack decisively, Sir Douglas
Haig would also attack. He asked, however, what alternative the Committee had
in view if the French would not attack decisively? In this respect, he suggested that
before answering the question the position of the Allies should be examined in the
Eastern theatre.

The Eastern Theatres of War
General Smuts expressed his opinion that Turkey is the weak point of the enemy.
If Turkey could be eliminated from the War the Dardanelles would be opened, we
should be sure of Russia, and Bulgaria could also, in all probability, be man-
oeuvred out of the War . . .
    In General Smuts's opinion . . . the best place at which to strike Turkey was
Alexandretta. Strategically, it was superior even to the Dardanelles, since the
railways to the Hejaz and Palestine, as well as to Baghdad, passed within 15 miles
of this port. If you were to occupy the railway you would strike Turkey a deadly
blow . . .
    He suggested, therefore, that our Salonica force ought to be replaced by the
Greeks and go into reserve; if the Russian plans should mature we would then be
in a position to help them. Otherwise, we ought to release the whole army now
engaged on our front, together with, perhaps, a portion of the French army and
some of the Italians, and fling them on Alexandretta in the autumn, thus cutting
the whole Turkish position to pieces. Troops might also be withdrawn from
Palestine if General Allenby found he was unable to advance . . .
    Lord Curzon recapitulated the objections that had previously been raised to an
attack on Alexandretta . . .
    The Prime Minister said that it was not necessary for us to decide to attack
Alexandretta today, but he would like the War Policy Committee to give their
minds to the general policy, namely, of making a special effort, which should be
diplomatic as well as military, elsewhere than on the Western Front.

Duff Cooper, ii, p 129: Robertson to Haig, 7 July

Prime Minister is more keen than ever on the Italian project! Several of the other members of the War Cabinet are equally keen on some other equally foolish strategical project. Alexandretta – the Balkans, for instance. Yet I suppose that these same Ministers will be held up in years to come as farsighted statesmen and the saviours of their country!

Wilson, ii, p 4; 7 July; Callwell writes:

Bonar Law expressed himself as opposed to Haig's offensive because of the loss that it would entail, to which Sir Henry rejoined that 'the loss of men might have been a good reason for not entering into the war, but a bad reason for not fighting when in the war'.

GERMANY

Ludendorff, ii, p 451

An outward indication of the falling-off of our spiritual capacity for war was afforded at the session of the Main Committee of the Reichstag on 6 July. Deputy Erzberger made a speech which utterly surprised us, in which he maintained that the submarine war was perfectly hopeless and that it was quite impossible for us to win the war at all. On this the spirit of the Reichstag broke down completely . . . Now it was perfectly clear how far we had sunk. If things continued in this way in Germany, if nothing was done to encourage and strengthen the people, military defeat was indeed inevitable.

Ibid, pp 451–2

The situation in Berlin became more acute. On 8 July the Chancellor,* although at that time he accurately gauged the enemy's destructive intentions, agreed to the peace resolution which was to be put forward by the Majority parties and, at the same time, definitely promised them to apply the Reichstag franchise law to the elections for the Prussian Diet. Both these measures must have strengthened the enemy's will to an incalculable extent. On the afternoon of the 10th the Imperial Chancellor felt obliged to hand in his resignation, which was, however, refused on the 11th . . .

After all that had happened I could no longer believe that the Chancellor was the right man to perform the task demanded of him by this war and lead the country out of the depths of its depression to victory. It had become evident to me that, in order to conquer in the field, the General Staff needed the co-operation of the statesmen at home, and the better acquainted I became with the general

*Theobald von Bethmann-Hollweg.

situation after assuming duty the more convinced I was. This co-operation we had
not obtained; national thought and feeling at home had fallen off. The political
leaders lacked creative force; they had no ideal which would take hold of the
people and thus develop their powers.

It is usually an ominous sign when military chiefs declare that 'the
political leaders lacked creative force'; this was no exception. Hindenburg and Ludendorff decided that Bethmann-Hollweg must go;
accordingly they tendered their own resignations on 12 July. These were,
of course, refused. Lacking the support of a Reichstag majority,
Bethmann-Hollweg had no option but to hand in his own resignation
again, and on 13 July it was accepted. The next day he was succeeded by a
nonentity, Georg Michaelis, with the blessing of the Army High Command which now became the effective ruler of Germany. Reichstag
acceptance of Michaelis was conditional upon acceptance of a 'Peace
Resolution' drafted by the majority parties (Centre, Progressives and
Socialists) calling for a negotiated peace and international conciliation.
Conceding that the terms of this resolution were loose enough to allow of
almost any interpretation, the High Command reluctantly agreed. The
resolution was passed on 19 July.

Ibid, p 458

From the tribune of the Reichstag the peace resolution went out into the world.
As anticipated, it produced on our enemies no political effect whatever; they took
it as a confession of weakness. Bulgaria and Turkey began to doubt our victory.
Nor was the effect in the country what the movers hoped.

Instead of drawing the proper conclusion from the refusal of the enemy and
strengthening the fighting spirit of the people, the Government gave no thought
to the enemy, but entangled itself further and further in the unfortunate idea of a
peace by understanding that could be had at any time. This was to prove the curse
of the peace resolution. The General Staff considered it a mistake from the
military point of view. But the Field-Marshal and I authorized the Imperial
Chancellor to announce our concurrence in his attitude towards it, because he
wished to avoid a conflict with the majority of the Reichstag in the interests of the
prosecution of the war. And so we also shouldered the responsibility for the
resolution which we thought a lesser evil than internal confusion. To that pitch
had things come in Germany.

A German seaman on leave from the High Seas Fleet in July noticed in
his travels an unusual calm.

The Private War of Seaman Stumpf, edited and
translated by Daniel Horn, Leslie Frewin, 1969,
p 342

I missed the lusty curses of the soldiers, the suspicious listening of the dock
workers and the complaints of the women. Does this mean that things are now
better in the land? I am afraid not. The people are so apathetic and hopeless that it
hurts my heart. It isn't so bad as long as the people still have the strength to vent
their anger by cursing. Only when they have lost all hope do they appear as
disconsolate and indifferent as they are nowadays.

Obviously, the German Government could not conceal everything that
was happening from foreign eyes and ears. The 'Peace Resolution', for
instance, was public property – but in the Allied capitals it was dismissed
as a trick to mask the continuing pursuit of a 'victor's peace'. Knowledge
of German home conditions was more fragmentary; each fragment would
receive serious attention from the Allied General Staffs as part of a
recognizable jigsaw. Others, however, having been misled for three years
by irresponsible Press reports and official statements, were likely to shrug
the new facts aside. What is now clear is that by mid-1917 Germany was
internally in a bad way – but that France's plight was (for the time being)
worse, that Italy was also in poor shape, and that Russia's condition was
abysmal. Thus, despite her own difficulties and the grave deterioration of
all her allies, Germany retained a marginal but definite advantage, which
the Russian collapse would improve.

SOLDIERS AND POLITICIANS

CAB 27/6; Fifteenth Meeting of the Cabinet
Committee on War Policy, 6 July

The Forthcoming Conference
The Prime Minister asked the Committee to consider what would be the position
of the British delegates at the forthcoming Conference in Paris? Their first task
would be to try and induce the French to attack strongly on the Western Front.
He, personally, was opposed to this policy, but as he understood it to be the
decision of the Committee he would support it. We should have to be sure,
however, that the French attack was a *bona fide* one. What would be their
position, however, if they were not satisfied that the French would do this? To him
there appeared to be three alternatives:
1. To continue to worry and harry the enemy with relatively minor attacks on
General Pétain's lines:
2. To throw in our lot with General Cadorna and strike a blow at Austria, which

would strengthen the hands of the Pacifist elements in that country. Italy could not abate her terms. No Italian Government would survive for 24 hours which made a separate peace which did not include Trieste. Hence, before there could be any question of a separate peace with Austria, Trieste must be won, for if Trieste was in Italian hands the Austrians might be willing to let it go rather than continue the War:

3. A concentration against Turkey. This involved immediate preparations, whether the object was Gaza, or Haifa, or Alexandretta. This alternative was not inconsistent with an attack on Italy (sic). The latter might take place in August, and if successful, would, as he had already pointed out, cut the umbilical cord of the enemy.

If the attack on Italy (sic), with the assistance of a very large force of heavy guns, failed, we could have a bargain with General Cadorna that 100,000 Italian troops would be sent to Turkey . . .

The Western Front

The Prime Minister asked the Committee to bear in mind that they were being asked to sacrifice hundreds of thousands of men on an operation on the success of which our principal Military Adviser refused to pledge his military reputation, his reason no doubt being that he knew quite well that the French would not support us effectively.

Lord Curzon demurred to this suggestion.

The Prime Minister said that if we were satisfied that the French would fight, then we would go on with the attack on the Western Front, but if we were not satisfied, what were we to do? To attack Turkey or help General Cadorna? These decisions ought to be taken before we went to France. The reason why he did not believe that the French would undertake a thorough attack was that General Pétain was the confidant of M. Painlevé, the Minister of War, who was known to be opposed to decisive operations on the Western Front.

General Smuts said he agreed with Field-Marshal Haig that his proposed operation was a very promising one, but it was essential that the French should cooperate.

The Prime Minister said that if the Western Front plan was adopted he thought it would be better that two of his colleagues should press it at Paris. It was not that he was unwilling to press it, but he did not believe in the plan, and they would put it with greater force.

Lord Milner asked how the Prime Minister proposed the question should be handled at Paris? It was evident that he had made up his mind that the French would not carry out any promise they might give. When the French gave assurances, what would be his reply?

The Prime Minister said that Field-Marshal Haig had fully explained his plans to the Committee, and had stated exactly how many divisions he intended to employ and the manner of their employment. We ought to insist on the French tabling their plans in exactly the same way. Before we could undertake any offensive we ought to know exactly what the French were going to do.

The Secretary reminded the Committee that General Robertson had informed them that General Foch had given an undertaking to attack with 18 or 20 divisions, and had indicated the point of attack. No doubt the reply would be precisely the same in Paris.

Lord Curzon suggested that the French ought to know before we came to Paris exactly what we were going to ask them for. He could not ask their Military Authorities to explain their plan in detail without giving them some warning. He agreed that it was necessary now that all the cards should be on the table.

The Prime Minister read a telegram from General Cadorna which had been communicated to him by the Italian Ambassador, the gist of which was that although he was preparing his next attack, it could not take place at the date originally arranged unless he was reinforced by Allied artillery, owing to the strength of the Austrian artillery opposed to him. Unless supported he might have to postpone his attack.

Conclusion

The Secretary was instructed to obtain the information asked for in regard to Austria.

(The Prime Minister asked the Members of the Committee on War Policy to consider the various proposals that had been put forward.)

Author's Papers: Haig to Robertson, 10 July

(M. Painlevé) assures me too that the French Army will be able to assist us by attacking on its own front, and that the French Govt. intends that it should do so.

Author's Papers: Robertson to Haig, 13 July

L.G. is still much in the mood as when you were here, and all French news tends to show hesitation on their part to do much. *This* L.G. uses for his own arguments.

FLANDERS

Author's Papers: Haig Diary

7 JULY.   The guns of the XIV Corps on his left were, (Gough) said, suffering considerably from the enemy's fire. 27 guns out of 36 had been damaged. He asked for a postponement for 5 days. I pointed out that the date of the attack could not be definitely fixed now . . . I was averse to delaying longer than was really necessary because the enemy is as yet in ignorance of our preparations. Every day is of consequence.

Repington, I, p 608

9 JULY . . . The Boche guns are busy and are doing better than usual with their counter-battery work, while their planes have been all over us.

On 10 July the Germans launched a successful surprise attack on the British XV Corps in the coastal sector at Nieuport. Two battalions of the 1st Division were practically annihilated, forward positions were lost, and in two days' fighting British casualties mounted to 126 officers and 3,000 other ranks.

Charteris, pp 234–5

11 JULY.   I have been out all day, up to the coast where we have taken a very nasty knock. It is the first German success against us since the Loos counter-attacks.* We had taken over some trenches from the French a short time ago, and the Germans, with complete justice, thought we were going to do something there and decided to forestall us. They attacked with great determination and we have lost practically the whole of a battalion, a real bad affair. Fortunately it does not affect the general situation, but it does show that the Germans have still plenty of kick left in them. The German attack was admirably planned and carried out.

Between 12 and 15 July Haig paid a number of visits to units preparing for the forthcoming attack.

Author's Papers: Haig Diary

12 JULY.   30th Division: (General Williams) seemed very confident, and said his troops had never been so well prepared for an attack.
    11th Division: Division in good order.
13 JULY.   8th Division: The men looked in splendid condition and marched very well.
14 JULY.   34th Brigade exercise:† I thought the subordinate commanders of companies and platoons had not had enough practice in meeting unexpected situations such as regularly arise during operations against a trained foe.
15 JULY.   24th Division: . . . in excellent order and all are full of confidence.

Author's Papers: Haig Diary

15 JULY . . . XIV Corps commenced bombardment of the enemy's trenches today in co-operation with the French First Army. This is the beginning of the great battle against the Passchendaele Ridge.

*This is incorrect; the Germans carried out several successful minor attacks in 1916.
† 11th Division.

The Official History says that the preliminary barrage of the Third Battle of Ypres opened on 16 July. The Fifth Army employed 752 heavy guns and howitzers and 1,422 field guns and howitzers (total, 2,174) against some 1,500 German pieces (according to the German Official Account). The *Statistics Of The Military Effort Of The British Empire*, published by HMSO for the War Office in 1922, inform us that during the period 17–30 July, 4,283,550 rounds were fired. A moment's reflection on the transportation problems involved in assembling this amount, plus an average of well over 2 million rounds per week for the battle itself, explains why High Commands were so reluctant to 'switch' or cancel major offensives for which preparations were well advanced.

FRENCH MORALE

Haig Diary: Blake, pp 244–5

MONDAY, 16 JULY.   General Pétain visited the First French Army and then came to see me at 6.30 pm and stayed to dinner. We were thus able to have a good talk before dining. He was most frank regarding the indiscipline which had shown itself in the French Army after the failure of Nivelle's Offensive. The situation had been very serious indeed but he thinks it is very much better, and the troops operating under Anthoine are now in excellent order. He also said that being next to the 'splendid British troops' had done these French Battalions no end of good.

As regards what the French Army can do to co-operate with me, he said that he 'intends to do his utmost'. At present the situation on the Chemin des Dames is not good, and hard fighting is going on;* also an attack by the enemy has forestalled his preparations at Verdun.† So it is impossible to say what attacks (or when) he will be able to carry out, but I may depend on him being able to prevent the enemy from withdrawing any Divisions from his front . . .

I found Pétain very cheery, with a straightforward soldier-like manner.

FLANDERS

Author's Papers: Haig Diary

17 JULY.   (Jacob) is . . . most confident . . . When officers live in such close touch with their men, look after their wants, and know what is going on, there can be little doubt as to the result of any operation.

*The Germans renewed their attacks on the Chemin des Dames and at Moronvilliers on 14 and 15 July.
† See Appendix II.

Ibid

18 JULY.   The artillery report for yesterday is satisfactory and hostile fire is said to have slackened as the result of our bombardments. Fifth Army report 45 destructive shoots, 44 pits hit and 17 explosions caused.

19 JULY.   Fifth Army reported tonight that the 'Hostile artillery was generally quiet' . . . The number of casualties in guns is much less than we expected! Very few guns have been seriously disabled.

General Jack's Diary, edited by John Terraine,
Eyre & Spottiswoode, 1964, pp 228–9

19 JULY . . . The Battle preparations have become more intensive. Further 'instructions' arrive nearly daily, constituting a kind of 'paper barrage'.

On most evenings we attend conferences at Brigade Headquarters, or lectures describing the plan of attack in the hall of this village, the largest room hereabouts. An exact clay model of the front at Ypres is at hand for study, and the lecturers are supplied with large-scale maps. Until yesterday most of those addressing us, with a comprehensive sweep of the pointer across the map, have declared that by 'Zero hour' all the German trenches will be 'obliterated' by our shells – a tale we have heard before. The last lecturer, however, on the artillery rôle, ominously omitted to provide this comforting assurance . . .

Our Air Offensive has already commenced. Now the Batttle Bombardments have opened at Ypres; it is whispered that they have drawn a considerable reply from the enemy . . .

All ranks are in great spirits in anticipation of smashing the Germans this time.

Author's Papers: Haig Diary

Haig visited II Corps again and interviewed Jacob and key members of his staff, as well as the staffs of the 8th, 18th, 24th, 25th and 30th Divisions.

20 JULY.   I spent an hour going through their schemes in detail. Every detail had been carefully worked out, every possibility it seemed to me had been foreseen and provided for. Every commander said he was satisfied that his plan was complete, and that it would succeed. All this gave me immense satisfaction and a great feeling of confidence.

Looking round the faces opposite me, I felt what a fine hard-looking determined lot of men the war had brought to the front.

*Brig-General J. L. Jack was at this time CO of 2/West Yorks, 8th Division.

Haig then visited XIX Corps, and

found the same thoroughness and the same confidence in victory.

Haig visited XVIII and XIV Corps and Fifth Army Headquarters.

21 JULY.   I told Gough how thoroughly satisfied I was with all the preparations
made by his subordinate commanders, and the confidence which I noticed existed
among all ranks.

As regards the artillery, we had passed the critical moment which was when we
started to place our batteries in position in the face of the enemy who had
observation. The artillery battle had already lasted over a fortnight and we were in
a fair way to win it. Our losses had been extremely small in guns and personnel.
We outnumbered the enemy's guns *tremendously*!

> Brig-General C. D. Baker-Carr,* *From Chauf-
> feur To Brigadier*, Ernest Benn, 1930, p 227

During the whole of the preliminary preparations, I never met one single soul who
anticipated success, with the exception of GHQ, who, either through ignorance of
the true state of affairs or for other reasons, endeavoured to inspire us with
confidence concerning the result.

SOLDIERS AND POLITICIANS

> Hankey, ii, p 683

16 JULY.   In the evening Lloyd George gave a dinner at 10 Downing Street to the
War Policy Committee (Curzon, Milner, Smuts and self). Balfour and Carson
being also guests. We went over much the same ground as at the last dinner at
Curzon's, and the final decision was to allow Haig to begin his offensive, but not to
allow it to degenerate into a drawn-out, indecisive battle of the 'Somme' type. If
this happened, it was to be stopped and the plan for an attack on the Italian Front
would be tried.

> Author's Papers: Robertson to Haig, 18 July

You will remember that when you left here the Cabinet had not definitely
approved your plans but said that you were to 'go on with your preparations'. The
War Policy Committee of the Cabinet, whom you met, have been continuing their
discussions ever since, when Mesopotamia† has allowed them to do so, but up to
the present no official approval of your plans has been given. I understand,

---

*General Baker-Carr commanded a Tank brigade.
† Repercussions of the publication of a controversial report on the Mesopotamia Campaign.

however, that the War Cabinet are now in favour of your plans, and I have daily been expecting that they would tell me so, but up to the present they have not done so. Apparently the Prime Minister is the only one who is sticking out against your plans, and who continues to be in favour of the Italian venture. I have twice reminded him that time is running short and that your preparations will soon be completed. However, this is mainly to tell you what has been taking place and is in no way meant to interfere with what you are doing or what you propose to do. The order to go on with your preparations still holds the field, and as the War Cabinet know that your preparations will soon be complete there is no more to be said on the matter. I daresay that tomorrow or the next day I shall be told that your plans are approved.

The Prime Minister had the War Cabinet Members to dinner on Monday night when there was a long discussion, and apparently while all the Members except the Prime Minister were in favour of accepting our advice they all expressed, so I am told, at different times the fear that you might endeavour to push on further than you were justified pending further artillery preparation, because they have all got in their mind, and correctly so, that the greatest losses sometimes occur in trying to take and hold positions too far in advance. I had a talk with one of the Cabinet on this subject yesterday and impressed upon him that I thought they need have no fear as it is well understood that the extent of the advance must, roughly speaking, be limited by the assistance of the guns until such times as a real breakthrough occurs. He replied that so long as this step-by-step system of advance was adhered to he would back your plan for all it was worth. I understand that the Prime Minister asked one of the Cabinet when your operations ought to be stopped, if they did not seem likely to achieve complete success – that is how many losses we ought to incur before stopping. The Cabinet Minister gave a good answer. He said that he could not answer the question merely with reference to losses, and that the time to stop would be when it appeared that our resources were not sufficient to justify a continuance of our effort.

The Allied Conference in Paris is fixed for the 25th instant. I should be glad if you would let me know your wishes as to attending. As by then there will be no question of discussing the situation on the West Front – because you will more or less be on the point of starting – I do not think there is any occasion for you to attend, and you know how useless these conferences are. Still, if you would like to attend I can arrange. In any case you may be sent for, but if I know your inclinations I shall know better what to do. I imagine you will be doing much better work with your armies.

Hankey, ii, p 683

18 July.   War Policy Committee in the morning, at which the conclusions agreed to at Monday's dinner were confirmed, and I was asked to write a report for circulation by Thursday evening (i.e. the very next evening). I said I could only do it by knocking off all other work. So from 4 pm until 9.15 pm I worked away at it,

locking my door, refusing all visitors and telephone calls . . . Just arrived at the club in time for a whisky and soda before the forbidden hour, but was too late for dinner and had to get a scrappy supper.

19 JULY.   Worked at report from 10 am until 2.30 pm and then on until 5 pm when I finished. It was sixty pages long and a very complete production, though I say it who shouldn't.

The Report may be found in CAB 27/6. It covers the whole field of the War Policy Committee's deliberations under six headings:

Part I: Existing War Policy (as of 8 June);
Part II: The New Factors:
    (a) Upheaval in Russia.
    (b) The weakening of the French army and people.
    (c) Recent events in Germany.
    (d) The deterioration of the situation in Austria.
    (e) The intervention of the United States of America.
    (f) The new situation in Greece.
    (g) The financial situation.
    (h) The British position in regard to man-power.
    (i) The shipping situation.
Part III: Entirely devoted to The Shipping Situation;
Part IV: Future Military Policy in the Main Theatres of Operations; (A recapitulation of 'Cadorna's plan' and 'Haig's plan'; on the latter, the report notes in Para. 124 that 'The preliminary bombardment began a few days ago . . .'; Para. 125 states: '. . . the Committee have decided to recommend that this plan shall be commenced. They feel strongly, however, that the offensive must on no account be allowed to drift into protracted, costly and indecisive operations as occurred in the offensive on the Somme in 1916, as the effect of this might be disastrous on public opinion . . . The Committee, therefore, attach the utmost importance to a frequent review of the results . . .')
Part V: Future Military Policy in Other Theatres;
Part VI: Summary of Recommendations;
    (The key recommendation was No. 2 (a): 'The Field-Marshal Commanding the British Expeditionary Force in France should be authorized to carry out the plans for which he has prepared, as explained by him to the Cabinet Committee on War Policy on 19 June.')

The Report, strangely enough, was dated 10 August, by which time the foregoing decision had been conveyed to Haig in another manner, as we shall see, and had already passed into history.

Cabinet Papers, CAB 23/13: War Cabinet No. 191a, 20 July

Military Policy in the Western and Southern Theatres.
2. The War Cabinet approved that the military policy in the Western and Southern theatres should be as follows:
(a) Report Recommendation No. 2 (a) verbatim, as above.
(b) If it appears probable in the execution of these plans that the results are not commensurate with the effort made and the losses incurred, the whole question should be re-examined by the War Cabinet with a view to the cessation of this offensive and the adoption of an alternative plan.
(c) The only alternative plan which at present commends itself to the Cabinet Committee is General Cadorna's proposal for a great offensive against Austria, supported by British and, if the French are prepared to co-operate, by French heavy artillery . . .
(e) The Chief of the Imperial General Staff should take immediate steps to give effect to these decisions.

Author's Papers: Robertson to Haig, 21 July

I am sending you today a copy of the Draft Conclusions recently reached by the War Cabinet. We had a rough and tumble Meeting yesterday. The fact is that the Prime Minister is still very averse from your offensive and talks as though he is hoping to switch off to Italy within a day or two after you begin. I told him that unless there were very great miscalculations on your part, and unless the first stage proved to be more or less a disastrous failure – which I certainly did not expect that it would be – I did not think it would be possible to pronounce a verdict on the success of your operations for several weeks. He seemed to have in mind what the French said last spring when Nivelle told them that he would be able to say in one or two days whether his operations had been successful or not.

He is also very keen on capturing Jerusalem and this of course I also had to fight, and I intend continuing to do so. Altogether I had one of the worst afternoons I have ever had, but I find that after all I generally get more or less what I want. But it is very disturbing all the same to have these hankerings after other plans and mistrust in present ones.

Haig Diary: Blake, p 246

22 JULY. Sir William Robertson (CIGS) arrived from England about 7 pm. After dinner we discussed the situation. He agreed with me as to the danger of sending forces to Italy. I urged him to be firmer and play the man; and, if need be, resign, should Lloyd George persist in ordering troops to Italy against the advice

of the General Staff. I also spoke strongly on the absurdity of the Government
giving its approval now to operations after a stiff artillery fight had been going on
for three weeks.* I handed him my reply to his official letter informing me of this
approval. In it I requested to be told whether I had the full support of the
Government or not.

Author's Papers: O.A.D. 564, Haig to
Robertson, 22 July

I beg to acknowledge receipt of your communication dated 21st instant, for-
warding for my information and guidance a copy of the draft Conclusions reached
by the War Cabinet at a meeting held on the 20th instant, and requesting me to
forward any observations I may wish to make in so far as the Conclusions affect
my Command.

I observe that with the exception of sub-paragraphs (a) and (b) of paragraph 2
of the War Cabinet's Conclusions the question of the operations of the Armies
under my Command was not dealt with directly at this meeting.

As regards these two sub-paragraphs, I note the decision recorded in (a). The
only remark which it appears desirable to offer on this now is that from the
postponement of their decision to such a late date I fear the War Cabinet cannot
have realized clearly the very serious objections to countermanding an attack at
the last moment, especially under existing conditions in France.

The preparations for this offensive have involved immense labour for Commanders, Staffs, and troops for many months – indeed some of these preparations,
such as railway construction and water supply arrangements, were commenced
more than a year ago.

The final concentration of troops, guns, and everything else required for such
an attack entails a very heavy strain on all ranks and services for many weeks and
involves the acceptance of risks on other parts of the front from the time when this
concentration commences until the attack is launched. These risks are seriously
increased if plans are liable to interference, after concentration has commenced,
by causes outside the carefully calculated chances of hostile actions.

The effect on the morale of the officers and men might have been so serious if it
had been decided, for no reason apparent to them, to abandon the attack at this
stage, after all their efforts to prepare for it, after a fierce struggle for artillery and
air supremacy has already been in progress for some days, and when the assault is
almost on the verge of being launched, that I earnestly hope the War Cabinet may
never again find it necessary to postpone such a decision to the last moment.

For sub-paragraph (b) I note that I may expect the cessation of the offensive to

---

*Haig is referring to the assembly period, as well as the bombardment, the hard beginning of
a hard battle for the Royal Artillery. In the words of his Despatch (25 December, 1917):
'The long preparatory bombardments had to be conducted from a narrow and confined
space, for the most part destitute alike of cover and protection, and directly overlooked by
the enemy.'

be ordered hereafter if, in the judgment of the War Cabinet, the results are not commensurate with the effort made and the losses incurred.

No doubt, before such an order is issued, the effort and losses of the enemy as well as on our side will be duly considered, as also the possible effect on both the enemy and our own Army of stopping the action, as foreshadowed in this Conclusion. On such points the judgment of the Commander on the spot, in close touch with the situation, is entitled to great weight, and I trust that my opinion may be taken and fully considered before a decision of such vital importance is arrived at.

From these sub-paragraphs, as well as from the Minutes generally, I have formed the impression that the plan of operations, although approved, has neither the full confidence nor the whole-hearted support of the War Cabinet. Such an impression adds very greatly to the responsibilities and anxieties of a Commander in entering on such a serious undertaking; and if the impression is not justified I respectfully ask for an assurance to that effect.

Author's Papers: Robertson to Haig, telegram,
25 July

Your O.A.D. 564 of 22 July. War Cabinet authorizes me to inform you that having approved your plans being executed you may depend on their whole-hearted support and that if and when they decide again to reconsider the situation they will obtain your views before arriving at any decision as to cessation of operations.

French Morale

Blake, pp 246–7: Notes by Haig, possibly an
aide-memoire

22 July.   The British troops are the only troops in the field at the moment on whose capacity to carry through successful attacks against Germans we can rely.

Encouraged by further British successes, the French will recover their capacity to carry through successful attacks, but it is very necessary they should have this encouragement . . .

The weariness and disappointment of the French is a factor of the greatest importance at the moment. Germany knows it, is trying to take advantage of it,* and will continue to do so. She is in a position to do so, which we are not in regard to Austria. If we have a really good success in our forthcoming operations, the value of the French troops will be much increased, and while their re-awakened enthusiasm lasts we should concentrate our endeavours on developing this success.

If we do not have a really good success our most urgent and serious care will be

*In Champagne and at Verdun.

to nurse France through the winter without impairing our offensive power for next year's campaign, which is practically certain to be the last campaign we shall induce France or Russia to face (even if we can get them to face that, which is doubtful).

To nurse France through the winter and to give ourselves the best chance of success next year will tax all our power. We cannot afford to dissipate any of it.

We could see Italy and even Russia drop out, and still continue the war with France and America. But if France drops out we not only cannot continue the war on land but our Armies in France will be in a very difficult position.

To keep France in does not entail our following her advice blindly, or committing further mistakes to please her politicians. But we must be prepared to lighten the burden of her Army by taking over all the line we can take *during the winter*, without detriment to our offensive next year.

Every man and gun that we send to Italy reduces our power in one respect or the other. I consider it so dangerous and so unsound to adopt such a course that, in my opinion, any responsible soldier who consents to issue an order for it must expect to be adjudged by history to have failed in his duty to his country.

FLANDERS

Haig Diary: Duff Cooper, ii, pp 130–1

25 JULY.   At 9.45 General Gough came to see me. All preparations are ready and he is anxious to stick to our date and attack on the 28th. If the French are not ready he thought it would be better to wait two or three days for them than to change our plan at the last minute. I agreed.

At 10 am I received General Anthoine, commanding French First Army. Owing to dull weather, observation had been bad and only 2¼ 'days of fire' had been expended instead of '7 days of fire'. I put the disadvantages of delay to him, but he was determined to have three more days of counter-battery work. So I had to choose between acquiescing with him or ordering him to attack on the 28th before the French are ready. For the future good relations of our two armies it is necessary to give the French every possible chance of gaining a big success this time. Also the present excited feeling in France would not brook a failure at this moment. So I agreed to put off the infantry attack for three days. I then saw Gough again and told him of my decision. He agreed that three days' delay was our best policy.

Charteris, p 236

25 JULY . . . Our bombardment has commenced, but time is passing. We should have attacked by now. All our weather statistics show that we cannot expect much dry weather after this month.

THE INVINCIBLE ENEMY

In his biography of Haig* Charteris later wrote: 'Careful investigation of the records of more than eighty years showed that in Flanders the weather broke early each August with the regularity of the Indian monsoon.' The Commandant of the Meteorological Section at GHQ, Colonel G. Gold, has commented:†

'This statement is so contrary to recorded facts that, to a meteorologist, it seems too ridiculous to need formal refutation.'

He points out that in August, 1915, there were 22 days without any rain, and that from the middle of July, 1916, to the middle of August there was no rain. A comparative table published in Lloyd George's *War Memoirs*, but unfortunately neither naming the meteorological station or stations nor giving a source for the statistics, shows:

	1914	1915	1916	1917	
July	4.88	2.91	3.86	4.095	inches
August	1.57	4.21	2.79	4.170	,,
September	2.95	2.56	3.07	.629	,,

By 1917 the Meteorological Section at GHQ had three stations operating in the northern sector; the nearest to the offensive front was at Vlamertinghe, some three miles west of Ypres. Their records for 1917 show:

	Vlamertinghe	Hazebrouck	Béthune
July	3.14	3.22	3.77
August	5.00	5.07	3.85
September	1.58	.55	.70
October	4.21	3.97	4.37

On this evidence Colonel Gold says 'The rainfall directly affecting the first month of the offensive was more than double the average; *it was over five times the amount for the same period in 1915 and in 1916.*'‡

Haig, by now, was residing at his Advanced Headquarters in a train in a specially constructed siding at Godeswaersvelde, roughly mid-way between Vlamertinghe and Hazebrouck. It was his habit to make a daily record of weather conditions in his diary. For the week before the offensive opened these entries read:

Field-Marshal Earl Haig, Cassell, 1929, p 272
†Letter in *The Spectator*, 17 January, 1958   ‡ Ibid. Col Gold's italics.

24 July. Glass steady. Fine warm day.

25 July. Glass fell at midnight, but steady after 8 am. Heavy thunderstorm from 9 till midday. Evening bright and clear.

26 July. Glass steady. Dull damp morning. Cleared later. Fine afternoon and clear evening.

27 July. Glass steady. Hazy morning, but cleared up about noon, when observation became good.

28 July. Glass steady. Fine morning. Fair observation. Cloudy at times. Warm.

29 July. Glass unsteady. Heavy thunderstorm between 9 am and midday. Afternoon fine.

30 July. Rain fell in the early morning. At noon glass was rising.

FLANDERS

26 JULY.   Charteris reported that the situation as regards the enemy was very favourable for our main attack.

O.H., 1917, vol ii, p 134

The air battles which took place during the last fortnight of July were the most bitter the War had yet produced. Clashes occurred between groups of about thirty aircraft on either side, and on the evening of the 26th an air battle took place above Polygon Wood involving about ninety-four single-seater fighters at heights from 5,000 to 17,000 feet. Throughout this struggle for air supremacy, and so far as the weather allowed, the British aircraft kept to their programme of artillery co-operation, air photography, reconnaissance and bombing. Towards the end of the month the enemy's opposition declined, nearly all encounters taking place on the enemy side of the line.

27 JULY.   General Birch reported that artillery counter-battery work is proceeding satisfactorily.

O.H., 1917, vol ii, p 136

(The German) batteries frequently changed position, each having three or more alternative emplacements, with occasionally a single gun firing from them as deception. For this reason . . . the method of calculating batteries destroyed by counting the successful shoots on gun-pits was misleading.

The actual results of the preparatory bombardment and counter-battery work could not be expected to compare with those obtained in the more favourable circumstances of the Messines battle; nor did they justify the optimistic report given to Sir Douglas Haig on 25 July by Lieut-General Sir Noel Birch, Artillery Adviser at GHQ, that he was 'confident the upper hand over the German artillery had been gained'. His report was particularly at fault in respect of the German artillery concentration in the Gheluvelt area.

General Jack's Diary, p 233

22 JULY.   The German shell fire on Ypres is persistent and heavy in reply to terrific poundings by our artillery. Shell splinters and masonry are constantly flying about while the concussion seldom ceases altogether. All troops not on duty must remain under cover; but even so, the casualties in and around the town are severe, amounting, I hear, to 400 or 500 daily. Between dusk and dawn working and carrying parties, as well as transport bringing stores along the Poperinghe road into Ypres, have nerve-wracking experiences in this ghastly area . . .

Our office is in a tin hut a few yards from the ramparts into which we may adjourn when the fire becomes too hot. Concealed amid the ruins near us are some 8-inch howitzers, two of which lie overturned in their shattered emplacements.

German Official Account, *Der Weltkrieg, 1914 bis 1918*, Mittler, Berlin; trans. Col R. Macleod [Author's Papers]

Under the mighty enemy artillery and trench mortar fire the German infantry suffered severely and even the artillery had a difficult time. As a result of the continuous fighting, which kept them all at maximum effort, it became possible to detect signs of exhaustion in a large number of batteries towards the end of July. The losses in men and equipment were enormous. The heavy field batteries' losses reached 50 per cent . . . The signs that intensive and long lasting battles were ahead were clearly visible. The main effort of the war would be in Flanders.

von Kuhl, *Der Weltkrieg*

In the last third of July the enemy's artillery fire mounted to a planned destruction bombardment. Heavy and extensive harassing fire – from experience always a sign of imminent assault – reached up to 20 km. in the rear areas behind the front line. Heavy enemy air attacks were carried out against Staff billets and against our balloons. The number of enemy balloons increased visibly. At times the artillery fire became drum fire. The big struggle for Flanders was imminent, the new 'Death of Ypres' was being proclaimed . . .*

The week-long, heavy fire brought to the defenders heavy and mounting losses. Some of the front line divisions had to be relieved before the storm broke, for their strength had been consumed. The trenches and entanglements were destroyed and the dug-outs smashed.

*An allusion to the heavy losses of young German volunteer formations in the First Battle of Ypres, 1914, called '*Der Kindermord von Ypern*': 'the death of the children at Ypres'.

Author's Papers: Haig Diary

Fifth Army reported that patrols were temporarily occupying parts of the German front line:

27 JULY.   We have never before found the enemy abandoning ground in this way before our attack. The situation looks most satisfactory.

General Jack's Diary, p 234

28 JULY.   At 6.45 pm the Battalion commences its march to the trenches. The companies, with platoons at 5-minute intervals, file through the Lille Gate . . . We proceed through the entrenched Field Artillery positions, the pieces of the battery nearest us all out of action, lying with broken wheels and shields, or overturned by the successive bombardments that sweep the extensive lines of guns from end to end, and necessitate large replacements after dark.

Haig was now receiving final reports from his various subordinates.

Author's Papers: Haig Diary

28 JULY.   Charteris reported situation satisfactory for our attack.

General Trenchard gave his report . . . Yesterday the fighting was *most severe* and the results highly satisfactory. Our aviators 'drove the enemy out of the Air' said T. to me.

General Birch reports that the artillery situation is satisfactory, and all gunner commanders most confident that *they have gained the upper hand over the hostile artillery* . . . In fact, my artillery adviser is of opinion that 'we have already cowed the enemy's artillery'.

General Anthoine is full of confidence and is pleased with the situation.

Lord Cavan (XIV Corps) is very pleased at the result of yesterday's operations.

29 JULY.   Prisoners report enemy's losses in artillery have been very heavy. One battery in the 49th Reserve Division is said to have had its gun detachments replaced 9 times, and its guns 5 times since the beginning of our bombardment . . .

Charteris reports that the enemy yesterday relieved 4 of his divisions on the battle front. Possibly the enemy may have heard that the 28th was the date of our attack . . . the divisions now in the line will have 3 days under our artillery fire.

30 JULY.   General Anthoine . . . was in excellent spirits and quite confident . . . all his divisional generals feel confident of reaching the final objective tomorrow.

General Birch reported . . . the artillery situation is quite satisfactory.

Charteris, pp 236-7

30 JULY.   Before this reaches you we shall have attacked again, the most important attack and, indeed, the only one that now matters for this year's fighting on
this theatre. It is impossible to forecast the result. The only thing that is certain is
that most unfortunate of all things, a big casualty list. All the preparations are, I
think, as good and as well advanced as those of our other two big attacks this year,
and if we get as much success in this as in the others, great things will happen. My
one fear is the weather . . . I do not think we can hope for more than a fortnight, or
at the best, three weeks of really fine weather. There has been a good deal of
pretty hot discussion, almost controversy, as regards the time of attack.

We cannot hope for a surprise; our preparations must have been seen, and even
if not, our bombardment must have warned the Germans, and no doubt they are
already moving up troops towards our battle area.* I had urged D.H. to attack on
these grounds some days ago in spite of the fact that our preparations were not
fully completed; it was a choice of evils. The Army Commanders wanted more
time; the last conference was definitely heated. The Army Commanders pressed
for delay; D.H. wanted the attack to go on at once, and in the end he accepted the
Army Commanders' view. He could, indeed, do nothing else, for they have to
carry out the job. I came away with D.H. from the conference when it was all
settled, and reminded him of Napoleon's reply to his marshals, 'Ask me for
anything but time'. D.H. was very moody, but once a decision is made he will not
give it another thought. With reasonable luck it will make little difference, but we
have so often been let in by the weather that I am very anxious.

SOLDIERS AND POLITICIANS

Blake, p 247, Haig to Derby, 29 July

Thank you very much indeed for your kind letter of 28th inst. . . . I am very
grateful for your generous expression of friendship and of your readiness to lift
some of the worries from my shoulders on to your own and Robertson's.

I have never for a moment doubted that you both mean to support me to the
utmost – I have no worries on that score. What has really been lacking has been
some practical indications on the part of the War Cabinet that they have confidence in my plan and mean to do their utmost to help me to achieve success.
Briefly that *they* know how to win! . . .

How different to the whole-hearted, almost unthinking support given by our
Government to the Frenchman (Nivelle) last January.

Never a word have I received that the Government is really *determined* to
concentrate all possible resources at this decisive point, at this decisive moment!

---

*The reader will note the contrast between the sober tone of this letter and the stream of
sanguine reports that Charteris proffered to Haig.

THE INVISIBLE ENEMY

Lloyd George, i, p 709

Statistics of Shipping Losses, July, 1917 — 359,539 gross tons sunk.*

FLANDERS

General Jack's Diary, p 236†

30 JULY.   A message arrives: 'Zero hour will be at 3.50 tomorrow morning, the 31st inst.' and is acknowledged. So we are for the 'high jump' once more.

I don't want to be mutilated, but death is a contemptible little enemy. Gone are the personal fears of the 1914 days. One has become accustomed to battles, besides being too strained, wearied and busy to care much about oneself. The certain loss of friends of all ranks will be the worst shock, a shock still keenly felt even after two and a half years of this bloody war. Tomorrow the French, British and German Press will all be hailing a victory, the first two for the capture of some ground, the last for losing so little. The National casualties will be described as 'slight', and those of the enemy as 'heavy'. One must however, keep these thoughts to oneself.

*Hereafter the convoy system began to contain the U-boat threat, as the rest of the table shows:

August	331,370	gross tons sunk
September	186,647	,, ,, ,,
October	261,873	,, ,, ,,
November	175,194	,, ,, ,,
December	257,807	,, ,, ,,

So the Invisible Enemy, though never entirely vanquished, ceased to be a major factor in the Flanders offensive of 1917.

† Colonel Jack was severely wounded a few minutes after Zero hour the next day, and invalided home.

IV

1917: THE WEB

--- ✠ ---

THE INVINCIBLE ENEMY

Haig Diary: Blake, p 249

31 JULY.   Glass steady. Morning dull and coldish. The bright weather reported as coming is slower in its progress than expected by our weather prophet.

FLANDERS: THE OPENING DAY:
THE BATTLE OF PILCKEM RIDGE

von Kuhl, *Der Weltkrieg*

In the early morning of the 31st July a storm of fire broke out the like of which had never been experienced before. The whole Flanders earth moved and appeared to be in flames. It was no drum fire any longer, it was as if Hell itself had opened. What were the horrors of Verdun and the Somme in comparison with this giant expenditure of power? Deep into the farthest corners of Belgium one could hear the mighty thundering of battle. It was as if the enemy wanted to announce to the whole world 'We are coming, and we shall overcome'. At 6.30 in the morning the British and French troops rose from their trenches, following the heaviest drum fire, and moved into the attack.

Ludendorff, ii, p 476

This formed the second great strategic action of the Entente in 1917; it was their bid for final victory and for our submarine base in Flanders . . . The fighting on the Western Front became more severe and costly than any the German Army had yet experienced.

CAB 23/3: War Cabinet No. 200, 31 July

6. The Chief of the Imperial General Staff read a communiqué from the Field-Marshal Commanding-in-Chief in France, which stated that at 3.15* that morning

*Actually 3.50 am.

the offensive had been resumed by the forces under his command to the north-west of Ypres and north of the Yser. General Robertson stated that there were three immediate objectives, which embraced a front of about 15 miles and a depth of about 2½ miles. Up to the time of the despatch of the communiqué the attack was progressing successfully, and the first objective had been achieved. French troops were co-operating in the attack.

Haig Diary: Blake, pp 249–50

31 JULY.   In the afternoon I visited General Gough with CGS . . . Fighting on our right had been most severe. This I had expected. Our Divisions had made good progress and were on top of the ridge which the Menin road crosses, but had not advanced sufficiently eastwards to have observation into the valleys beyond. Further to the west, our troops had established themselves beyond the Steenbeek and the French had taken Bixschoote and the Cabaret Kortekeer (which was so frequently attacked in October and November, 1914). This was a fine day's work . . .

As regards future operations, I told Gough to continue to carry out the original plan; to consolidate ground gained, and to improve his position as he may deem necessary, for facilitating the next advance; the next advance will be made as soon as possible, *but only after adequate bombardment and after dominating the hostile Artillery.**

Charteris, p 238

You ask for news of the progress of the battle.

The chief peculiarity of the fighting on the 31st was, of course, that owing to the weather we could make practically no use of our aircraft. This was most disappointing. The Flying Corps had worked for weeks for superiority in the air, and they had obtained it, only to find that owing to the bad visibility their efforts were in vain. To show what this means, it is enough to say that during the Messines battle in June we received two hundred of what we call 'N.F.'† calls. These are calls sent down by the aeroplanes of fresh targets not previously identified, and which are then taken up by our artillery under direction from the air; on the 31st of July we did not receive a single call of this nature, owing to the bad visibility.

In spite of this the attack on the left, on the centre and on the right centre, was a complete success up to the ultimate objectives. It was, in fact, too much of a success; the troops obtained their objectives without too much loss, and almost in advance of time. In consequence, they attempted to move forward to fresh objectives, and in doing so suffered a very considerable loss of life on the extreme right. The full result of the lack of aircraft visibility was felt at once.

*Haig's italics.   † Now Firing.

Gough, p 202

The enemy, during the night of the 31st, and all through the following day, made constant counter-attacks against the right and centre with the object of regaining his lost possessions. Sometimes these counter-attacks succeeded in driving us back, but our men recountered almost immediately in all cases, and usually succeeded in regaining any ground lost.

Author's Papers: Personal reminiscence by Colonel R. Macleod, Royal Artillery; 31 July

About 2 pm an intense German barrage fell on our forward troops east of the Steenbeek, some from guns at Gheluvelt which enfiladed their positions as far north as St Julien. The 2nd Corps had unfortunately not been able to seize the Gheluvelt plateau and rain and mist made aeroplane observation impossible, so counter battery work was ineffective. Shortly afterwards the Germans attacked and S.O.S. rockets went up. We answered and several times more as more rockets kept going up. I began to be a little alarmed about our ammunition situation. Our infantry were forced to fall back slowly to the Steenbeek, fighting every inch of the way and inflicting casualties. The Germans were stopped short of the Steenbeek, but succeeded in recapturing St Julien.

At 4 pm the drizzle turned to heavy rain and our infantry along the Steenbeek were up to their waists in water. At 6 pm the Germans, up to their knees in mud and water, made their last attack. They were stopped by a heavy S.O.S. barrage and withdrew up the slope leaving many casualties.

Sir Douglas Haig's Despatches edited by Lieut-Colonel J. H. Boraston; Dent, 1919, p 116*

The weather had been threatening throughout the day, and had rendered the work of the aeroplanes very difficult from the commencement of the battle. During the afternoon, while fighting was still in progress, rain began, and fell steadily all night. Thereafter, for four days, the rain continued without cessation, and for several days afterwards the weather remained stormy and unsettled. The low-lying, clayey soil, torn by shells and sodden with rain, turned to a succession of vast muddy pools. The valleys of the choked and overflowing streams were speedily transformed into long stretches of bog, impassable except by a few well-defined tracks, which became marks for the enemy's artillery. To leave these tracks was to risk death by drowning, and in the course of the subsequent fighting on several occasions both men and pack animals were lost in this way. In these conditions operations of any magnitude became impossible, and the resumption of our offensive was necessarily postponed until a period of fine weather should allow the ground to recover.

*This Despatch is actually dated 25 December, 1917.

O.H., 1917,vol ii, pp 177–9

Compared with the first day of the Battles of the Somme 1916 . . . when the casualties reported were 61,816 (reduced later by the return of absentees to 57,540), the losses, 31,850 (for the three days 31st July–2nd/3rd August), were moderate, although in themselves severe.

A general advance of about three thousand yards had been made, whereas at the Somme only three divisions on the right had made fair, but less, progress, and two others only achieved small isolated advances.

Although expectations had not been entirely realized and considerable casualties had been suffered, valuable results had been gained. The enemy's observation areas on the highest part of Gheluvelt plateau (near Clapham Junction) and along the long rise via Bellewaarde to Pilckem had been captured, and nine of his divisions had been badly mauled. Apart from an unusually large number of German dead on the battlefield, over six thousand prisoners (including 133 officers) and 25 guns had been captured. It is now known, as might have been expected, that the front divisions had been so badly shattered that they had to be replaced within a few days by fresh divisions. This relief implied the provision of a new complement of counter-attack divisions in close support. Thus began that steady stream of German divisions to the Flanders front which was to drain the resources of the enemy during the next four months, and keep him from attacking the French.

The situation was, however, only relatively satisfactory. The nine leading divisions of the four corps of the Fifth Army had been intended to reach the third and fourth objectives on the first day, and then to carry out the subsequent advance to the Passchendaele–Staden ridge before relief. Actually, they were less than half-way to the first day's objectives, and had already lost 30 per cent to 60 per cent of their fighting strength . . .

Apart from actual losses the conditions under which the battle was fought were most exhausting for all the troops concerned.

Ludendorff, ii, pp 478–9

On 31 July the English, assisted by a few French divisions on their left, had attacked on a front of about thirty-one kilometres. They had employed such quantities of artillery and ammunition as had been rare, even in the West. At many points along the whole front the enemy had penetrated with tanks. Cavalry divisions were in readiness to push through. With the assistance of the counter-attack divisions, the 4th Army, whose Chief of Staff was now Colonel von Lossberg, succeeded in checking the hostile success and localizing its effect. But, besides a loss of from two to four kilometres of ground along the whole front, it caused us very considerable losses in prisoners and stores, and a heavy expenditure of reserves.

German Official Account

The results of the first heavy blow, which the enemy with his massive superiority in men and equipment had prepared and carried out, were a gap about 16 kilometres wide and up to 3 kilometres deep between Poesele and Hollebeke as well as smaller gains between Hollebeke and the Lys. The losses were heavy. From 21 to 31 July, the Fourth Army had lost 30,000 men of whom about 9,000 were missing, together with 35 guns.*

Repington, ii, pp 8, 10

WEDNESDAY, 1 AUGUST . . . Much pleasure about the battle which began yesterday and has won for us a large area east of Ypres . . . It is thought that the Huns will hate this battle, and we mean to do a lot more before we finish.

*No precise British equivalent exists, but an approximation may be arrived at by adding:

20–7 July (*O.H.*, p 137 f.n.)	7,354
28–30 July (say)	3,500
31 July (Haig estimates 15,000, but say)	16,000
Total (approximately)	26,854
+ French (26–31 July inclusive)	1,800
	28,654

The British Official Historian would add a further 30 per cent to the German figure for unrecorded lightly wounded, a practice not universally admired (see pp 346–7).

August

—————————————— ✠ ——————————————

The Flanders offensive had opened under those most equivocal of auspices, partial success. All along the front men scanned the sky for further omens.

THE INVINCIBLE ENEMY

Author's Papers: Haig Diary

1 AUGUST.   Glass fell a tenth after midnight. Heavy rain began to fall about 3 am and continued all day.

Author's Papers: Haig to Lady Haig, 2 August

The ground now is in a terrible state . . . I see that in New York the heat is intense.

Author's Papers: Colonel Macleod's diary, 3 August

It has rained solidly for three days and the place is knee deep in mud . . . It is extraordinary weather for August.

Charteris, p 241

4 AUGUST.   All my fears about the weather have been realized. It has killed this attack. Every day's delay tells against us . . . We can do nothing but wait.

Author's Papers: Haig Diary

5 AUGUST.   Glass rising. Fine day but cloudy, observation bad, warmer.
6 AUGUST.   Glass steady. Warm foggy morning. Ground is drying up, but observation bad.

Author's Papers: Haig to Lady Haig, 7 August

It has stopped raining here, but is still very cloudy and misty in the mornings. This is rather disappointing especially as the weather is brilliantly fine in Paris I hear.

Author's Papers: Haig Diary

8 AUGUST.   Glass falling. Haze in morning. Cleared later, but several heavy thunderstorms during the day.

Charteris, p 243

9 AUGUST.   The rain keeps on and with each day's rain our task gets more difficult . . . the front area now baffles description. I went up again yesterday towards dusk. It is just a sea of mud, churned up by shell-fire. There was very little firing, and indeed nothing of what we call in the communiqués 'activity', only the endless toil of moving reliefs and rations and ammunition under incredibly difficult conditions.

FLANDERS

Author's Papers: Haig Diary, 1 August

Haig visited Fifth Army HQ and the corps commanders. He began to entertain a misgiving that Gough was not conforming to the battle programme that Haig had put to him with considerable emphasis at the end of June,* and was trying to thrust his army forward on a wrong axis. The name of Broodseinde, first heard in 1914,† came back into history.

II Corps.
(Jacob's) advance was stopped by hidden machine guns in concrete emplacements . . . (he) is quite condifent of being able to capture and hold the ridge in his next attempt.

XIX Corps
Obliged to retire owing to artillery fire from the main ridge to the east. This confirms my view that progress cannot be made by an advance towards the Forêt d'Houthoulst until the main Broodseinde–Staden ridge is taken.

2 AUGUST.   At 10 am I saw Gough and N. Malcolm . . . I showed him on my relief map the importance of the Broodseinde–Passchendaele ridge, and gave it as my opinion that his main effort must be devoted to capturing that. Not until it was in his possession could he hope to advance his centre. He quite agreed.‡

I also told him to have patience, and not to put in his infantry attack until after two or three days of fine weather, to enable our guns to get the upper hand and to dry the ground.

*See p 180.   †See p 8.
‡See p 112. This was the consequence of Gough's 'slight change in the plan' on 6 and 7 June.

Gough, p 202

We were now to encounter a different system of defence, impelled by the
terribly wet and muddy ground . . . It was not possible for the enemy – or in fact
for ourselves – to maintain long and continuous lines of heavily-wired entrench-
ments. The defence now took the form of small machine-gun posts in the most
defensible localities and in the driest places, supporting each other. The Germans
during the course of the previous two years had also built small but very powerful
concrete shelters. These were covered with mud and scattered throughout the
desert of wet shell-holes which stretched in every direction. They were impossible
to locate from a distance, and in any case were safe against anything but the very
heaviest shells.

The farms, most of them surrounded by very broad wet ditches, or moats, had
also been heavily concreted within their·shattered walls; every one of these was a
fort in itself.

The Germans were the first to make such use of concrete in field defences. They
were indeed thorough and efficient enemies.

The concrete shelters were christened 'pill-boxes'; many are there to
this day, incorporated in Flemish farms, and inspection of their massive
walls and roofs explains why they were able to resist the fire of 6-inch
howitzers, and even 8-inch howitzers needed to score a direct hit. An
officer of GHQ, Lieut-Colonel J. H. Boraston, says that 'the result of the
concentration of artillery fire upon them was to create around them a sort
of moat of mud and water – an addititional obstacle to infantry attack'.*
The 'pill-boxes' were first encountered on a large scale at Messines, and
new tactics were devised to deal with them.

Cyril Falls, *The First World War*, Longmans,
1960

In many cases the infantry tackled the forts – 'pill-boxes', as they called them –
with skill, working round them under cover of Lewis-gun fire and then killing the
defenders at close quarters with rifles and grenades. However, even with good
tactics, the human body is lucky to prevail over ferro-concrete, and many brilliant
attacks failed, with nothing to show but a few corpses sprawled about the strong
points.

Charteris, p 240

3 AUGUST . . . With regard to the enemy's casualty list, I do not like very much
giving an official estimate, which, as you know, can only be academic, and the
Germans have always six to four of the best of us in making official estimates of

*G.A.B. Dewar and Lt-Colonel J. H. Boraston, *Sir Douglas Haig's Command*, Constable,
1922, p 374 f.n.

their casualties. But there is no doubt, from the evidence of reliable, competent and independent observers, that the number of German dead, anyhow on the left flank of our advance, was greater than in any of the previous advances this year or last year. The reason for this is that we have a better organized artillery bombardment, and that owing to the nature of the ground the Germans had no proper dug-outs to take refuge in.

General Headlam,* who makes the point of wandering over each battlefield, and in the path of the infantry, tells me that this is the only one in which he has seen a remarkably greater number of German than British casualties, and he certainly does not err on the side of being optimistic.

Haig Diary: Blake, p 251

4 AUGUST.   Fifth Army are relieving all the Divisions in front line on account of the wet weather.

In view of the bad weather and wet ground, General Gough has cancelled the orders which he issued for the continuance of his attack.

German Official Account

The bad weather continued. With the exception of the 5th heavy rain fell from 2 to 6 August turning the ground in many places into a swamp. In the fighting area in front of the Ypres and Wytschaete Groups† vast areas of water were visible. The men in the trenches suffered severely from these weather conditions. There were only a limited number of dug-outs in their battered positions and they could find no shelter in the water-filled craters. The number of sick and wounded increased.

AMERICA

Haig Diary: Blake, p 250

1 AUGUST.   I saw Colonel de Bellaigue soon after 9 am before he left for French GHQ to see General Pétain. I asked him to urge the latter to start his attack as soon as possible in order to prevent reinforcements from being brought against the British by the enemy from the French part of the front . . . I told him to call Pétain's attention to the certain results of the policy advocated in Paris during the May Conference, viz. to 'wait and do nothing serious on the Western front *this year* until Americans arrive'. This would have suited the Germans admirably because they would then have concentrated all their available reserves against Russia so as to gain a decision in that theatre before the winter. In my opinion, now is the critical moment of the war, and the French must attack as strongly as possible and as soon as possible, so as to co-operate with the British in dealing the enemy as strong a blow as possible. I mentioned the bad state of discipline in the

---

*Later Lieut-General Sir John Headlam.   † Equivalent to British army corps.

6th Bavarian Reserve Division – one of the enemy's crack units – and that the prisoners taken yesterday suffered from malnutrition due to shortage of food.

GERMANY

The Private War Of Seaman Stumpf, pp 344–8

Today's date is 2 August. It is the third anniversary of the declaration of war on France and Russia . . .

If I were called upon to render a medical diagnosis of the present state of feelings among the enlisted men,* it would read something like this:

High state of excitement caused by a total lack of confidence in the officers. Persistence of the fixed notion that the war is conducted and prolonged solely in the interests of the officers. Manifestations of bitter anger due to the fact that the enlisted men are starving and suffering while the officers carouse and roll in money.

Is it therefore any wonder that the men should now inevitably turn to revolt as a means of improving their sordid lot? As far as I have been able to tell, the mutiny raged most strongly on the ships of the Kaiser class, especially on *Prinzregent Luitpold* and *König Albert*. Apparently the Captain† bears most of the blame. He arrested a stoker for collecting subscriptions to *Vorwärts*.‡ The joint protests of two crews of stokers compelled the Captain to set him free again . . . One might almost laugh if it weren't so terribly serious. Before these people will admit their guilt a few heads will have to roll. What a shame that a good and industrious nation like Germany is ruled so miserably . . . I am convinced that an actual revolutionary situation exists in the fleet.§

Author's Papers: Haig Diary

3 AUGUST.   Everything points to a distinct deterioration of the enemy's morale. We hear of their men refusing to stay in the front trenches, and, guns no longer being accurate through wear, German infantry are losing faith in their own artillery.

Author's Papers: Haig to Lady Haig, 5 August

It is highly satisfactory to see that the morale of the German troops is steadily getting worse. In fact quite a change has occurred since Messines.

*Naval personnel.
† Of the *Prinzregent Luitpold*.   ‡ Organ of the Social Democratic Party.
§ Stumpf's further account of the episode, based on dockyard rumour, is fanciful, but the facts were serious enough, as his editor makes clear in a footnote on p 347. The secret of this mutiny was so well kept that it did not reach the ears of the British War Cabinet until 12 October.

MANPOWER

Author's Papers: Haig Diary

5 AUGUST. I went into the state of *our reserves*, and find they are likely to be sufficient; but, owing to lack of men, divisions after having been once in the battle cannot be made up again, but must go forward a second time *below* war establishment. Also divisions on the defensive fronts must be allowed to fall to 8 or 9,000 infantry. This is due to lack of drafts.

Ibid, Haig to Robertson, 9 August

The country will never forgive Govt. for its failure in this vital matter.

FLANDERS

A note of increasing anxiety may be detected at GHQ, not only about the Fifth Army's strategic dispositions, but also about its tactics. On 7 August GHQ issued new Tactical Notes.

Author's Papers

1. From recent information of the enemy's dispositions and views as well as from our experience in the most recent battles, including 31 July, it appears that there has been a modification in the enemy's system of tactics, and that his present tendency is to reserve his most serious counter-attacks until the later stages of the fight. We know that, recently, he has drawn back his guns before our attack, and that he now holds counter-attacking divisions behind the divisions detailed to hold the lines of defence. We know also that some, at least, of his heaviest counter-attacks were launched on 31 July against our troops after they had reached the black line* and pushed on beyond it; doubtless on the theory that our troops at that stage, tired by their previous efforts, weakened by losses, and in some disorder, would be more easily overcome than earlier in the fight.
2. If we accept this as the enemy's system of 'major' tactics, the question arises whether our dispositions for attack do not require some modification in order to ensure the defeat of such counter-attacks.

A primary consideration with us in fixing the depth to which to push an attack is the factor of artillery preparation and the final artillery barrage to cover the troops in their final objective. Do we take sufficiently into consideration the physical capacity of the infantry? That requires to be gauged with even more care

*Objectives were designated by colours, as follows: 1st objective, 'Blue'; 2nd, 'Black', 3rd, 'Green'; 4th 'Red'.

and accuracy than the limits of the artillery barrage, especially in the earlier stages of the offensive when our object is the exhaustion of the enemy and when gain of ground is only of value in so far as it assists us in attaining that object. We must exhaust the enemy as much as possible *and ourselves as little as possible* in the early stages of the fight. Later, when he is so exhausted and disorganized that he cannot hit back effectively, we can push our advance to its utmost limits and call on our men to the utmost limits of their endurance; at that stage all the ground we desire to gain can be taken with comparative ease.

In short, in the earlier stages of the offensive our furthest objective must be not only within the power of our artillery, but within the power of our infantry (having regard to the state of the ground existing at the time of the attack, and to the discipline and state of training of the divisions) so that we may gain the great advantage of beating off the enemy's counter-attacks. The next blow should then follow as quickly as possible, and this object is assisted by not pushing our infantry to exhaustion in the first instance, so that, without relief, they may be capable of advancing again after three or four days, or if possible even less.

On 31 July certain divisions which pushed on beyond the black line with the greatest gallantry, in some cases reaching and even passing the green line, were then thrown back with loss. Exposure of flanks and some delay in obtaining artillery assistance against counter-attacks – due to unfavourable weather and consequent lack of air observation – partly accounts for this; but it does not account for it entirely, and there is some reason to suppose that the forces which reached the green line were too weak and too exhausted to maintain the positions won. If they were too exhausted, this points to the green line having been beyond their physical powers.

If they were too weak in numbers, it points to a need to reconsider our dispositions. In almost all cases where (e.g) 2 brigades were detailed to take the black line the task of pushing on to the green line was entrusted to only one brigade. If it be true that the heaviest counter-attacks were made by the enemy beyond the black line, and that the latter was captured, in most cases, with comparative ease, should we not reverse this procedure and detail 2 brigades for the further objective and only 1 for the nearer ones? Or at least should we not have equal forces for each?

These points require close, full, and immediate investigation before the depth of our next advance and the disposition of the troops for it are decided on.

3. The other points for immediate investigation are:

    (a) the arrangements for mopping up;

    (b) the use made of machine gun barrages in offence and defence.

4. Mopping up appears to have been carried out more effectively by some divisions than by others. The systems adopted in each case require very close investigation in order that full value may be obtained from experience. The results of this investigation should be communicated to General Headquarters as soon as possible for circulation to all Armies.

Amongst other points to be investigated under this head is that of the use made by the enemy of shell-holes for machine guns.

Statements have been made of much trouble being experienced by fire from such shell-holes taking our men in reverse. If these statements be correct the arrangements made for examining such shell-holes by moppers-up cannot have been sufficient.

It may be that their enemy occupants have in some cases shammed death and all moppers-up should be warned to take the obvious precautions against this.

5. Barrages and covering fire, offensive and defensive, by massed machine guns have, in many recent cases, been brought to a high pitch of perfection. If made full use of, these massed machine guns can afford very great assistance to an attack and can render counter-attack almost, if not quite, impossible.

We are at present well ahead of the enemy in the use of massed machine guns in this manner, and it is most important to develop it to the utmost.

All Corps and Divisional Commanders should satisfy themselves that the methods now taught at our machine gun schools, and successfully practised in battle on many occasions, are fully understood and applied in their commands.

6. The value of rifle fire both in attack and defence has again been demonstrated by divisions which – probably as a result of careful and methodical training – have made full use of it, though it appears, unfortunately, that in several divisions it is not yet sufficiently appreciated.

This paper seemed worth reproducing in full as an example of how GHQ, with the battle only a week old, sought to distil its lessons for future general use. Unfortunately, in a war of continuous innovation, every battle experience was likely to be a fresh one. The opening of the Battle of Arras showed that the Army had come a long way since the Somme – but the later stages showed that so had the Germans. The Battle of Messines showed that it had fully mastered techniques for capturing the enemy's front – but being a strictly limited operation had nothing to teach about maintaining momentum. The Battle of Pilckem Ridge showed that the Army had absorbed the lessons of Vimy and Messines – but that once more the Germans had been doing some thinking too.

Tactically, it may be said that the whole of the First World War on the densely occupied, heavily armed Western Front revolved around the problem of how to maintain an advance through deeply entrenched positions, defended by barbed wire, machine guns and plentiful artillery. The early Marks of tanks were helpful, but not an answer in themselves. This was, from beginning to end, basically an artillery war, and there never was a time when the problem of attack was susceptible of solution without the use of artillery; it was a matter of making this use as judicious as possible. Merely multiplying guns did not provide an answer: heavy and protracted bombardments, particularly in wet weather, intensified the obstacle that the infantry (with or without tanks) would have to overcome. Spreading targets, either in width or depth, nullified the advantage of increasing numbers. More and more, all armies moved towards short, intense, surprise bombardments, concentrated on precise targets.

What was difficult to appreciate was the dialectical proposition that only rigidity could ensure tactical flexibility. This was to be fully demonstrated in 1918. In 1917 the difference between a 'thruster' like Gough, and a 'methodical' general like Plumer, satisfied with smaller gains, is difficult to discern in actual plans or orders. It was nevertheless there, communicated more by what they did *not* say to their subordinates than by what they did say. Gough would not prohibit attempts to advance if 'opportunity' seemed to offer; Plumer would be less concerned with that, but would dwell upon the problems of holding and consolidating the gains made. In 1918 the Australian General Monash *positively forbade* any departure from plans once agreed, no matter how tempting the opportunities. What this meant was that his artillery always knew where his infantry was, and could support and protect it accordingly. Opportunism defeated itself by silencing its own artillery; Monash's rigid method, by ensuring the co-operation required for the success of each stage, made possible a flexible approach to the direction and timing of the next bound. When truth is hidden in such contradictions, it takes some time to bring it to light. Plumer's success at Messines, and his advances in September–October at Ypres, were the beginnings of the process.

SOLDIERS AND POLITICIANS

> Field-Marshal Sir William Robertson, *Soldiers And Statesmen*, ii, pp 250–1; Blake, pp 251–2: Robertson to Haig, 9 August

An Anglo-French-Italian conference took place in London on 7–8 August.

The Conference lasted two days. It was of the usual character and resulted in the usual waste of time . . .

Foch and I were told off to say what amount of heavy artillery could be sent from the West Front in time for operations on the Italian Front on 15 September, and it was suggested by Thomas, Sonnino,* and Lloyd George that it would

*Italian Foreign Minister.

perhaps be a good thing to postpone the contemplated Italian offensive, due to begin in a week's time, till 15 September. The Italian General here pointed out the impossibility of doing this, and Foch and I later weighed in with the opinion that we could send no more heavy artillery to Italy in time for 15 September. This was very distasteful to Mr Lloyd George and his colleagues. I may say here that Baron Sonnino, and for that matter Cadorna, are both anxious to get heavy artillery out of us, and even divisions, and urged that they could then dispose of Austria. This is also Mr Lloyd George's plan for winning the war, with the result that there was a further long discussion on the subject yesterday. I expressed my opinion pretty freely in the morning, and said, amongst other things, that I was surprised to receive the impression I had from what Ministers had said, which showed that they attached no importance to the great and serious operations now taking place or about to take place on the West Front and in Italy . . .

Unfortunately, Lloyd George has got the French with him as well as the Italians . . . (Foch) seems to have made up his mind that it is hopeless looking for good results on the West Front. This will make my task much harder . . .

But Lloyd George being keen on the Italian project for the time being and knowing that I am against it and that the French are for it, and as the French keep rubbing in that it is necessary to have a Central Staff at Paris, I can see Lloyd George in the future wanting to agree to some such organization so as to put the matter in French hands and to take it out of mine. However, we shall see all about this. His game will be to put up (the useless) Foch against me as he did Nivelle against you in the Spring. He is a real bad 'un. The other members of the War Cabinet seem afraid of him. Milner is a tired, dyspeptic old man. Curzon a gas-bag. Bonar Law equals Bonar Law. Smuts has good instinct but lacks knowledge. On the whole he is best, but they help one very little.

Author's Papers: General Sir R. Whigham* to
Haig, 9 August.

I am taking on myself the responsibility of writing you a few lines privately to let you know that the CIGS has been having a real bad time with the Prime Minister this week. He (the PM) said openly before the whole Conference of the Allied representatives that he had no confidence in the General Staff or their plans and that he had known all along that this latest offensive was doomed to failure, and a good deal more in the same strain . . . this week he has surpassed himself in his methods of treating his principal military adviser . . . By constant fighting, however, CIGS has persuaded the War Cabinet to adhere to the prosecution of your present plans and there is therefore no question of a change at present.

Esher, iv, pp 132–3: Esher to Haig, 9 August

All the politicians, English, French and Italian, are drunk with their own verbosity. They talk themselves into the belief that they are winning the war, when

*Deputy CIGS.

they are losing it hard. Lying at the root of our failures, English and French, is the defensive attitude of mind. Disheartened by the Gallipoli catastrophe, the governing politicians have been afraid of their shadows ever since. They have always disliked in their hearts your offensives of the Somme, Arras and Messines. They were ready to sacrifice you at the first check. At sea, on land and in the air their eyes have been fixed on the problems of defence against the enemy's attack.

THE INVINCIBLE ENEMY

Author's Papers: Haig Diary

10 AUGUST.   Glass rising. Fine clear morning.
11 AUGUST.   Fine morning, but heavy thunderstorms took place during the day.
12 AUGUST.   Heavy rain fell in the night but morning was fine, and day bright and clear. Observation good.

Author's Papers: Haig to Lady Haig, 13 August

We are anxiously waiting for fine weather. We want 3 or 4 days to enable our aeroplanes to regain their supremacy over the enemy's flying men. As August up to date has been very wet I hope that the rest of the month and September may be fine.

Author's Papers: Haig Diary

14 AUGUST.   Fine day, two or three heavy thunder showers.
15 AUGUST.   Glass steady. Local thunder showers during the day, observation good in the afternoon.

FLANDERS

O.H., 1917, vol ii, pp 184–5

The preparations for the proposed operations were hampered, and their prospect of success spoilt, by the undiminished strength of the German artillery concentration on and behind the Gheluvelt plateau. This mass of guns continued to harass, by day and by night, the 6,000-yard frontage and the back areas of the II and XIX Corps between Stirling Castle and St Julien, whilst those of the XVIII and XIV Corps northwards from St Julien were left in comparative quiet. The counter-batteries of the Fifth Army, on the other hand, continued to spread their fire over the whole Army frontage of 12,000 yards in preparation for the renewed general offensive . . . As a result, the German artillery concentration opposite the II Corps remained unmastered. From the evening of 31 July onwards it pounded the new battery emplacements, so that their construction and occupation became a long and costly task, which was not completed until 8 August. Artillery casualties were severe both in men and in guns, and as early as 4 August many batteries were reduced to half-strength; and some brigades had to be reorganized from four into two batteries. The recurring wastage of artillery fire-power, due to the German counter-battery work, was a severe handicap to the artillery programme.

Author's Papers: Personal reminiscence by
Colonel R. Macleod

On 8 August I had two men killed and eleven wounded, and more on other days. Trained men were precious, so, when a strafe* started, I withdrew the detachments to a trench the other side of Boundary road behind us.

Now and again the shelling set fire to the camouflage netting over the guns, making shells on the racks below explode. The fires had to be put out with buckets filled with water from shell holes.

The battery 100 yards ahead of us, which I passed on my way to the OP, was twice completely destroyed in the strafes, every man killed or wounded and every gun knocked out. We, at the back end of the strafe, were luckier because the shelling was not so intense.

I think the muddy ground saved us many casualties because shells were often buried a long way down before they exploded, thus blanketing much of their effect.

The Battle of Gheluvelt Plateau, 10 August

This attempt by II Corps to clear the area due east of Ypres which Haig had always recognized as vital, but had failed to make Gough see in the same light, is bluntly described by the Official History as a 'failure'.

Author's Papers: Haig Diary

10 August.   The attack was most satisfactory . . . our guns killed vast numbers of the enemy when forming up for counter-attacks. Six of these were attempted but all failed.

Gough, p 203

The Germans realized that merely passive defence was not sufficient. They therefore threw their troops forward to constant counter-attacks immediately we had gained any new position. These cost them extremely heavy losses but they delayed and hampered us – nor did we escape our share of casualties in all the fierce fighting entailed by their energetic and resolute action.

On the afternoon of the 10th August they launched no less than five counter-attacks against the front of the II Corps, all of which were repulsed except the last, which forced our line back out of a wood known as Glencorse.

*Slang for 'enemy bombardment'.

Author's Papers: Haig Diary

10 AUGUST.   Owing to the rain Gough has had to postpone his further operations
for two days.

SOLDIERS AND POLITICIANS

Author's Papers: Haig to Robertson

13 AUGUST.

My Dear Robertson,

Very many thanks for your letter of the 9th inst telling me of the doings of the
recent London Conference.

You already know my views. Briefly, this being the decisive point, the only
sound policy is for the Govt. to support me *whole-heartedly* and concentrate all
possible resources here. And do it *now* while there is time, instead of continuing to
discuss other enterprises.

In this Army we are convinced we can beat the enemy, provided units are kept
up to strength in men and material. Our opinion is based on actual *facts*, viz: the
poor state of the German troops, high standard of efficiency of our own men,
power of artillery to dominate enemy's guns, etc, etc; an occasional glance at our
daily intelligence summaries would convince even the most sceptical of the truth
of what I write. Moreover I have been in the field now for 3 years and know what I
am writing about. The Foreigners have certainly misled our Govt. Yet, from what
you say, I see the Prime Minister prefers the advice which they tender to your and
my opinion.

The views which I have always held and expressed as to the decisive effect on
the enemy of a blow N. of the Lys are daily shewn to be sound – 'We must hold our
positions between the Sea and the Lys, or we shall lose the war entirely – The fate
of Germany is now being decided in Flanders' – so write the German newpapers
with the approval of their Government.

In my opinion the war can only be won here in Flanders. Even if the Austrians
were driven from Trieste, the Germans will still hold the Belgian Coast &
Antwerp!

As to the paper of Foch's which you sent me, I can hardly believe *he* could have
produced such an utterly stupid document. I fear the old man is done; but in any
case the idea of organizing an Allied Staff in Paris is quite unsound, even if a really
good French Staff Officer were in existence.

I am in complete agreement with your views on that hand, as on all the main
Military questions. The only point I am not in accord with you on is the desirability
of issuing such pessimistic estimates from your Intelligence Branch. They do, I
feel sure, much harm and cause many in authority to take a pessimistic outlook,
when a contrary view, based on equally good information, would go far to help the
nation on to victory. Personally I feel we have every reason to be optimistic; and if

the War were to end tomorrow, Great Britain would find herself not merely the Greatest Power in Europe, but in the World. The chief people to suffer would be the Socialists, who are trying to rule us all, at a time when the right-minded of the Nation are so engaged on the country's battles that they (the Socialists) are left free to work mischief.* But whatever views may be held on the Socialist problems, there is only one possible plan to win the war and that is to go on attacking in Flanders until we have driven the German Armies out of it. If we relax our determination to do this then Germany will attain her end in the War.

Please accept my hearty thanks for the way you supported the sound policy at the recent Conference, and my heartfelt wishes for your continued success.

Hankey, ii, p 693

15 AUGUST . . . I had a short talk with the Prime Minister and Robert Cecil. I impressed strongly on the former that he ought to investigate the question of the Flanders offensive, which seems to be rather hung up, with a view to the possible adoption of the alternative Italian plan before Cadorna had started. I found him unresponsive, though he sent for Robertson in order to instruct him to report on Haig's next objective. In this connection it must be noted that Robertson is going to France tomorrow. The PM is obviously puzzled, as his predecessor was, how far the Government is justified in interfering with a military operation.

Lloyd George, ii, p 1382

As the futile massacres of August piled up the ghastly hecatombs of slaughter on the Ypres Front without achieving any appreciable result, I repeatedly approached Sir William Robertson to remind him of the condition attached to the Cabinet's assent to the operation. It was to be abandoned as soon as it became evident that its aims were unattainable this year and our attention was to be concentrated on an Italian offensive. He was immovable.

Haig Diary: Duff Cooper, ii, pp 145–6

16 AUGUST . . . Sir William Robertson arrived from England at 3 pm. I had a talk with him till 4.30 pm. The Prime Minister sent me a friendly message by him, with an expression of confidence in me. This was, I gather, due to his having said at the recent London conference (with reference to my present operations) that 'he thought we had put our money on the wrong horse. We ought instead to have reinforced the Italians'.

In reply, I told Robertson to thank the Prime Minister for his message, but what I want is *tangible* support. *Men, guns, aeroplanes.* It is ridiculous to talk about

*The International Socialist Conference at Stockholm had been very much in the news. The Labour representative in the War Cabinet, Mr Arthur Henderson, who was also Secretary of the Labour Party, resigned his Cabinet post on 11 August following a dispute with his Cabinet colleagues about whether the Party should be represented at Stockholm. This event no doubt accounts for Haig's unusual incursion into domestic politics.

supporting me 'whole-heartedly' when men, guns, rails, etc. are going in quantities to Egypt for the Palestine expedition; guns to the Italians, to Mesopotamia
and to Russia. Robertson agreed, and said he was entirely opposed to any Italian
venture.

FLANDERS

Author's Papers: Haig to Lady Haig, 15 August

This day 3 years ago I landed at Havre, and the Germans then thought that they
had ample time left before winter in which to beat the French and ourselves! Why
should *we* not have time left this year to beat the Germans before winter? If our
Govt. would only stir themselves it is to be done! We have made a good start with
our attack near Lens.

Charteris, pp 244–5

15 AUGUST.   The weather is improving and there are indications that we may
have a few days clear of rain. The centre of gravity has shifted . . . to the old Loos
area, where the Canadians brought off a very successful little attack this morning.* It is only preparatory to another attempt here, but it gained ground and
captured a couple of thousand prisoners. If only we had enough troops to attack
hard in two places simultaneously we could accomplish much. Today's attack
found the Germans unprepared and with tired troops. Tomorrow we go on up in
the north, without some expectation – at least so far as 'I'† is concerned – of doing
more than gain some ground.

Author's Papers: Haig Diary

15 AUGUST.   At 10.30 am I met General Gough and his CGS . . . I told Gough
that, looking at the development of his advance, I did not wish a direct attack
made on the Forêt D'Houthoulst It would be very costly, and would be playing the
enemy's game to embark on a large battle in a forest. My view is that the forest
should be turned on both flanks and that, at the right moment, the Belgians should
launch an attack via Dixmude to capture the Clercken ridge. Gough should
arrange to establish a strong flank on the southern edge of the forest and push a
line of skirmishers assisted by Tanks into the southern part of the forest to clear up
the situation there. If the enemy is found to be in force, we can cause him great loss
by our artillery: on the other hand, if not strongly defended, all ground gained by
the Tanks and skirmishers can be consolidated. After Gough has thought over the
matter and reported to me, I will then arrange with General Anthoine what his
rôle will be.

*Officially known as the Battle of Hill 70, near Lens.
† The Intelligence Branch at GHQ.

The Invincible Enemy

Author's Papers: Haig Diary

16 August. Glass rising steadily. Fresh wind from S.W. Considerable amount of cloud with bright intervals. Observation fairly good.

17 August. Glass rising steadily. Fine bright morning. A few clouds . . . in the afternoon.

18 August. Glass rather unsteady. Day at times looked threatening but kept up all right.

19 August. Fine bright day. Wind from west. Glass rising slightly. Observation good.

20 August. Glass steady. Day fine and observation good.

21 August. Glass steady. Fine and bright day . . . Observation good.

22 August. Fine day. Very warm. Observation only moderate on account of haze.

23 August. Glass falling. Dull morning and some heavy showers. Cleared up in the afternoon.

24 August. Glass rising. High wind. Occasional showers.

Flanders: The Battle of Langemarck

Haig Diary: Duff Cooper, ii, pp 144–5

16 August.   Fifth Army attacked at 4.45 am. We heard at breakfast time that the attack was progressing well, execpt on the right flank where the country is very wooded and much broken up by our heavy shell fire, so that progress was slow. At 9.45 our troops of II Corps were reported in Polygon wood, and flank had been formed along southern edge of Glencorse wood.

XIX and XVIII Corps had both got Green line. XIV Corps had passed beyond Langemarck.

At 10.30 a telephone message stated that our troops had been seen coming back from Nonne Boschen* and Gallipoli.† It is very difficult in these battles quickly to discover what the real situation is . . .

XIV Corps are on the Red line, i.e. has taken all objectives and over nine hundred prisoners. On the left of the latter corps, the French occupied the whole of the ground up to the Martjevaart as well as the bridgehead at Drie Gratchen. Also 300 prisoners. So the French have done well and are in good spirits. 'Casualties extremely small', they report.

Charteris, p 245

16 August.   We attacked at dawn. I was up with the Corps HQ. We did fairly

*In II Corps sector.   † Gallipoli Farm in XIX Corps sector.

well on the left, but failed elsewhere.* . . . Back to office at 11 pm to write a report on the German methods in this battle, which have changed greatly, and concerning which some wild rumours are getting about in our own army.

Gough, p 205

The state of the ground was by this time frightful. The labour of bringing up supplies and ammunition, of moving or firing the guns, which had often sunk up to their axles, was a fearful strain on the officers and men, even during the daily task of maintaining the battle front. When it came to the advance of infantry for an attack, across the water-logged shell-holes, movement was so slow and fatiguing that only the shortest advances could be contemplated. In consequence I informed the Commander-in Chief that tactical success was not possible, or would be too costly, under such conditions, and advised that the attack should now be abandoned.

I had many talks with Haig during these days and repeated this opinion frequently, but he told me that the attack must be continued. His reasons were valid. He was looking at the broad picture of the whole theatre of war. He saw the possibilities of a German victory, a defeat of the whole Allied cause. There was only one Army in the field in a position to prevent this disaster, and that was the British Army in France. On it fell this heavy burden.

Ludendorff, ii, p 479

10 August was a success for us, but on the 16th we sustained another great blow. The English pressed on beyond Poelcappelle and, even with an extreme exertion of strength on our part, could only be pushed back a short distance. During the following days fighting continued with diminished intensity.

GERMANY

Author's Papers: Colonel Macleod's diary

15 AUGUST.   The Bosches are fighting with the utmost stubbornness. Their morale does not appear to be bad and their troops seem well fed, so they are nowhere near cracking yet.

CAB 23/3: War Cabinet No. 217, 17 August

German Desertions
7. The Director of Military Intelligence pointed out recent cases of desertion on the part of the enemy, indicating deterioration of morale in certain units. In the

---

*A fair summary: the Official History sketch shows almost no gains on II and XIX Corps fronts. The front begins to shift perceptibly on the left of XVIII Corps; only XIV Corps and the French did really well. Over 2,100 prisoners and 30 guns were taken.

206th German Division, composed of Prussian troops, at Verdun, on the left bank of the Meuse, a whole platoon of 40 men had deserted, and yesterday another batch of 70 men had deserted.

Charteris, pp 245–6

18 AUGUST.   Just finished a report for D.H. on German tactics in recent fighting. The principal changes are: no attempt made to hold a line of trenches; defence organized in strong points and immediate counter-attacks, first by regiments in immediate support, and second, within twelve hours by a reserve division. Artillery rely for protection on a number of alternative positions . . . The morale has been very uneven. In some divisions it has been noticeably low, e.g. 119th and 3rd R. Division. We expected good morale in 6th Bavarian R. Division* and 3rd Guards Division. Both of them proved to be suffering from bad morale. On the other hand the 38th Division and the 52nd R. Division fought better than was anticipated. On the whole the morale was about as expected, not noticeably lower than at Arras . . .

The idea that groups remained behind 'shamming dead', and then reappeared to resist our mopping-up parties, is not borne out by investigations, but the shell-holed area has enabled small parties of Germans to dodge our mopping-up parties from one shell-hole to another.

The Fifth Army reports 'the general morale of the Germans is undoubtedly lowered' since the commencement of the attack. Several captured orders seem to indicate that the German Higher Command is much exercised about the fall in morale.

I summed up the report:

The two vital factors which from a military point of view will be decisive in this war are:

Morale, of which the evidence shows a steady deterioration in the German Army, and

Manpower, of which calculations . . . show that even the resources of the German Empire cannot stand the strain of war on its population for more than a limited number of months (a maximum of twelve months) *provided the fighting is maintained at its present intensity in France and Belgium.*

FLANDERS

von Kuhl, Der Weltkrieg, 1914–1918

The situation in Crown Prince Rupprecht's army group was serious and caused its commander considerable worry. With anxiety he had to look at other fronts, to the areas of LENS, ARRAS and ST QUENTIN, where an enemy attack could be

*See p 219.

expected at any time, even if it took the form of a Secondary Attack. During the battles on the Somme in the previous year it had been possible to contain the Anglo-French attack through weakening, to an absolutely dangerous degree, the other fronts, and putting all the forces collected into the one big battle area. Even a relatively light enemy attack upon one of the other areas would have been a most serious danger. But such Secondary Attacks had to be reckoned with in the summer of 1917 following the transfer, by the Army Group, of all dispensable men and materials to the 4th Army in Flanders for the big defensive battle.

In the second part of August the German High Command was distracted by both French and Italian operations – added reasons why Haig could not call off the British offensive, even if he had wanted to. On 17 August General Cadorna launched the Eleventh Battle of the Isonzo. Meanwhile the first phase of the Canadian diversion at Lens was coming to its conclusion (18 August).

> Col. G. W. L. Nicholson, *Canadian Expeditionary Force 1914–1919; The Official History of the Canadian Army in the First World War*; The Queen's Printer, Ottawa, 1962, p 292: Lieut-General Sir Arthur Currie's* personal diary, 18 August

There were no fewer than twenty-one counter-attacks delivered, many with very large forces and all with great determination and dash . . . Our casualties so far about 5,600 but in my opinion the enemy casualties must be close to 20,000. Our gunners, machine gunners and infantry never had such targets, FOOs† could not get guns for all their targets . . . It is a great and wonderful victory. GHQ regard it as one of the finest performances of the war.

> Von Kuhl, *Der Weltkrieg*

The fighting at Lens cost us, once again, the expenditure of considerable numbers of troops who had to be replaced. The whole previously worked-out plan for relieving the fought-out troops in Flanders had been wrecked.

On 20 August General Pétain launched his long-promised attack at Verdun.

> Repington, ii, p 28

MONDAY, 20 AUGUST   lunched at the Bath Club with Sir W. Robertson. He had been over to France for twenty-four hours and returned on Friday last. He admitted that the Low Country positions which I had warned him and others about were pretty horrible, but of course they had been made worse by the rain

---

*Commanding the Canadian Corps.   † Forward Observation Officers.

... This was hard luck on Haig ... The French this morning had attacked on both banks of the Meuse at Verdun, and up to 8 am had taken 2,000 prisoners. R. hoped that the number might be increased to 10,000 and thought that Pétain, who had 18 divisions in the fight, and more hanging about, had a good chance of a fine success. The Italians had taken 4,700 prisoners: their right had done better than their left.

The French attack at Verdun is officially reckoned to have continued until 9 September, by which time the French had taken over 10,000 prisoners. In fact, sporadic fighting continued at Verdun well into October, with particularly violent German counter-attacks on 21 and 22, 27 and 28 August, 24 September and 1 October. During all this time the Aisne and Champagne fronts were also active. These important facts seem to have become lost to the sight of history, but they must have had an important influence on thinking at British GHQ during the autumn months. By 31 August the Italians claimed 27,000 prisoners.

Ludendorff, ii, p 479

The main French effort took place at Verdun on 20 and 21 August. The 5th Army was not suprised. As had been provided for weeks before, certain areas such as the Talou ridge, were abandoned in time. The assault, which was not accompanied by tanks, again penetrated far into our positions. On the left bank, close to the Meuse, one division had failed, nor had we been fortunate on the right bank; and yet both here and in Flanders everything possible had probably been done to avoid failure. The 21st and 26th also brought success to the enemy and loss to us. The French Army was once more capable of the offensive. It had quickly overcome its depression.

MANPOWER

Repington, ii, p 29

MONDAY, 20 AUGUST (Robertson) said that we were about 50,000 infantry down in France in the aggregate, but this meant a larger deficit proportionately at the actual front. If we were not more down it was because our estimated losses of 100,000 men a month had not been reached lately. We had only lost 50,000 since 31 July. But we would certainly be much more down before the end of October, though he had just scraped up 21,000 men of all sorts at home and was sending them out, and was not enlisting men for cavalry and engineers.

I asked about his 500,000 A men by August.* He said that everybody knew that

*See p 99.

they had not been obtained. I denied this, and asked how people could know if they were not told, and that I did not know. R. said that nearly two-thirds had been obtained. Smuts and Milner formed a sub-committee of the War Cabinet to look after manpower, but Milner was all for men for agriculture, and we were just giving him 80,000 whom he said he could not do without. The War Cabinet tried to make out that the country could not find more men, but R. did not agree with them. R. admitted L.G.'s difficulties, but still we could not win battles without men. R. said, in reply to a question from me, that the War Cabinet were all right about peace and meant to see the thing through, but war was a hard business, and the Cabinet was not very well manned for waging war.

> Author's Papers: Extract form Haig's notes for
> Army Commanders' Conference, 21 August

We are now fighting what may well be the decisive battle of the war. We are confronted with a situation that we cannot continue to fight this battle out to a finish without more infantry. We all know the present shortage in the infantry and the reinforcements that can be supplied us from home, and it is clear that the Divisions cannot be maintained in a position to fight by normal reinforcements alone.

It is essential that we should be in a position to *continue the battle well into November*.* By this means, and by this means only, can we ensure final victory by wearing out the enemy's resistance.

Under the circumstances there is no alternative but to throw into the battle, as a fighting man, every single able-bodied man in France who is not directly concerned with the prosecution of operations.

For these men to be of use, it is essential that they should be withdrawn at once and trained as infantry soldiers, ready to take their place *in the ranks of the Divisions from the beginning of October onwards*.*

Then is the time when, so far as can be foreseen, we shall be at our lowest ebb, and unless these men materialize in large numbers, we shall be forced to close down operations at a moment when complete success may be within our grasp.

To get these men it is necessary that *every Service and Department should immediately give up every man who is in any way likely, by training, to become fit** for service in the infantry, and the remainder must be prepared to work seven days a week instead of six, and twelve or fourteen hours a day.

> Lieut-Colonel J. H. Boraston and Captain C. E.
> O. Bax, *The Eighth Division in War, 1914–1918*,
> Medici Society, 1926, p 154

The division was once more sadly reduced in numbers. Its casualties in this last encounter† amounted to 81 officers and 2,074 other ranks and when the infantry were inspected by Sir Douglas Haig on 21 August the full strength on parade numbered no more than 3,950 all ranks.

*Haig's italics.   †Langemarck, 16–18 August.

Author's Papers: Haig to Robertson, 22 August
You must force the Govt. to give me the means to keep going.

Author's Papers: Haig Diary
31 August.   What is wanted is a Prime Minister *with courage* to tell the people that in order to win we must have men!

GERMANY

Charteris, pp 247–8
21 August.   Fifth Army reported a rather remarkable instance of low German morale. One whole regiment of the 75th R. Division is reported to have 'fairly taken to its heels on the 16th and seven officers of the same regiment, found hiding in a dug-out, surrendered without even showing fight'. The report seemed so extraordinary that I questioned it, and eventually went myself to Army HQ to sift the evidence. It seems completely true. Even as an isolated incident it is very remarkable.

D.H. has not only accepted *in toto* my report on fighting up to 16th, but has gone much farther. He has reported to War Office that 'time is fast approaching when Germany will be unable to maintain her armies at their present numerical strength'. 'In front of the XIVth Corps a large portion of their defending troops are reported by both our own men and by prisoners to have run away.' 'For all these reasons, although the struggle is likely to continue severe for some while yet, there is good reason to hope that very considerable results will then follow and with more rapidity than may seem likely at present.'

Author's Papers: Haig to Lady Haig, 24 August
There is no doubt but that the Germans realize that their existence depends on the issue of the present struggle in Flanders. I am glad that the French General Staff realize it too!* I *think* the Germans mean to put forward definite peace proposals soon. They are in a terrible state I gather in Germany.

FLANDERS

Author's Papers: Haig Diary
17 August.   The cause of the failure to advance on the right centre of the attack of the Fifth Army is due, I think, to commanders being in too great a hurry! Three more days should have been allowed in which (if fine and observation good) the artillery would have dominated the enemy's artillery and destroyed his concrete

*Haig's Deputy Chief of Staff had just returned from GQG.

defences. After Gough has got at the facts more fully, I have arranged to talk the matter over with him.

Repington, ii, pp 30–1

MONDAY, 20 AUGUST . . . (Robertson) thought that there was nothing for us but to go on. Haig thought that he was killing a lot of Germans.

Charteris, pp 247–8; 21 August

Haig's report to the War Office continues:

'If we are favoured with a fine autumn . . . I regard the prospects of clearing the coast before winter sets in as still very hopeful, notwithstanding the loss of time caused by the bad weather during the first half of August. At the least, I see no reason to doubt that we shall be able to gain positions from which subsequent operations to clear the coast will present a far easier problem than we had to cope with at the outset of this offensive, and in which the losses and hardships suffered round Ypres in previous winters will be much reduced. In these circumstances the right course to pursue, in my opinion, is undoubtedly to continue to press the enemy in Flanders without intermission and to the full extent of our powers, and if complete success is not gained before the winter sets in, to renew the attack at the earliest possible moment next year. Success in clearing the coast may confidently be expected to have such strategical and political effects that they are likely to prove decisive.'*

Gough, p 206

On 22 August another general attack was made by the three corps on the right – the II, XIX and XVIII. The objectives in this attack had been reduced to those within a short distance of our line, as it was impossible for the men to go forward over any long distance; my object was to spare the troops to the utmost possible degree, while at the same time complying with my orders from GHQ to the effect that the battle must be continued.

The II Corps as usual met with a violent opposition, and counter-attacks were launched against its 14th Division which continued during 23 and 24 August, and involved very heavy fighting.

Author's Papers: Personal reminiscence by Col-
onel R. Macleod

I now† had only three guns left for the barrage next day . . . At the usual time of

---

*It is this passage that impelled Sir James Marshall-Cornwall, who served at GHQ under Charteris, to call the latter's influence on Haig 'calamitous' (*Haig as Military Commander*, Batsford, 1973, p 241).
† 21 August.

4.45 we opened fire on our creeping barrage. We were not much worried during it by the German artillery. The attack was partially successful.* When it was over the German artillery turned on to our batteries. Another gun was soon knocked out and I withdrew the detachments into the trench behind. As I stood with Lieut Allday watching the shelling three German shells fell on one of my two remaining guns. When the smoke had cleared we examined the large crater made and there was no sign of the gun or any part of it. I now had one gun left. I reported this to the Colonel and he ordered me to hand it over to the battery next door, which was a gun or two short, withdraw my battery to the wagon lines and draw six new guns from Ordnance. I went down with about twelve men and a few signallers – all that remained of the battery.

On 23 August I went to Ordnance for my six new guns. They flatly refused to believe that I had lost a gun completely destroyed and no trace left, in spite of my certificate, and would only give me five. If I wanted a new gun I must at least produce a part of it. I had to send up two men to dig round the crater and they eventually found the fore end of the buffer . . .

I found four young officers and some men at the wagon lines to replace the casualties. The officers, enlisted, I think, under the 'Derby' scheme, were straight out from home, had never been in action before and knew little of guns or gunnery. Most of the men also were only semi-trained.

On 22 August Haig decided, after consulting General Rawlinson and Admiral Bacon, that military reasons did not justify carrying out the landing near Ostend, and in default of sufficiently weighty naval reasons, the operation was indefinitely postponed. Meanwhile his anxieties about the fighting for the central ridge, traversed by the Ypres-Menin road, had come to a head.

Haig Diary: Duff Cooper, ii, p 147

24 AUGUST.   I directed the CGS to consider, in view of the apparent difficulty of holding Inverness copse,† and of the decisive nature of the fight for the ridge, whether it would not be necessary to enlarge the front of our attack so as to include Zandvoorde on our right. This will cause the enemy to disperse his artillery fire, and may also mislead him as to the objectives of our attack.

After dinner I discussed the situation with Kiggell and Davidson. The former was opposed to attacking Zandvoorde because it would use up more divisions and the time for preparation would come to three or four weeks, i.e. to the end of September. I arranged to see Generals Plumer and Gough on the situation tomorrow.

---

*Gough says a general advance of some 500 yards was made.
†The Germans counter-attacked Inverness Copse 4 times on 22 August, again on 23 August, and again on 24 August.

25 AUGUST. I had a talk with (Plumer) on the situation on the ridge on which is Inverness copse. He did not think it was necessary to attack Zandvoorde in order to capture Polygon wood and the ridge beyond. I pointed out that unless Zandvoorde were attacked, the enemy could enfilade, from the present positions of his batteries in the hollow east of Zandvoorde, not only the Inverness copse spur, but also the Broodseinde ridge. I accordingly told him that as soon as the II Corps (Jacob) had terminated the operation for the capture of Nonne Boschen (which the 23rd Division was just starting) the left of the Second Army would be extended to the Ypres–Roulers railway, and he would have as his objectives the capture of the Broodseinde-Polygon wood ridge, in order to cover the right of the Fifth Army. He is at once to make his arrangements to capture Zandvoorde, but if he found that he could capture the Gheluvelt spur without doing so, he need not do it.

At 3 pm I saw General Gough. He explained his plan, and stated that in his view Zandvoorde ought to be attacked. I then told him what Plumer's orders were, and asked him to consider what day would be most suitable for handing over the II Corps front to the Second Army.

From this date the main rôle in the offensive was played by the Second Army. General Sir Herbert Plumer, Major-General Harington and the Army staff brought to it the same deliberation, the same detailed and scrupulous planning that they had displayed earlier in the year at Messines. They were not, of course, any more than their colleagues in the Fifth Army, able to control the elements.

THE INVINCIBLE ENEMY

Author's Papers: Haig Diary

25 August. Glass rising steadily. Fine clear day.

26 August. Glass began falling at midnight . . . day was fine until 8 pm. Heavy rain then began to fall.

27 August. Glass continued to fall at a rapid rate. Showery morning until noon when a regular heavy downpour with high winds began and continued till after dark. Day dark and cold, like November.

28 August. Owing to storm of wind and rain the military activity on the front was much reduced today . . . All boats across the Channel stopped.

Oliver, p 205

29 August. It is very odd how each of the attacks we have delivered in the west this summer has been accompanied by an exceptional storm. I had never really believed in a personal devil until this summer.

Author's Papers: Haig Diary

30 August. Glass rising. A few showers in the morning, but later day became bright and clear.

31 August. Heavy rain all night . . . Forenoon showery. Cleared up later.

To Haig's observation, rain fell on 18 days of August, 1917.

FLANDERS

Von Kuhl, *Der Weltkrieg*

About 25 August, the first part of the great struggle was ended. The British target was quite clear. It was their intention to obtain the high land east and north of Ypres as a spring-board for a break-through into the Flanders plain. So far their efforts had been contained. But the fighting strength of numerous German divisions was being used up, the prompt replacement by fresh divisions from the whole area of the Crown Prince Rupprecht's Army Group was already difficult.

Author's Papers: Haig Diary

27 AUGUST.   Charteris reported that the state of the enemy's reserve is today the most favourable for us since the war began! Apparently he has only 4 'fresh' divisions available . . . i.e. divisions which have not been hammered during the last 3 months.

O.H., 1917, ii, p 449, Appendix XX: Kiggell to
Gough, 28 August

With reference to O.A.D. 606, dated the 26th instant,* it may be expected that the Second Army preparations for attack will be complete in about three weeks.

In view of the unfavourable weather, of the inadvisability of pushing forward too far on your centre and left before the capture of the main ridge, and of the need that you should have in hand a thoroughly efficient force for the capture of the Staden Ridge hereafter in combination with the advance of the Second Army, the Commander-in-Chief considers it inadvisable that you should attempt any operations on a great scale before the Second Army is ready to co-operate.

He therefore desires that in the present circumstances your operations may be limited to gaining a line including. Inverness Copse and Glencorse and Nonne Boschen Woods, and to securing possession, by methodical and well-combined attacks, of such farms and other tactical features in front of your line farther north as will facilitate the delivery of a general attack later in combination with the Second Army. Proceeding on this principle he trusts that you will be able so to

*The formal order to the Second Army to extend its front northwards.

arrange for reliefs, and for the rest and training of your divisions, as to ensure having a fresh and thoroughly efficient force available for the severe and sustained fighting to be expected later. He considers these questions of relief, rest and training to be of great importance.

O.H., 1917, ii, pp 208–10

The casualties during the four weeks of August (31 July–28 August) since the opening day of the main offensive had amounted to 3,424 officers and 64,586 other ranks;* and the expenditure of artillery and munitions had eaten deeply into the available reserves.† In all, 22 British divisions (including one twice) had been engaged on the Fifth Army front, of which 14 had been relieved and withdrawn to refit: and, in spite of the large nucleus of officers and men withheld from battle to reconstitute the units, these 14 divisions could not be considered fit to be engaged for some weeks . . .

During the period 25 July to 28 August, 23 German divisions (17 in the first three weeks) had been exhausted and withdrawn out of the 30 which had been engaged (two of them twice) opposite the Fifth Army alone . . . and . . . 7 more with heavy losses, opposite to the French First Army. Of this total of 37 divisions – as against 26 Allied (4 French, 22 British) divisions – 9 had come from Champagne and Alsace-Lorraine, thereby relieving anxiety in that direction; information, too, had been received by GHQ of a diminution of 70 per cent in the German heavy gun ammunition in the French sector, indicating that the Germans had had to concentrate their available heavy artillery ammunition in Flanders. More important than this, Sir Douglas Haig's purpose to draw all available German reserves to the British sector was proving effective. The French battle-front had been left unmolested,‡ and German plans for an attack on the Russian front had had to be postponed.

Soldiers and Politicians

Author's Papers: Haig to Robertson, 22 August

The one black spot in the whole picture of the war is our PM's desire to gain ground in secondary theatres as if he did not believe in our ability to beat the Germans themselves and wished to gain something with which to bargain at a Peace Conference.

---

*See Appendix III.
† In the II Corps sector alone, the artillery fired off 2,766,824 rounds between 25 June and 31 August.
‡ If receiving not less than 30 German attacks or counter-attacks on the Aisne, in Champagne and at Verdun can be called 'unmolested'.

Wilson, ii, pp 10–11

23 AUGUST.   (Lloyd George) explained the position as follows: He was satisfied with Haig, but dissatisfied with Robertson. He was quite clear in his mind that we were not winning the war by our present plans, and that we never should on our present lines; but he did not know how, or what, we should do, and he had no means of checking or altering Robertson's and Haig's plans though he knew they were too parochial. He said that he was not in the position, nor had he the knowledge, to bring out alternative plans and to insist on their adoption, as it would always be said that he was overruling the soldiers . . . He is evidently inclined to stop Haig's offensive in another ten days because of our losses, which, he says, we cannot stand.

Author's Papers: Lloyd George to Robertson, 28 August

The Italian attack seems to me to be developing well, and judging by the reports that come from Delmé Radcliffe there are great possibilities in it if fully and promptly exploited. I can of course only judge by what he says, but his account of the Austrian demoralization and of their lack of reserve – both confirmed by the number of prisoners and guns captured and the extent of the ground occupied – seems to me to indicate immediate prospects of a signal military victory on that front. I need hardly point out that the overthrow of the Austrian army might produce in the present condition of Austrian public opinion decisive results on the whole campaign. I was therefore very distressed to find from one of Delmé Radcliffe's reports that Cadorna apprehended that these brilliant possibilities might be rendered unattainable owing to the imminent exhaustion of the Italian reserves of ammunition. Do you not think that a new situation has arisen there which requires immediate action on the part of the Allies to support the Italian attack, make up their deficiencies and enable them to convert the Austrian retreat into a rout? It would indeed be a severe reflection upon us all if later on it were discovered that we missed a great chance of achieving a signal and far-reaching military success for the Allied cause through lack of readiness to take advantage of an opening made for us by the Italian army.

I feel confident that you are watching events with anxious scrutiny. If you think that the Italian victory is capable of being pressed to important conclusions would it not be worth while your paying an immediate visit to that front to judge for yourself and to form an independent opinion as to what might be accomplished if the French and ourselves were to make a sacrifice which would enable Cadorna to press on until the Austrian army completely breaks?

Once more I would impress upon you and the War Cabinet the enormous responsibility that rests upon us not to allow the most promising opening which events have thrown in our way in any western theatre to come to nought for want of opportune support.

I should be obliged if you would mention this communication to the Cabinet*
this morning. I am writing Mr Bonar Law on the same subject.

CAB 23/13: War Cabinet No. 225a, 28 August

Bonar Law was in the chair, the other War Cabinet members present
being Milner, Carson, Smuts and George Barnes, who had replaced
Arthur Henderson as Labour's representative. Also attending were
Derby, Robertson and Lord Robert Cecil. The meeting took place in the
afternoon and was devoted to the question of support for Italy.
Robertson opened the discussion with a résumé of military policy, beginning with the Asquith Government's directive of November, 1916, and
touching on the Rome and London Conferences in January, the Calais
Conference in February, and the Paris Conference in May.

Finally, General Robertson continued, in June and July of this year, the War
Cabinet appointed a Committee to investigate the whole question of Military
Policy, and after hearing his views and those of a number of other Officers, and
holding a number of meetings, at many of which the Chief of Imperial General
Staff was not present, decided upon the plan which is now being carried out. The
Prime Minister, however, raised the question of the Italian plan at these meetings
and also at the recent Allied Conferences in Paris and London. It is now raised
again, and this indicated to the Chief of the Imperial General Staff that the War
Cabinet have no real confidence in the plan they adopted after very long and
careful consideration. If this is so, then they cannot hope it will succeed, for no
plan is of any good unless carried out with confidence and resolution.

The War Cabinet, therefore, had now to come to an important decision, viz.
whether to adhere to their plan or to change it. If they considered that strong
support should be given to General Cadorna so as to enable him to achieve a
victory of far-reaching results and of a decisive character, this would entail
breaking off the great battle now in progress in Flanders. But there were many
great objections to this, and as General Maurice had pointed out (War Cabinet
224) the effect of such a decision on the morale of our Army in France would be
very grave.

General Robertson said that he did not see how any support we could give to
General Cadorna could arrive in time to affect the situation on the Isonzo Front.
Fighting was now proceeding in mountainous country where there were no roads
and where big guns could not be quickly brought up. In the course of a fortnight
or so the issue would be known; either General Cadorna would have defeated
and scattered the enemy or he would be against a fresh wall of resistance. It

---

*Lloyd George was taking a short 'rest' at the home of Sir George (later Lord) Riddell
(proprietor of *The News Of The World*) at Lindfield.

was impossible to transfer large numbers of guns to that Front in less than a month.

General Robertson's own view was that it was false strategy to close down the offensive on the Western Front in order to give General Cadorna support which would only reach him too late to be effective.

It was pointed out that the reason why the suggestion of helping General Cadorna to the utmost was put forward was that his present offensive seemed to hold out a possibility of attaining infinitely greater results than had been anticipated by him or by the Allies; and the chance of a complete victory on any main front would justify concentration of all available resources on that front. If, however, military opinion was convinced that any assistance now rendered to General Cadorna would arrive too late to be fully effective, and that in any case the event of a great victory in that theatre could not justify a cessation of the offensive in Flanders, the suggestion would not be pressed.

The War Cabinet decided:

That it was desirable that the Prime Minister should be acquainted with the views of the Military Authorities in regard to his suggestion and that if the Prime Minister were unable to attend the Cabinet on the following day, the Chief of the Imperial General Staff should visit him and place those views before him.

Hankey, ii, p 694–5

29 AUGUST.   Robertson and Maurice arrived* about 11 am and an agreement was reached that a telegram should be sent to the British Ambassador at Rome . . . warning him that we could only assist at the expense of an abandonment of the Flanders offensive; that this would be trumpeted by the Germans as a defeat to our arms; that we could even consider facing this, if we were assured that a really great victory could be won with our aid on the Italian Front; but that we knew by experience the optimism of generals, and we should therefore require a convincing appreciation. Robertson . . . on the previous day had dissented strongly from the idea, and I am certain that he only agreed to this telegram because he was sure that the Italians could not convince us. Maurice, with whom I had a talk, was also strongly opposed.

FLANDERS

Ibid.

(Maurice) told me that Haig, and still more Kiggell, his Chief of Staff, still believed we could clear the Flanders coast – his reason being that there only remained five German divisions that had not passed through the mill, and that the

---

*Hankey was also staying at Lindfield, and describes how unrestful it was.

reserves with which they were filled up were the poorest material. I am bound to say that I could not share this optimism. A private letter I received about this time from a valued former member of my staff, now a brigadier-general and a corps Chief of Staff, described the German shelling as heavier than he had ever encountered, and the difficulties of dealing with the myriads of machine-guns in wooded country as very great. And he, though a sober judge, has always been an optimist.

O.H., 1917, ii, pp 209–10

The casualties alone do not give the full picture of the situation; for, apart from actual losses, the discomfort of the living conditions in the forward areas and the strain of fighting with indifferent success had overwrought and discouraged all ranks more than any other operation fought by British troops in the War, so that, although the health of the troops did not suffer, discontent was general: the soldier hates discomfort more than he fears danger. The memory of this August fighting, with its heavy showers, rain-filled craters and slippery mud, was so deeply impressed upon the combatants, who could not be told the reason for the Commander-in-Chief's persistency, and such stories of it were spread at home by the wounded, that it has remained the image and symbol of the whole battle, overshadowing the subsequent successful actions of the campaign and preventing the true estimation of them, even in some cases stopping any knowledge of them from reaching the public ear.

Ludendorff, ii, p 480

The costly August battles in Flanders and at Verdun imposed a heavy strain on the western troops. In spite of all the concrete protection they seemed more or less powerless under the enormous weight of the enemy's artillery. At some points they no longer displayed that firmness which I, in common with the local commanders, had hoped for.

The enemy managed to adapt himself to our method of employing counter-attack divisions. There were no more attacks with unlimited objectives such as General Nivelle had made in the Aisne-Champagne Battle. He was ready for our counterattacks and prepared for them by exercising restraint in the exploitation of success. In other directions, of course, this suited us very well.

I myself was being put to a terrible strain. The state of affairs in the West appeared to prevent the execution of our plans elsewhere. Our wastage had been so high as to cause grave misgivings, and had exceeded all expectation.

September

✠

During the first three weeks of September, military activity in Flanders was confined to minor operations, not affecting large numbers of troops though unpleasant enough for those who were involved, while General Plumer perfected his careful preparations for renewing the main offensive. Political activities, on the other hand, were lively, and conducted against a background of unusual anxiety and strain due to an unprecedented German air attack on Britain. There were seven raids during the month, only one less than in the whole of the preceding four months. These had the added terror of being carried out at night, by Gotha and Giant* bombers; their attack on the Chatham naval barracks, Sheerness and Margate on the night of 3–4 September was by far the worst in terms of human loss, with 132 dead (mostly naval ratings) and 96 injured. By the end of the month the bombers had killed 206 and injured 388 – a small number by Second World War standards, but alarming enough at the time, and contributing an unwelcome extra to the stress of war for Ministers and the civilian population, especially of London which was attacked five times.

Battle preparations in Flanders proceeded amid the usual difficulties.

THE INVINCIBLE ENEMY

Author's Papers: Haig Diary

1 September. Glass falling slightly. Weather unsettled. Heavy showers of rain fell throughout the day. Owing to bad weather, there has been little military activity.
2 September. Heavy rain fell in the night and showery morning. Glass rising. Day cleared in the afternoon.
3 September. Glass steady. Fine day. Weather seems to have taken up.

---

* Riesen, or R-type machines. These were four-engined biplanes, with a bomb-load of nearly two tons and range of 300 miles. They carried a crew of 7 to 9 men, and their wing-span (138 ft. 5½ in.) was only three feet less than that of the B-29 Superfortress.

GERMANY

Charteris, p. 249

1 SEPTEMBER.   D. H. has called for a minute on German manpower. The results
of the twelve months, September '16 to September '17, are very interesting.

September 1916	September 1917
Class 1916 Finishing as a source of drafts	Class 1918 Finishing as a source of drafts
Class 1917 Just commencing to be identified in front line	Class 1919 Just commencing to be identified in front line
Class 1918 Not yet called up	Class 1920 Partially called up throughout Germany (?)

The 1916 class comprise men of 21
„ 1917 „   „   „   20
„ 1918 „   „   „   19
„ 1919 „   „   „   18
„ 1920 „   „   „   17

This means that in one year Germany has expended two years of her income in
manpower. *At the same rate* by this time next year, she would be calling up her
boys of 15 or, alternatively, she would not be able to maintain her present number
of units at their present strength.

Actually even now her *company* strength has fallen from 230 in September,
1916, to an average of 175 now.

Author's Papers: Esher to Haig, 3 September.

Yesterday, from two sources, Holland and Belgium, there were rumours of a
'strategical retirement' of 20 kilometres under preparation. A lady at whose
house the Crown Prince has been staying for many months was liberated last week
. . . The Crown Prince, in giving her the necessary passports, spoke freely of the
necessity of immediate peace, of the hopelessness of the struggle, and said that his
father was so worn out and enfeebled that his judgment was valueless, and his
authority nil. The eagerness of the Crown Prince and of the Emperor Karl to end
the War at once is symptomatic of their very natural desire to preserve their
thrones. This type of story, potin, rumour, call it what you will, would be neg-
ligible if it stood alone: but it must be weighed in the balance of general evidence
on the subject of German morale. The German papers in commenting on Wilson's Encyclical* show more disappointment than fury. This too is highly sig-

*The American reply to the Pope's peace proposals, actually signed by the Secretary of
State, Robert Lansing, on 27 August. It contained the statement: 'We cannot take the word

nificant. Every paper quoted sounds the same note. Bitter disappointment at the reception of the Pope's intervention. Had the Germans felt confidence, their attitude would surely (have) been different.

FLANDERS

Gladden, *Ypres 1917*, p. 116

On the first of September we were ready for battle. The band and some other fortunates had gone back to act as reserves, but final orders had not yet been received. Towards the late evening unexpected rumours began to travel round the camp. The attack, it was said, had been cancelled. A joyous leap of relief in my breast was almost immediately stilled by a feeling that such a miracle at the eleventh hour was impossible. When I awoke the following morning the camp was already in a state of tremendous excitement. The miracle had really happened: for once rumour had proved true. The morning light seemed to shine in a new way. We had been reprieved – and reprieved, it seemed, not from the normal toll of battle but from certain annihilation.

Author's Papers: Haig Diary

3 SEPTEMBER.   General Anthoine saw me by appointment . . . to ask permission to send certain guns on railway mountings and others to support General Pétain in Champagne. It seems that the enemy has prepared a gas attack on a big scale and Pétain wishes to demolish the enemy's arrangements before he can complete them.* The guns will return as soon as possible. I said that since Pétain had supported me so generously I felt most anxious to give him all that he asked for as soon as possible, and rely upon him to return the guns in good time for our next operation.

SOLDIERS AND POLITICIANS

Haig Diary: Blake, pp. 252–3

3 SEPTEMBER.   At breakfast I received a telegram from the CIGS that 'General Foch arrives London 3 September on behalf of French War Cabinet to press British War Cabinet to agree to his sending 100 heavy guns from French First Army to Italy at once; if, as I suppose, this will affect your plans, it is very desirable that you should come over and see War Cabinet.' I decided to go to London today.

of the present rulers of Germany as a guarantee of anything that is to endure, unless explicitly supported by such conclusive evidence of the will and purpose of the German people themselves as the other peoples of the world would be justified in accepting.'
*There was heavy fighting in Champagne on 15, 16, 17 September, without particular advantage to either side.

Stephen Roskill, *Hankey: Man of Secrets*, Collins, 1970, vol. i, p. 432: Hankey Diary, 3 September. [This entry is fuller than in *The Supreme Command 1914–1918*]

We received at the morning meeting (of the War Cabinet) a telegram from our liaison officer in Paris,* actually addressed to the Director of Military Operations, stating that the French Govt. wanted to send 100 guns to Italy; that General Foch and Pétain wanted to take them from the first French army in Flanders attached to Haig's command; that Foch was coming at once to London to see Robertson; and that if Robertson could not agree to his proposals the French Govt. hoped the British Govt. would over-rule the CIGS! Fancy addressing such a communication to the DMO! Robertson was at once recalled; Haig was brought to England; and Ll. G. telephoned up† that he would hold a Cabinet after dinner . . . At 9.15 pm the War Cabinet met – all rather sulky at being hauled out. Practically no business was done, as Foch had not arrived,‡ and there was no fresh news. Ll. G. appeared to be funking the row with Robertson, which had seemed inevitable.

Author's Papers: Haig Diary

3 SEPTEMBER. I . . . told (Anthoine) of the reason for my visit to London, and asked his views. He said that it was impossible for him to spare any guns for Italy without upsetting our plans. Further, in his opinion, any guns withdrawn now from our front for Italy would be lost to both theatres.

Charteris, pp. 250–1

3 SEPTEMBER . . . The whole tone of the letters from London show a very marked weakening of trust in D.H., combined with the fatal wish to transfer our strength to side-shows. It is confined to a few persons, but those few are in power. Neither the Press nor the public share the view at present. Apparently the discontent is due to the dissatisfaction in the new Government at not being able to justify themselves by parading big results before the public, combined with a genuine belief that 'old-fashioned methods' will not win, and that strategical knowledge reposes in their brains. The difficulty is bringing facts home to them, and when we do we only get resentment. Probably that is natural. It is the slaughter of the theory begotten of their brains, and someone once said the only real tragedy in life is the killing of a theory by a fact. Robertson is a master of hard facts, but I do not know whether his slaughter of theories is done tactfully – if slaughter can ever be tactful. Certainly the dislike in the Cabinet of the soldiers seems just as much against Robertson as against D.H.

Our present line here is to keep clear of it all, for if we give any handle to the present powers that be, they would seize it to sack D.H. and Robertson, or both

*Spiers
†Lloyd George was at his house at Walton Heath.
‡Foch's crossing was delayed by mines in the Channel.

[sic], and Wilson is always lurking in the background to squeeze his way back to power.

CAB 23/13: War Cabinet 227c, 4 September

At this meeting Lloyd George was in the chair, and those present were, on the civil side, Milner, Bonar Law, Carson, Smuts and Lord Robert Cecil, Acting Foreign Secretary; on the military side, Robertson, Haig and Brig-General J. H. Davidson, Head of the Operations Branch at GHQ. The proceedings began with an explanation by Haig of the progress of his operations, the general military situation on the Western Front, and his future plans. The War Cabinet then turned to consider support for Italy.

General Robertson admitted that it would be very awkward to refuse General Cadorna's request for assistance. He thought that the Field-Marshal was better qualified than himself to decide whether any guns could be spared from the British front. From the purely military point of view it was very undesirable to withdraw heavy artillery from the Flanders theatre while the present big battle was in progress. Any guns so withdrawn could not take part in the operations on the Isonzo in less than a month, and it was probable that they would then arrive too late to be of use. Diplomatic considerations could not be ignored, but he thought that General Pétain . . . should have gone into the whole question with General Foch and Sir Douglas Haig. Whatever decision the War Cabinet might arrive at on the question, he strongly urged that not more than 50 guns should be taken from the British Front.

Haig then reported Pétain's request for guns for Champagne and his conversation with General Anthoine on the previous day; he drew attention to the valuable uses of the French First Army's heavy guns, the possible bad effects on the Belgians of taking these away, and his own shortage of guns of certain calibres. Lloyd George disagreed with the military view, and referred to the lunch he had just had with Foch, Carson and Lord Robert Cecil having also been present.

General Foch had stated to him in their presence that, as a soldier, he was not in the least convinced that it would be dangerous to remove 100 guns from the British Front; his view was that a comparatively small success on the Isonzo Front might achieve great results and might even have a decisive effect on the War, whereas a much more considerable success in the West might have proportionately small results; the Germans were a much more stubborn and tenacious enemy than the Austrians, and consequently it would be far more difficult to make an impression upon them; General Anthoine would attack whether he had

250 guns only, or 350; in General Foch's view too many guns were concentrated on the British Front, and their employment in such large numbers might almost be regarded in the light of a luxury and not a necessity.* General Foch evidently considered that we could well spare 100 guns for the support of Italy on a Front where good and far-reaching results might be anticipated.

Foch had told Lloyd George that the French Army could not spare the guns because of the length of its front; Lloyd George then suggested that Pétain should send 50, while Haig sent the other 50 from Anthoine's front.

Mr Lloyd George said he wished both Sir Douglas Haig and General Robertson to realize the possible consequences of a refusal to let these guns go. The Italians had appealed to the French and the British for artillery support. The French had agreed to release 100 of their own guns, which happened for the present to be under the Field-Marshal's command. If the British refused to permit the withdrawal of these guns, the Italians would say the French were willing to render them support and to send French guns on which the lives of French soldiers depended; whereas the British refused to let the French guns go. If, ultimately, our own operations were not successful, the unfortunate impression created by this attitude would be accentuated.

Lloyd George said he thought it impossible to send a blank refusal to the Italians, but suggested the War Cabinet should agree that if Haig would release fifty guns the French should be asked to send the remainder from their own front.

The French had arranged rather astutely to place us in a dilemma, and (the Prime Minister) felt that it was important, from the diplomatic point of view, for us to do nothing which might offend our Italian Allies . . . He fully realized the very difficult position in which the Field-Marshal was placed, but he desired him to remember the great difficulties which faced the War Cabinet in their endeavours to keep the Alliance together . . . While admitting the force of the military arguments, he felt it was almost impossible to refuse the request of our Ally to release what was, after all, a comparatively insignificant number of guns compared with the large numbers disposed of in the Western theatre.

Lord Robert Cecil said that the point which had impressed him in General Foch's remarks had been that he did not expect very great success on the Italian Front. He himself did not attach so much importance as the Prime Minister to the

*It is difficult to resist the thought that Lloyd George was to some extent embroidering Foch's statements, which bear a striking similarity to views which he himself had so often expressed.

political aspects of the case. The differences between the French and the Italians were unfortunately so great that our refusal on sound strategical grounds to release the guns would not have any very marked effect on the respective political relations of Great Britain and France with Italy. Moreover, he did not believe that the addition of 50 guns to the Italian Army would have a decisive influence towards influencing Austria to make a separate peace. In these circumstances, he objected altogether to a decision which might involve a change in the plans on which the War Cabinet had decided. From the political point of view also we had to remember not only our relations with foreign countries, but the effect on our own people.

After a brief further discussion the War Cabinet decided that:

The Prime Minister, on their behalf, should make the following proposals at the forthcoming meeting with General Foch:

1. That Field-Marshal Sir Douglas Haig ... should examine the military situation on his front in detail with a view to the release, if possible, of 50 guns of medium calibre from the French 1st Army now under his orders:
2. That the British Government would consent to the release of these guns, provided that Field-Marshal Sir Douglas Haig could spare them and provided that an equal number of French medium guns could be released from other parts of the French front in order to provide a total reinforcement sufficient to give a substantial support to the Italian Army:
3. That an immediate conference between Field-Marshal Sir Douglas Haig with the Chief of the Imperial General Staff, if possible, and Generals Pétain, Foch and Anthoine should be held in order to give effect, as far as possible, to the above proposals.

Haig Diary, p. 253

4 SEPTEMBER.   Finally, it was agreed that the matter should be placed in my hands. After explaining that it was the wish of the Cabinet that the guns should be sent, if I could possibly spare them, Lloyd George spoke to me alone, and said that it was very desirable to help the Italians at this juncture because the French were trying to supplant us in their affections! We must not give the French the power of saying that *they wanted* to send 100 guns, but the British would not let them go. I said that I would review the whole gun situation on the battlefront, and if we could possible liberate 50 guns, it would be done. He said he was very grateful.

Roskill, *Hankey: Man of Secrets*, p. 433: Hankey Diary

4 SEPTEMBER.   I have no doubt that M. Thomas, who had at Lindfield the previous week shown great enthusiasm for the Italian idea, had inspired the

French message. Then Ll. G. had been very truculent about the idea of overruling the soldiers, but when he came to the point, he funked it. In fact, after the meeting with Foch, he said to me 'I think this is the best we can do, don't you? I do not think this is the moment for a row with the soldiers'. Haig again showed himself very confident, though I could discover no good reason for his confidence.

Wilson, ii, p. 14

5 SEPTEMBER.   I believe that Lloyd George, knowing that Haig will not do any good, has allowed him to keep all his guns, etc, so that he can, later on, say, 'Well, I gave you everything. I even allowed you to spoil the Italian offensive. And now, owing to gross miscalculation and incapacity you have entirely failed to do anything serious except lose a lot of men.' And in this indictment he will include Robertson, and then get rid of both of them.

Haig Diary: Blake, pp. 253–4

Haig and Lord Derby met Pétain and Foch at Amiens.

7 SEPTEMBER.   I began by making a statement that I had considered the question, etc. (and) I was prepared to liberate 100 guns (about) from French First Army provided General Pétain could replace them in time for the attack as planned.

It is to be noted that this *may* result in the abandonment of the attack on Lens which I had hoped to carry out with the British First Army this Autumn.*

General Pétain at once agreed that he could meet my request. He had recently reorganized his heavy artillery which gave him a reserve of heavy guns to employ as the situation required. This ended the discussion on the question of the guns in the most friendly way . . .

Foch seemed on arrival at Amiens to have all his 'hackles' up but my few friendly words quickly calmed him, and we all were on the best of terms. His experiences in London should have done him good. He had gone there behind the back of Pétain and myself to get the British War Cabinet to sanction 100 French guns being withdrawn from *my* command. The War Cabinet then handed the question to me to arrange with Pétain. This we have done satisfactorily for all. I found Pétain today straightforward and clear in his views, and most businesslike. And, as he said himself today, 'The Marshal and I never argue and haggle over such matters.'

Duff Cooper, ii, p. 153: Telegram, Lloyd George
to Haig, 11 September

My colleagues and I are much gratified at the manner in which you have met them in regard to Italy. Please accept our best thanks for the promptitude with which you have carried out our wishes in a matter which was of great importance to the interallied policy.

*An operation to capture Lens, planned for October, was abandoned because of lack of troops.

Manpower

Repington, ii, p. 46

THURSDAY, 6 SEPTEMBER TO SUNDAY, 9 SEPTEMBER . . . The military news of the week is that L.G.'s plan of sending an army to Italy is once more temporarily abandoned . . . There has also been defeated a plan of taking part of our army away to the French front.* All these things entail a vast amount of unnecessary work, but I do not think it bad that the railway projects of a move to Italy should be ready, as they now are. We remain much down in numbers in France, 64,000 in the aggregate, but in the divisions it is 104,000, or was a few days ago, and we may have 10,000 casualties a week. Drafts are going out at the rate of 4,000 a day, and it is hoped that Geddes† will get the men right if the Government do not impede him. Haig is still bent on getting the Passchendaele Ridge, but not just yet.

The Invincible Enemy

Author's Papers: Haig Diary

7 September. Glass rising. Dull morning, but cleared up about 11 o'clock. Hot.
8 September. Glass rising slowly. Foggy morning. Fine day but hazy.
9 September. Glass rising slightly. Slight fog in the morning, but day fine and warm. Observation poor.
10 September. Glass steady. Foggy morning. Fine day though rather hazy.
11 September. Glass steady. Foggy morning. Fine day though rather hazy.
12 September. Glass rising slightly. Wind stronger from north. Bright sun. Clear. Observation better.

Flanders

Author's Papers: Haig Diary

FRIDAY, 7 SEPTEMBER . . . I discussed with Kiggell the wisdom of making small attacks on farms and isolated strong points, such as Gough has been doing on the Fifth Army front. In my opinion, unless we have dominated the enemy's artillery completely, our troops cannot retain a small area captured, because of the hostile artillery fire which can and will assuredly be concentrated on it; and also because our own guns have destroyed the defences, before our troops attack them, that little is left to consolidate. These small operations are also very wasteful in ammunition. I decided therefore to stop Gough from going on with these little attacks.

*We see how rumour had enlarged reality, not for the first or last time.
†See p 99 f.n.

SATURDAY, 8 SEPTEMBER . . . Total number of German divisions engaged by II Corps since 23 July (date of our artillery bombardment) is 16 . . . This shows importance which the enemy attached to this portion of his line, and the sacrifices which he was willing to make in order to maintain possession of the high ground which dominated all our forward positions east of Ypres.

This ridge is now completely in our hands and the only portion from which the enemy can obtain any close ground observation over our communications is the high ground just east of Nonne Boschen; also, to a limited extent, from Anzac.

We have obtained a position from which excellent observation over the enemy's area is now obtained. The immediate consequence is the withdrawal of the hostile artillery to a considerable distance . . . The result in our rear areas has been very apparent.

Haig Diary: Blake, p. 254

10 SEPTEMBER.   General Kiggell reported that he is afraid that some of Gough's subordinates do not always tell Gough their true opinion as regards their ability to carry out an operation. I therefore decide to go tomorrow and see the GOC 5th Corps (General Fanshawe) with reference to the small attacks prepared for the 13th.

The state of affairs in the Fifth Army was serious. Sir Philip Gibbs, then reporting for the *Daily Chronicle*, says: 'Battalion officers, and divisional staffs, raged against the whole Fifth Army organization, or lack of organization, with an extreme passion of speech.

"You must be glad to leave Flanders," I said to a group of officers trekking towards the Cambrai Salient.

One of them answered violently:

"God be thanked we are leaving the Fifth Army area!"'

(Gibbs: *Realities of War*, Heinemann, 1920, p. 389).

For a recent examination of this state of affairs, and the rôle of Major-General Neil Malcolm, Gough's Chief of Staff, see Farrar-Hockley, *Goughie*, pp. 226–32. For the details of Haig's intervention in the matter of the proposed small attacks by V Corps, see *Douglas Haig: The Educated Soldier*, pp. 350–2. I there remarked: 'It should not be necessary for the Commander-in-Chief of a great force of over sixty divisions to supervise the engagements of companies and platoons.' Here we need only note the upshot.

Author's Papers: Haig Diary

12 SEPTEMBER.   Report from Fifth Army. General Gough has decided to give up the minor operations which he proposed to make before the main operations.

German Official Account

On 10 September General von Kuhl had a conference with the Dixmude and Ypres Groups, at which divisional General Staff officers were present, in order to acquaint himself with the situation at the fighting front. His impression was that the generally unsystematic counter-battery fire and the passive attitude of the enemy infantry indicated that a major assault on a wide front was not likely; but that the British had completely given up their offensive designs for that year was unacceptable because of their well-known tenacity . . . It was too early to say that the battle of Flanders had already ended. Because of other information received, General von Kuhl came to another point of view a few days later. On 13 September he wrote: 'My innermost conviction that the battle of Flanders has finished is strengthened more and more.' In a telephone conversation with the staff of Fourth Army he repeated his point of view but also said 'I cannot prove all my points. Caution is still required.' . . . Assessments of the situation which the Army Group sent in to the Supreme Command on 12, 14, 17 and 19 September reported that the situation was still unclear . . . Special care must be taken around the areas of Lens, Havrincourt and St Quentin, even though change in the enemy order of battle before the Sixth and Second Armies had not yet been discovered . . . Even so fighting strength of the (Fourth) Army was weakened by the surrender of two divisions, 25 batteries, including 13 heavy ones, together with three fighter squadrons and four air force units.

THE INVINCIBLE ENEMY

Author's Papers: Haig Diary

13 September. Glass steady. Wind north-west. Cold morning. Observation fair.
14 September. Glass steady after a fall. Some rain fell during the night.
15 September. Glass steady. Wind from west. Fine day. Observation not good till afternoon.

Charteris, p. 253

16 September. A glorious day, bright sun and very warm. If only we had had this weather last month, but even now it may not be too late.

Author's Papers: Haig Diary

17 September. Glass fell during the night, but began to rise this morning. Fine day but strongish westerly wind.
18 September. Glass steady . . . occasional showers.

Author's Papers: Haig to Lady Haig, 19 September

The weather is splendid today and everything looks favourable for a big success tomorrow.

Soldiers and Politicians

Hankey, ii, p. 697

14 September . . . Found the Prime Minister had been quite seriously ill with a very high temperature. He was still looking out of sorts and only convalescent. I spent an hour after dinner . . . discussing the general situation, after which he went straight to bed. I found him rather despondent at the failure of this year's campaigning, and disgusted at the narrowness of the General Staff, and the inability of his colleagues to see eye to eye with him and their fear of overruling the General Staff.

Haig Diary: Blake, p. 254

Winston Churchill, appointed Minister of Munitions in July, was visiting GHQ and had a two-hour talk with General Kiggell on strategy.

13 September. Winston admitted that Lloyd George and he were doubtful about being able to beat the Germans on the Western Front. This confirms the opinion I formed some time ago, based on my discussions at the War Cabinet in London and a talk with L.G. in Paris last May: namely, that the latter does not believe it possible for the Allies to be victorious on the Western Front.

14 September. Sir F. E. Smith came to lunch. He is now Attorney-General. After several glasses of wine, port and old brandy he was most communicative and very friendly. He stated *privately* to me after lunch that he, Lloyd George and Winston Churchill dine regularly together once a week, and that although he (Smith) is not in the War Cabinet, he is in a position to influence the Prime Minister very considerably. He assured me that he (Smith) is all out to help us soldiers on the Western Front because he has seen the splendid work which has been and is being done by the Army under my orders.

Winston Churchill had a long talk in the afternoon with Birch and Butler over guns and our requirements, and left for Amiens at 7 pm. I have no doubt that Winston means to do his utmost (as Minister of Munitions) to provide the Army with all it requires, but at the same time he can hardly help meddling in the larger questions of strategy and tactics; for the solution of the latter he has no real training, and his agile mind only makes him a danger because he can persuade Lloyd George to adopt and carry out the most idiotic policy.

15 September. I had a talk with Sir E. Carson before he went out this morning. He considers that Lloyd George has considerable value as PM on account of his driving powers, but he recognizes his danger. He has no knowledge of strategy or military operations, yet he thinks he is well qualified to direct his Military Advisers!

Hankey, ii, p. 697

16 SEPTEMBER . . . Lloyd George . . . rediscussed military policy. He wants to abandon all activity on the Western Front and to concentrate our efforts against Turkey.

17 SEPTEMBER.   Milner arrived this morning . . . it was agreed that our proper course in the war was to concentrate on Turkey, as there is little hope of achieving definite success on the Western Front. I felt it my duty to warn them that the Turkish operation involved considerable risks.

18 SEPTEMBER . . . Milner seems to have come completely round to Lloyd George's view that the Western Front affords no opportunity for achieving complete success and that it is necessary to devote our main efforts against Turkey. He agrees fully with me, however – having reached his decision quite independently – that success in the Turkish theatre can only be achieved if the soldiers are in it whole-heartedly.

Haig Diary: Blake, p. 255

19 SEPTEMBER.   Lord Derby said that Lloyd George is scheming to get rid of him and Robertson from the War Office. L.G. and Painlevé . . . are desirous of forming an Allied General Staff in Paris to direct operations. This I feel certain cannot possibly work. It seems to be an effort of the French to retain control of operations, notwithstanding that their Army has ceased to be the main factor in the military problem; in fact the French Army has not only ceased to be able to take the offensive on a large scale, but, according to Pétain's opinion, its discipline is so bad that it could not resist a determined German offensive.

FRENCH MORALE

O.H., 1917, vol ii, p. 235

On 19 September the French Commander-in-Chief was again imploring that the offensive in Flanders should be continued without further delay. During this special visit to British headquarters he assured Sir Douglas Haig that between the British right and Switzerland he had not a man upon whom he could rely. Not only, he said, had the French army ceased to be able to make any considerable offensive, but its discipline was still so bad that it would be unable to resist a determined German offensive: France was nearing the limit of her manpower, and the danger existed that the French Government would – as indeed GHQ had feared in the two preceding winters – demand a separate peace rather than withstand another German offensive and its resulting casualties. Even after making allowances for General Pétain's pessimistic outlook, Sir Douglas Haig appreciated the urgency of his repeated requests for a breathing space for the recovery of the French army.

This is a puzzling passage. In *Douglas Haig: The Educated Soldier* (pp 363–4, f.n.) I have discussed in detail Haig's view of the condition of the French Army, and the proposition that the Flanders offensive was conducted 'to save the French'. It is a subject fraught with contradictory evidence, but the general run of Haig's diary entries does not bear out what the Official History says above, or his letter to Charteris of March, 1927, in which he said: 'It was impossible to change sooner from the Ypres front to Cambrai without Pétain coming to press me not to leave the Germans alone for a week, on account of the *awful* state of the French troops!' As we shall see, on 29 September he would be writing in a very different sense in his diary. But on 19 September the only explanation of Pétain's highly alarmist statement is some unrevealed incident or incidents during the heavy fighting in Champagne on 15, 16 and 17 September (referred to on p 249) or at Verdun on 17 September. The probability is that these dates contained the single mutinous incident of September to which Pétain refers in his narrative (see p 127) and that this had severely shaken his nerve.

THE INVINCIBLE ENEMY

Author's Papers: Haig Diary

20 SEPTEMBER.   Glass steady. Cloudy morning, following 2 or 3 hours heavy rain in the night. Cleared up about noon – fine afternoon and evening. Clear. Observation good.

FLANDERS: THE BATTLE OF THE MENIN ROAD RIDGE

For the renewal of the main offensive General Plumer brought in two fresh army corps to occupy the ground previously held by II Corps: X Corps (Lieut-General Sir T. L. N. Morland) and I Anzac Corps (Lieut-General Sir W. R. Birdwood). On the right flank of the Fifth Army, V Corps (Lieut-General E. A. Fanshawe) had relieved XIX Corps on 7 September. The special feature of General Plumer's revised plan was the increased weight of artillery fire, especially of heavy and medium calibres – 'more than double the allotment to the same frontage for the offensive on 31 July' (*O.H.*, p 238).

Haig Diary: Blake, p 255

20 SEPTEMBER.   About midnight General Gough proposed that operations should be postponed on account of rain, but General Plumer between 1 and 2 am,

after consulting his Corps and Divisional Commanders, decided to adhere to plan. Zero hour was 5.40 am. The attack was launched on a front of about 8 miles from Langemarck on the North to Hollebeke on the Ypres–Comines Canal on the South. Our attacks were everywhere successful.

O.H., 1917, vol ii, pp 253–5

During August many thousands of British troops had moved forward over this same ground when zero hour arrived with high hopes of success, but on this occasion they were inspired with more than the usual confidence. Behind them was the new organization of supports and reserves . . . in front, they were screened to a depth of a thousand yards by an artillery barrage of an extent and weight beyond all precedent. General Plumer's insistence on a great increase in the proportion of heavy and medium howitzers enabled the bombardment groups to form two belts of heavy high-explosive shell to creep ahead of the two field artillery belts of the barrage. Thus, together with the machine-gun barrages, five belts of fire, each accountable for two hundred yards, preceded the infantry. Beyond the barrage belts lay the fire of the four heavy artillery counter-battery double-groups, consisting of 222 guns and howitzers covering a 7,000-yard frontage; they were ready to neutralize with gas and H.E. shell any German batteries which might open fire.*

Massively supported in this manner, it is no wonder that the four assaulting divisions advanced with the utmost resolution. The three sunny weeks of September had hardened the ground between the shell craters, and, although it was slippery after the night's rain, the infantry were able to pick their way and generally keep pace with the artillery time-table . . . The western half of the plateau was soon covered with small assault groups, worming their way in single file between the shell craters deep into the German defence system. In general, unnerved and stunned by the concentrated blast of the heavy high-explosive shell in the two forward belts of the barrage, many of the Germans in the front line, and even in the more distant lines, were completely demoralized.

Field-Marshal Lord Birdwood, *Khaki and Gown*,
Ward, Lock & Co, 1941, pp 314–15

Our own artillery barrage was magnificent – quite the best that the Australians had ever seen. Creeping forward exactly according to plan, the barrage won the ground, while the infantry followed behind and occupied all the important points with a minimum of resistance. Our main difficulty, indeed, was to keep the ardent infantry sufficiently in hand to prevent their running into their own barrage. Our gun-fire was so concentrated and effective that even the enemy sheltered in strong pill-boxes seemed impotent to resist us. Three lines of objectives had been laid down, and the third of these was reached by 10.15 am, our men being in great

---

*The fine September weather had greatly helped the preparatory work of the 26 squadrons of the Royal Flying Corps on the Second and Fifth Army fronts.

heart. At 3.15 came the expected German counter-attack, but so effective was our artillery fire that by 7 o'clock the attack had been killed. Not a single German reached our front line, and the first stage of our task was satisfactorily accomplished.

Gladden, *Ypres 1917*, pp 137 & 139

Gladden's division, the 23rd, advanced on the right of the Australians. His own experiences on 20 September (pp 129–139) were as hair-raising as battle usually is; his comment is therefore the more interesting.

Our new line was now on the far side of the ridge. Certainly the day's advance was more than sufficient to justify the paeans of victory which we knew would fill the newspaper headlines at home. It was so easy to overlook the price paid in lives. Even we, who knew how it all had happened, were inconsistent enough to feel elated at having taken part in a military victory . . . There had been a feeling after the battle that there was no resistance ahead.

Gough, p 208

As usual in this battle, the Germans counter-attacked fiercely. On the V Corps front they launched no less than six counter-attacks. These were either beaten off, or our supporting troops immediately counter-attacked in their turn and once more drove the Germans out. Their losses were very heavy and we captured over 1,300 prisoners. By the end of the day we had captured all our objectives with the exception of two farms – an average penetration of 1,000 yards along the front of attack.

O.H., 1917, vol ii, p 277 f.n.

(The German Official Account)* xiii, p 75, sums up: 'The German Eingreift† divisions were at 8 am assembled at their stations in readiness to move at any moment. In spite of this, the counter-attacks did not take effect until the late afternoon; for the tremendous British barrage fire caused most serious loss of time and crippled the thrust power of the reserves.

Ludendorff, ii, p 488

After a period of profound quiet in the West, which led some to hope that the Battle of Flanders was over, another terrific assault was made on our lines on 20 September. The third bloody act of the battle had begun. The main force of the attack was directed against the Passchendaele–Gheluvelt line. Obviously the English were trying to gain the high ground between Ypres and the Roulers–Menin line, which affords an extensive view in both directions. These heights

Der Weltkrieg, 1914 bis 1918: Die militarischen Operationen zu Lande, prepared by the Military History Research Institution of the Forces; vol xiii, 1942.
† Counter-attack.

were also exceptionally important for us, as they afforded us ground observation posts and a certain amount of cover from hostile view.

The enemy's onslaught on the 20th was successful, which proved the superiority of the attack over the defence. Its strength did not consist in the tanks; we found them inconvenient, but put them out of action all the same. The power of the attack lay in the artillery, and in the fact that ours did not do enough damage to the hostile infantry as they were assembling, and, above all, at the actual time of the assault.

O.H., 1917, vol ii, p 278

Thus ended, with complete success except at Tower Hamlets, the first step in Sir Douglas Haig's first trial of step-by-step advance; the much-vaunted new German defence tactics had failed to stop the new method. The change was not appreciated in England or in France, and the success was underrated by the public, but not by the troops themselves, or by their adversaries.*

GERMANY

During August and September, 1917, various moves and tentatives towards peace were made on 1 August Pope Benedict XV had put forward proposals (published on 14 August) to all belligerents for a peace based upon 'freedom of the seas', no annexations or indemnities, diminution of armaments, etc. We have noted the American reply (see p 248 f.n.) An Imperial Council in Berlin on 11 September, with the Kaiser, Chancellor Michaelis and the Army and Navy chiefs, considered closely the kind of peace that Germany should settle for; there was substantial divergence of opinion on the crucial question of Belgium. Ludendorff tried to clarify the discussion with a long memorandum on the general situation and his conclusions; he began by admitting Germany's internal difficulties, but continued:

Lloyd George, ii, pp 1224–8: Ludendorff to Michaelis, 14 September

On the other hand, the position of the Entente is considerably worse.

Russia is tending even more obviously towards internal dissolution. She thus progressively falls out as an effective enemy . . .

Italy is apparently reckoning on a victory in the twelfth Isonzo battle. It will be denied her. The internal situation will then tend to precipitate a crisis. The coal shortage must be very great.

*For casualties see *O.H.*, p 279.

It is not to be believed that the new ministry in France will be permanently more bellicose than its predecessor. We may anticipate the contrary. France, too, is faced with a coal crisis.

All recent reports from England agree that the U-boat campaign is effective,* the food situation is serious, and the English Government has to contend with great social difficulties. The pressure for peace is becoming stronger. I need go no further into this matter. If England took really serious steps it would be a sign that she no longer believed she could win. It is no long step from that to the conviction that she might lose.

Since Russia's downfall, America has become the hope of the Entente. Although she is not to be under-estimated, she must not be over-estimated. At the moment England seems to be afraid that the leadership of the Entente will pass to America . . .

So far the year 1917 has not brought the Entente great military successes. England has only won Mesopotamia. The great victories on land† and sea (U-boats) have been on our side.

I draw the following conclusions:

Our military situation is more favourable than that of the Entente. Our alliance is firmer. Our internal difficulties are less than those of the Entente.

Yet, notwithstanding all this, I am of opinion that it is desirable that we should try to get a peace before the winter sets in, so long as it brings us those essentials which we need to secure our economic position hereafter and gives us an economic and military position which allows us to face another war of defence without anxiety.

With his eye already fixed upon the needs of the next war, Ludendorff urged that Belgian territory should be annexed up to the line of the Meuse. Even that, he said, would not give Germany complete security.

That can only be secured by binding Belgium so closely to us economically that she will seek political union also. The economic association will not be realized without strong military pressure – a considerable period of occupation – and without our possessing Liège. The neutrality of Belgium is a phantom on which no practical reliance can be placed.

This view brought the High Command into conflict with the new Foreign Secretary, Richard von Kühlmann, who preferred to think of Belgium as one of his biggest potential bargaining counters. Kühlmann now began to pursue initiatives of his own.

*See p 210 f.n.
† The Germans captured Riga on 3 September.

Lloyd George, ii, p 1231

German statesmanship was still anxious to entice the Allies into a Peace Conference at a moment so favourable to the Central Powers. It continued to pursue what was known as the Peace Strategy . . . Von Bethmann-Hollweg, Michaelis, the Pope and the Emperor Karl having failed, the German Foreign Minister, von Kühlmann, tried his hand. He was the ablest diplomat who had yet appeared on the scene . . . Had he been complete master of the situation in Germany, no one could tell what might have ensued. But he was not. He had the unstable Kaiser, the weak Michaelis, the stubborn and arrogant Great Headquarters of the Army, and the Prussian aristocracy to overcome before he could put through any settlement which had the slightest chance of acceptance by the Allies. He nevertheless made an attempt.

The complicated story of the German peace feeler through neutral Spain is well documented in Lloyd George's *Memoirs*, pp 1231–7. By 20 September the British Foreign Office was taking a grave view of the matter.

Lloyd George, ii, pp 1237–1240: Balfour to
Lloyd George, 20 September

From Austria, Bulgaria and Turkey, hesitating and inconclusive advances have . . . been made to us and, I believe, to France also . . .

The last to enter the diplomatic field is Germany.

A private telegram just received from Sir A. Hardinge,* which I have circulated to the Cabinet, shows beyond question that the German Foreign Office is desirous of entering into conversations with the British Government; *probably* with a view of arriving at some basis of discussion as regards terms of peace, *possibly* with the amiable purpose of sowing dissension among the Entente powers . . .

We need not fear, indeed, that any of the Allied Governments will prove willingly faithless: but, with the exception of Britain and America, they each have to deal with a public opinion which is moved in the main by national considerations. If, therefore, either France or Italy (for example) were offered *now* all, or more than all, that a successful war could ultimately give them, it might be exceedingly difficult for any Government to induce them to go on fighting for interests that were not their own.

I do not see any method of effectually parrying this danger. But our best chance is perfect frankness, and it seems therefore clear that we should do nothing without fully informing France, Italy, America, Russia and Japan. It is quite possible that if, and when, we communicate our intention to the Germans they may drop the whole matter. This does not, however, alter my opinion that we should lay ourselves dangerously open to misconception if we indulged in even the most noncommittal conversations behind the backs of our friends.

*British Ambassador in Madrid.

Repington, ii, p 53

FRIDAY, 21 SEPTEMBER . . . Lunched at Mr Balfour's house with him, General Smuts, and Sir William Robertson . . . We discussed Germany's position, and were agreed that Germany was all for peace. We imagined that she had some difficulties which we did not fully know, but we thought that want of men, raw material, and especially wool, transport, food, and so on were quite enough to account for her chastened mood.

No sooner had Balfour composed his memorandum to Lloyd George than he learned from the French Ambassador that an approach had also been made to France. A German official in Brussels, Baron von Lancken, had made a roundabout approach to the French ex-Premier, Aristide Briand, suggesting that the latter should meet a German representative in Switzerland. Briand reported this approach to his successor, Painlevé, who passed the information on to London. It was decided that Lloyd George should discuss the question with Painlevé; the conference took place in Boulogne on 25 September.

Lloyd George, ii, p 1242

According to a note taken at the time, I ascertained from the conversation with M. Painlevé that the German peace approach to France was serious. The suggestion was that M. Briand should meet in Switzerland either an ex-Chancellor, the present Chancellor, or some more exalted person. M. Painlevé had said that M. Briand had fluctuated somewhat in his reports of what terms the Germans were prepared to offer. At one moment he had said that they were willing to give up everything that the Allies desired in the West – e.g., Belgium and Alsace-Lorraine. Afterwards he had said that they were willing to *discuss* Alsace-Lorraine. One of the most serious considerations was that M. Briand was in favour of entering into this negotiation. M. Painlevé and M. Ribot, however, were both opposed to it. What M. Painlevé seemed to fear was not that the approach was not bona fide, but that it *was* bona fide. He evidently doubted whether France would continue fighting if it were known that the Germans had offered both nine-tenths of Alsace-Lorraine and the whole of Belgium. French Ministers took the same general view about the desirability or otherwise of peace *pour-parlers* with Germany as we did – that it was undesirable to enter into any negotiations until the German military power was broken.

My views as to the policy we ought to adopt depended on the military prospects.

FLANDERS

Author's Papers: Haig Diary

21 SEPTEMBER.   I spoke to Kiggell, Birch and Davidson regarding the nature of our next operations. In view of the fine weather which our weather experts think is likely to last for a week, it is most desirable to take full advantage of it, and of the superiority which we have now gained, for the time being, over the enemy's aeroplanes and artillery. Our next attack should therefore be made on as wide a front as possible. In this way it will be more certain of succeeding, and more German divisions will be used up. Our subsequent attacks should therefore encounter less opposition.

Repington, ii, pp 54–5

21 SEPTEMBER.   All [Balfour, Smuts, Robertson] happy about the second day of Haig's new offensive. R. says that Plumer is a good man and that Tim Harington and the 2nd Army Staff have done splendidly. Gough was promised the command in the Yser fight before Messines had proved the efficiency of the 2nd Army Command and Staff, and the latter having again shown their competence would be given a wider control in future . . .

Saw Maurice. He says that Plumer will go on again in five or six days if the weather serves. Haig was only anxious about the second day of the fight, as the Huns had accumulated great reserves for counter-attacks. All had been beaten back and we now seemed secure. All Haig's interest was in the attack on the Menin Road.

Author's Papers: Haig Diary

23 SEPTEMBER.   Gough was disinclined to make his plans to take all Poelcappelle village when he attacks, because it would form a pronounced salient. My opinion is that we shall be able to accomplish things *after* the next offensive which we could not dare even to attempt now. So Kiggell is to see him this afternoon, and ask him to *make preparations to take the whole* village if all goes well during the next attack. Such an operation is necessary to cover the flank of our attack against Passchendaele . . .

I told (Admiral Bacon) that it would be impossible to carry out the combined operation on 6 October, which is the last date for favourable tides.

SOLDIERS AND POLITICIANS

CAB 23/4: War Cabinet 237, 21 September

With reference to War Cabinet 232, Minute 2, the Chief of the Imperial General Staff reported that the guns which the Allies had sent from France had now arrived in Italy. He stated, however, that he had received information of a serious nature, to the effect that General Cadorna had modified his plans and did not propose to take the offensive again during the rest of the year; he was going to wait for the Austrians to attack, and then he would make a counter-attack.

The Secretary of State for War pointed out that it had been laid down by General Pétain, at the time when it had been decided to send the guns to Italy, that if there was no further offensive on the part of the Italian army, the 100 guns were to be returned to the French front . . .

The War Cabinet decided that:

The Secretary of State for Foreign Affairs, in consultation with the Chief of the Imperial General Staff, should send a telegram to Baron Sonnino saying that we had heard of the abandonment of the Italian offensive with extreme surprise; that it was inexplicable to us, having in view the recent despatch of 100 guns in compliance with General Cadorna's earnest request;* and that the decision was very embarrassing to our military operations on other fronts.

Author's Papers: Robertson to Haig, 24 September

You will be pleased to hear that as Cadorna has said he must go on the defensive the Cabinet are awfully sick with him, and I think also with themselves! I do not anticipate that we shall ever hear any more about your sending divisions to the Italian Front.

Duff Cooper, ii, p 158: Robertson to Haig, 24 September

The Prime Minister has been away during the last fortnight, and his mind has consequently been very active. I have recently had to knock out a scheme for operations in the Aden hinterland involving the employment of not less than a division. I have also had to destroy one for landing *ten* divisions at Alexandretta, all of which would have had to come from you. Further, I have had to fight against sending up more divisions to Mesopotamia. Generally, all round, I have been quite successful, although the expenditure of energy which ought otherwise to be employed has been a little greater than usual.   .

Repington, ii, p 58, 25 September

(Maurice) thought that we ought have a Chair at some University to teach budding statesmen the rudiments of war, and that it would be a very interesting one. 'A sort of Senior Officers' Staff College Course,' I said. 'Yes,' said M., 'to make them understand all the things that the War Cabinet has not been able to grasp throughout the war and cannot grasp now.' I told M. that I had said to the Frenchmen that after the war it would be found that 50 per cent of the time and

---

*Cadorna was alarmed at the arrival of Austrian reinforcements from the now dormant Eastern Front, already estimated at four divisions.

energy of soldiers had been expended in fighting their own politicians. M. thought that my percentage was much too low.

Haig Diary: Duff Cooper, ii, pp 158–9

26 SEPTEMBER.   At 9.30 am I had a meeting in my room with the Prime Minister, General Robertson and Colonel Hankey, who made notes. I was asked to submit my views as to the rôle of the British forces in the event of the Russians dropping out of the war – and the Italians and French doing (as they are doing now) very little. I am to give a considered opinion. My opinion without having gone into details is that we should go on striking as hard as possible with the object of clearing the Belgian coast. We should be prepared to make and win the campaign . . .

Lloyd George mentioned that Painlevé had referred to their desire that the British should take over more line. I said that we must set our face against doing any such thing. In my view, the plan for next year should be settled first and the necessary troops for *attack* be selected and specially trained for the purpose. I gathered from what the P.M. said that some members of the Government think that no offensive will be possible by the Allies on the western front next year.

Author's Papers: Haig to Lady Haig, 26 September

Lloyd George has just gone. Most friendly, but one never knows what rascality he may not be plotting.

MANPOWER

Repington, ii, p 58: 25 September

[Maurice said that] the War Cabinet had still taken no decision respecting men. We had swept everybody in the Army for the fighting line, including even experts, motor-drivers, and so on, but unless something were done we should be compelled to reduce strengths. We had 64 divisions in France. They were the equivalent of about 80 German, and 10 of our divisions were from the Dominions. The Cabinet wanted to reduce the strength of our divisions in order to evade their duty of calling up more men.

THE INVINCIBLE ENEMY

Author's Papers: Haig Diary

21 September. Glass rising slightly. Fine clear night. Cold. Bright morning and day. Very fine. Observation good.
22 September. Glass steady. Fine day with bright intervals. Colder.

23 September. Glass fell slightly. Day overcast at times, but no rain fell. Observation fair.
24 September. Glass steady. Cold morning with slight haze. Bright warm day.
25 September. Glass steady. Morning hazy but bright, sunny and very warm.

FLANDERS

Repington, ii, p 55

TUESDAY, 25 SEPTEMBER . . . Maurice says that Plumer and his Staff are now
responsible for the main attack on the Menin Road, and that Gough is on his left
now, with Rawlinson to come in presently. All goes well. M. hopes that the
Passchendaele Ridge may be taken by 10 October, and that before the close of the
campaigning season in November we may have the next ridge on the way to
Roulers, when our long-range naval guns which are in readiness will be able to
bombard Ostend and Zeebrugge, and render them and the Bruges Canal useless
for naval purposes. I hope that this may pan out, but it all seems a trifle petty in
itself, and one can only approve because it entails killing Germans all the time.

Lloyd George, ii, p 1315

I visited General Headquarters some time about the end of September.* I found
there an atmosphere of unmistakable exaltation. It was not put on. Haig was not
an actor. He was radiant. He was quiet, there was no swagger. That was never one
of his weaknesses, but he had the satisfied and confident demeanour of a leader
who was marching his army step by step surely and irresistibly, overcoming all
obstacles, including good advice from Gough and Plumer and the Prime Minister,
forward to the penultimate triumph of the War. This time it was purely his own.
The politicians had tried to thwart his purpose. His own commanders had timidly
tried to deflect him from his great achievement.† He magnanimously forgave us
all. He received me hospitably and pleasantly, without any of the humiliation of
Canossa. The French could claim no share in this victory, which was breaking the
might of the great army of Germany and leaving it a nervous wreck to be finally
disposed of in 1918. Something must be left for the Americans, otherwise they
would be disappointed.

Hankey, ii, p 699

25 SEPTEMBER . . . Lloyd George, Robertson . . . and I motored up to GHQ in a
village outside St Omer. I sat next to Haig at dinner. He was rather preoccupied
about tomorrow's attack, which has been somewhat dislocated by a big unsuccessful German counter-attack this afternoon.

*25–26 September.
† Harington (p 109) writes: 'I can say without any hesitation that my Chief, General Sir H.
Plumer, welcomed and endorsed the plan (of the Flanders offensive).

Harington, *Plumer of Messines*, pp 116–17

With our plans all complete for our offensive to take place early on 26 September, it was very disconcerting to be attacked ourselves on the 25th and it appeared at one time as if our plan for the 26th would not materialize.

At 6 am on 25 September, the enemy attacked in force our positions between Tower Hamlets and the Polygon Wood. The attacking troops penetrated our front and support lines in the Veldhoek trench north of the Menin Road, and for 500 yards south of the Polygon Wood. The support lines of the Veldhoek trench were re-captured by the Queens and Highland Light Infantry.

About 12 noon, a second heavy attack developed on the same front, which succeeded in driving in our line again in several places. The situation was, however, restored later during the afternoon . . .

During the night 25/26 September, the situation quietened down.

THE INVINCIBLE ENEMY

Author's Papers: Haig Diary

26 September. Glass falling slightly. Cloudy day. Dull morning but fine. Observation bad early but better in the afternoon.
27 September. Glass rising steadily. Slight drizzle early, then fine warm day.
28 September. Glass steady. Dull and coldish morning, but fine and warm later.
29 September. Glass rising slightly. Fine day. Morning dull, but fine and warm later.
30 September. Glass falling a little but day beautifully fine . . . morning was frosty.

FLANDERS: THE BATTLE OF POLYGON WOOD

Harington, *Plumer of Messines*, p 117

At 5.50 am on 26 September, the attack was launched on a frontage of 5,500 yards* extending from the Bitter Wood opposite the southern extremity of the Tower Hamlets Spur to 500 yards north of Anzac. The Fifth Army continued the attack to the north . . .

All day on the 26th our aeroplanes were very active; contact patrols flew low over the enemy's positions from early morning onwards, searching for reserve troops, and harassing hostile troops and transport from an average height of about 300 feet. A considerable amount of artillery co-operation was carried out and several special reconnaissances made. Several tons of bombs had been dropped daily and nightly during recent operations on enemy dumps, railheads, assembly areas, and traffic routes. Hostile aircraft were very active on the 26th, both trying

*Second Army.

to hinder our own machines and also flying low over our lines. Five of these low-flying aeroplanes were shot down by our machine-gun fire.

Birdwood, *Khaki and Gown*, p 315

On 26 September began the second stage. Our chief initial difficulty was that the ground over which our advance was to be made had been so churned up by artillery fire that there was no prospect of moving our guns across it till tracks or roads or light railways could be improvised. The distance involved was in places as much as 4,000 yards, and the ground had patches of swamp in it. Circuit roads, too, were essential. For the last five days the weather had been beautiful, but hazy ... At 5.50 am on the 26th our barrage came down; it was perfect, breaking out with a single crash and raising a dense wall of dust. Under this screen my 4th and 5th [Australian] Divisions, in conjunction with British formations, swept forward, and after much hard fighting captured the prearranged objectives round Polygon Wood and Zonnebeke. Our losses were again heavy – over 4,000. The German casualties were later found to have been about the same.

Hankey, ii, p 699–700

26 SEPTEMBER. Conference in morning with Haig, Prime Minister and Robertson ... There was a big attack that morning. All the time at the conference messages were coming in from the front. Haig had a great map showing the line we wanted to reach, and it was very interesting the way first one bit was filled in on the map, then another, until by the time we finished (11.30 am) the picture was complete except for a small section, where two brigades had been held up. In the evening, when we came back to GHQ for tea *en route* to Boulogne, news came that this bit was also captured, and the whole picture was complete like a jigsaw puzzle.

Ludendorff, ii, p 488

Another English attack on the 21st was repulsed; but the 26th proved a day of heavy fighting, accompanied by every circumstance that could cause us loss. We might be able to stand the loss of ground, but the reduction of our fighting strength was again all the heavier. Once more we were involved in a terrific struggle in the West, and had to prepare for a continuation of the attacks on many parts of the front.

O.H., 1917 ii, p 292–4

Although the frontage attacked was considerably less than on the 20th (8,500 yards compared with 14,500 yards) the demands made on the artillery during the Polygon Wood battle were said to be proportionately as great, and the forward move of the majority of the heavy and field batteries added a longer carry to the difficulties of the ammunition supply. It had been necessary for the protective artillery barrages, especially those laid by the I Anzac Corps, to be maintained almost without a break from dawn to dusk; in addition the X Corps artillery had been heavily engaged during most of the 25th . . .

Three German divisions had been sent in on the battle day to support three front divisions, compared with three sent up to support six front divisions on 20 September, and despite this added density of infantry, the German system of defence by organized counter-attack had completely failed.* Not a yard of ground lost by the enemy had been recaptured, and the counter-attack divisions had to be utilized to reinforce the new line to which the front divisions had been withdrawn.

Not only had the objective of the second step been gained and held, but the destruction also of German divisions and artillery was being carried out faster than they could arrive through the bottle-neck of communication into Western Belgium. The great advantage in the choice of Flanders as the battlefield area which accrued from this limitation of enemy entry was now manifest.

CAB 23/4: War Cabinet 240, 27 September

The Prime Minister remarked on the poor condition of the German prisoners whom he had seen on the 26th instant, during his recent visit to the British front in Flanders, and upon the very good spirit which prevailed among all ranks of our own army that he had seen and conversed with. The enemy system of concrete block-houses, commonly known as 'pill-boxes', appeared to have been mastered by our troops.

Charteris, p 257

27 SEPTEMBER.   While our minds have been turned on the theoretical discussion of future policy, the armies attacked again yesterday towards Passchendaele. Again the fighting was very heavy, with numerous counter-attacks. We gained ground but did not reach the ridge.† Nevertheless our position is improved, and there is now no reasonable doubt but that we can secure the whole ridge next month. That is the minimum. If the weather holds fine we may do much more. But the weather is now the dominant factor. As the sun loses power, it necessarily takes much longer to counteract each fall of rain. The general situation as regards the battle is strangely like the Somme. Now, as then, we had worn down the German resistance to very near breaking-point; then, as now, the weather went against us. It is a race with time, and a fight with the weather. One thing is certain, no other army but ours could fight on as we are fighting. D.H. is asking for the last ounce from it and getting a wonderful response.

---

*The German Official Account (xiii, p 77) says: 'The Eingreif divisions for the most part again struck against an already well dug in enemy, in some places against new enemy attacks . . . In the face of the British barrages, they took $1\frac{1}{2}$ to 2 hours to advance one kilometre, their formation broken and their attack-power lamed.'

† Charteris evidently had some difficulty in grasping the strategy of step-by-step advances; all objectives were taken on 26 September.

The casualties are awful;* one cannot dare to think of them. The temptation to stop is so great, but the obviously correct thing for the nation is to go on. I would not have believed that any troops would have faced what the Army is facing. But the Army knows it is winning. It is easy enough here for us, with all our information about the Germans, to count the cost coldly, to strike a balance sheet and see what is right to do. But for the men, and even more so for the regimental officers, it must seem a pretty hopeless outlook. Yet it is not at the front, but in England, that the calamity of casualties affects resolution.

Author's Papers: Haig Diary

Haig held a meeting with Plumer and Gough.

28 SEPTEMBER.   I urged the necessity for preparing to exploit our success after the attack, following that of 4 October. I am of opinion that the enemy is tottering, and that a good vigorous blow might lead to decisive results. If we could destroy, or interrupt for 48 hours, the railway at Roulers there would probably be a débâcle, because the enemy would then have to rely on only one railway line for the supply of his troops between Ghent and the sea. In order to exploit our success with good results, there must be *fresh* troops available, also Tanks and cavalry. Army commanders are to work out details.

Gough, p 212

On the 28th Haig held a conference, at which he expressed somewhat optimistic views, and gave the opinion that our repeated blows were using up the enemy's reserves and that we might soon be able to push on with no definite and limited objectives as heretofore. He thought that it might be possible that Tanks and even cavalry could get forward. The Germans were undoubtedly feeling the strain very seriously, and from the strategical point of view the Commander-in-Chief's operations were fully achieving their object; from a tactical outlook, however, his hopeful opinion was not justified when one considered the ground, the weariness of our own men, and the stout hearts which, in spite of all, were still beating under the German tunic.

Gough was always a most loyal subordinate of Haig, so his dissenting opinion requires serious attention. It must be said, however, that his attitude towards the campaign changed somewhat when the main rôle was transferred to Plumer, and on this day (28th) the relief of his V Corps by II Anzac reduced the Fifth Army from its original four to two corps, in effect merely a flank guard for the Second Army. There appears to have been an unresolved strategic disagreement between Fifth Army and GHQ at this juncture.

*Casualties for 26 September were 15,375 in the seven attacking divisions (*O.H.*, p 293, f.n. 3)

FRENCH MORALE

On 27 September Haig had once more asked General Anthoine to urge Pétain to mount an attack. On 29 September Colonel de Bellaigue reported that the French could not attack before 10, or possibly 15 October.

Author's Papers: Haig Diary, 29 September

What a wretched lot the majority of the French are! Here is an attack which was promised for the *middle of September* not ready to go in till 15 October. I doubt if it will go in then! If the 'intention to attack' existed the attack would have been ready to time. Gemeau* tells me that the morale of the French troops is now excellent,† what is wrong is the 'material' . . . History will doubtless conclude that the French are not playing the game!

GERMANY

Charteris, pp 256–7

25 SEPTEMBER . . . The immediate problem for the Allies' strategy resolves itself into:
(a) Whether a temporary defensive should not be assumed and maintained until such time as the full force of the American armies can be developed; or,
(b) Whether continuous pressure should be maintained and developed from now onwards, increasing and developing as the greatest manpower becomes available.

In favour of (a) is the argument that it is in the national interest to husband our resources of manpower so that the nation is not so exhausted that even victory in the field may spell catastrophe in the future. Against this, great though the effort of Great Britain has been, it has not involved her so far as loss in her manhood goes, in any way proportionate to that of France and Germany. But still more important is the argument that if we stop the offensive, Germany will recover and France may give way. The relative advantage of a breathing space is greater for Germany than for her enemies. We are fighting the willpower of the German nation as much as, if indeed not more than, the German armies in the field. That willpower is being steadily undermined by the drain on Germany's manhood. It will rapidly recover if the pressure is relaxed. Quite apart, therefore, from any actual progress that we may hope to make this autumn, in terms of ground captured, we must keep up our pressure in order to:
1. Protect our Allies

*French liaison officer at GHQ.   † See p 259.

2. Facilitate our task next year
3. Prevent the recovery of the power of resistance of the German people and the German Army.

Author's Papers: Robertson to Haig, 27 September

With reference to the Paper you are preparing on the Military Outlook ... there is no doubt that Germany is much more anxious at the present time for peace than she has ever been before. Information showing this comes before me in some form or other, sometimes from very good sources, nearly every hour of the day. But at the same time the terms stated to you yesterday* were I think probably exaggerated. If such terms were offered we should do very well to consider them, but I do not think they will be offered until the German Armies have been further defeated . . .

The view taken, and quite naturally, by certain people here is that the collapse of Russia would make our task very much greater, and no doubt it would. Germany has some 90 divisions on the Russian Front while Austria has between 30 and 40. I do not think that the latter would be likely to come to the West Front but the heavy artillery might, and the Austrian divisions might be sent to the Italian Front. Of the 90 German divisions some would no doubt have to stay in and about Russia for a long time to come but the withdrawal to the West Front during the winter of even 30 divisions would make a considerable difference. There is also the question of the large number of German and Austrian prisoners that would be released. Against these things is the entry of America into the war and the effect of that you are as well able to judge as I am.

But the result of it all is that certain people here think it would be exceedingly difficult to bring about a decision on the West Front if the German troops there are materially reinforced, and therefore they are frequently looking about for means of detaching some of the hostile Powers. To detach them they maintain that more punishment is required, and that naturally takes away from our concentration on the West.

My views are known to you. They have always been 'defensive' in all theatres but the West. But the difficulty is to *prove* the wisdom of this now that Russia is out.† I confess I stick to it more because I see nothing better, and because my instinct prompts me to stick to it, than to [sic] any convincing argument by which I can support it. Germany may be much nearer the end of her staying power than available evidence shows, but on the other hand France and Italy are not much to depend upon, and America will require a long time. Further, it is argued that

---

* When Robertson came to GHQ with Lloyd George and Hankey; Lloyd George informed Haig of the German peace feelers, and the possibility that Germany would be willing to give up Belgium and Alsace-Lorraine. (See pp 000–0)

† During September the Russian Provisional Government was assailed from the Right by an Army revolt under the Commander-in-Chief, General Kornilov, and from the Left by the increasing agitation and influence of the Soviets.

stagnation will destroy the Nation's determination. It is not an easy business to see through the problem when present resources of both sides and hostile gains are considered.

Author's Papers: Haig Diary

29 SEPTEMBER.   Charteris reported on the enemy's situation which is very favourable to us.

30 SEPTEMBER.   Charteris reported that the situation is most favourable for continued success. The enemy is very short of reserves.

October

✠

Author's Papers: Haig Diary

1 October. Glass falling slightly, but day fine and warm, after frosty night.
2 October. Glass falling steadily, but fine after a cold night. Very warm during day.
3 October. Glass steady since midday yesterday. Some heavy showers . . . fell during the night. Dull morning but day fine with occasional bright intervals.

Flanders

Ludendorff, ii, pp 488–9

October came, and with it one of the hardest months of the war. The world at large – which began in my immediate neighbourhood – saw only Tarnopol,* Czernovitz,† Riga,‡ and later Oesel,§ Udine, the Tagliamento and the Piave.¶ It did not see my anxiety, nor my deep sympathy with the sufferings of our troops in the West. My mind was in the East and Italy, my heart on the Western Front.

It may be noted that in the eight days, 26 September–3 October, the Germans launched not less than 24 attacks and counter-attacks in Flanders, viz.: 26 September: 'at least 7'; 27 September: 7; 30 September: 3; 1 October: 5; 3 October: 2.

Ludendorff, ii, p 489

After each attack I discussed the tactical experiences with General von Kuhl and Colonel von Lossberg,‖ sometimes at the front, sometimes on the telephone . . .

---

*Captured by the Germans, 24 July.
†Captured 3 August.
‡Captured 3 September (See p 264 f.n.)
§Oesel Islands, captured 15 October.
¶Stages of the Caporetto offensive (see below).
‖Fourth Army Chief of Staff.

Our defensive tactics had to be developed further, somehow or other. We were all agreed on that. The only thing was, it was so infinitely difficult to hit on the right remedy. We could only proceed by careful experiment. The proposals of the officers on the spot tended rather in the direction of our former tactics; they amounted to a slight, but only a slight, reinforcement of our front lines, and the abandonment of the counter-attack by the counter-attack divisions, local counter-attacks being substituted for this. These local counter-attacks were to be made by a division in the second line, to be brought close up and spread over a wide front, before the enemy's attack began. So, while the front was to be held rather more densely once more, in order to gain in power, the whole battlefield was to be given more depth than ever. GHQ would thus, generally speaking, have to provide a second division for every fighting division in the front line, an unheard-of expenditure of force.

Author's Papers: Haig Diary

2 OCTOBER.   I held a Conference at my house at Cassel at 11 am. Kiggell, Davidson and Charteris accompanied me. Generals Plumer and Gough were also present with their senior Staff Officers and General Nash (Director-General of Transport). I pointed out how favourable the situation was and how necessary it was to have all necessary means for exploiting any success gained on the 10th, should the situation admit, e.g., if the enemy counter-attacks and is defeated, then reserve Brigades must follow after the enemy and take the Passchendaele ridge at once. Masked guns for this object should be placed behind Gravenstafel ridge as soon as we have captured it. Tanks must also be arranged for. The cavalry corps to have its head on the Ypres canal ready to move up early on the 11th . . . Both Gough and Plumer quite acquiesced in my views, and arranged wholeheartedly to give effect to them when the time came. At first they adhered to the idea of continuing our attacks for limited objectives.

   Charteris emphasized the deterioration of German Divisions in numbers, morale and all-round efficiency.

Casualties in the Flanders offensive, 31 July–3 October, were reported by the British Representatives to the Supreme War Council (see below) on 25 February, 1918, as 138,787.* The *Statistics of the Military Effort of the British Empire During the Great War* (HMSO 1922) p 334, Table xviii, give for the period 31 July–5 October, 163,769. The Official History gives losses of 20,472 for the two days, 4–5 October, making a total of 159,259, which may be taken as the corrected version of that given in the *Statistics*, based on first returns.

*See *O.H.*, 1917, ii, p 361

THE INVINCIBLE ENEMY

Author's Papers: Haig Diary

4 OCTOBER.   Glass fell half inch from midday yesterday to midday today. High wind all night with slight rain, increased to a gale during the day. Storm in Channel so boats did not cross. Wet afternoon. Fine night.

FLANDERS: THE BATTLE OF BROODSEINDE

O.H., 1917, ii, pp 303–5

At dusk on the 3rd the assaulting brigades began to march up to the line; most of the Australians, of whom three divisions were going into battle side by side for the first time, passed out of Ypres by the Menin Gate . . .

A full moon was hidden by clouds when, by 4 am on this 4 October . . . the men lay crowded on the wet ground behind the jumping-off tapes. Brigades had assembled well forward to escape the expected German defensive barrage about zero hour; but at 5.20 am, forty minutes earlier, intense German artillery fire suddenly fell on most of the front of the two Anzac corps. It seemed that the waiting mass of men had been detected, and, in order to minimize losses, they were squeezed still closer to the German outpost groups, taking any available cover in shell holes . . . Even so, heavy casualties were suffered during forty minutes' shelling, particularly by the brigades of the I Anzac Corps, which lost, it was estimated, one man in seven killed or wounded before the assault started.

At 6 am the British barrage suddenly crashed down on the whole depth of the German position. The infantry stood up, unperturbed by their ordeal, and, lighting cigarettes, the men surged across no-man's-land to escape a renewal of the German shelling. The companies then shook out into groups and small columns, with their proper distances and intervals, as rehearsed. It was twilight, and a drizzling rain, driven by a south-west wind, limited visibility to about thirty yards . . .

Before the leading companies had crossed no-man's-land they saw in the dim light, close ahead, lines of men rising up from shell-holes. Some were already on the move forward with bayonets fixed, and the Australians opened fire. The assault was only momentarily delayed. As the Australians advanced they found Germans in every shell-hole waiting for the signal to advance.

Although the first two belts of the barrage were noticeably thinner and more ragged than on 20 September, owing to the weakened artillery support, the same confident resolution and determined driving power which had characterized the assault by (the 1st and 2nd) Australian divisions on 20 September quickly gave them mastery of this unexpected situation. Many of the enemy would not face the onslaught and fled back, risking the barrage, whilst numerous sharp and merciless encounters took place with any survivors who offered resistance.

Birdwood, *Khaki and Gown*, pp 315–16

Once more complete success was achieved, the objectives of Broodseinde Ridge and Zonnebeke being taken. By something of a coincidence, our attack had hardly commenced when our men encountered German troops who had evidently been launched on a similar attack against us; but these were swept away in many individual combats by my Australians. There could be no doubt as to the completeness and importance of our success. The Germans, who had recently been holding their front lines in vastly increased strength, not only suffered heavily but had lost one of their most vital positions on the Western Front; and this despite their knowledge that the blow was coming. The German official history says: 'The black day of 4 October was extraordinarily severe, and again we only came through it with enormous losses.'*

Harington, *Plumer of Messines*, pp 122 & 124

During the day the enemy delivered no less than ten counter-attacks . . .

The total number of prisoners who passed through the Corps Cages and Casualty Clearing Stations from 6 pm, 3 October, to 6 pm, 6 October, was 114 officers and 4,044 other ranks.†

German Official Account

Once again the losses had been extraordinarily severe . . . The new combat methods had not proved themselves successful on 4 October. The more heavily manned front line which had suffered heavy losses from artillery fire had been overrun by enemy infantry who had attacked in superior numbers with tank support. All the counter-attack divisions behind the Ypres Group and the Wytschaete Group had had to be used. The Army High Command came to the conclusion that there was no means by which the positions could be held against the overpowering enemy superiority in artillery and infantry. Loss of ground in these heavy enemy attacks was unavoidable. Up to now the High Command had tried to cover the heavy losses suffered in these giant battles but it would not be possible to do this for very long . . .

In connection with the new regulations regarding the fighting methods, the Supreme Command asked for opinions regarding the amount of ground which could be given up without prejudicing the safety of the U-boat bases: in particular also how to retain its fighting strength in Flanders throughout the winter . . . The Army Group stressed that it was less concerned with a determined retention of the marked fighting zones than in a more elastic defence – where necessary, a limited yielding at the main points of pressure and counter-attacks against the flanks of an attack.

*The monograph *Flandern 1917* issued by the Reicharciv in 1928. The German 212th Reserve Regiment, encountered by the Australians, lost 36 officers and 1,009 other ranks.
†In addition, the Fifth Army captured 12 officers and 589 other ranks.

With this in mind an offensive had been suggested for 5 October, in the area of GHELUVELT against the right flank of the British advancing in the YPRES SALIENT . . . Every major enemy attack won from one kilometre to one and a half kilometres gain of ground by reason of his overwhelming arms and ammunition. One could not hope to do any better than this oneself. Such a success would constrict the British, would compel them to regroup and would bring their offensive to a halt. It would be of great significance if we could win just eight days until the onset of winter. But as the Army Group could not supply the necessary forces, the offensive plan had to be cancelled.

> *Official History of Australia in the War*, vol. iv, p 875

An overwhelming blow had been struck and both sides knew it. The objective was the most important yet attacked by the Second and Fifth Armies and they had again done almost exactly what they proposed to do . . . This was the third blow struck at Ypres in fifteen days with complete success . . . Let the student, looking at the prospect as it appeared at noon on 4 October ask himself, 'In view of three step by step blows' (20 September–26 September and 4 October) 'what will be the result of three more in the next fortnight?'

> Haig Diary: Blake, p 257

4 OCTOBER.   Today was a very important success . . . In order not to miss any chance of following up our success if the enemy were really demoralized, I met Generals Plumer and Gough with their Staff Officers at my house in Cassel at 3 pm. Plumer stated that in his opinion we had only up-to-date fought the leading troops of the enemy's Divisions on his front. Charteris, who was present, thought that from the number of German regiments represented amongst the prisoners, all Divisions had been seriously engaged and that there were few more available reserves.

After full discussion I decided that the next attack should be made two days earlier than already arranged, provided Anthoine could also accelerate his preparations. At 4 pm I saw the latter. He was most anxious to do everything possible to hasten matters. Finally it was found possible to advance the attack by *one* day.

> Lloyd George, ii, p 1319

The Times has two leading articles on successive days on the Broodseinde victory, as it was called. Who remembers the name now? (Try it on one of your friends.)

> Wilson, ii, p 16

5 OCTOBER.   Lloyd George has no illusions about Haig's 'victory' of yesterday. At the same time I again insisted on Lloyd George giving Haig *all* the men and guns that he possessed, up to the time of the mud, to which he agreed. The fact is that Lloyd George is profoundly dissatisfied, but does not know what to do.

Charteris, pp 258–9

5 OCTOBER.   We are far enough on now to stop for the winter, and there is much to be said for that. Unless we get fine weather for all this month, there is now no chance of clearing the coast. With fine weather we may still do it. If we could be sure that the Germans would attack us here, it would be far better to stand fast. But they would probably be now only too glad to remain quiet here and try elsewhere. Anyhow, there are reasons far more vital than our own interests here that give us no option. But it is a tremendous responsibility for D.H. Most of those at the conference,* though willing to go on, would welcome a stop.

Author's Papers: Haig Diary

5 OCTOBER.   In my opinion when we have gained the Passchendaele ridge as far north as Stadenburg the enemy will be forced to withdraw from the Dixmude front and Forêt d'Houthoulst because he cannot risk his troops being cut off in that area . . . My view is *first*, capture the Passchendaele-Stadenburg ridge; *second*, clear Forêt d'Houthoulst by advancing to Staden on the east side of it, so as to turn it; *third*, Second Army to take Moorslede ridge and Roulers, Fifth Army Hooglede and Thourout. The French to take Cortemarck, Zarren and Hill N.E. The Belgians to cover flank.

SOLDIERS AND POLITICIANS

Haig Diary: Blake, p 256

3 OCTOBER.   A great bombshell arrived in the shape of a letter from CIGS stating that the British Government had 'approved in principle' of the British Army in France taking over more line from the French, and details are to be arranged by General Pétain and myself. This was settled at a Conference at Boulogne on 25 September at which I was not present.† Nor did either L. George or Robertson tell me of this decision at our interview.‡ All the P.M. said was that 'Painlevé was anxious that the British should take over more line'. And Robertson rode the high horse and said that it was high time for the British now to call the tune, and not play second fiddle to the French, etc, etc, and all this when shortly before he must have quietly acquiesced at the Conference in Painlevé's demands! R. comes badly out of this, in my opinion,§ especially as *it was definitely stated (with the War Cabinet's approval) that no discussion re operations on the Western front would be held without my being present.*

---

*The Army Commanders' Conference with Haig on 4 October.
† See p 272.
‡ See p 269.
§ In *Douglas Haig: The Educated Soldier* (p 364) I wrote: 'This entry marks the beginning of a perceptible decline of confidence and co-operation between Haig and Robertson.'

Roskill, *Hankey: Man of Secrets*, i, p 440: Hankey Diary

6 OCTOBER.   Saw Lord Milner in the morning, who told me that on the previous day they had a highly unsatisfactory meeting of the War Policy Ctee; Robertson had apparently strongly opposed the despatch of two divisions to Egypt as a reserve for Palestine or Mesopotamia, and the Prime Minister had handled him very badly with much recrimination and reminders of the past deficiencies of military advice.

Author's Papers: Robertson to Haig, 6 October

You are getting on splendidly, and your forecasts as to the cumulative effect of your efforts are proving well-founded. One would think that the fine successes you are winning would suffice to satisfy even the people with whom I live, but it is not so apparently or they would drop the Palestine rot. On the contrary, they are more full of it than ever. The War Policy Cttee: P.M. (1), B. Law (2), Curzon (3), Milner (4), Smuts (5) recommenced their labours yesterday. (1), (2), (4) are for Palestine, (3) I think not. (5) has really no definite views. He talks one day one way, another the other day. The idea is to give the Turk such a blow as will make him come to terms. When I try to show it is neither likely nor possible, I am accused of being a hide-bound west-fronter with no imagination. The usual arguments are adduced against the possibility of a decision in the West. The condition of France is ignored. Naturally I insist that Palestine must be considered with the whole question, and that troops sent there must be lost to you next year. The answer is (1) A few less troops to you will make no difference. (2) They will be back in time to resume with you. (3) But you won't want them as the Americans will be a great addition next year, and the French will fight next year etc. Time, space, human strength, concentration at decisive point are all ignored. However, I am, I hope, making my arguments in a direct and clear way and will avoid being jockeyed by degrees into a wrong course. I shall, I hope, keep the issue and consequences clear, and so have a good field of battle on which to fight these people. Then I can beat them, or have a row. But of course the politician's cunning has shown itself. L.G. says, if I will send Allenby* sufficient troops – probably 5 or 6 divisions more – he will fight the French against your taking over more line. Alternatively, I *know* he will *not* fight them if I refuse – as I shall – to agree to this plan. You shall hear more later.

Once more, best congratulations. It is a hard war – not because of the Boche but because of these people here.

FRENCH MORALE

CAB 23/4: War Cabinet No. 243, 2 October

In connection with a French offensive on the Western Front, the Chief of the

*General Sir Edmund Allenby, GOC Egypt and Palestine.

Imperial General Staff reported that . . . Sir Douglas Haig . . . was satisfied that active preparations were now being pressed forward by General Pétain.

The Prime Minister reminded the War Cabinet that at the Paris Peace Conference on 26/27 May he had been convinced that the French did not intend to attack.

The War Cabinet felt that the coincidence of the delays on the part both of the French and Italians to attack was unsatisfactory and difficult to explain.

Author's Papers: Haig Diary

6 OCTOBER. General Pétain . . . came to see me at 4 pm. He said that he was heartbroken (*navré*) at the delay in putting in his attack on the Aisne. He could not override the decision of the Generals on the spot, and sending the guns to Italy had further delayed things . . . He was . . . anxious to support my offensive to the fullest extent possible and had told General Anthoine that he was free to make use of his reserves, and that he would send him more troops to replace them.

Repington, ii, pp 77, 83

SUNDAY, 7 OCTOBER. Went to look up Joan Wodehouse, who has been helping to nurse 700 French soldiers most of the war at the *Hôpital Complémentaire* . . . She tells me that the morale of the French troops at the front was bad in June after Nivelle's failure, but is now good. She says, however, that the wounded in hospital are gloomy, and that they are much upset by the French papers with the accounts of all the scandals and treacheries, and ask whether such a Government and such rascals are worth fighting for. I advised her to tell them that they were fighting for France, and that all the Allied Armies had rotten Governments . . .

Reached Compiègne three-quarters of an hour late for dinner and found Pétain nearly finished . . . We . . . discussed the morale of the French, and Pétain told me of the terrible time he had passed through last June. The morale was now completely re-established at the front. He only feared the rear and the effect of current scandals and treacheries.

Throughout the year political agitation – Socialist, Pacifist, Anarchist, sometimes infiltrated by German agents and supported by German funds – had been very active, especially in Paris. John Williams (*The Home Fronts, 1914–1918*, p 209) says:

'In and around the large railway termini, especially the Gare de l'Est and Gare du Nord – stations for the front – lurked (anti-war) agents, mingling with the troops in transit to distribute anti-war pamphlets and urge them to desert. Near the stations were illicit clothing agencies, at which deserters could obtain civilian clothes. This year the toll of desertions, either spontaneous or induced, was to reach the record total of 27,000.'

The manager of the pacifist news-sheet *Le Bonnet Rouge* was found with a cheque for 150,000 francs signed by the paymaster of a German espionage ring. He (Duval) and his editor Almereyda were arrested and the paper suspended. A round-up of similar trouble-makers brought 1,700 arrests by the end of the year. The Minister of the Interior, Malvy, resigned in August; in November he was himself arrested and charged with treason. There was widespread industrial unrest.

THE INVINCIBLE ENEMY

O.H., 1917, ii, p 325

The rain which had set in during the afternoon of the 4th continued in a steady drizzle, with occasional heavy showers, throughout the next two days, and on the 7th came squalls of cold drenching rain.

Author's Papers: Haig to Lady Haig, 8 October

Bright and clear with a high wind which is drying the ground nicely. But yesterday's rain made the mud very bad beyond Ypres in the low ground and stopped all the guns we wanted getting forward, but we have enough for tomorrow's attack.

Author's Papers: Haig Diary

9 OCTOBER.   Gale blew all night. Morning still very windy but fine.

FLANDERS

The War Letters of General Monash, Angus & Robertson, 1925; 7 October

Great happenings are possible in the very near future, as the enemy is terribly disorganized, and it is doubtful if his railway facilities are good enough to enable him to re-establish himself before our next two blows, which will follow very shortly and will be very severe . . . Our success* was complete and unqualified. Over 1,050 prisoners and much material and guns. Well over 1,000 dead enemy counted, and many hundreds buried out of reach. We got absolutely astride the main ridge.

Repington, ii, pp 82–3

7 OCTOBER.   (Pétain) had the greatest respect for Haig and admired his tenacity

*The 3rd Australian Division on 4 October.

and the great achievements of our Armies, but could not think that our attack in Flanders was good strategy. What did I think of it, and was not the strategy imposed upon us by our Admiralty?

I replied that on the latter point I had no information, but that I thought killing Boches was always good business, and that Haig was killing a lot. Also, he had freed Ypres from strangulation, and now on his whole front had the best of the ground and could, at need, hold it defensively with reduced effectives. This was worth doing. But if the strategical objective were the submarine bases, I thought this of second-rate importance, as the best German submarines came from German and not Flanders ports.

Charteris, p 259

8 OCTOBER. We go on again tomorrow, and yesterday and today there have been heavy downpours of rain, a last effort. Documents taken on the 4th show that the Germans are very hard pressed to hold their ground. They have given up their new plan of thinly held front lines and gone back to their old scheme, which is all to the good; but unless we have a very great success tomorrow it is the end for this year so far as Flanders is concerned, and next year the Germans will have their troops from Russia. With a great success tomorrow, and good weather for a few more weeks, we may still clear the coast and win the war before Christmas.

Haig Diary: Blake, pp 257–8

8 OCTOBER. I called on General Plumer and had tea. It was raining and looked like a wet night. He stated that 2nd Anzac Corps* (which is chiefly concerned in tomorrow's attack) had specially asked that there should be *no postponement.* Plumer was anxious lest the French should want to postpone. I told him that Cavendish (attached to General Anthoine) had reported at noon by telephone that 'the situation on First Army (French) for attack on 9th is on the whole satisfactory' though the bombardment had not been effective. But Anthoine is 'quite ready to carry out his attacks as already arranged.' . . . Gough telephoned to Kiggell as to postponement; he said Cavan was against it, but Maxse wanted to postpone. I ordered them to carry on.

THE BATTLE OF POELCAPPELLE

Birdwood, Khaki and Gown, p 316

My men were weak and tired, and when Plumer consulted me I had to advise against any further advance. However, since only one division of my Corps was to be involved in the next stage, and since the other Corps Commanders were in favour of pushing on, Haig decided to do so.

In a sense, I was reminded of our final effort to capture Sari Bair at Gallipoli, for here again it was a case of 'so near and yet so far'. Haig's view was that if we held

*Lieut General Sir A. J. Godley.

the main Passchendaele Ridge overlooking and commanding all the country to the east, this would involve so decisive a break in the German line that our cavalry could be used to good effect; and there is little doubt that if the weather had held, and if we had been able to prepare and rehearse our advance as carefully as in the first three stages, we should have been able to take Passchendaele. But the weather defeated us.

von Kuhl, *Der Weltkrieg*

4 and 9 October were also days of severe fighting which stretched the German forces to their limit. The enemy succeeded in mounting repeated attacks and gradually forced the German front at Ypres back on a stretch about 33 km. wide. The penetrations at their deepest were from five to seven kilometres. But the British had made no breakthrough.

In the middle of October there was a pause in the fighting and the enemy moved up his guns and relieved his fought out divisions by new ones. On the German side it became even more difficult to procure the reserves to continue the defence.

O.H. 1917, ii, pp 327–30

The roads and tracks across the battle area had gravely deteriorated. Three months of persistent shelling had blocked the water-courses, and the mass of shell-holes frustrated every attempt to drain the water away. It must be emphasized, however, that the chief engineers of the corps and the divisional CREs are unanimous in stating that up to 4 October there had been no serious difficulty in maintaining the communications to the front, weather and ground conditions being tolerable and damage by the enemy being readily repairable. Some even say this was the case until the 12th; but in certain areas conditions did become impossible. The entire valley of the upper Steenbeek and its tributaries (behind the II Anzac Corps) was, in the words of one divisional CRE, 'a porridge of mud'.

On such a foundation, despite the concentrated and untiring efforts of the engineers of the two Anzac corps, no progress could be made with the plank roads for the forward move of the guns: the planks either sank in the mire or floated away. The field batteries of the II Anzac Corps which were to have been near the Zonnebeke-Winnipeg road to support the main attack had to remain west of the Steenbeek on hurriedly constructed and unstable gun-platforms. Until these were made many of the guns were up to the axles in mud, and some even to the muzzles. [A footnote here adds: Each gun-platform had to have a foundation of fascines and road metal, on which was placed a double-decked platform of beech-slabs nailed together. It required two days' hard work to make, and a temporary plank road had to be built from the platform to the main roadway for the ammunition supply by pack transport. Even after this labour, many of the platforms began to sink into the mud after a few rounds had been fired.] The morning objective of the 9th would be at (field guns') extreme range (6,000 yards); Passchendaele village, whose church spire was visible from many of the battery positions, was seven thousand yards distant, so the mass of the German field batteries which were about and behind that locality would be beyond reach . . .

The dug-outs at the wagon lines and the shelterless gun platforms were soon flooded, and the men had to sleep on wet blankets or sodden straw, resulting in a rapid dwindling of the effective artillery strength through sickness and exhaustion . . .

These conditions equally affected the infantry in the forward area . . . The difficulty was to get the assaulting troops up to the jumping-off tapes at all, and in some condition to make an attack. The chief cause of the great discontent during this period of the Flanders fighting was, in fact, the continuous demands on regimental officers and men to carry out tasks which appeared physically impossible to perform, and which no other army would have faced.* It must be emphasized again, too, that in all that vast wilderness of slime hardly tree, hedge, wall or building could be seen. As at the Somme no landmarks existed, nor any scrap of natural cover other than the mud-filled shell-holes. That the attacks ordered were so gallantly made in such conditions stands to the immortal credit of the battalions concerned.

> Sholto Douglas (Marshal of the Royal Air Force
> Lord Douglas of Kirtleside), *Years of Combat*,
> Collins, 1963, pp 239-40

With the start, on 9 October, of the attack on Passchendaele itself, after two days of continuous and heavy rain, our work was changed to that of carrying out low-flying attacks against enemy concentrations on the ground. It was supposed to be an effort on our part to assist our troops, who were struggling in what had become nothing more than an appalling morass. In this job there was very little fighting in the air, and since we were flying at heights of only two or three hundred feet we were supposed to be able to see plenty of what was going on below us. What I saw was nothing short of horrifying. The ground over which our infantry and light artillery were fighting was one vast sea of churned-up muck and mud, and everywhere, lip to lip, there were shell-holes full of water.

These low-flying attacks that we had to make, for which most of my young pilots were quite untrained, were a wretched and dangerous business, and also pretty useless. It was very difficult for us to pick out our targets in the morass because everything on the ground, including the troops, was the same colour as that dreadful mud.

> Charteris, p 259

10 OCTOBER.   I was out all yesterday at the attack. It was the saddest day of this year. We did fairly well but only fairly well. It was not the enemy but mud that prevented us doing better. But there is now no chance of complete success here

---

*The Germans, of course, were facing identical conditions at the front and in their endless counter-attacks, though their rear areas were 'clean country'.

this year. We must still fight on for a few more weeks,* but there is no purpose in it now, so far as Flanders is concerned. I don't think I ever really had great hope of a big success yesterday, but until noon there was, at least, still a chance. Moving about close behind a battle, when things are going well and when one is all keyed up with hope of great results, one passes without much thought the horrible part of it – the wounded coming back, the noise, the news of losses, the sight of men toiling through mud into great danger. But when one knows that the great purpose one has been working for has escaped, somehow one sees and thinks of nothing but the awfulness of it all. Yesterday afternoon was unutterably damnable. I got back very late and could not work, and could not rest. D. H. sent for me about 10, to discuss things. He has to bear the brunt of it all. He was still trying to find some grounds for hope that we might still win through here this year, but there is none.

SOLDIERS AND POLITICIANS

It was precisely as the Flanders offensive took this gloomy turn that the year-long contest between the Prime Minister and his responsible military advisers came to its head. On 8 October Haig submitted the paper on the *Rôle Of The British Forces Should Russia Fall Out Of The War* that Lloyd George had asked for on 26 September (see p 269). The military philosophy expounded in it could not fail to infuriate Lloyd George, who refers to the paper in his memoirs as an 'inebriated document'. Haig's fundamental belief about the war, from which he never departed, was succinctly expressed in his diary as early as March, 1915: 'We cannot hope to win until we have defeated the German Army'. Lloyd George entirely disagreed with this view, and cannot have enjoyed finding it re-stated now:

O.H., 1918, vol i, Appendix 1

The first factor to be taken into account is that not only Germany but her allies rely primarily and practically entirely on the invincibility of the German armies to secure for them favourable terms of peace.

It is evident to the whole world that it is belief in Germany's military strength, hope of eventual safety based thereon, and fear of incurring her resentment, which hold her allies in the field; and that if the power of resistance of the German armies were once broken down completely, or even manifestly on the point of breaking down, Germany and her allies would gladly accept such terms of peace as the allies might offer.'

*A footnote by Charteris says: 'The French were still appealing for the protection provided by our attacks.' He does not state his evidence for this. As we have seen (p 275) Haig was urging Pétain to attack.

The question, then, was whether it was feasible to overcome German resistance by direct attack, and if not, what to do instead. Haig dealt with the second question first, reaching the unpalatable conclusion that:

It would be not only unsound but highly dangerous to undertake any of the various indirect means which have been suggested to sap Germany's power by operating against her allies.

Writing with the Broodseinde victory still fresh, and before the setback of Poelcappelle, he was fortified in this view by his hope of breaking through in Flanders.

Our offensive in front of Ypres continues to make good progress. The enemy is undoubtedly considerably shaken and the ground we have already gained gives us considerable advantages and renders us less dependent on weather in following up our success further. Our troops are elated and confident; those on the enemy's side cannot but be depressed and we have good evidence of it.

In these circumstances it is beyond question that our offensive must be pursued as long as possible. I have every hope of being able to continue it for several weeks still and of gaining results which will add very greatly to the enemy's losses in men and morale, and place us in a far better position to resume an offensive in the spring.

Haig then analysed the conditions of a 1918 offensive, with Russia knocked out, and concluded:

Even if the German forces on this front are increased to the extent assumed, I am confident that the British Armies in France, assisted by the French and American armies, will be quite capable of carrying through a sustained and successful offensive next year under certain conditions which I understand to be realizable.

This brought him to a sore point – the question of the extension of the British line.

Though the French cannot be expected to admit it officially, we know that the state of their armies and of the reserve manpower behind the armies is such that neither the French Government nor the military authorities will venture to call on their troops for any further great and sustained offensive effort, at any rate before it becomes evident that the enemy's strength has been definitely and finally broken. Though they are staunch in defence and will carry out useful local offensives against limited objectives the French armies would not respond to a call for more than that, and the authorities are well aware of it. In these circumstances, since the British armies alone can be made capable of a great offensive effort it is beyond argument that everything should be done by our allies as well as ourselves to enable that effort to be made as strong as possible and for this as much training, leave and rest as possible is absolutely essential for our men.

The French authorities will no doubt insist strongly on an extension of our front, but the weight of argument is all against it and our troops are entitled to be protected against what is really an unfair demand on them. They are in a foreign country, the French are at home. They get little leave and at long intervals, the French soldiers get ten days leave every four months and their Government dare not refuse it. Our men have borne more and accomplished more than the French this summer, and though France may plead that the weight of the war has fallen on her, it cannot be expected that the British soldiers in the field who have done so much and borne so much, and who have come voluntarily from the ends of the earth to fight in France will be content to see preferential treatment given to their allies. This aspect of the case must not be overlooked any more than the purely military arguments, and it is on popular feeling amongst the French people rather than on military argument that the French demand on us to take over more line is based . . .

We cannot afford to assist (our allies) directly, and it is not in their own interests that the efforts of the only really effective offensive army which will exist next year in the alliance should throw away what is a good prospect and practically the only prospect of a real victory by disseminating its forces. Victory against a strong and determined foe has never been won by such a course and never can be. We must insist that our allies shall rely on themselves for defence, and the most effective assistance we can give them is by forcing Germany to use up her troops in guarding herself against our blows . . .

Everything goes to show that the power of endurance of Germany and her allies is so severely strained that the mere fact of our ability and evident determination to maintain the struggle to the end may suffice to turn the scale at any moment.

Even if they hold out until next year and if our success in the field then is of a limited nature our enemies cannot possibly face a further prolongation of the war, with the full development of America's strength, which will then be developing, to be reckoned with.*

In the present state of the German armies and of ours I am confident that if the course I have recommended be adopted whole-heartedly we shall gain far more than a limited success in the field next year; and I urge unhesitatingly the continuance of the offensive on the Western Front, with all our strength, as the correct rôle of the British forces even under the conditions laid down by the Prime Minister for the examination of the problem.

Blake, p 259: Robertson to Haig, 9 October.

Your memorandum is splendid . . . I gather . . . that you are perhaps a little

*The ration strength of U.S. forces in France on 13 November, 1918, was 1,876,000.

disappointed with me in the way I have stood up for correct principles, but you must let me do my job in my own way. I have never yet given in on important matters and never shall. In any case, whatever happens, you and I must stand solid together. I know we are both trying to do so . . . *

(Lloyd George) is out for my blood very much these days. Milner, Carson, Curzon, Cecil, Balfour, have each in turn expressly spoken to me separately about his intolerable conduct during the last week or two and have said they are behind us . . . Since then, he has got my Future Policy Paper and your Memo. A Cabinet is now sitting. He will be furious and probably matters will come to a head. I rather hope so. I am sick of this d——d life.

I can't help thinking he has got Painlevé and Co. here in his rushing way so as to carry me off my feet.† But I have big feet! The great thing is to keep on good firm tactical ground. This is difficult for he is a skilful tactician but I shall manage him.

> Roskill, *Hankey: Man of Secrets*, i, pp 440–1:
> Hankey Diary

9 OCTOBER.   In the afternoon the War Policy Ctee assembled again . . . Ll. G. still refuses to recognize any merit in Sir Douglas Haig's offensive. A letter from the Prime Minister to M. Painlevé was approved, urging decisive operations this winter against Turkey. Gen Smuts strongly favours a landing operation at Haifa. He told me after the meeting that he would be willing to assume the command. Personally I am opposed to heroic measures of this kind at this stage of the war, as I believe that if we pursue even a western front policy steadily we shall exhaust the Central Powers.

> CAB 23/13: War Cabinet 247a, 10 October

The view was freely expressed that Field-Marshal Haig's Memorandum of 8 October, O.A.D. 652, did not provide a convincing argument that we could inflict a decisive military defeat on Germany on the Western Front next year, even if Russia was still able to retain the same number of German troops on the Eastern Front as at present, and that if Russia collapsed and the German forces on the Western Front became equal, and, perhaps, greatly superior, to the Allies, both in men and guns, there was no reasonable probability of a decisive victory . . . [The War Cabinet then dicussed an offensive in Palestine.]

The Prime Minister pointed out that the War Cabinet had a very grave decision to take. He reminded them that at the outset of the War, when equally grave decisions had had to be taken, Mr Asquith, who was then Prime Minister, had called a War Council, including, besides the Members of the Army Council, the following Military experts:

Field-Marshal Lord Roberts
Field-Marshal Lord Kitchener

*See p 283 f.n.
* Painlevé came to London to argue for further extension of the British front and an attack on Syria.

Field-Marshal Lord French
General Sir Ian Hamilton
General Wilson
General Haig
General Grierson
General Sir Archibald Murray

He proposed that a similar course should be taken at the present juncture. In reply to a suggestion that the Chief of The Imperial General Staff might resent this procedure, the Prime Minister pointed out that neither General Sir Charles Douglas, then Chief of the Imperial General Staff, nor Field-Marshal Lord French, the Commander-in-Chief Designate of the British Expeditionary Force, had resented the War Council held in August, 1914, and he himself would undertake to explain the matter fully to General Robertson.

The War Cabinet decided that:
The following Generals should be invited to attend a Meeting of the War Cabinet:

The Chief of the Imperial General Staff
Field-Marshal Sir Douglas Haig
Field-Marshal Lord French
General Sir Henry Wilson

At the first meeting the situation should be fully explained to them, and they should be shown all the papers bearing on the decisions to be taken in regard to the Western Front and Palestine. After a preliminary discussion they should then withdraw, and at a second meeting should be asked to give their advice independently. The Prime Minister undertook to see the Chief of the Imperial General Staff in the afternoon and to explain to him the reasons for this decision.

The Council of War of 5–6, August 1914, was an extraordinary occasion, considering that, in Asquith's own words, through the agency of the Committee of Imperial Defence (over which he himself presided), 'the Government had by (1909) investigated the whole ground covered by a possible war with Germany'. As Sir William Robertson wrote (*Soldiers and Statesmen*, i, p 152) the majority of the distinguished soldiers consulted 'had no status qualifying them either to give advice or take executive action'. The gathering, says Robertson, displayed that 'the warning given by Lord Salisbury in 1900 as to the unsuitability of our constitutional methods for war purposes was unheeded' – or, in other words, the extreme difficulty experienced even by well-intentioned Liberals in grasping the different organizational necessities of peace and war.

In *The Western Front* (Hutchinson, 1964, pp 44–5) I wrote: 'The thought of such a gathering offends against every modern conception of

war direction; it is almost impossible to imagine what they could usefully
have discussed at this stage, in view of the very different levels of their
information and responsibility. What they did discuss was, first, where
should the BEF be sent? and, secondly, what should it consist of? Since
these were both elementary questions which had been under consideration and had received their answers in the very act of creating the
Expeditionary Force years before, the discussion that followed could
scarcely fail to be confusing . . .' The worst confusion, however, was
undoubtedly the resurrection of a bad precedent for bad reasons by Lloyd
George in October, 1917. (For a fuller treatment of this and the consequences, see *The Western Front* pp 98–113).

Robertson, Soldiers and Statesmen, ii, pp 257–8

Mr Lloyd George (told me the Cabinet's decision) implied no want of confidence
in the General Staff, but that, in view of the very serious situation in which the
country was placed, and the heavy loss of life that was being suffered, he felt it his
duty to obtain a second opinion, just in the same way as a second doctor was called
in when a serious case of illness occurred. He claimed, in fact, that he was
following the precedent set by Mr Asquith on 5 August, 1914 . . .

I was not impressed with the 'precedent' argument as the circumstances were
different, nor could I pretend to be satisfied that no lack of confidence was
implied. The analogy of the two doctors was also rather far-fetched. When a
second doctor is called in he consults with the first, the two together decide on a
method of treatment, and the first then carries it out. Mr Lloyd George's procedure was to be quite different. He was to call in not one additional doctor, but
two, and far from consulting with the first doctor (the General Staff) these
newcomers were to keep severely apart from him. They were to prepare a
joint prescription of their own, and then Mr Lloyd George, after comparing it
with the prescription of the first doctor, would himself decide which of the two
should be administered. As events turned out, the two new doctors differed in
their views as to the treatment required, and accordingly they submitted separate
prescriptions, thus making a total of three, from which Mr Lloyd George had to
choose one.

It is not forgotten that Mr Lloyd George was carrying very heavy responsibilities, and if he felt that outside advice would help him one may concede that
he was entitled to have it, provided it was obtained in the right way. The outside
advisers could not possibly be acquainted with all the details affecting their
advice, and consequently unless, before being accepted, it was reviewed by those
who had that acquaintance – the General Staff – it might be productive of more
harm than good. I suggested this to Mr Lloyd George, but he objected that he
must have an opinion independent of the General Staff, and that it must be sent
direct to the War Cabinet. The matter was discussed in Cabinet, and as my

suggestion was favoured by most of the members a compromise was made, the two Generals [French and Wilson] being instructed to send their reports neither to me nor to the War Cabinet, but to the War Minister, who would transmit them to the War Cabinet after obtaining such comments as I might wish to make.

Hankey, ii, pp 712–13

10 OCTOBER. The Prime Minister saw Robertson in the afternoon, but the interview was unsatisfactory. At 7.20 pm Curzon called on me and told me that Derby had told him that Robertson had just offered his resignation. Derby had, in order to gain time, refused to accept it that night, and had asked Robertson to dinner. Curzon had then explained to Derby . . . that there was no lack of confidence in Robertson; that the War Cabinet was merely following Asquith's precedent in August, 1914, in calling a War Council before taking a great decision; and that it was like calling an independent medical opinion. Curzon then went on to tell me that, if the Prime Minister drove out Robertson, Robert Cecil, Balfour, Derby, Carson, and he himself, probably, would leave the Government, which would then break up.

Roskill, Hankey: Man of Secrets, pp 441–2: Hankey Diary

11 OCTOBER. Before the War Cabinet I walked round St James's Park with Ll. G . . . I repeated Curzon's warning in very straight terms and he took the hint very quickly. The result was that at the War Cabinet, which was the first 'War Council', French and Wilson being present, he was quite at his best, handling Robertson (who was as sulky as a bear with a sore head) quite admirably, and explaining the whole situation, including the Western Front and Palestine alternative plans, quite impartially and judicially. I told Curzon what I had done and he said I had rendered a very considerable public service. Balfour, with whom I walked to the Foreign Office after the meeting, remarked on how admirable the P.M. had been . I told him of my warning to Ll. G. which he warmly endorsed.

Haig Diary: Blake, p 259

11 OCTOBER. General Whigham arrived (by special boat) from London about noon. He came from General Robertson to ask my advice . . . R. thinks he should resign. I wrote him a note and said that he ought not to resign until his advice has been rejected. In any case he must send in a protest showing with reasons why the Government ought not to call in outside advisers, now that the General Staff has been organized and is in existence for the main purpose of advising the Government and giving a reasoned opinion on strategical problems.

Author's Papers: Robertson to Haig, 11 October

The War Cabinet met this morning and discussed general policy, French and Wilson being present. The Prime Minister made a speech for an hour on the lines with which you are familiar. He said much the same as he said to you when he last saw you. French and Wilson are to prepare their advice and they hope to have it ready for a meeting on Monday when it will be considered by the War Cabinet . . .

I do not much care what advice is tendered by French and Wilson as I shall not budge an inch from my paper and I do not suppose you will budge from yours.

I have just heard from Whigham that I am to do nothing till he returns. I have done nothing. But I have thought a lot. The fact is it is a *very* weak-kneed, craven-hearted cabinet, and L.G. . . . is allowed to run riot. We shall see what we shall see.

Hankey, ii, pp 713–14: Hankey Diary

12 OCTOBER.   I lunched alone with Eric Geddes who told me that Robertson had consulted him about resigning but that he had told him that it would be bad ground for resignation merely because the War Cabinet wanted to have someone else's views. He promised me to use all his influence with Robertson to prevent him resigning . . . In the afternoon motored down to Chequers . . .

14 October (Sunday). The PM, Balfour, Smuts, Franklin Bouillon*, Foch and I had an informal conference in the library in the morning. The PM horrified me by raising the question of an inter-allied War Council *and permanent General Staff* in Paris. Of course Franklin Bouillon and Foch leaped at it. I had no time to warn PM that in Robertson's present hurt, bruised and suspicious frame of mind he willl see in it merely a proposal further to upset his authority and may resign. When I warned him of this afterwards he was astonished, and hardly credited it!

THE INVINCIBLE ENEMY

Author's Papers: Haig Diary

10 OCTOBER.   Heavy rain fell in the morning, but day cleared after lunch and evening was fine. Observation then good. Glass rising.

11 OCTOBER.   Fine bright morning. Glass rising. Clear and cold day. Wind began to rise at 10 pm.

O.H., 1917, ii, p 341, f.n. 1: 12 October

Crown Prince Rupprecht notes in his diary on this day: 'sudden change of the weather. Most gratifying – rain: our most effective ally.'

FLANDERS

Author's Papers: Haig Diary

10 OCTOBER.   The 3rd Australian Division and New Zealand Division go into the

*French Foreign Minister.

line again tonight. Gough told me they are determined to take Passchendaele in
the next attack and will put the Australian flag on it! The advance will be then over
2,000 yards. But the enemy is now much weakened in morale and lacks the desire
to fight.

Charteris, p 260

11 OCTOBER.   We are attacking again tomorrow. It is the weather and the ground
that we are fighting now. We have beaten the Germans, but winter is very close,
and there is now no chance of getting through.

O.H., 1917, ii, pp 338-9

General Plumer's sanguine expectation that Passchendaele would be captured in
the next attack was based on misleading information. The failure of the main
attack on the 9th against Poelcappelle was assumed to have been due to the mud,
and it was not until the morning of the 11th that reports from patrols . . . disclosed
the strength of two formidable and continuous belts of new wire entanglements.
This obstacle, thirty yards in breadth, protected the pillboxes of the Flanders I line
on the Wallemolen spur, and in fact had been the real stumbling-block to the
advance . . . The conditions, too, were lamentable. The sodden battleground was
littered with wounded who had lain out in the mud among the dead for two days
and nights; and the pillbox shelters were overflowing with unattended wounded,
whilst the dead lay piled outside. The survivors, in a state of utter exhaustion, with
neither food nor ammunition,* had been sniped at by the Germans on the higher
ground throughout the 10th, with increasing casualties.

O.H., ii, p xiv

Under 11 October, Crown Prince Rupprecht records in his diary: 'most per-
turbing is the fact that our troops are steadily deteriorating'.

Harington, *Plumer of Messines*, pp 110–12

I reconnoitred the Bellevue position under the most appalling conditions prior to
the attack on 12 October. It has been said that it was between the above dates†
that Sir Douglas Haig should have abandoned all further operations. On that I can
make no criticism. I was not in a position to know the various factors that
influenced him. I certainly never heard the question either raised or mentioned . . .
One writer‡ has stated that my Chief was always opposed to the Passchendaele
operations and urged Sir Douglas Haig to abandon them and also that he is
reported to have written a letter opposing or throwing cold water on the whole
operations . . . It is . . . inconceivable to me that his agreement with the views of the
Commander-in-Chief was anything but one of *'utter loyalty'* and desire to carry
out his Chief's orders to capture Passchendaele. He knew well what that ridge

---

*Reserve ammunition supplies could not be brought to the forward troops.
†4–12 October.   ‡Lloyd George.

would mean to his beloved troops and I am sure that once within grasp, as it was after his successful capture of the Broodseinde Ridge on 4 October, he never gave a thought to stopping and turning back . . . I said earlier that I had studied that ground in front of Passchendaele. I have studied it since both from where our line was on 4 October and from the Passchendaele–Staden Ridge. I still ask the critics to state where our advanced troops could have spent the winter of 1917.

In theory anywhere. In practice nowhere. We find these convenient lines in War Games but not in war. I have knelt in Tyne Cot Cemetery below Passchendaele* on that hallowed ground, the most beautiful and sacred place I know in this world. I have prayed in that cemetery oppressed with fear lest even one of those gallant comrades should have lost his life owing to any fault or neglect on the part of myself and the Second Army Staff. It is a fearful responsibility to have been the one who signed and issued all the Second Army orders for those operations. All I can truthfully say is that we did our utmost. We could not have done more.

German Official Account

In a report prepared on 11 October, Crown Prince Rupprecht laid down that the consumption of strength in Flanders on 4 and 9 October had grown so much that technical difficulties had arisen on the railway during the relief of divisions. Such demands on the strength could no longer be made good. The bringing up of reinforcements from other Army Groups would become quite impossible as soon as the French returned to the attack. Bringing the divisions up to strength was becoming more difficult. The Fourth Army must adapt itself to manage with less strength. The necessity of saving strength and men was more necessary than that of retaining ground. If it became absolutely necessary the Front would have to be withdrawn so far from the enemy that he would be compelled to undertake a new artillery deployment. In addition the Supreme Command suggested on 13 October that, in order to relieve the railway problem,† divisions which had not lost more than 1,500 to 1,800 men‡ should be kept in Flanders and given a three to four week rest for retraining and refitting.

THE FIRST BATTLE OF PASSCHENDAELE

CAB 23/4: War Cabinet 248, 12 October

The Western Front

The Chief of the Imperial General Staff reported that our troops were attacking

---

*Tyne Cot is the largest British military cemetery in the world, with 11,956 burials.
† Referring to the constant need for reliefs and replacements, von Kuhl says: 'This continual movement of divisions behind Prince Rupprecht's Army Group . . . grew to such proportions that the railways had difficulty in obtaining the transport.'
‡ This represents a loss of 20–25%.

on a front of 5 or 6 miles, with Passchendaele as objective, and that satisfactory progress was reported.

Author's Papers: Haig to Lady Haig, 12 October

I expect we will have Passchendaele Village today all right. The N.Z. and 3rd Australian Divns. are to put the Australian flag on the Church there!

Birdwood, *Khaki and Gown*, pp 317–18

Haig and Plumer both felt that far-reaching strategic success was within their grasp, and the latter proposed objectives which, I had to tell him, were far beyond the capacity of my troops in their now exhausted condition. I insisted that my action must be limited to safeguarding the flank of the II Anzac Corps on my left, whose commander, Godley, shared the optimism of Plumer and Haig.

Rain continued, and in spite of tremendous efforts by gunners and roadmakers it was found impossible to get the guns forward to their intended positions. The supply of planks failed, and the ground was utterly impassable. Guns had to be halted on the forward slopes of the Frezenberg ridge in full view of the enemy, and it is hard to understand how any of these survived. Nor could any progress be made by the pack animals on which the ammunition supply depended; horses sank into the mud and disappeared, and in one instance a journey that normally occupied an hour took 17 hours to accomplish. Moreover, when at length some ammunition did reach the guns it was so coated with mud as to be unusable, till cleaned. The conditions were simply indescribable, and a state of havoc ensued. The whole system of reliefs broke down, and even on the 12th many of the guns had to be left lying about, temporarily abandoned.

The work of my Pioneer Battalions during this period was beyond all praise. Out in all weathers, day and night, with little chance of ever getting into dry clothes, they laboured magnificently and without complaint. Without their work the Corps could not have carried on at all, and their casualties were in much the same proportion as the infantry's.

All this time the back areas were having a terrible time from attacks of mustard gas, which virtually finished off the Australian attempts on Passchendaele Ridge.

The Letters of General Monash

During the battle of 12 October the work was very heavy. The average 'carry' from the front line was over 4,000 yards, through a heavy morass, and each stretcher took sixteen bearers, in four relays of four men each – instead of two men as normally.

O.H., 1917, ii, 341–2

The artillery barrage intended to support the advance of the New Zealand Division, weak and erratic at the start, became even thinner and more ragged as the troops advanced up the slope, howitzer shells burying themselves in the sodden ground and merely splashing the pillboxes with fountains of mud. In consequence, the New Zealanders found themselves confronted with broad belts of unbroken wire entanglements . . . This splendid division lost a hundred officers and 2,635 other ranks within a few hours in brave but vain attempts – its only failure – to carry out a task beyond the power of any infantry with so little support, and had gained no ground except on the left.

Although a patrol of the 3rd Australian Division succeeded in entering the village of Passchendaele (which it found deserted), no permanent progress of any significance was made except by XIV Corps (Fifth Army) on the extreme left, where the Guards Division reached the edge of the Forêt d'Houthoulst.

O.H., 1917, ii, p 345 f.n.l

The Guards Division thereby made the record of gaining the final objective allotted to it in every assault in this campaign. From the Yser Canal to Houthoulst Forest its successive advances had, to quote the divisional diary, 'been made so quickly and so quietly that its achievement is in danger of being forgotten'.

Haig Diary: Blake, p 260

12 OCTOBER.   Second and Fifth Armies continued their attack at 5.25 this morning. Troops reached points of assembly up to time in spite of the very bad state of the ground . . . Owing to rain and bad state of the ground, General Plumer decided that it was best not to continue the attack on the front of his Army.

Ludendorff, ii, p 491

There were further severe engagements on 9 and 12 October. The line held better than on the 4th, although in some places the enemy penetrated to a considerable distance. The wastage in the big actions of the Fourth Battle of Flanders* was extraordinarily high. In the West we began to be short of troops. The two divisions that had been held in readiness in the East, and were already on the way to Italy, were diverted to Flanders . . . These days were the culminating point of the crisis.

Haig Diary: Blake, p 260

13 OCTOBER.   I held a Conference at Cassel at noon with Generals Plumer, Gough and their Staff Officers . . . The Army Commanders explained the situation; all agreed that mud and the bad weather prevented our troops getting on yesterday. I said that our immediate objective was the mass of high ground about Passchendaele. Once this was taken the rest of the ridge would fall more easily. The Canadians would join Second Army at once . . . The enemy seems to have increased the number of his machine guns in front. This necessitates a larger bombardment. We all agreed that our attack should only be launched when there

---

*Ludendorff's five phases of the campaign were: 31 July–9 August; 9 August–25; 20 September–1 October; 2 October–21; 22 October–10 November.

is a fair prospect of fine weather. *When the ground is dry* no opposition which the enemy has put up has been able to stop our men. The ground is so soft in places, the D.G.T. (Nash) told us, that he has light engines on the 60cm. railways sunk up to the boilers in the mud. The track has completely disappeared.

SOLDIERS AND POLITICIANS

Roskill, *Hankey: Man of Secrets*, Hankey Diary

15 OCTOBER.   Breakfast with Ll. G. Afterwards we had a great argument about war policy.* I supported Haig's policy and Ll. G. opposed it. Eventually he committed himself to the view that we could only win in 1919 and that we must conserve our strength for this. This, I pointed out was a new idea, which he had never told his colleagues, and I suggested he ought to lose no time in doing so.

CAB 23/4: War Cabinet 250, 16 October

A suggestion was made that a message of congratulation should be sent, on behalf of the War Cabinet, to Field-Marshal Sir Douglas Haig on his continuous, persistent, and dogged advance of $4\frac{1}{2}$ miles in conditions of great difficulty.

Some discussion took place as to the date on which the message should be sent – whether immediately or after Sir Douglas Haig's next successful advance.

The War Cabinet decided that –

A message of congratulation should be sent immediately, and the Secretary of State for War was asked to draft a telegram on the subject, the draft to be shown to the Prime Minister.

Haig Diary: Blake, p 261

16 OCTOBER.   Telegram of congratulation received from the Prime Minister. 'The War Cabinet desire to congratulate you and the troops under your command upon the achievements of the British Armies in Flanders in the great battle which has been raging since 31 July. Starting from positions in which every advantage rested with the enemy, and hampered and delayed from time to time by most unfavourable weather, you and your men have nevertheless driven the enemy back with such skill, courage, and pertinacity, as have commanded the grateful admiration of the peoples of the British Empire and filled the enemy with alarm. I am personally glad to be the means of transmitting this message to you, and to your gallant troops, and desire to take this opportunity of renewing my assurance of confidence in your leadership, and in the devotion of those whom you command.'

This is the first message of congratulation on any operations by the War

---

*See Hankey, *The Supreme Command* pp 703–7 for full record.

Cabinet which has reached me since the War began! I wonder why the Prime Minister should suddenly have sent me this message.

Wilson, ii, p 18

17 OCTOBER.   Tonight Lloyd George, Johnnie* and I dined again at Johnnie's house. It became very clear to me tonight that Lloyd George means to get Robertson out, and means to curb the powers of the C in C in the field. This is what I have been advising for 2½ years, and this is what the whole of my paper is directed at – *not* to getting Robertson out, but to forming a Superior Direction over all the CGSs and C in Cs. . . . . . . Lloyd George referred to the Press campaign which is working up against him on the basis that he is interfering with the soldiers.

FLANDERS

Repington, ii, pp 98–9

SUNDAY, 14 OCTOBER.   Motored to Advanced GHQ to have lunch and a talk with Charteris, the head of Haig's Intelligence. I find that he is strongly set upon continuing the Flanders offensive next year, and is most optimistic as usual. He has great ideas of the hurt that we have caused the Huns, and the number of divisions which we have 'exhausted' as he terms it. I doubt whether they are much more exhausted than those which we take out of our own line after an attack. He believes that we can gain our present objectives, and next spring clear up to Ghent, and then be on the flank of the German line. So we should be, but on the wrong flank strategically. I was given papers to show all the Hun divisions drawn from the French front to oppose us, and assuming these to be correct, it would appear that we have been fighting most of the Western Germans, and the best of them, this year . . .

Motored on to Cassel and found Plumer . . . very happy about his successes. His day of the 12th could not be put through because the ground was impossible owing to the weather. So he is going to hold the thing up for ten days until he can complete his communications again. At present some of his light railways are bodily embedded in the mud up to the top of the little locomotives; the whole railway has subsided into the morass, and until he can get his ammunition up he cannot get on. It is a race against time, as the season grows so late. He wants to take Passchendaele, and Gough Westroosebeke, while there are a couple of other points east and south-east of the ridge which the Huns must be turned out of to make a clean job of it. I found Plumer heart and soul for the Flanders offensive. I asked him whether he was thinking of his present tactical objectives, or whether he had in his mind the strategy of next year and its possibilities. He said that he had both, and had fully considered the future possibilities. But I think that he nears the

* French.

end of his tether for this year, as he admits that he has nearly come to the end of the troops available for his operation, and that he must soon think of resting them and beginning the winter training . . . The Huns still fight well, and Plumer is rather sarcastic about Charteris's optimism . . . Not much chance of a talk with Harington, but he told me that they meant to have Passchendaele.

O.H., 1917, ii, p 347

After the middle of October the weather improved. The German artillery, however, became more aggressive in its efforts to hinder progress in the laying of plank roads, and to delay other offensive preparations, which could be seen from Passchendaele Ridge. Almost nightly from 14 October onwards to mid-November enemy aircraft bombarded the back areas with high-explosive, and drenched the low ground of the Steenbeek valley with gas shell. Sneezing gas (blue cross = diphenyl chlorasine), which made it difficult to keep on respirators, was followed by mustard gas (yellow cross = dichlorethal sulphide), which blistered the body and damaged throat and eyes. Although only a few deaths were caused, some thousands of men of the infantry in support and reserve positions, of the artillery and of the working parties were disabled during this period. Large areas, too, including battery positions and bivouacs, became saturated with mustard oil and could not be reoccupied for some time.

Repington, ii, pp 101–2: 15 October

I found Haig as firmly set upon the Flanders offensive as possible. He does not believe that the French can or will attack, and so does not see why he should change his plan to please the French. He cannot take over the front named by Pétain without so weakening himself that he will be unable to attack. If he goes south to co-operate with Pétain, the Huns will give way as they have done before and leave us stranded. Whereas, Haig thinks, in Flanders the Huns cannot go back without letting go their hold on the Belgian coast, and therefore here they must fight. Haig will, therefore, not compromise, and does not know what the decision at Boulogne means, nor what it will entail, nor why he was not called in. He has been told nothing by Robertson. Haig likes Pétain very much, but thinks that the politicians dominate the soldiers in France.

We had lunch and *banalités* . . . Kiggell then went fully into the strategy . . . He was firmly convinced that to abandon our plan would be fatal . . . The loss of the Belgian coastline would be a heavy blow to Germany, and no excuses could palliate it. He was prepared to stake his reputation that the Germans could not retreat without fighting foot by foot on the Flanders front, and that next year in from one to two months the operation would be concluded . . . If the Government took a political decision which interfered with the prosecution of this plan, then the matter passed out of his hands. He was only talking strategy, and these were his views.

German Official Account

In a conference on 18 October, General von Kuhl proposed that in view of the coming shortage at the main pressure points, the line must be taken back eastwards to that limit to which it would be possible to withdraw it. General Sixt von Armin and his Chief of Staff were opposed to this. Every step backwards made the position more difficult as there were no bomb-proof shelters and it would be impossible to errect sufficient before the onset of winter. For the enemy things were easier; he would be coming forward from a cratered area into country which, from previous experience it was known, was passable in winter. And if this line were to be broken then the U-boat bases could no longer be defended. The Army must, therefore, if at all possible, hold the fighting forward of the proposed line. General von Kuhl ended his argument with the remark that, in this connection the Army Group did not wish to issue orders: he did not believe that the Supreme Command would do this either. He asked, however, that the proposals be considered.

THE INVINCIBLE ENEMY

Author's Papers: Haig Diary

13 OCTOBER.   Glass falling steadily until midnight. Gale blowing most of night. Weather very unsettled, rain and wind all day.

Ibid, Haig to Lady Haig, 14 October

The rain has upset our arrangements a good deal, but I still hope that the weather may take up before long and the ground become as dry as it was in 1914 at the end of October.

Ibid, Haig Diary

15 OCTOBER.   Glass rising steadily and fine weather prophesied. A few drops of rain in the morning, but the day was fine with sunny intervals. Observation good.
16 OCTOBER.   Glass steady. Fine morning and day. A few drops of rain in the afternoon. Observation on the whole good.
17 OCTOBER.   Very fine day until 2 pm. Glass falling slightly.
18 OCTOBER.   Glass rising slightly. Fine sunny day. Observation good and ground on the battle front reported to be drying nicely.
19 OCTOBER.   Glass rising slightly. Fine morning and day. Slight haze but occasionally the sun came through.
20 OCTOBER.   Glass still rising . . . Fine bright morning and day fine but hazy.
21 OCTOBER.   Frost last night, but warm day. Sun bright but haze in places.
22 OCTOBER.   Glass falling slightly. Early morning hazy . . . then clear and sunny: day quite mild.

FLANDERS

Author's Papers: Haig Diary

20 OCTOBER.   The enemy's artillery fire is heavy against the rear areas and communications of Second Army. Owing to haze, it has not been possible to do much counter-battery work with aeroplane observation. 'Concentration shoots' have been carried out.

German Official Account

The Fourth Army High Command asked the question in a report dated 21 October how long it would be possible to fulfil the Army's rôle in 'pure defence' . . . In the three months between 1 July and 10 October the 63 divisions which had been in action had lost 159,000 men. To this could be added the 'morale pressures to which even the finest troops are subject', especially in the case of the infantry upon whom the 'continuous enemy fire and the effects of the weather in the soaked crater area fall most heavily, without having the opportunity of rest and relief because of the enemy attacks which follow each other so quickly'. Even if the troops 'almost without exception perform to the best of their ability' it must be reckoned with that in view of the enemy's superior strength he would slowly gain ground. In the long term he could only be held by attack.

Charteris, p 261: 22 October

Another small attack this morning gained a little ground. It had no particular strategic purpose. We have to keep up pressure here.* But plans are afoot now for another final effort elsewhere before the winter sets in.†

Ludendorff, ii, pp 491–2

The fifth act of the great drama in Flanders opened on 22 October. Enormous masses of ammunition, such as the human mind had never imagined before the war, were hurled upon the bodies of men who passed a miserable existence scattered about in mud-filled shell-holes. The horror of the shell-hole area of Verdun was surpassed. It was no longer life at all. It was mere unspeakable suffering. And through this world of mud the attackers dragged themselves,‡ slowly, but steadily, and in dense masses. Caught in the advanced zone by our hail of fire they often collapsed, and the lonely man in the shell-hole breathed again. Then the mass came on again. Rifle and machine-gun jammed with the mud. Man fought against man, and only too often the mass was successful.

What the German soldier experienced, achieved, and suffered in the Flanders

---

*Because of the imminence of the long-awaited French supporting action (see below).
† The Third Army's attack at Cambrai on 20 November.
‡ Ludendorff is referring to the British attacks, but it has to be borne in mind that the Germans themselves made not less than 42 counter-attacks in October.

Battle will be his everlasting monument of bronze, erected by himself in the enemy's land.

The enemy's losses were also heavy. When we occupied the battle field in the spring of 1918 we encountered the horrible spectacle of many unburied corpses. They lay there in thousands. Two-thirds of them were enemies, one-third German soldiers who had found a hero's grave there.

And yet it must be admitted that certain units no longer triumphed over the demoralizing effects of the defensive battle as they had done formerly.

On 23 October Pétain at last delivered his long-promised supporting attack along the Aisne, known to the French as the Battle of Malmaison, and to the Germans as the Battle of the Laffaux Salient. Attacking on a front of about 7½ miles, the French, between 23–6 October, took 11,157 prisoners and 180 guns, at a cost of 14,000 to themselves.

Ludendorff, ii, pp 492–3

The French attack on 23 October was successful. One division succumbed to the effects of an exceptionally heavy gas bombardment and gave way before the hostile assault. The enemy advanced towards Chavignon and so caused a narrow but deep indentation in the salient. This forced us to order its evacuation, and the line was withdrawn behind the Oise-Aisne Canal. The losses were very serious; once more several divisions were destroyed.

This withdrawal of our line inevitably entailed the evacuation of the Chemin des Dames ridge. It was ordered, and carried out on the night of 1–2 November, after the stores and equipment had been removed. In itself it was of no consequence whether we stood north or south of the Ailette, but after having fought all through the summer for possession of the Chemin des Dames it was very difficult to order it to be given up. To hold on, however, would only have involved continuous wastage . . . As at Verdun in August, the French, supported by remarkable masses of artillery, had fought very vigorously.

Author's Papers: Haig to Lady Haig, 24 October

The French did well yesterday . . . If the French had only made this attack 6 weeks ago, it would have had a much more decisive effect.

SOLDIERS AND POLITICIANS

On 19 October Field-Marshal Sir John French and General Sir Henry Wilson completed their memoranda on the future conduct of the war.

Wilson, ii, p 18: 19 October

It seems to me that there will be a holy row over all this, and, of course, the Frock Coats will quote Johnnie and me against Haig and Robertson. We must avoid this as much as possible. It is the system and machinery that I am aiming at, and not the men.

The inevitability of a 'holy row' was confirmed by the acrimonious tone of Lord French's paper, and the direct attacks in it on Robertson and Haig. Lord Derby (recipient of the reports) at the War Cabinet of 23 October doubted the wisdom of sending them on to Robertson as they stood; such a course 'he felt might involve friction, replies, rejoinders, and delay'. The War Cabinet itself discussed the problem somewhat ineffectively on 23, 24 and 25 October. By that date, as we shall shortly see, the general situation had been transformed. Meanwhile Hankey had been exercising his very considerable personal diplomacy. On 24 October he interviewed French and Wilson, to try and persuade them 'to soften some of the phrases to make them less offensive to Robertson.'

Roskill, *Hankey: Man of Secrets*, pp 446–7

French flatly refused 'to praise Haig's tactical handling of the situation', and declared that 'he was always repeating the same mistake'. French frankly admitted that his object was to get rid of Robertson.* 'We shall do no good,' he said, 'until we break down the Haig-Robertson ring.' 'There was envy, hatred and malice in the old boy's heart as he spoke', remarked Hankey perceptively . . . However, he succeeded in getting French to modify his critical paper, and on the 25th handed Derby the revised version.

The gravamen of French's attack on Robertson lay in the following passage of his memorandum:

Lloyd George, ii, pp 1429–3

When it is a question of directing a war which is going on over half the world, offering for this reason so many alternative possibilities, the conclusions arrived at and the recommendations made by any individual Commander in the field must be subjected to the crucial test of exhaustive examination by the General Staff . . . After making a close examination of the papers submitted to me, I have, rightly or wrongly, formed the opinion that this has not been done.

This, of course, was music to Lloyd George, as was French's conclusion:

*In 1915, when French was C–in–C of the BEF, Robertson was his Chief of Staff. He attributed his dismissal to intrigue by Robertson and Haig.

It is my fixed belief that . . . co-ordination and economy can only be obtained by establishing a common co-ordinating authority over the whole front from the Adriatic to the North Sea . . . I would therefore emphasize the extreme desirability of establishing at once a Superior Council of the Allies. It is only such a body that can thoroughly examine a joint scheme of action in all its bearings. The weight and influence of such a Council must carry conviction to the minds of the several Allied Governments.

Sir Henry Wilson's paper had the advantage of being less recriminatory, and better written. Professing himself 'an ardent "Westerner"', he nevertheless added, to Lloyd George's pleasure:

Lloyd George, ii, pp 1431–4

It is no use throwing 'decisive numbers at the decisive time at the decisive place' at my head if the decisive numbers do not exist, if the decisive hour has not struck or if the decisive place is ill-chosen.

Frequently the master of a felicitous or striking phrase, as far back as August* Wilson had intrigued Lloyd George with the proposal of 'three Prime Ministers and three soldiers, to be over all CIGSs and to draw up plans for the whole theatre from Nieuport to Baghdad'. Such language, as arresting as it was confusing, appealed greatly to Lloyd George;† Wilson now developed the theme:

The superior direction of this war has, in my opinion, been gravely at fault from the very commencement – in fact, it is inside the truth to say that there has never been any superior direction at all . . . we have tried many expedients but always with most disappointing, sometimes even with disastrous results . . .
What can be done to remedy a state of affairs which is undoubtedly prolonging the War to an unnecessary, even to a dangerous extent?
The answer to this question lies in the establishment of an intelligent, effective and powerful superior direction. And by this I mean a small War Cabinet of the Allies so well-informed, and above all, entrusted with such power that its opinion on all the larger issues of the War will carry the weight of conviction and be accepted by each of the Allies as final . . .
Such a body will be above all Sectional Fronts, it would view the War as a whole, it would treat the line of battle from Nieuport to Mesopotamia as one line, and it would allot to each of the Allies the part which it would play . . .

*See Wilson, ii, p 10.
† As CIGS, himself in 1918, Wilson soon realized that while Baghdad was in a relatively unimportant area, Nieuport was not. But in his CIGS capacity, he also found that Superior Direction was not the panacea that he proclaimed it to be while looking for a job in 1917.

In short, such a Superior Direction would take over the Superior Direction of the War – a thing which has not yet been done, and for the lack of which we have suffered so grievously in the past and without which we shall, as certainly, suffer even more in the future.

Author's Papers: Robertson to Haig, 24 October

I gather that both (French and Wilson) are opposed to Eastern enterprises and that W. is inclined to wait for the Americans, while apparently French is not very definite as to what he would do. It would all be rather amusing if it were not so serious and did not involve such a waste of time.

It was on 24 October that the Austrians, backed by 7 German divisions made available by the success of the operations at Riga (see p 278), attacked the Italians on the Isonzo front, the Battle of Caporetto. By the end of the month the Austro-German forces claimed over 180,000 prisoners.

Charteris, p 262: 25 October

The storm has broken in Italy and the news is very alarming: but we have not full information yet and often first reports are unduly pessimistic. The Italians have a great numerical superiority both in men and guns, and should be able to hold. But as D.H. caustically observed, 'It is the spirit that quickeneth'.

Haig Diary: Blake, p 262

27 OCTOBER.   Telegram from CIGS tonight: 'HM's Government have decided to despatch two Divisions to Italy as quickly as possible.' This decision has been come to without the War Cabinet asking me as to the effect which the withdrawal of troops from this front would have on the situation. If the Italian Army is demoralized we cannot spare enough troops to fight their battles for them.

Two high-quality divisions, 23rd and 41st, were sent at once to Italy, under Lord Cavan. In November three more (7th, 48th and 5th) followed, requiring the appointment of an Army Commander, and on 8 November General Plumer was designated by Government request to take command.

Roskill, *Hankey: Man of Secrets*, pp 448–9: Hankey Diary

27 OCTOBER.   War Cabinet 11.30. Ll. G. very upset and snappy about Cadorna's defeat and at having to make a speech to move a vote of thanks to our sailors and soldiers. Owing to the Italian affair he has to re-write his speech and left the

Cabinet early for this reason. Before he left he had an outburst, in the course of which he sneered at the General Staff. Lord Derby threw me across a note, announcing his intention of resigning. I threw it back with a note on the back pointing out that Ll. G. was upset, and that this was a moment when the wisest heads must keep cool. He then said he would not resign, but felt inclined to . . . After lunch I saw the PM for a moment. He told me that he would not go on unless he obtained control of the war. He meant to take advantage of the present position to achieve this . . . I went to tea with General Maurice, the Director of Military Operations, who is acting for Robertson during the latter's visit to Italy. I told him that in my opinion very serious trouble was brewing for Robertson, unless he could see his way to drop the idea that the only way to win the war was by hammering away at the same spot on the western front. Maurice took a very sensible line, and I promised to try and arrange for Ll. G. to see him with a view to a reconciliation with Robertson.

Charteris, pp 262–3: 28 October

The reports from Italy are worse even than the first. The Italians apparently panicked and put up no fight at all, and are going back everywhere. One report says 'running like hares'! Apparently not more than half a dozen German divisions were employed – the rest all Austrian. D.H. has called for a paper on the possibilities of the new situation . . . this Italian debâcle will give a tremendous stimulus to all opponents of our policy and plans here.

The Invincible Enemy

Author's Papers: Haig Diary

23 OCTOBER.   Rain fell off and on all day till afternoon. 'Meteor' reports this to be only a temporary depression.
24 OCTOBER.   Fine bright morning . . . Wet and dull afternoon. High wind sprang up at 10 pm.
25 OCTOBER.   Glass fell sharply . . . Very windy and stormy night . . . no boats crossed from either side of the Channel today.
26 OCTOBER.   Glass steady, but heavy rain began to fall soon after midnight and continued off and on till evening.
27 OCTOBER.   Last night was fine. Sky clear. Morning and day fine and bright.
28 OCTOBER.   Frost last night. Fine bright cold day. Observation fair.
29 OCTOBER.   Glass steady. Frost last night. Fine until 4 pm.
30 OCTOBER.   Night was fine . . . until 11 am. Then rain began to fall, but cleared about 4 pm and evening fine.
31 OCTOBER.   Some rain during night. Glass rising and day fine and bright. Milder.

FLANDERS

Charteris, p 262: 25 October

We attack again tomorrow; the weather today is good, with a strong drying wind, and the forecast for tomorrow not unfavourable.

THE SECOND BATTLE OF PASSCHENDAELE

Harington, *Plumer of Messines*, p 127: 26 October

Our troops having been successfully assembled without serious interference by the enemy an attack was launched at 5.40 am on the fronts of the X and Canadian Corps.

Very heavy fighting took place during which our troops succeeded in capturing Gheluvelt village and Polderhoek Spur but were unable to hold on to either owing to the powerful enemy counter-attacks.*

The weather conditions and the state of the ground had a very great influence on the day's operations.

Two features, apart from exhaustion and the difficulties of movement, seem outstanding:

(i) The mud, in a semi-liquid state and splashed up by shell-bursts, got into everything, and was especially troublesome for rifles and machine guns.

(ii) The very soft nature of the ground apparently affected the detonation of percussion shells to such an extent that prisoners have on several occasions remarked on the harmlessness of the bursts, or the failure to detonate.

Gough, pp 213–4

Very little progress was made either by us or by the Second Army. The state of the ground had been frightful since 1 August, but by now it was getting absolutely impossible. Men of the strongest physique could hardly move forward at all and became easy victims to the enemy's snipers. Stumbling forward as best they could, their rifles soon became so caked and clogged with mud as to be useless.

German Official Account

On the northern wing of the front under attack . . . the French threw back the German division holding the line, which had suffered in a gas attack, about a kilometre and reached their objective without severe losses. Counter-attacks were unsuccessful . . . On other areas of the battlefield . . . the British were initially successful in breaking into the main defence line, but during the course of the day

---

*The Official History records at least four.

they were thrown back and in part driven out of the outpost area. Only on the boundary between the Staden and Ypres Groups were they able to make a salient about a kilometre wide . . . Even if the German losses had been severe in some places (the enemy announced the capture of over 1,200 German prisoners) the British seem to have suffered many more. South of the Ypres–Menin road about 500 dead British were counted in one regimental sector alone and the numbers of the fallen were said to be many more in the area north of the road. The number of British prisoners was more than 300. It seems that once again the outpost system had proved itself.

Author's Papers: Haig Diary

26 OCTOBER.   In the evening General Gough communicated with General Kiggell (CGS) that he found that the ground on his front was so very bad that he recommended delaying further operations until frost set in! K. proposed a conference tomorrow with General Plumer to discuss this question. I said: 'No. Let Army Commanders go round their troops tomorrow and ascertain the situation, and report to me personally on Sunday at Cassel whether they considered any delay of date for the next attack was necessary.' In my opinion today's operations at the decisive point (Passchendaele) had been so successful that I was entirely opposed to any idea of abandoning the operations till frost set in! If the wet continues, a day or two's delay may be advisable before we launch the next attack.

Haig visited X Corps.

28 OCTOBER.   The 7th Division were really engulfed in mud in some places when they attacked Gheluvelt. Rifles could not be used.

Haig Diary: Duff Cooper, ii, pp 170–1

28 OCTOBER.   At 12 noon I had a conference in my house at Cassel. Generals Plumer, Gough, with their staff officers were present – also with me were Kiggell, Davidson, Birch and Charteris.

We discussed the situation on each of the army fronts and fixed the depth to be aimed at in the next two advances, and points of junction of the two armies etc. It was agreed that the date already fixed for the next attack should hold, but that the date of the second attack should be settled at a conference subsequent to our attack on the 30th. Incidentally Gough stated that it was not the mud which prevented the XIV Corps' attack progressing the last day, but the enemy's defences which were very strong and had not been sufficiently bombarded.

Haig Diary: Blake, p 262

30 OCTOBER.   Second and Fifth Armies attacked at 5.50 am with the object of advancing our line still closer to the ridge on which Passchendaele village stands. The operation was most successful and we are now round the village on the south west and north-west.

Gough p 214

On 30 October the Second Army again attacked, and by now it was closing in on
Passchendaele itself. We attacked with part of two divisions, but being in the low
ground and operating in the valleys of the small streams that run westwards off the
ridge, we could not get far forward – an advance of 300 yards or so being the limit
of the day's objectives.

This was the last active operation undertaken by the Fifth Army in Flanders in
1917.

Harington, *Plumer of Messines*, p 128

During the course of the day the 3rd Canadian Division was counter-attacked no
less than five times from the north of Passchendaele. All these attacks were
successfully repulsed.

Again, the factor which chiefly affected the situation during the battle was the
condition of the ground.

Canadian Expeditionary Force 1914–1919, p 323

The step by step battle was gradually accomplishing its purpose. In this second
attack towards Passchendaele the Canadian Corps had achieved gains of up to a
thousand yards on a 2,800-yard front. The cost had been high.

German Official Account

The capture of Passchendaele was once again denied to the British. However
there was a salient in the Geman lines . . . Contact was lost between the Staden and
Ypres Groups.

On the morning of 31 October the left wing of the Staden Group threw the
British back some way and closed the gap. On the same day and on 2 November
the right wing of the Ypres Group tried to recapture the heights west the
south-west of Passchendaele. The first attempt was not carried out because of
strong enemy defensive fire, the second gained some ground but did not reach the
desired objective. Other than this there were only small operations on both sides
until 5 November. The numerous enemy attempts to press forward into the
outpost area showed that a new big attack was imminent.

Author's Papers: Haig to Robertson, 31 October

In the first place I desire to point out that, subject to the necessary force being left
at my disposal, it is my intention to continue the offensive on the Flanders front
for several weeks yet. The situation there, despite the advanced season and the
delays caused by bad weather, is still favourable for a considerable and important
further measure of success. From the positions already reached I see no reason to
doubt that PASSCHENDAELE and the high ground round it will be in our possession
by the middle of November, if not sooner, and the ground in question is the most

formidable stronghold still left to the enemy on the ridge extending from the south-west through PASSCHENDAELE and thence to near DIXMUDE.

The capture of this stronghold should ensure the eventual capture of the remainder of the ridge, thereby forcing the enemy to evacuate HOUTHOULST Forest.

The political, moral and strategical advantages of gaining this ridge have been stated by me in previous memoranda. I may point out here, however, that tactically possession of the ridge will be of extraordinary value at the opening of next year's campaign, while as a defensive line for the winter it offers very great advantages, giving us dry trenches, excellent cover in rear of them, and secure flanks.

On the other hand, if it should be necessary to abandon any further advance before the ridge has been captured, a portion of our line for the winter on the west of the ridge will be low-lying, waterlogged, and overlooked; difficult to hold against a determined attack, which must be regarded as a possibility especially if the enemy regains the initiative, and expensive in wastage both from the enemy's fire and from sickness.

The loss of the troops already detailed to proceed to Italy will not compel me to abandon my plans on the Flanders front, although it will throw a much greater strain on my resources and involve heavier demands and greater hardships on the troops remaining at my disposal.

A decision to send larger forces to Italy, however, will reduce the forces in France below what is required for the continuance of the offensive, and I trust the effects of this will be very thoroughly considered before such a decision is formed.

When Haig wrote this paper, only the 23rd and 41st Divisions were ordered to Italy. On 8 November, however, he had to send two more, and on 14 November another two were demanded (only one actually went). Meanwhile the Cambrai attack was being prepared in deep secrecy.

GERMANY

Charteris, pp 263–4: 30 October

The Munitions Department have issued a typically carping document, leading to the deduction that we must sit still for at least another year. It is full of the most amazing ineptitudes, so far as my own branch is concerned . . .

The pundits in London are also sceptical about much of what both GQG and ourselves now regard as almost axiomatic. They question whether a German division, after having been heavily engaged in battle, is rightly considered as of lower fighting value. We know that Germany does not engage a division after it has been withdrawn from battle for at least two months, and we also know from actual experience that when re-engaged after two months it is of less fighting value

. . . They also question our estimates of German casualties. The official casualty lists of Germany showed 50 per cent of their infantry engaged as casualties before a division was withdrawn. This year the fighting has been at least as hard, and we have based our estimates, as does GQG, on the same scale with allowance for lower establishments . . .

However much we may wish to adopt a passive defensive in 1918 to avoid casualties, we should either be forced to retreat in front of a German onslaught, or ourselves take the offensive elsewhere . . .

All this may be put to the proof.

SOLDIERS AND POLITICIANS

Wilson, ii, p 19: 30 October

I had a long talk with Winston. He is enthusiastically in favour of my paper, and has written a whole paper – which he sent me – on the paragraph in which I urge an enormous increase of material – guns, tanks, aeroplanes, railways etc. Winston's paper is admirable, and full of ideas. Winston is quite clear that we must have a Superior Direction. He tells me that Lloyd George thinks this also, but is afraid to take the plunge because of the opposition of Haig, Robertson and Asquith.

I told Winston that I did not think Asquith would take up the challenge for one moment, for neither Haig nor Robertson would have a leg to stand on. I quoted the new case of the French sending 4 divisions to Italy and our only sending 2, as another example of how we lose a chance of getting a grip of the situation. Winston entirely agreed. I quoted also my example of the different strategies – ours and the Boches': 1, we take Bullecourt, they take Rumania; 2, we take Messines, they take Russia; 3, we don't take Passchendaele, they take Italy.

What passes understanding is that no one, apparently, ever asked Sir Henry Wilson to explain what he meant by phrases like 'getting a grip of the situation', 'take Russia', 'take Italy'. We have already noted Ludendorff's assessment of Germany's showy successes on other fronts, in contrast to his deep anxiety about the West.

Roskill, *Hankey: Man of Secrets*, p 449: Hankey Diary, 30 October

War Cabinet at 11.30 . . . The proposal for an inter-Allied Council and General Staff practically accepted in principle . . . At 7.15 I called on Ll. George, who had just returned from meeting Painlevé at the station and gossiped with him. He was very gloomy owing to the loss of Udine by the Italians, but pleased at the hope of 'dishing' the soldiers by establishing the allied council.

Haig Diary: Blake, p 262:

31 OCTOBER.   I read the papers by Lord French and General H. Wilson on the General Military Policy of the Allies. The former belittles the work of the British Armies in France since he left and comes to the conclusion that we ought to wait and do nothing until the Americans are organized in 1919. He will not admit that the German Divisions have lost much of their fighting value, nor does he foresee that the enemy if left alone will also become stronger in manpower. It is a poor production and is evidently the outcome of a jealous and disappointed mind. H. Wilson came to no conclusion but advises an 'Inter-Allied Council' being formed with (presumably) himself as head of the British Staff section.

November

———————————— ✠ ————————————

In November the offensive foundered, as much in the morass of politics which had surrounded it from its earliest days as in the morass of Flanders mud.

SOLDIERS AND POLITICIANS

Haig Diary: Blake, p 262

1 NOVEMBER. Pétain showed me a short note which he had written on the question of an Allied Commander-in-Chief (à la Hindenburg). It was possible amongst Allies only when one Army was really the dominant one as in the case of the Central Powers. Our case was different. The British and French Armies were now in his view on an equality. Therefore, he and I must exercise command, and if we disagree, our Governments alone can settle the point in dispute.

Charteris, pp 264–5

1 NOVEMBER The Cabinet are in full cry against D. H. and against our strategy ... Henry Wilson's paper resolves itself into a recommendation for an International Board of Control of politicians, with military advisers, to co-ordinate the decisions of the Cabinets of the various countries. Admirable in theory, but no Council of War has ever yet won a war. D. H.'s criticism is that this will only provide machinery for further discussion and delays ... All the same, the fact that L. G. has even called for these papers shows that he is out again to interfere, to try to win the war without fighting. Wilson will do anything and say anything to get back into power, and L. G. will probably have his way. If he does, heaven only knows what may happen next spring.

Repington, ii, p 126

FRIDAY, 2 NOVEMBER. Saw Sammy Scott* in the morning, and we put our heads together about the set being made at the General Staff by the *Manchester Guardian, Evening Standard*, and other papers, all the attacks obviously inspired from the same source, and no one doubts that Downing Street is this source.

*Major Sir Samuel Scott, MP.

Ibid, p 127

3 NOVEMBER. The dead set being made at Robertson and the General Staff continues. David Davies* began it in the *Sunday Times* three weeks ago. Then Scott† and the *Manchester Guardian* took it up this week, Monday and Thursday, while the *Evening Standard's* London Diary man is also hard at it. Complete ignorance and rank injustice are the characteristics of these attacks, which display a common origin and imply an attempt to create a fictitious public opinion.

Esher, iv, p 151, 3 November

I dined with D. H. this evening. He has come to meet L. G., who arrives tonight... D. H. spoke with no bitterness or even criticism of L. G., or of Henry Wilson, who under the General Staff scheme would be 'Military Member' representing Great Britain.

Haig Diary: Blake, pp 263–4

4 NOVEMBER. At 10.15 I attended a meeting in the Prime Minister's sitting-room (Hotel Crillon) at which he (Lloyd George), General Smuts, General Maurice and I with General Davidson were present.

The Prime Minister first made a few remarks regarding the necessity for forming an Inter-Allied Supreme War Council and Staff and asked my views. I told him that the proposal had been considered for three years and each time had been rejected as unworkable. I gave several reasons why I thought it could not work, and that it would add to our difficulties having such a body. The PM then said that the two Governments had decided to form it; so I said, there is no need saying any more then! . . .

Incidentally, he complained about attacks being made on him in the press which he said were 'evidently inspired by the Military'. He intended to make a speech and tell the public what courses he proposed and how, if he had his way, the military situation would have been much better today, but that the Military Advisers had prevented him from carrying out his intentions! He took special exception to articles in the *Morning Post, Spectator, Nation, Globe,* and he said that one editor had come back from my Headquarters and said that I had complained that he (L.G.) had interfered with tactics. I at once said, 'What is his name, because it is not true?' He said 'Spender, of the *Westminster Gazette*'. I said 'I will write to him', but L. G. at once said, 'Oh, please do not do that'!

I thought L.G. is like our German enemy who, whenever he proposes to do something extra frightful, first of all complains that the British or French have committed the enormity which he is meditating. L.G. is feeling that his position as PM is shaky and means to try and vindicate his conduct of the war in the eye of the public and try and put the people against the soldiers. In fact, to pose as the

*Major David Davies, MP.
†C. P. Scott, Editor of the *Manchester Guardian.*

saviour of his country, who has been hampered by bad advice given by the General Staff!

One important point to bear in mind is that he has never taken the soldiers' advice, namely, to *concentrate all our resources* on the Western Front.

I gave L. G. a good talking to on several of the questions he raised, and I felt I got the best of the arguments. He seemed quite 'rattled' on the subject of Italy.

About 12 o'clock he asked me to go out for a walk, and I went with him up the Champs Elysées to the Arc de Triomphe. Quite a pleasant little man when one had him alone, but I should think most unreliable.

THE INVINCIBLE ENEMY

To the end, the 1917 weather continued its treacheries.

Author's Papers: Haig Diary

1 NOVEMBER.   Glass rising slightly. Dull day but no rain. Observation bad.
2 NOVEMBER.   Glass rising slightly. Dull misty day. Bad observation.
3 NOVEMBER.   Glass rising steadily . . . Dull foggy morning.
4 NOVEMBER.   [Paris] Fine day but dull.
5 NOVEMBER.   Dull dark day but no rain fell.
6 NOVEMBER.   Sunrise was red and the sky looked 'lowering', but only a few drops of rain fell about 9 am, and then the day was fine.

FLANDERS

Wilson, ii, p 20, 2 November.

Kigg came in for an hour before dinner. He pleaded that in another eight days Douglas Haig would take enough of the Passchendaele Ridge to make himself secure for the winter, and that this operation ought to be stopped. Also that Haig had another secret operation in view, which promised satifactory results provided no more troops were sent to Italy. Kigg said that the Boches had skinned the whole front in a manner they had never done before, and that this was a great chance. I could not help saying that, if this was so – i.e. the skinning – then all our attacks had had a very disappointing result, as they had not saved Russia, nor Italy, nor prevented the Boches weakening the front in face of us.

Canadian Expeditionary Force 1914–1919, p 324: 6 November.

At 6.00 am on the sixth a powerful barrage, tremendously satisfying to the assaulting infantry, exploded across the front as the attack was launched under a clear sky that later became cloudy but shed no heavy rain. So quickly did the assaulting companies break out of their starting position that the enemy's retaliatory fire, opening a few minutes later, fell mainly behind the advancing troops. Afterwards prisoners reported that the infantry followed their barrage so closely that in most cases the Germans could not man their machine guns before the attackers were on top of them. Almost everywhere the attack went well. The 2nd Division encountered its chief opposition from pill-boxes at the north end of Passchendaele, but less than three hours after zero the village that had so long been an Allied objective was securely in Canadian hands.

Haig Diary: Blake, p 264

6 NOVEMBER. The operations were completely successful. Passchendaele was taken, as also were Mosselmarkt and Goudberg. The whole position had been most methodically fortified – yet our troops succeeded in capturing all their objectives early in the day with small loss – 'under 700 men'. The left Battalion of the 2nd Division had hard fighting. 21 officers and 408 other ranks were taken prisoners. Today was a very important success.

Charteris, p 266, 7 November

We have now got to where, with good weather, we should have been in early September, and with two months in front of us to carry on the operation and clear the coast. Now, from the purely local point of view, it is rather a barren victory, and if the home people decide on a defensive next year, it will be almost altogether lives and labour thrown away. We have beaten the Germans nearly to breaking point.

German Official Account

The intention of mounting a counter-attack on the next morning met with the objection of the Army High Command. The location and state of available troops – so said General von Lossberg in conversation during the night with the Ypres Group – was unknown; whether the orders would come through at the right time was questionable; the British would have established themselves by the next morning; without strong artillery preparation an attack would be hopeless; on the morning of 7 November after reviewing the situation it could be decided whether an attack following thorough artillery preparation would have any chance of success. The undertaking was not carried out.

German losses around Passchendaele were once again considerable.* The British took over 400 prisoners, but they also, according to German troops' reports, seem to have suffered heavily. They had succeeded in taking the bitterly fought-for Passchendaele, which Field-Marshal Haig had wanted to take before the end of July and which had been his immediate objective since 12 October. The success was meaningful inasmuch as the rise in the ground gave good observation into the German artillery positions. The British had a favourable base for further

*In the 11th Infantry Division alone about 1,700.

attacks against the inner wings of the Ypres and Staden Groups. A speedy renewal of their offensive had to be reckoned with.

Charteris, p 266: 8 November

Full news is now in about the fighting on 6 November. The enemy appear to have made every effort to hold on to the ridge. They sent in five counter-attacks. Their artillery fire was very slight early in the day, but became intense in the afternoon and died away altogether in the evening. Apparently, the Germans only got warning of our attack one hour before we began. There are at present no indications that the Germans will attempt to retake the ridge.

Author's Papers: Haig Diary

8 NOVEMBER.   Examination of prisoners shows that the capture of Passchendaele on 6 November was carried out in face of a fixed determination of the enemy to retain it at all costs . . . I expect he will withdraw *after a suitable lapse of time* so that the world may not be able to say that he was kicked off the ridge.

FRENCH MORALE

Charteris, p 266, 5 November

News from Paris is mixed. The Ministry there is very shaky. Clemenceau* is said to be the first favourite as successor to Painlevé. He would stiffen up the French nation greatly. Rumour has it that it is only by the threat that Clemenceau will succeed him that Poincaré can make Painlevé carry on. Clemenceau would have the support of the whole French Army, owing to his frequent visits to the front. But Poincaré both hates and fears him. The bad news is that Albert Thomas is said to be going round the French munition works lecturing on the immediate need of peace.

SOLDIERS AND POLITICIANS

On 6 and 7 November a French-British-Italian conference was held at Rapallo.

Hankey, ii, p 720

6 NOVEMBER.   Before breakfast I had a stroll with Lloyd George, returning

---

* Georges Clemenceau, Radical Senator, aged 76; editor of *L'Homme Enchaîné* (previously *L'Homme Libre*). He became Prime Minister on 15 November and declared his programme to the Chamber of Deputies on 20 November: 'We have accepted the government in order to conduct the war with redoubled energy . . . We shall carry on this programme . . . there will be neither treason nor half-treason – only war. Nothing but war!'

before him for a talk at 8.30 with Robertson, who was to breakfast alone with Ll. G. I had promised Ll. G. that I would make it quite clear to Robertson that the war Cabinet was absolutely committed to this scheme of a Central Council of Allies, and that it was useless for him to kick against it . . . Robertson made no secret of his objections to the scheme, and I deduced from his manner that he was half inclined to chuck the appointment of CIGS. Shortly after breakfast the conferences commenced and continued on and off all day.

Lloyd George, pp 1439–40

I. The representatives of the British, French and Italian Governments, assembled at Rapallo on 7 November, 1917, have agreed on a scheme for the organization of a Supreme War Council with a Permanent Military Representative from each Power, contained in the following paragraph.

SCHEME OF ORGANIZATION OF A SUPREME WAR COUNCIL

II. (1) With a view to the better co-ordination of military action on the Western Front a Supreme War Council is created, composed of the Prime Ministers and a Member of the Government of each of the Great Powers whose armies are fighting on that front. The extension of the scope of the Council to other fronts is reserved for discussion with the other Great Powers.
(2) The Supreme War Council has for its mission to watch over the general conduct of the War. It prepares recommendations for the decisions of the Governments and keeps itself informed of their execution and reports thereon to the respective Governments . . .
III. The Permanent Military Representatives will be as Follows:

For France	General Foch
For Great Britain	General Wilson
For Italy	General Cadorna

Rapallo, 7 November, 1917.

We should note that in this context 'Western Front' includes the Italian Front. The Rapallo Conference constituted its session on 7 November into the first session of the Supreme War Council, and its first decision was to direct the Permanent Military Representatives to 'report immediately on the present situation on the Italian Front' (still in very grave disorder after the Caporetto disaster).

Hankey, ii, p 722

The limitation to the Western Front was adopted in order to keep the situation open vis-à-vis Russia. It was impossible to include Russia at that stage, partly because the Russian Government was not represented at Rapallo, and partly because it was becoming more and more doubtful whether that country would play any further part in the war. But it was felt to be of great importance to do nothing which would offend Russian susceptibilities.

Lloyd George, pp 1440–1

Sir William Robertson ostentatiously declined to attend the discussions on the Supreme War Council. His general sulkiness was apparent to all. He left the room with a flaunting stride the moment the idea of a Supreme Inter-Allied Council was mentioned, just stopping on the way for an instant to instruct Sir Maurice Hankey to make a note of the fact that he was not present during the discussions. He wished Sir Maurice to send for him when the Conference passed on to other subjects. He said: 'I wash my hands of this business.' His whole attitude during the Rapallo Conference was sullen and unhelpful, and it was ominous of acute trouble to come in our future relations. He meant to fight the Inter-Allied Council.

The story of the Supreme War Council is outside the scope of this book; however, since it has already bulked so large, it does require a little further consideration. What is important to note is that it contains two threads. There is Lloyd George's loathing of the Western Front in general and the Flanders offensive in particular, his dread of any repetition of this strategy, and his distrust of the Military advisers responsible for it, which caused him to see in the new inter-Allied machinery a useful device for over-riding them. It was awareness of this motive that provoked Robertson's unwise and provocative reaction.

The list of Military Representatives underlines the point: Wilson was appointed as an *alternative* adviser, independent of the Chief of Staff (Robertson); Foch *was* the Chief of Staff, and when Lloyd George objected to this, was replaced by Weygand, his staff officer and mouthpiece; Cadorna, 'kicked upstairs' after Caporetto, could be nothing but the mouthpiece of the Italian General Staff; when the Americans joined the new organization, their Military Representative was the Chief of Staff, General Bliss. Thus, as his biographer* says, 'Wilson's position was, in fact, going to be the exceptional one' – naturally, in view of the exceptional reasons for his appointment. Everyone else understood that military advisers *must* be responsible advisers.

There remains the larger question of of the desirability of an inter-Allied co-ordinating machinery. This cannot be disputed, but neither can the fact that with a polyglot Coalition the difficulty of setting up such a machinery is very great. Even when there are no language problems, dif-

---

* Callwell, *Wilson Diaries*, ii, p 33.

ficulties abound, as the Germans and Austrians discovered in the First World War, and the British and Americans in the Second, However, as that war also showed, they can be overcome, by such devices as a Joint Chiefs of Staff Committee, instructing Supreme Allied Commanders in the theatres of war. By contrast, in November, 1916, we find the extraordinary spectacle of an inter-Allied political conference on the future conduct of the war taking place in Paris sumultaneously with an inter-Allied military conference on the same subject at Chantilly, neither, apparently, taking cognizance of the other. It did not require a Supreme War Council to resolve that absurdity, only a little common sense and mutual trust between soldiers and politicians which, as we have seen, was lacking throughout the year.

In the event, the Supreme War Council did not have a distinguished history. Its chief recommendation for 1918 was an Allied blow against Turkey. It failed to foresee or recommend useful steps against the great German offensives in the West, March–July; it proved to be quite helpless when the offensives were launched. When unity of command was obtained under Foch (later Marshal) the Supreme War Council quietly faded into oblivion, though its secretariat served the Paris Peace Conference in 1919. So enticing, however, was the idea of such a Council that it was revived in 1939, only to fade away again under the impact of war's realities in 1940. Probably the truth about Coalition war was best expressed by Pétain when he said that unity of command 'is only possible amongst Allies when one Army (or Navy, of course) is really the dominant one' (see p 318).

While the Western statesmen were busy at Rapallo, in the East a new tremendous event cast a fresh cloud of confusion over a year which was not lacking in that element. It was on 7 November (25 October by the old calendar) that the Bolsheviks seized power in Petrograd, and within a week were masters of Russia (though a long and bloody civil war would be required to confirm that mastership). The Bolshevik programme was 'Peace, Land and Bread', and they lost no time in trying to obtain the first of these.

Esher, iv, pp 155–6: Esher to Lord Stamfordham, 9 November

At last some credence may be felt in the collapse of Russia. Kerensky has met his inevitable fate. The adulation of him has been one of the worst features of the war. Either our War Cabinet knew that Russia was hopelessly 'out of it' and they dissimulated and deluded the nation, or they were crassly ignorant.

And now Italy is following exactly the same course. Preliminary collapse to a revolutionary finale . . . If her King can stave off revolution and stifle the potential Soviets, he is a lucky fellow.

And next in the scale comes France. Do not mistake these internal squabbles. They go far deeper than any personalities and reach down to revolutionary depths. There is no doubt about this.

I found L.G. in a curious mood. Bad-tempered would perhaps describe it. He thinks that he has been misled by his military advisers. It is his own fault. Over and over again he has been warned that the political factors in this war were the grave danger; that unless he gripped the situation hard for England, the Allied vessel would drift on to the rocks. He never realized the peril. It is now a bit late.

The one solid *point d'appui* is the British Front, and the character of the Commander-in-Chief. From this pivot we may even at the eleventh hour man-oeuvre ourselves into a fairly favourable peace. But far more insight will be required than the War Cabinet has shown. If L.G. thinks that an 'Allied General Staff', mainly military in character, is going to free him from his entanglements, he is deluding himself.

The Invincible Enemy

Author's Papers: Haig Diary

7 NOVEMBER.   . . . Some rain in forenoon. Afternoon fine and colder.
8 NOVEMBER.   Glass steady. Slight frost last night. Bright morning but day became overcast.
9 NOVEMBER.   Glass falling, but morning and forenoon bright and fine.
10 NOVEMBER.   A wet night and wet morning . . . some fine intervals during the day.

Flanders

Canadian Expeditionary Force 1914–1919, pp 325–6

On the day after the capture of Passchendaele General Currie gave orders for the ninth and final phase of the battle to be launched on 10 November . . . From the unsystematic pattern of their defences and the indifferent morale of several Germans who had already been taken prisoner, the enemy do not seem to have considered the area attacked as vital ground. This was later borne out by their generally light resistance to the attack. Officers in a group of eleven who were taken in one dug-out were obviously embarrassed when questioned as to the circumstances of their capture.

It was raining heavily when the 7th and 8th Battalions jumped off from positions north and north-east of Mosselmarkt on 10 November, shortly after six o'clock. By 7.30 am both units were on the first objective, only 500 yards away; but to secure its goal the 7th Battalion on the right had to push on another 300 yards to quell troublesome German machine-guns in a nearby trench . . . On the left of the Canadians the 1st British Division's advance ran into difficulties when a German counter-attack got between two diverging battalions . . .

The frontage of the Anglo-Canadian attack, narrow enough to begin with and reduced by three-fifths by the failure on the left, allowed the enemy to concentrate an unusual weight of artillery against the new line. In all, the counter batteries of five German corps were turned on the Canadian front. 'Almost as bad as Pozières*. . .' an Australian diarist was to note. 'The night is simply vile – and the day too . . . If the Canadians can hold on they are wonderful troops.' . . . During the afternoon a German counter-attack was turned back by the 20th Battalion's small-arms fire; another was broken up with artillery. But the Canadians held grimly on . .

This attack on 10 November brought to an end the long drawn-out Third Battle of Ypres.

German Official Account

After this there were only engagements in the outpost area and assault troop patrols. Artillery fire remained lively. The enemy's conduct was no different to that in the earlier pauses in the major assaults. The conclusion that the battle was at an end could not be drawn. Although the Supreme Command as well as the High Command of the Army Group and Army had long been of the opinion that Field-Marshal Haig was not capable of continuing the offensive through the winter, it was, however, quite uncertain when he would finally stop.

Ludendorff, ii, p 492

On 26 and 30 October and 6 and 10 November the fighting was again of the severest description. The enemy charged like a wild bull against the iron wall which kept him from our submarine bases. He threw his weight against Houthoulst Forest, Poelcappelle, Passchendaele, Becelaere, Gheluvelt and Zandvoorde. He dented it in many places, and it seemed as if he must knock it down. But it held, although a faint tremor ran through its foundations.

The impressions I continuously received were very terrible. In a tactical sense, everything possible had been done. The advanced zone was good. The effectiveness of our artillery had considerably improved. Behind every division in the front line there was another in support; and we still had reserves in the third line. We knew that the enemy suffered heavily. But we also knew he was amazingly strong and, what was equally important, had an extraordinarily stubborn will.

---

*Where the Australians entered the Battle of the Somme in 1916, and where their dead lay thicker than on any other battlefield of the war.

Lloyd George wanted victory.* He held England in his hand. Only one thing we did not know; how long the battle would continue. The enemy must tire some time.

Author's Papers: Haig Diary

12 NOVEMBER.   I sent letter to Kiggell, and said my view is that we must stop the offensive in Flanders, except for bombardment and simulated attacks for the next fortnight.

O.H., 1917 ii, pp 360–1

The (casualty) figures submitted to the Supreme War Council on 25 February, 1918, by the British Section of the Military Representatives were:

31 July–3 October	138,787†
4 October–12 November	106,110
Total	244,897

This total includes normal wastage‡

Les Armées Françaises dans la Grande Guerre
(Paris: Imprimerie Nationale) V (ii), p 719 f.n.

Du 8 juillet au 31 octobre, la Ire armée a perdu 1,625 tués et 6,900 blessés.
(From 8 July to 31 October the First Army lost 1,625 killed and 6,900 wounded.)
[Total: 8,525]

German Official Account, xiii, p 96

The battle lasted over four months and had led to enormous consumption of strength. A total of 73 German divisions had taken part in it from 15 July to 10 November.§

The German Fourth Army lost from 21 July to 31 December, 1917, about 217,000 men, of which 35,000 were killed and 48,000 missing.¶

---

*The ironies will not escape the reader. It must be remembered that in September 1916 Lloyd George had given an interview to an American correspondent in which he proclaimed what became known as 'The Policy of the Knock-Out Blow'. Britain, he said, would continue the war 'until the Prussian military despotism is broken beyond repair . . . There is neither clock nor calendar in the British Army today. Time is the least vital factor . . . It will not take 20 years to win this war, but whatever time is required, it will be done.' This interview fixed the image of Lloyd George as an implacable enemy irrevocably in German minds.
    It is interesting to note Ludendorff's estimate of the value of 'stubborn will' – one of the qualities for which Lloyd George blamed Haig most.
† See p 279.
‡ Normal Wastage, 2 Armies × 3½ months = 49,000 approx. (See p 345).
§ Von Kuhl says 77 divisions; Prince Rupprecht says '86 . . . including 22 used twice'.
¶ See pp 346–7.

Harington, *Plumer of Messines*, pp 129–30

Thus ended what may be called the Passchendaele operations with Passchendaele in our hands and a substantial footing on the Passchendaele–Staden Ridge. Critics will say and have said 'Yes, and at what a price!'

I cannot dispute that. Those stages up to Passchendaele have always been a nightmare to me as they were to my Chief. They were all right up to and including Broodseinde, 4 October. After that Fate was very cruel to us.

von Kuhl, *Der Weltkrieg*

The suffering, privation and exertions which the soldiers had to bear were inexpressible. Terrible was the spiritual burden on the lonely man in the shell hole, and terrible the strain on the nerves during the bombardments which continued day and night. The 'Hell of Verdun' was exceeded by Flanders. The Battle of Flanders has been called 'The greatest martyrdom of the World War'.

No division could last more than a fortnight in this hell. Then it had to be relieved by new troops . . . Looking back today it seems that what was borne here was superhuman. With respect and thankfulness the German people will always remember the heroes of Flanders.

Soldiers and Politicians

On 12 November at a luncheon in Paris, Lloyd George made an important speech explaining the purposes of the Supreme War Council. He dismissed all previous attempts to arrive at an Allied military policy.

Lloyd George, pp 1442–4; Duff Cooper, ii, pp 86–7

Great Generals came from many lands to Paris with carefully and skilfully prepared plans for their own fronts . . . they all sat at the same table and metaphorically took thread and needle, sewed these plans together, and produced them to a subsequent civilian conference as one great strategic piece; and it was solemnly proclaimed to the world the following morning that the unity of the Allied war organization . . .

You have only to summarize events to realize how many of the failures from which we have suffered are attributable to this one fundamental defect in the Allied war organization . . .

Unity – not sham unity, but real unity – is the only the only sure pathway to victory.

He also said, among other things:

We have won great victories. When I look at the appalling casualty lists I sometimes wish it had not been necessary to win so many . . . When we advance a kilometre into the enemy's lines, snatch a small shattered village out of his cruel grip, capture a few hundred of his soldiers, we shout with unfeigned joy.

This obvious reference to the Flanders communiqués he then contrasted with the Austro-German achievement at Caporetto; Duff Cooper remarks:

German agents were busy in every allied and neutral country spreading propaganda in words that were almost identical.

Repington, ii, p 132: 13 November

This morning comes the report of our PM's astonishing speech at the Paris luncheon, in which he castigated every one concerned in the past conduct of the war except himself, and exalted himself as the only wise man. A dreadful, self-righteous speech, with severe indictment of the soldiers, but not by name.

Oliver, p 291: 14 November

Ll. G. has . . . made a speech at Paris, the core of which is as sound as anything could possibly be, viz. *the need for unity*; but I never in my life read anything which showed less tact or consideration for the feelings of people who have to be considered – the Army above all. Regarded as an appeal to the inhabitants of the United Kingdom, of the Dominions, France and America, the speech is one of the finest pronouncements that has been made during this or any other war, but in the most gratuitous way it casts, or appears to cast, aspersions not only upon his own military advisers, but upon the British Army as a whole. The result over here for the time being is a tremendous row.

I expect most people in London who know anything about the inside of the matter are inclined to think that Asquith will succeed in getting Ll. G. out next Monday. I don't; for the Goat* is a very downy animal and very quick at turning.

Haig Diary: Blake, p 267

14 NOVEMBER.   A letter from Lord Derby . . . re Lloyd George's Paris speech last Monday. 'I feel that it is a speech which you will possibly think reflects on you and your men. I want you to allow me to again express my entire confidence in you – and I shall probably have to show that confidence in an outward and visible way.† You will understand what I mean.' I have not read L.G.'s speech but from Reuter's summary of it, I gather that it is more likely to hearten the enemy and discourage the Italians than any other language!

Charteris, pp 268–9: 15 November

There is a lull in the attack from home on GHQ, but it is only a lull. If we have a big

*Lloyd George's nickname, attributed to well-known propensities.
† Derby meant the offer of a peerage; Haig had already refused a similar offer in June.

success next week the whole thing may blow over. If we fail, or have only a modified success, it will blow up again worse than ever. The mainspring of the attack is the PM himself, and he has willing helpers in French, Churchill and Wilson . . . I wish I could think that all those who are attacking D.H. are doing so solely on patriotic grounds. The only consoling thought at present is that D.H.'s position is so strong that his enemies have not yet dared to attack him openly. But the attack on the Staff is only a means of getting at him.* There is an alarming similarity between all these intrigues and manoeuvres against him and those against Joffre in 1916. They ended in the Nivelle disaster in 1917. I hope these do not bring a similar catastrophe in 1918.

FLANDERS

Blake, pp 267–8: Haig to Robertson, 15 November

Any further offensive on the Flanders front must be at once discontinued though it is important to keep this fact secret as long as possible.

The positions already gained on that front fall short of what I had wished to secure before the winter . . . Our present position . . . may be difficult and costly to hold if seriously attacked . . . I think this latter contingency must be expected as soon as the enemy realizes that he has regained the initiative . . .

In view of the advanced season and the existing state of the enemy's infantry on this front such attacks are, for the present, unlikely to aim at more than local and limited objectives on which a heavy concentration of hostile artillery can be brought to bear.

The situation next year, however, may give cause for more serious anxiety if the measures outlined in your letter are carried out.

The British personnel in France is urgently in need of rest and training. A serious reduction in their numbers will deny them the opportunities for both and throw a considerably increased strain on the forces left in France.

But little activity can therefore be maintained during the winter and the enemy will have time and opportunity to recuperate. The increased expenditure of energy and manpower on this front and in Italy during the winter will render impossible any serious offensive by the Allies on this front next spring, and under these conditions the enemy is not unlikely to seize the initiative in attack, the power of the British and French Armies to resist which will be comparatively low.

The bringing up to establishment of units sent to Italy, their maintenance at full establishment, the relief from this front of divisions exhausted in Italy,† the

* Under Government and War Office pressure, Charteris himself was removed in December. In January, 1918, there were further changes at GHQ, the most important being Kiggel and Butler (Deputy CGS).
† Fortunately, this contingency did not arise; British losses in Italy, December, 1917 – November 1918 were less than 7,000. Two divisions returned to France in April, 1918.

probable extension of the British front, all following on the strenuous efforts made continously since the beginning of last April, must undoubtedly not only deprive the British Armies of offensive power next year, but will reduce very considerably their fitness to meet and repulse a serious attack.

> Crown Prince Rupprecht of Bavaria: Order of the Day, 5 December, 1917

Sons from all parts of Germany have shown heroic bravery and powers of endurance and brought to nought the attempts by the British and French to achieve the breakthrough which, had it succeeded, would have brought about a decision because it would have meant the capture of Flanders and our U-boat bases. Despite the use of unheard-of masses of men and material the enemy has not achieved this. A narrow strip of completely destroyed crater land is his only gain. He has bought this gain with extremely high losses while our own casualties have been less than in any previous defensive battle.

Thus the Battle of Flanders is a severe defeat to the enemy and is for us a great victory. He who was present can be proud to have been a Flanders warrior.

> German Official Account

Above everything else the battle had led to a vast consumption of German strength. Losses had been so high that they could no longer be replaced and the fighting strength of battalions, already reduced, was further reduced. That the enemy, despite the most thorough preparation, numerical superiority, bravery and perseverance had been able to achieve so little, was partly due to the adverse weather conditions which made movement in the Flanders soil extremely difficult. But water and mud were no less a disadvantage to the defenders . . . These conditions, more than the bloody fighting, led to a rapid wearing out of the troops and were, along with the lower numerical strength of the German divisions and the serious inferiority in guns and ammunition, among the reasons why the German defence required a more rapid relief of divisions than (during the enemy's attacks. [sic. 'the attacking enemy'?]). . .

The 73 German divisions which had fought in Flanders* within the space of four months could only be brought together by replacing the fought-out divisions of the Fourth Army by fresh troops from other Armies. A reserve worth mentioning was never available.

> Field-Marshal von Hindenburg, *Out of My Life*, Cassell, 1920, pp 288–9

From the point of view, not of scale, but of the obstinacy which the English displayed and the difficulties of the ground for the defenders, the battles . . . in Flanders put all our battles on the Somme in 1916 completely in the shade . . . these actions kept us in great and continual anxiety. In fact, I may say that with

*See p 328 f.n.

such a cloud hanging over our heads we were seldom able to rejoice wholeheartedly over our victories in Russia and Italy.

It was with a feeling of absolute longing that we waited for the beginning of the wet season . . .

The flames of battle did not die down until December. As on the Somme, neither of the two adversaries could raise the shout of victory in Flanders.

Sir Douglas Haig's Despatches, ed. Boraston, pp 133–5: 'The Campaigns of 1917', 25 December 1917

This offensive, maintained for three and a half months under the most adverse conditions of weather, had entailed almost superhuman exertions on the part of the troops of all arms and services. The enemy had done his utmost to hold his ground, and in his endeavours to do so had used up no less than seventy-eight divisions, of which eighteen had been engaged a second or third time in the battle, after being withdrawn to rest and refit. Despite the magnitude of his efforts, it was the immense natural difficulties, accentuated manifold by the abnormally wet weather, rather than the enemy's resistance, which limited our progress and prevented the complete capture of the ridge.

What was actually accomplished under such adverse conditions is the most conclusive proof that, given a normally fine August, the capture of the whole ridge, within the space of a few weeks, was well within the power of the men who achieved so much. They advanced every time with absolute confidence in their power to overcome the enemy, even though they had sometimes to struggle through mud up to their waists to reach him. So long as they could reach him they did overcome him, but physical exhaustion placed narrow limits on the depth to which each advance could be pushed, and compelled long pauses between the advances. The full fruits of each success were consequently not always obtained. Time after time the practically beaten enemy was enabled to reorganize and relieve his men and to bring up reinforcements behind the sea of mud which constituted his main protection.

Notwithstanding the many difficulties, much has been achieved. Our captures in Flanders since the commencement of operations at the end of July amount to 24,065 prisoners, 74 guns, 941 machine guns and 138 trench mortars. It is certain that the enemy's losses considerably exceeded ours. Most important of all, our new and hastily trained Armies have shown once again that they are capable of meeting and beating the enemy's best troops, even under conditions which favoured his defence to a degree which it required the greatest endurance, determination and heroism to overcome . . .

In the operations of Arras, Messines, Lens and Ypres as many as 131 German divisions have been engaged and defeated by less than half that number of British divisions.

The number of prisoners and guns captured by us is an indication of the progress we have made. The total number of prisoners taken between the opening of our spring offensive on 9 April, 1917, and the conclusion of the Flanders offensive, exclusive of prisoners captured in the Cambrai Battle, is 57,696, including 1,290 officers. During the same period and in the same offensives we have also captured 393 guns, including 109 heavy guns, 561 trench mortars and 1,976 machine guns.

Without reckoning, therefore, the possibilities which have been opened up by our territorial gains in Flanders, and without considering the effect which a less vigorous prosecution of the war by us might have had in other theatres, we have every reason to be satisfied with the results which have been achieved by the past year's fighting. The addition of strength which the enemy has obtained or may yet obtain, from events in Russia and Italy has already largely been discounted, and the ultimate destruction of the enemy's field forces has been brought appreciably nearer.

von Kuhl, *Der Weltkrieg*

The terrible fighting conditions in Flanders already described meant that the expenditure of divisions was unexpectedly high . . .

With such continuing wastage it is understandable that it became more and more difficult to withdraw the fought-out divisions from the battle line and to find, promptly, sufficient replacements for the losses they had suffered. The number of field replacement depots behind the Front was soon insufficient. Strong demands were made upon the replacement authorities in Germany. Because of the mounting demand it was found that replacements coming from the Homeland were often so little advanced in their training and so little instructed that they could not be put straight into the line. Filling the ranks with insufficiently trained replacement, it was found by experience, did not increase the fighting strength of the divisions in any way; rather, valuable replacements were uselessly lost. Raw recruits could not, therefore, be used on the Western Front for the purpose merely of bringing establishments up to strength. It was necessary to limit the supply to those divisions proceeding to the Front in order, where possible, to bring them up to adequate strength. Other divisions on quieter sectors were left with many gaps in their ranks. In general it was made more difficult in that the fought-out divisions, usually with only a rest of a few days and sometimes without any rest at all, were sent to other sectors before they had received their replacements.

By the end of November the average fighting strength of battalions on the Western Front was approximately 640 men. The Supreme Command was compelled to announce that an improvement in the replacement position was unlikely. In Germany the demands of industry and agriculture had to be met and the situation had reached the lowest admissible point. Apart from the men of 1899, that is the 18-year-olds,* only convalescents and drafts from the Eastern Front were available.

*cf. Charteris's estimate in September, pp 248–9.

It is necessary to bear these conditions in mind if a picture of the position of Germany after the Flanders battle is to be correctly gained. The supply of replacements would become even more difficult in the coming year and this would tend to affect the conduct of the War. In this, Field-Marshal Haig was correct: even if he had not broken through the Flanders front he had weakened German strength to a point where the damage could not be made good. The German sword had become blunted. Although most of the German divisions contained enough men to carry out their duty, even if they were to serve several times on the Flanders front, there were signs here and there in some formations that the terrible burden could not be carried for long. Even if these were exceptions the concern was justified whether the Army could retain its strength for a further year of war.

Ludendorff, ii, pp. 541–3

The Army had come victoriously through 1917; but it had become apparent that the holding of the Western Front purely by a defensive could no longer be counted on, in view of the enormous quantity of material of all kinds which the Entente had now at their disposal . . . The enormous material resources of the enemy had given his attack a considerable preponderance over our defence and this condition would become more and more apparent as our best men became casualties, our infantry approximated more nearly in character to a militia, and discipline declined . . .

The troops had borne the continuous defensive with extreme difficulty. Skulkers were already numerous. They reappeared as soon as the battle was over, and it had become quite common for divisions which came out of action with desperately low effectives to be considerably stronger after only a few days. Against the weight of the enemy's material the troops no longer displayed their old stubbornness; they thought with horror of fresh defensive battles and longed for the war of movement . . . The interests of the Army were best served by the offensive; in defence it was bound gradually to succumb to the ever increasing hostile superiority in men and material. This feeling was shared by everybody. In the West the Army pined for the offensive, and after Russia's collapse expected it with the most extreme relief . . .

The condition of our allies and of our Army all called for an offensive that would bring about an early decision. This was only possible on the Western Front.

Conclusion

───────────────────── ✠ ─────────────────────

The purpose of this book is to let the Third Battle of Ypres and those who took part in it, or influenced it, or reported it, speak for themselves. However, some final comment is probably required from me. I would say this:

The strategy of launching an offensive in Flanders has been criticized on account of the fierce resistance encountered there. This misses the point that a large reason for Haig's preference for Flanders was that there the Germans could not retire, as they had done after the Battle of the Somme, but *must* stand fast and fight. German sources confirm this. The Flanders U-boat bases, though not as important as was supposed in England at the time, were important to Germany nevertheless. Even more important, as study of the peace discussions in Germany in 1917 reveals (see pp 263–6), was the determination to hold on to as much of Belgium as possible, as a bargaining counter in peace negotiations. The military leaders went even further; in his memorandum of 14 September Ludendorff said: 'We should only be absolutely safe . . . if we were in military occupation of the whole of Belgium and held the coast of Flanders.'

Powerful political and strategic reasons thus held the Germans in Flanders. On the other hand, as their own sources also confirm, this was an awkward area to defend, because of the constriction of communications there, making it difficult to supply. Von Kuhl tells us: 'the Flanders fighting was the climax of the effort which the German railways made in the defensive battles.' Between 15 June and 15 November, 6,591 troop trains alone ran in the area of the Fourth Army, reaching a peak of 90 a day, a very formidable strain. There is no doubt that German transportation problems became acute. Passchendaele is only 5 miles from the rail junction of Roulers; if Passchendaele could have been taken by September . . .

Granted the strategic possibilities, we yet have to ask whether these were not cancelled out by tactical disadvantages. My own view is that the tactical problems, though great, were not in themselves insurmountable. Reading some of the highly articulate British (or American) critics of the campaign, one sometimes wonders whether they are talking about the battle in which the German Army took part, or something else altogether. All the conditions adduced as overwhelming barriers to offensive success are presented by the Germans as extreme disadvantages to the defence. Thus von Kuhl:

'In the Flanders battle there were no trenches, no dug-outs. With ground water just below the surface it was not possible to drive tunnels into the soil . . . The defenders cowered in their water-filled craters without protection from the weather; hungry and freezing, completely without cover from continual enemy artillery fire. Even the staffs of the forward units had no cover, except perhaps a thin corrugated iron roof over their shell-hole. Movement in the muddy soil was very difficult and men and horses sank into the slime; rifles and machine guns, coated with mud, refused to function. Only rarely was it possible to supply the defenders with a hot meal. Distribution of orders in the forward area was difficult in the extreme as telephone and line communication had been shot to pieces. With difficulty runners made their way through the mud.'

Even the 'pill-boxes' of evil fame in British accounts, which often present them as another example of fiendish German ingenuity, look different to their designers: 'The few concrete bunkers which were erected were placed on top of the earth, and offered tempting targets to the enemy artillery' (von Kuhl). The vile summer of 1917, in fact, which did so much to spoil the attacks, also bade fair to ruin the defence. I would add this, however: the appalling ground conditions did affect the British more gravely inasmuch as their forward movements (especially of guns and ammunition) were slowed and sometimes halted, whereas the Germans had only to 'stay put', even though their situation was abominable, and when the British did advance, it was *into* the shell-crater morass, while when the Germans retired, it was *away* from it. The difference made by the weather is clearly proved by Plumer's successes at Messines and by 20 September–4 October, when the ground was relatively dry.

Apart from the effect of the exceptional weather, it must be said that the offensive's prospects were also marred by other factors, including command errors. The Battle of Arras, fought in conformity with Nivelle's demands, as well as gravely weakening the Army, contributed to a delay of 53 days – nearly eight weeks – between the first phase in Flanders, Messines (7 June) and the next, Pilckem Ridge (31 July). Transferring matériel from the Second to the Fifth Army caused more delay. In

Douglas Haig: The Educated Soldier (p 336) I said 'A great deal of the misfortune and the misery that followed is attributable to this protracted delay.'

Much misfortune stemmed from Haig's decision to give the Fifth Army the principal rôle in the main offensive. With all those splendid advantages that hindsight confers, one can see now that the most profitable plan would probably have been to spread the battle northward stage by stage: first, the Messines–Wytschaete Ridge; next (and soon),* the Gheluvelt plateau; soon after that, the Broodseinde–Staden Ridge. Success on those lines should have obviated much of the necessity of fighting across the Steenbeek valley, where the bulk of the Fifth Army was deployed, and where the pulverizing of the drainage produced the worst swamp. It is clear that Gough never fully grasped the vital importance of his right flank. It was not a case of 'pivoting on the left' (see p 112); it was a case of absolute concentration on the right, which would then draw the left up beside it as it made progress, by enfilading the enemy's positions. But in fairness to Gough it must be pointed out that this could only have been done by extending the main attack *southward*, i.e. into the Second Army area; which brings one back again to the fundamental thought that this should always have been Plumer's battle, with Gough in support, never vice versa. This was Haig's most serious mistake, because it affected time, and it affected method.

Another mistake, but one for which it is difficult to lay reasonable blame, was his acceptance of Pétain's repeated promises to help with a large diversionary offensive. It is now obvious that Pétain was behaving very deviously – an understandable and patriotic reluctance to expose France's weakness even to an ally being his most probable motive. Haig always liked Pétain (even after the latter's moral collapse in March, 1918) and got on well with him. It is a good thing, in a coalition, for the two commanders-in-chief to agree; but in 1917 this amity had dire consequences.

Then there is the question of Intelligence, and the rôle of Charteris. Captain Cyril Falls, a level-headed historian, summarizes this in the sentence: 'On the basis of optimistic intelligence reports, (Haig) magnified a deterioration in the German Army into something far more serious than it was in fact.' Once more, examination of German accounts (in conjunction with conditions in Germany herself) show that the gap between GHQ's view of the enemy's state and the reality was con-

---

*The logistical problem would, of course, have been much simplified.

siderably less wide than even Falls suggests. But wide or narrow, that gap
was crucial – as it turned out. In those hideous final stages of the battle, it
is clear that the Germans did come close to cracking point; but not close
enough for the exhausted British to clinch the matter.

Optimism itself is not a fault – in the frightening crises of 1918 this
quality in Haig proved to be a major asset of the Allies. Optimism
founded simply on ignorance, however, can be a liability. Haig and his
staff have been accused of ignoring the conditions in which the Army was
fighting. There is the story* of how General Kiggell, looking at the
battlefield afterwards, burst into tears and said, 'Good God, did we send
men to fight in that?' Whatever may be the explanation of this occasion
(fact or fiction) there can be no doubt that Haig himself knew full well
what the conditions were. The language of his own Despatch (substantially quoted verbatim without acknowledgment in the Official History) could hardly be more eloquent (see p 213). But that apart, when we
find him quoting the D.G.T. as saying that the narrow-gauge railway
engines were 'halfway up to the boilers in mud' (13 October) and on the
same day telling his wife that 'the ground became quite impossible';
noting 'rifles unusable owing to mud' (22 October); or the 7th Division
'really engulfed in mud' (28 October), we know that, as a fairly literal-
minded man, he is speaking from certain knowledge. How was it
acquired?

Haig, like the Duke of Wellington before him and Field-Marshal
Montgomery after, made regular use of liaison officers touring the front
as his 'eyes and ears'. One of them, Mr. E. A. Osborne, then a GSO II in
the Operations Branch (under General Davidson) who generally worked
in the Fifth Army area, described in *The Spectator* on 10 January, 1958, a
visit to the 34th Division in front of Poelcappelle in October, 1917:

'I went up and spent some hours at brigade and battalion HQs. I could
see, and heard much about, the awful conditions. I felt very bad about it
all, probably to an increased extent as so many valued friends were
involved. On return that evening I dictated and signed what could only
be described as a violent report. After dinner I was sent for by the CGS,
General Sir Launcelot Kiggell. He took me straight to the C-in-C's
room. There was nobody else there. Sir Douglas took me across the
room to a big wall map and told me to elaborate my report. I did this at
considerable length and with great emphasis. As far as I remember,

*Captain B. H. Liddell Hart in *The Spectator*, 3 January, 1958.

though very attentive, he made little or no comment. At the end he said, 'Thank you, Major Osborne. Good night.'

I left with a great feeling of relief. I had unburdened my soul to a great man and a real commander.'

As we have seen, Charteris himself and other GHQ officers regularly inspected the front and reported. There was no blind ignorance: just a determination to beat the enemy despite the conditions, and a marginally excessive belief that this could be done.

It should be apparent to every careful reader of this book that misunderstanding, in various degrees and on various subjects, haunted the Flanders campaign from beginning to end. Throughout, in both France and Britain, there was deep misunderstanding between soldiers and politicians which could not fail to have bad effects. Equally dangerous was the misunderstanding between soldiers themselves; we have noted that between Haig and Pétain; another mischievous one was between Haig and Wilson; but saddest and most serious of all was that which arose between Haig and Robertson. When the professional head of the Army and the commander of its most important field force are not in full accord, trouble is bound to ensue.

We have seen how Robertson's misgivings about Haig's information, and sometimes about his strategy, developed. Robertson's biographer, Victor Bonham-Carter, percipiently writes:*

'What he could not do, and what he should have felt free to do, was to talk the whole thing over with the Prime Minister. But that was impossible. Relations with Lloyd George were such that they prevented any possibility of unbiased judgment. Both Wully and Maurice were hag-ridden by the constant fear that if they failed to support Haig, then the Prime Minister would step in, and profit from the situation to launch some far-fetched enterprise and let the Western Front go hang: in their view the surest way to destroy the Army and lose the War.'

In other words, CIGS and C-in-C were thrust into an undesirable form of solidarity, and an even more undesirable reticence with each other, because any hint of a divergence of views between them would be seized upon, lawyer-fashion, by Lloyd George for his own ends. I am perfectly sure that the hopes of success in Flanders were already placed in deadly jeopardy when the British and French Governments decided to set aside the strategy agreed by the military leaders of the Allies at Chantilly on 16

*Soldier True, Frederick Muller, 1963, p 286.

November, 1916; when they both committed themselves to their flirtation with Nivelle without consulting their advisers; and above all when Lloyd George's infatuation caused him to undermine every prospect of future mutual confidence at the Calais Conference in February, 1917. Queen Mary Tudor is said to have proclaimed that she would die with 'Calais' graven on her heart; in 1917 there were others who could have said the same. If there is any unforgivable guilt to be associated with the Flanders offensive, it is here, in this fatal destruction of trust. It is possibly some faint stirring of consciousness of this that accounts for the shrill venom of Lloyd George's attempt to exculpate himself in his *War Memoirs*, a document as shabby as his behaviour at Calais.

To conclude: there is no denying the tragic quality of 'Third Ypres'; it has an Aeschylean ring. I would not for one moment dispute with Sir Philip Gibbs when he says:* 'For the first time the British Army lost its spirit of optimism, and there was a sense of deadly depression among many officers and men with whom I came in touch.' Fortunately, the depression was not permanent. But for those who endured the battle, or its aftermath, the trial was severe indeed. The 29th Division took over a sector of the stricken field in January, 1918, and its historian, describing what it found there, writes:†

'By universal consent the Third Battle of Ypres represents the utmost that war has so far achieved in the way of horrors.'

'So far'; Leningrad, Okinawa,‡ fire-storms, atomic bombs were yet to come. But for the men of the 29th Division and others like them, the Ypres Salient was a horrible place to begin a new year.

Nevertheless, among those who had shared the responsibilities of command at different levels, mixed with natural revulsion there was also a sense of achievement, tempered by the sadness of lost opportunity. We have noted the steadfast views of two such humane soldiers as Plumer and Harington, and General Monash's conviction that 'great things are possible'. Marshal of the Royal Air Force Lord Trenchard told the Official Historian years later:

*Gibbs: *Realities of War*, p 396.
†Captain Stair Gillon, *The Story of The 29th Division*, Thomas Nelson, 1925, p 122.
‡In Leningrad, in January 1942, people were dying at the rate of 3,500–4,000 a day; the final total has been estimated at 900,000. Of Okinawa the American Official History says: 'There was only one kind of Japanese casualty – the dead.' They numbered 100,000 out of 110,000 combatants.

'Tactically (the offensive) was a failure, but strategically it was a success, and a brilliant success – in fact, it saved the world.

There is not the slightest doubt, in my opinion, that France would have gone out of the War if Haig had not fought Passchendaele, like they did in 1940 in this war, and had France gone out of the War I feel, as all our manpower was in France, we should have been bound to collapse, or, at any rate, it would have lengthened the War for years.'*

Gough, whose enthusiasm for the offensive waned early, nevertheless says: 'Haig's strategy was sound . . . he was right in shouldering the main part of the Allied military burden.' Birdwood, who had certainly had enough of it by the time his Corps came out, said: 'I still feel that if only the weather had held, Haig might well have achieved an epic victory.' Closer to the mud, a staff officer of the 'engulfed' 7th Division, Colonel the Hon H. B. Robson, wrote to me:

'There can be no doubt at all as to (the offensive) being rightly under-taken, nor any question of the immense contribution it made to the winning of the war.'

Once more we may leave the last word to the enemy:†

'Now that we know the circumstances of the situation in which the French Army found itself during the summer of 1917, there can be no doubt that in fact the stubbornness shown by the British bridged the crisis in France. The French Army gained time to restore itself and the German reserves were drawn to Flanders. The casualties which Britain sustained in defence of the Entente were not in vain.'

*O.H., 1917, vol ii, p xvii.
†Von Kuhl

Note on Casualties

———————————————— ✠ ————————————————

CASUALTIES IN THE THIRD BATTLE OF YPRES

As might be supposed, the question of casualties in the Flanders Offensive of 1917 has always been vexed with controversy. The discrepancies in the figures offered by various sources are considerable. Against the official figures (British, (French and German) quoted on p 328, we may set the following:

'For these "purposes of distraction" the killing, maiming or capture of over 400,000 British soldiers was apparently considered a reasonable price to pay.'

(Churchill: *The World Crisis*, Odhams Ed, ii, p 959)

'The total casualties on the whole British Front during the progress of the battle mounted up to the appalling figure of 399,000 men – three times the official estimate.'

(Lloyd George, ii, p 1496)

'It is reasonably certain that the British losses in the three and a half months of the Passchendaele offensive were near 300,000 at the lowest – while probably they were more – and that the losses among the German troops facing them on that sector were a little under 200,000.'

(Sir Basil Liddell Hart: 'The Basic Truths of Passchendaele', *Journal of the Royal United Services Institute* November, 1959, p 438)

'The British casualties were something over 300,000; the German under 200,000 – a proportion slightly better than on the Somme.'

(A. J. P. Taylor, *The First World War*, Hamish Hamilton, 1963, p 148)

'In March, 1922 the British War Office published its *Statistics of the Military Effort of the British Empire During the Great War*. Released as soon as possible after the event, it flatly lists British casualties between July and December 1917 (the Flanders campaign and Cambrai) at 448,614. This does not include French losses on the north flank, which may be conservatively reckoned at 50,000 for the same period. Thus the total Allied loss comes to half a million . . . In the same report German casualties are listed as 270,710.'

(Leon Wolff, *In Flanders Fields*, Longmans, Green & Co, 1959, p 259)

It has to be stated that in some ways that most valuable compilation, *Statistics of the Military Effort of the British Empire* has much to answer for. It will generally be found that the very high British totals originate in that volume – but in fairness to the compilers it must also be said that this is due to a failure to consult it properly.

Let us examine Mr Leon Wolff's assertion that 'it flatly lists British casualties between July and December, 1917 (the Flanders campaign and Cambrai) at 448,614'. Even if this were so, it would still be necessary to subtract the Cambrai losses, which were not part of the Flanders campaign. These are to be found in Table xiv, v (p 327):75,681 – which at once reduces the Flanders total to 372,933. It is strange that Mr Wolff does not attempt this simple sum.*

The *Statistics* do not, in fact, 'flatly list' anything. The British total of 448,614 (and German 270,710) is arrived at by adding figures for the 'Summer battles in Flanders' and 'Autumn battles in Flanders; Battle near Cambrai' in a comparative table of British and German losses in 1917 on p 361. This is not, however, the only word that the *Statistics* have to offer on the subject.

On pp. 263–5 we find tables showing the 'Approximate Casualties by months in the Expeditionary Force, France'. Here the July–December total adds up to 479,340. But again, we have to deduct Cambrai, making it 403,659. And of course, as with Mr Wolff's total, further deductions are needed for the first 30 days of July and the last 24 days of December (after Cambrai). Nor is this all.

If we return to Table xiv (pp 326–7) we find two tables covering the period of the Third Battle of Ypres:

31 July – 19 September	136,447
20 September – 31 December	263,374.

It is specifically stated that the second figure includes Cambrai, so again a deduction is required, making it 187,693, and the full total 324,140. And this is still not all.

On p 334 there is yet another table, comparing casualties and gains in the Battles of Arras, Messines and Third Ypres (but only to 5 October). Here we find that British casualties (to 5 October) are stated as 162,796 (and estimated German, 255,000). Evidently there is nothing 'flatly listed' about the *Statistics*; on the contrary, they offer an embarrassing range of choice.

In any case, whichever of these totals the student chooses to accept, there is a further exercise to be performed. The table on p 361 selected by Mr Wolff shows casualties 'on the Western Front'; Table xiv (pp 326–7) shows 'casualties in the Expeditionary Force'; so does the table of casualties by months (pp 263–5); the only one that limits itself to a battle front is the last one quoted (Table xviii, p 334), and as we have seen it is unfortunately incomplete.

---

*If he had troubled to consult the French Official Account, he would not have offered the ludicrous 'conservative reckoning' of 50,000 for them.

What this means, clearly, is that from every one of the other totals given we have to deduct something further for 'normal wastage' (which would include the fronts of the inactive Armies (First, Third, Fourth), as well as what the 'battle Armies' would have lost in any case, had they not been conducting a major operation. According to a statement by the Director of Military Operations to the War Cabinet on 2 November (CAB 23/4; War Cabinet 263, Para. 6) 'the normal average monthly casualties, when there was no severe fighting, was 35,000'.

That being so, from Mr Wolff's preferred total of 448,614 we need to deduct not only the Cambrai losses but 'normal wastage' (July–December, 6 × 35,000) making the Flanders Offensive total 162,933. Deducting from the monthly totals (July–December, 6 × 35,000) we end with 193,659. Deducting from Table xiv (31 July–31 December 5 × 35,000) we end with 149,140.

I think I have said enough to show that, valuable as they are in many other respects, as regards casualty figures the *Statistics* are unhelpful, and this can no doubt be attributed to the fact that, as Mr Wolff says, they were 'released as soon as possible after the event'. It was obviously too soon.

Now what of the figures supplied by Sir James Edmonds in the Official History, which I quote on p 328? These, too, have been severely criticized. In *The Spectator* on 6 December, 1957, the late Sir Basil Liddell Hart referred to General Edmonds's 'preposterous assertions' and said: 'The way he "cooked" the figures shocked those who had been concerned in working them out. In old age his treatment of the evidence became deplorably misleading.'*

It would hardly be supposed from this that on pp 364–5 of '1917', vol ii, Sir James Edmonds supplies weekly casualty totals extracted from the Summaries furnished to GHQ by the Second and Fifth Armies, the Second Army from the week ending 2 August to that ending 10 November, Fifth Army from week ending 3 August to 9 November, and that he arrives at his grand total by the straight-forward method of adding them all together. The resulting total is 238,313 – slightly less than that submitted to the Supreme War Council which he settles for on p 361.

How was that figure arrived at? The veil of Official Secrecy has now lifted from that distant period, and I may therefore quote from a letter which I received in June, 1963, from Mr A. W. Sarsey, who was Sir James Edmonds's confidential clerk in the Historical Section of the Committee of Imperial Defence during the whole period of the compilation of the Official Histories. He told me:

> All the British totals, with *one important exception given below*, were compiled direct from the War Diaries of the Units and Formations engaged and in addition the Army, corps, divisional and even brigade aggregates were checked each against each and then given a final scrutiny before being incorporated in the official draft. I know this for a fact, as I did a great number of them *myself*. . . .
>
> I repudiate with all honesty the statements made (by Liddell Hart) . . . I am

*Sir James Edmonds, being dead, could make no reply.

very much puzzled and bewildered as to what the accusation of 'cooking' the figures is based upon. The use of the word in this sense is, inter alia, to manipulate or falsify for an ulterior motive. Now, the figures for 'The Third Battle of Ypres', 'The Battles of Ypres 1917' or 'Passchendaele' were *not* compiled in the Section. They were accepted ready-made from the records of the Supreme War Council.

I well remember taking it to the General, who was quite pleased about it and remarked in words to the effect – 'Well, that saves lots of work.' . . . The war diaries were not consulted in the matter* as there was the total ready-made by a 'rival firm' to the Field-Marshal so to speak . . . Of course the records of the S.W.C. are Cabinet documents . . . I catalogued them, and found the document, taken out of the records without alteration. So I do know definitely that there was no kitchen activity of any kind in the figures.

Now we must ask, how did the Supreme War Council obtain its figures? The only possible answer – the only possible source – is the Adjutant-General's Branch at GHQ. Did GHQ 'cook' the figure? If so, with what aim in view, in February 1918? It must be remembered that this was a very critical moment in the war. It was clear that the Germans were about to deliver a heavy blow on the Western Front and evidence was mounting that this would fall on the fronts of the British Third and Fifth Armies. The whole BEF was seriously under strength (the infantry alone were 100,000 below establishment); it had just taken over 25 miles of front from the French; it was in process of reorganizing its divisions from 12 battalions to 9, not, as other countries had done, in order to create new divisions, but simply because of the manpower crisis; this meant the physical disbandment of 141 battalions in the field on the eve of the German attack. At the same time, GHQ was being pressed to provide divisions for a central Allied Reserve, to be directed by a committee of Military Representatives at the Supreme War Council.

In other words, every temptation at GHQ at that stage would have been to exaggerate losses and weakness, rather than disguise or minimize them, in order to obtain more men to fill the gaps in the BEF and enable it to fulfil the demands that were being made of it. But of course, there is no evidence whatever that any 'cooking' was done at GHQ, any more than in the Historical Section. For myself, for reasons which I have stated at length in *Douglas Haig: The Educated Soldier*, pp 371–2, I can see no reason for not accepting the figures submitted to the Supreme War Council as the nearest possible approximation to the truth.

When we turn to the German figures, and their interpretation, once more we find Sir James Edmonds under fire. The German Official Account of the year 1916 admits that in its casualty totals it does not count 'the wounded whose recovery was to be expected within a reasonable time' – i.e., the lightly wounded who would quickly return to their units, but who, having received attention at First Aid Posts, Advanced Dressing Stations or Casualty Clearing Stations, are included in the British figures. Sir James Edmonds reckons these to amount to

*As we have seen, the War Diaries were, in fact, consulted as well.

some 30% of the total, and regularly adds that proportion to all German returns. In the case of Flanders, this would bring their total to 'about 289,000'.

As I have stated above (p 215 f.n.) this practice has incurred considerable criticism (see in particular the *Journal of the Royal United Services Institute*, February, 1964: "Thirty Per Cent: A Study in Casualty Statistics' by M. J. Williams). My own feeling is that the addition of a flat 30% at all times is very arbitrary, that it makes no allowance for the endless possibilities of variation in circumstance. On the other hand, it is clear that the German figures are *not* exact; they always require further calculation before acceptance, and what this amounts to, basically, is *adding* something. But what? The answer, I suspect, is a variable: sometimes, perhaps, Edmonds's 30%; sometimes nearer 25%, or 20%; I should be surprised if it was ever as low as 15%.

Without in any way sponsoring this figure, I may remark that an addition of 20% to the figure stated in the German Official Account (p 367) gives a total of 260,400 which, taking into account the extra span of time (to 31 December) is roughly equal to the combined total of the British and French. Having regard to the absolute minimum of 135 attacks or counter-attacks conducted by the Germans by 20 November which I have been able to identify (there were more in December) this would seem unlikely to be an overstatement. Every German account emphasizes the sense of heavy loss throughout the battle.

APPENDIX I

———————————— ✠ ————————————

The following throws some light on a vexed subject:

'The first four months of the year saw strikes in the Ruhr, Berlin and elsewhere. A basic pretext was the insufficiency of food. The Ruhr disturbances were so serious that the troops were called in. Here the workers were demanding that either they receive more food or that they be paid higher wages to obtain food on the black market. In the Ruhr coal mines a further cause was the temporary unemployment produced by the transport crisis. The reduction of the bread ration in mid-April provoked a wave of strikes in Berlin and Leipzig. On the 16th some 220,000 workers struck in the capital, staging huge non-violent demonstrations. After negotiations, they were promised an increase in the meat ration, on which most of the strikers returned to work. The Leipzig stoppages had a more political character, for besides demanding more food and coal the strikers called for a Government declaration stating, among other things, its readiness to conclude a peace without annexation. The strike quickly ended after a Government under-taking to raise wages and reduce the working week to fifty-two hours. Meanwhile more Berlin workers had struck, making claims similar to those of the Leipzig men. Only after their workplaces – two branches of the German Weapons and Munitions Factories – had been occupied by troops and the strikers ordered to return under pain of fines and imprisonment, did the stoppage end. There was more trouble in June, notably in the Ruhr where, in the calls for peace and political reform, a new radical note was evident. July brought strikes in Düs-seldorf and Upper Silesia, the latter resulting in losses of half-a-million tons of coal.'

(John Williams, 'The Home Fronts: Britain, France and Germany', Constable, 1972, pp 232–3)

APPENDIX II

-- ✠ --

What the French actually *were* doing is a subject largely ignored in every British history of the war that I have read. The suggestion is that when Nivelle's great effort failed on 16 April fighting on the French front soon died down. This was by no means the case, and both Haig and Robertson must have had some inkling of that fact. The French communiqués after all were not silent, though under Pétain they may have been more cryptic than previously. What they reveal is that, after heavy fighting on the Aisne-Champagne front all through May, at the beginning of June the Germans launched a powerful counter-offensive, which continued throughout the month. The points selected for attack were the Vauxaillon area, at the western end of the Chemin des Dames, the California Plateau between Hurtebise and Craonne in the centre, and the Moronvilliers *massif* east of Rheims. Here, the German attacks reached a climax on 30–31 May, prompting a French counter-attack on 18 June, and a German reaction on 21 June. The main German assault was in the centre, beginning with five attacks on the California Plateau on 3 June; fighting here continued until 6 June, then died down until the 17th, when the Germans attacked again. On 25 June, after a fierce struggle with lavish use of flame-throwers, the French captured the notorious 'Dragon Cave' shelter, 70 feet deep, at Hurtebise, and won positions which enabled them to inflict a sharp repulse on the Germans at the end of the month. At Vauxaillon the serious fighting began with a German attack on the 20th, a French counter-attack on the 21st, violent German attacks on the 22nd, more on the 23rd, and a French retort on the 24th. The high peak of the offensive was reached on 4 July when the Germans attacked along a 17-kilometre front on the Chemin des Dames in the Craonne-Cerny area – provoking, needless to say, sharp French reactions on the 7th and the 9th. And so the pattern continued.

Perhaps even more significant than this action in Champagne in the wake of Nivelle's offensive was a flaring-up of activity entirely on the German initiative at Verdun. On 29 and 30 June the Germans attacked the French positions on Hill 304 and Mort-Homme, continuing right through July and into August. This offers a new perspective in which to view Pétain's attack on 20 August. All in all, for an army still racked by mutiny (see p 127) this French effort, both defensive and offensive, was considerable. However, it was not until 25 July that any of this activity was brought formally to the War Cabinet's attention, when Macdonogh reported that the Germans had made 70 attacks on the French front since 5 May, and there had been fighting on 53 days out of 80 (War Cabinet 195, CAB 23/3). The significance of this information appears neither to have been grasped by the War Cabinet at the time nor by many historians afterwards.

APPENDIX III

— ✠ —

Officers			Other Ranks			
Killed	Wounded	Missing	Killed	Wounded	Missing	Total
684	2,563	177	9,582	47,598	7,406	68,010

It will be noted (see p 242) that the casualties for the first *month* in Flanders were only about 10,000 more than for the first *day* on the Somme in 1916 – due chiefly to the appalling weather on so many days. It may also be noted that the total of known dead in Flanders was 10,266, compared with 19,240 on the Somme on 1 July, i.e. rather more than one seventh of the total, as compared with one third. Evidently, a proportion of the 7,583 missing must be added to the dead – but what proportion? In not less than 36 attacks and counter-attacks during August the Germans must have taken prisoners. We do not know how many, but I suggest, as a very conservative estimate, ¼ of the total of missing, in which case the proportion of dead rises to rather less than a quarter. But as the official breakdown for the Somme does specify an exact number of prisoners, we should add all the Somme missing to the dead, giving a proportion of more than a third. I can only account for this difference by suggesting that there was never, in August, 1917, an occasion when a very large number of casualties lay out all day, under enemy artillery, machine gun and rifle fire, as on 1 July, 1916, when many wounded men must have died of their second, third or even fourth wounds. Also, the soggy ground reduced the lethal effect of shelling at Ypres. Total casualties for the first *month* of the Somme were 164,709.

I. INDEX OF 'THREADS'

See p. 21

THE INVISIBLE ENEMY
(*U-boats*)

MANPOWER

SOLDIERS AND POLITICIANS

II. GENERAL INDEX

III. INDEX OF MILITARY FORMATIONS